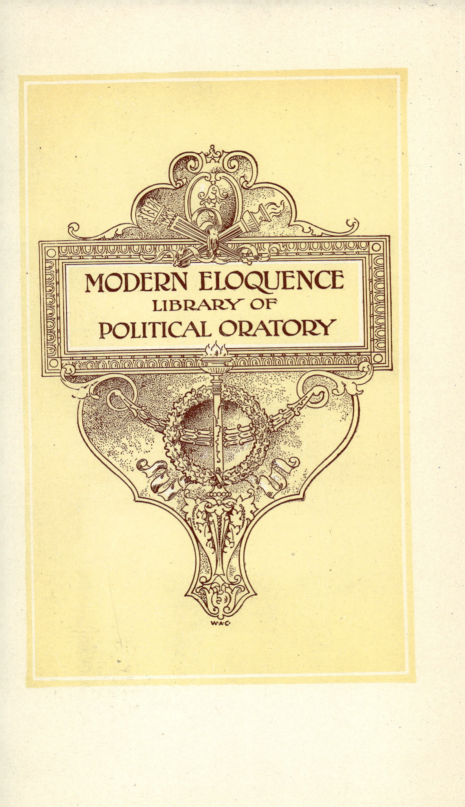

MODERN ELOQUENCE
LIBRARY OF
POLITICAL ORATORY

GEORGE WASHINGTON

Photogravure after a painting by Gilbert Stuart

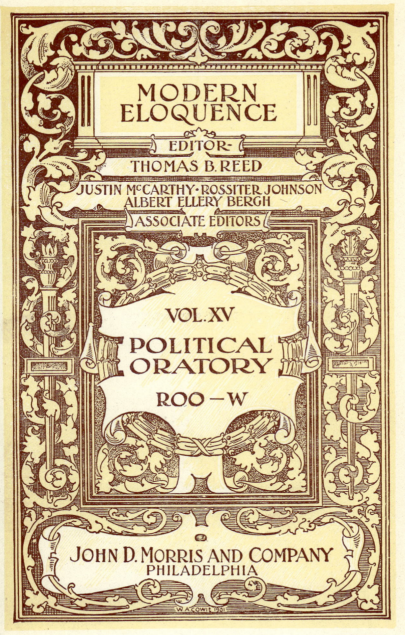

MODERN ELOQUENCE

EDITOR-
THOMAS B. REED

JUSTIN McCARTHY · ROSSITER JOHNSON
ALBERT ELLERY BERGH
ASSOCIATE EDITORS

VOL. XV

POLITICAL ORATORY

ROO — W

JOHN D. MORRIS AND COMPANY
PHILADELPHIA

W.A.COWIT 1901.

COMMITTEE OF SELECTION

EDWARD EVERETT HALE, Author of "The Man Without a Country."

JOHN B. GORDON, Former United States Senator.

NATHAN HASKELL DOLE, Associate-Editor "International Library of Famous Literature."

JAMES B. POND, Manager Lecture Bureau; Author of "Eccentricities of Genius."

GEORGE McLEAN HARPER, Professor of English Literature, Princeton University.

LORENZO SEARS, Professor of English Literature, Brown University.

EDWIN M. BACON, Former Editor "Boston Advertiser" and "Boston Post."

J. WALKER McSPADDEN, Managing Editor "Édition Royale" of Balzac's Works.

F. CUNLIFFE OWEN, Member Editorial Staff "New York Tribune."

TRUMAN A. DEWEESE, Member Editorial Staff "Chicago Times-Herald."

CHAMP CLARK, Member of Congress from Missouri.

MARCUS BENJAMIN, Editor, National Museum, Washington, D. C.

CLARK HOWELL, Editor "Atlanta Constitution."

EPIPHANIUS WILSON, Managing Editor.

INTRODUCTIONS AND SPECIAL ARTICLES BY

THOMAS B. REED,	HAMILTON WRIGHT MABIE,
LORENZO SEARS,	JONATHAN P. DOLLIVER,
CHAMP CLARK,	EDWARD EVERETT HALE,
GEORGE F. HOAR,	CHARLES W. EMERSON,
ALBERT J. BEVERIDGE,	ALBERT ELLERY BERGH.

NOTE.—A large number of the most distinguished speakers of this country and Great Britain have selected their own best speeches for this Library. These speakers include Whitelaw Reid, William Jennings Bryan, Henry van Dyke, Henry M. Stanley, Newell Dwight Hillis, Joseph Jefferson, Sir Henry Irving, Arthur T. Hadley, John D. Long, David Starr Jordan, and many others of equal note.

INTRODUCTION

ORATORY AND ELOQUENCE

SELECTIONS FROM VARIOUS AUTHORS

Oratory.—Oratory is like music; it must have tone and time. *G. Grote.*

The Injudicious Orator.—An orator without judgment is a horse without a bridle. *Theophrastus.*

Perfection in Oratory.—Oratory and poetry are of little value unless they reach the highest perfection. *Pliny.*

Logic and Eloquence.—Sound logic is the sinews of eloquence; without solid argument, oratory is empty noise, and the orator is a declaimer or a sophist. *J. Wilkins.*

Oratory Rare.—We have a hundred speakers, but where is the orator? Where shall we find one from whose soul pours eloquence as naturally as poetry from the poet's lips? *E. Hildreth.*

End of Oratory.—Oratory is an engine invented to manage and wield at will the fierce democracy, and like medicine to the sick, is only employed in the paroxysms of a disordered state. *Montaigne.*

Affectation in Oratory.—In oratory, affectation must be avoided; it being better for a man by a native and clear eloquence to express himself, than by those words which may smell either of the lamp or inkhorn. *Lord Herbert.*

Use of Oratory.—The art of oratory is designed to instruct people, express their passions, and reform their manners; to support the laws, direct public counsels, and to make men good and happy. *Fénelon.*

Effect of Oratory.—The really great orator shines like the sun, making you think much of the things he is speaking of; the second-best shines like the moon, making you think much of him and his eloquence. *R. Whately.*

The Power of Oratory.—There is no power like that of oratory; Cæsar controlled men by exciting their fears, Cicero by captivating their affections and swaying their passions; the influence of the one perished with its author, that of the other continues to this day. *H. Clay.*

Great Oratory of Slow Attainment.—The orator whose eye flashes instantaneous fire, and whose lips pour out a flood of noble thoughts, startling by their unexpectedness and elevating by their wisdom and truth, has learned his secret by patient repetition and after many disappointments. *Smiles.*

Universality of Oratory.—The matchless eloquence of oratory is applicable everywhere, in all classes of life; the rich and the poor experience the effects of its magic influence; it excites the soldier to the charge, and animates him to the conflict; the guilty are living monuments of its exertion, and the innocent hail it as the vindicator of their violated rights and the preserver of their sacred reputation. How often in the courts of justice does the criminal behold his arms unshackled, his character freed from suspicion, and his future left open before him with all its hopes of honors, station, and dignity. *Melvill.*

The Orator's First Step in His Art.—The beginning of the art of oratory is to acquire a habit of easy speaking; the next step is the grand one—to convert this style of easy speaking into chaste eloquence. Though speaking, with writing beforehand, is very well until the habit of easy speech is acquired, yet, after that, one can never write too much; it is laborious, no doubt, and it is more difficult, beyond comparison, than speaking offhand; but it is necessary to perfect oratory, and at any rate it is necessary to acquire the habit of correct diction. But I go further, and say, even to the end of a man's life he must prepare, word for word, most of his finer passages. *Brougham.*

Advantages of Clearness and Conciseness.—The public orator who presents in a clear, concise, and forcible manner the strong points of his case, whose every sentence strikes home, who says just all that is necessary, and there stops, is always listened to with a marked attention, unknown to those who indulge in flights of oratory, plucking flowers from the regions of fancy, drawing more largely upon imagination than upon sound logic and plain common sense. *L. C. Judson.*

Tediousness.—The orator must never bore; he must never be obscure; he must never seem hesitating in his assertions; he must not be minutely refining, nor metaphysically subtle, in his philosophical deductions; all the knowledge he thinks fit to press into his service he must seek to render clear to the commonest understanding; all his imagination must be employed, not in creating new worlds of thought, but in bringing thoughts the most generally admitted as sound into brilliant light. *S. A. Allibone.*

Persuasion.—Oratory is to be estimated on principles different from those which are applied to other productions. Truth is the object of philosophy and history. Truth is the object even of those works which are peculiarly called works of fiction, but which, in fact, bear the same relation to history which algebra bears to arithmetic. The object of oratory alone is not truth, but persuasion; but the criterion of eloquence is different. A speaker who exhausts the whole philosophy of a question, who displays every grace of style, yet produces no effect on his audience, may be a great essayist, a great statesman, a great master of composition, but he is not an orator. *T. B. Macaulay.*

Clear Thinking.—Whenever men think clearly and are thoroughly interested, they express themselves with perspicuity and force. *F. W. Robertson.*

Canons of Perspicuity.—The three canons of perspicuity are, the word that is necessary, the quantity that is necessary, and the manner that is necessary. *Catherall.*

What is Perspicuity?—Perspicuity consists in the using of proper terms for the thoughts which a man would have pass from his own mind into that of another. *Locke.*

The Fundamental Quality of Style.—Perspicuity is the fundamental quality of style; a quality so essential in every kind of writing that for the want of it nothing can atone. Without this the richest ornaments of style only glimmer through the dark, and puzzle instead of pleasing the reader. *H. Blair.*

A Good Argument.—A chain of reasoning ought to have an adequate number of links, a hook for the nose of the auditor, a grapple for the subject, and a swivel to every pair of propositions to relieve the kinks. *L. Dow.*

Rules of Rhetoric.—The two best rules of a system of rhetoric are: first, have something to say; and next, say it. *Emmons.*

Reasoning and Rhetoric.—By reasoning we satisfy ourselves; by rhetoric we satisfy others. Most modern orators and rhetoricians content themselves with fulfilling the first part of this proposition. *P. B. Randolph.*

What is Rhetoric?—Without attempting a formal definition of the word, I am inclined to consider rhetoric, when reduced to a system in books, as a body of rules derived from experience and observation, extending to all communications by language, and designed to make it efficient.

W. E. Channing.

The Idleness of Sophistry.—Genius may dazzle, eloquence may persuade, reason may convince; but to render popular cold and comfortless sophistry, unaided by these powers, is a hopeless attempt. *J. Hall.*

Use of Words.—Words borrowed of antiquity do lend a kind of majesty to style, and are not without their delight sometimes; for they have the authority of years, and out of their intermission do win themselves a kind of gracelike newness; but the eldest of the present and newest of the past language is the best. *Ben Jonson.*

Wisdom Learnt through Emotion.—Lessons of wisdom have never such power as when they are wrought into the heart through the groundwork of a story which engages the passions; is it that we are like iron, and must first be heated before we can be wrought upon; or is the heart so in love with deceit that where a true report will not reach it, we must cheat it with a fable in order to come at the truth? *Sterne.*

Antithesis.—Antithesis may be the blossom of wit, but it will never arrive at maturity unless sound sense be the trunk, and truth the root. *Colton.*

Falsehood in Wit.—I give you full credit for your elegant diction, well-turned periods, and Attic wit; but wit is oftentimes false, though it may appear brilliant; which is exactly the case of your whole performance. *Junius.*

The Human Face.—Look in the face of the person to whom you are speaking, if you wish to know his real sentiments; for he can command his words more easily than his countenance.

Chesterfield.

The Countenance of the Orator.—As the language of the face is universal so is it very comprehensive; no laconicism can reach it; it is the short-hand of the mind, and crowds a great deal in a little room. A man may look a sentence as soon as speak a word; the strokes are small, but so masterly drawn that you may easily collect the image and proportions of what they resemble.   *Jeremy Collier.*

Expression of Features More than Sound of Words.—The face of a man, as a rule, speaks more eloquently and in a more interesting manner than his mouth, for it is the compendium of everything which the latter has to say, since it is the monogram of the thinking and acting of the man. Besides the mouth only utters the thoughts of nature; wherefore every man is worth being closely observed, though every man is not worth being talked to.   *Schopenhauer.*

Vain Speaking.—Some in their discourse desire rather commendation of wit, in being able to hold all arguments, than of judgment, in discerning what is true; as if it were a praise to know what might be said, and not what should be thought. Some have certain commonplaces and themes wherein they are good and want variety; which kind of poverty is for the most part tedious, and when it is once perceived, ridiculous.   *Bacon.*

Something for All.—A speech being a matter of adaptation, and having to win opinions, should contain a little for the few, and a great deal for the many. Burke hurt his oratory by neglecting the latter half of this rule, as Sheridan must have spoilt his by his carelessness about the former. But the many always carry it for the moment against the few; and though Burke was allowed to be the greater man, Sheridan drew most hearers.   *Guesses at Truth.*

The Orator's Eye.—Oratory may be symbolized by a warrior's eye, flashing from under a philosopher's brow. But why a warrior's eye, rather than a poet's? Because in oratory the will must predominate.   *Guesses at Truth.*

Sincerity.—How many faithful sentences are written now? —that is, sentences dictated by a pure love of truth, without any wish, save that of expressing the truth fully and clearly— sentences in which there is neither a spark of light too much, nor a shade of darkness?   *Guesses at Truth.*

Fox and Demosthenes.—What made Demosthenes the greatest of orators was that he appeared the most entirely possessed by the feelings he wished to inspire. The main use of his action was that it enabled him to remove the natural hindrances which checked and clogged the stream of those feelings, and to pour them forth with a free and mighty tor-

rent that swept his audience along. The effect produced by
Charles Fox, who by the exaggerations of party spirit was
often compared to Demosthenes, seems to have arisen wholly
from this earnestness, which made up for the want of almost
every grace, both of manner and style. *Guesses at Truth.*

Feeling and Speech.—Eloquence is speaking out—out of
the abundance of the heart—the only source from which truth
can flow in a passionate, persuasive torrent. Nothing can be
juster than Quintilian's remark (X. 7, 15): "Pectus est, quod
disertos facit, et vis mentis: ideoque imperitis quoque, si
modo sint aliquo affectu concitati, verba non desunt." (It is
the heart and the power of intellect that make eloquence,
and thus language never fails even the unskilful, provided
their passions are excited.) This is the explanation of that
singular psychological phenomenon, Irish eloquence; I do
not mean that of the orators merely, but that of the whole
people, men, women, and children. *Guesses at Truth.*

Prayer and Eloquence.—The ancient Romans used the
same word to express the act of prayer and the act of public
speaking, as if to imply that pleading with the Deity and
pleading with the people were in some points essentially the
same function. This puts the office of the orator on a plane
as high as it raises the power of the people. If, as Dupan-
loup says, "Omnipotentia supplex," the suppliant is omnipotent, the orator is omnipotent, too. The will of the people
is indeed the supreme arbiter in a republic, and he who could
sway by eloquence this mighty power seemed to the fancy of
the ancient world in some way to control the weapons of
omnipotence, to brandish the bolts of Zeus, and shake the
world with the thunder of his words.

Epiphanius Wilson.

The Preëminence of the Orator.—There are three ways in
which a public speaker must be superior to those whom he is
anxious to influence: he must know more, he must feel more
keenly, and he must be able to express more clearly than they.
The Hebrew prophet is represented as standing on the sum-
mit of a tower, from which he could see beyond the horizon
of the audience gathered at its base. Thence he might dis-
cern the distant tempest gathering up the dust of the plain,
or the cloud of locusts advancing like an armed host, or the
first streaks of dawn invisible to the people in the valley.
From this wide vision would come the deeper realization of

the woe or the joy which was approaching. By the gift of vivid speech he would convey his own impressions to his auditors. Perhaps the best example of this intellectual breadth and loftiness, this profound and earnest feeling, and their expression in words that thrilled and illuminated, is to be found in the speeches of Daniel Webster.

Epiphanius Wilson.

The Telling Phrase.—To make the effect of an oration lasting in the memory of the hearers it is good to use some telling phrase or catchword in which the point of the contention is summarized or suggested. Unlettered people carry all their knowledge or wisdom in short rhymes and proverbs, which are delightful even to the most cultivated as being portable, racy, and seasoned with a kind of wit. As models of this sort of watchword we may point to the "Peace with honor" of Beaconsfield, the "toujours l'audace" (always to dare) of Danton, "the Cross of Gold" of W. J. Bryan, the "plumed knight" of Ingersoll, and the "iridescent dream" of Ingalls.

Epiphanius Wilson.

True Eloquence.—When public bodies are to be addressed on momentous occasions, when great interests are at stake, and strong passions excited, nothing is valuable in speech, farther than it is connected with high intellectual and moral attainments.

Clearness, force, and earnestness are the qualities which produce conviction. True eloquence, indeed, does not consist in speech. It cannot be brought from far. Labor and learning may toil for it, but they will toil in vain. Words and phrases may be marshaled in every way, but they cannot compass it. It must exist in the man, in the subject, and in the occasion. Affected passion, intense expression, the pomp of declamation, all may aspire after it. They cannot reach it. It comes, if it come at all, like the outbreaking of a fountain from the earth, or the bursting forth of volcanic fires, with spontaneous, original, native force. The graces taught in the schools, the costly ornaments, and studied contrivances of speech, shock and disgust men when their own lives and the lives of their wives and children, and their country, hang on the decision of the hour. Then, words have lost their power. Rhetoric is vain, and all elaborate oratory contemptible. Even genius itself then feels rebuked and subdued as in the presence of higher qualities. Then, patriotism is eloquent. Then, self-devotion is eloquent.

The clear conception, outrunning the deductions of logic, the high purpose, the firm resolve, the dauntless spirit, speaking on the tongue, beaming from the eye, informing every feature, and urging the whole man onward to his object—this, this is eloquence, or rather it is something greater and higher than eloquence ; it is action, noble, sublime, godlike action.
Daniel Webster.

CONTENTS

VOLUME XV

PAGE

ROOSEVELT, THEODORE

Address at State Fair of Minnesota. (*Delivered in Minneapolis, Sept., 1901*) 1759

On Reading the Bible. (*Delivered before the Members of the Bible Society, 1901*) 1770

Trusts and the Tariff. (*Delivered in Cincinnati, Sept. 20, 1902*) 1776

ROSEBERY, LORD

Questions of Empire. (*Delivered before the University of Glasgow, as Lord Rector, in 1900*) . . 1785

SALISBURY, LORD

On the Abandonment of General Gordon. (*Delivered in the House of Lords, in 1885*) . . . 1808

Tampering with the Constitution. (*Delivered at a public meeting held in London, 1875, to protest against Mr. Gladstone's Redistribution Bill*) . 1821

SCHURZ, CARL

The Policy of Imperialism (*Delivered in Chicago, in 1899*) 1834

SEWARD, WILLIAM HENRY

The Irrepressible Conflict. (*Delivered in Rochester, N. Y., Oct. 25, 1858*) 1849

SHEIL, RICHARD LALOR

Ireland's Part in English Achievement. (*Delivered in the House of Commons, 1837*) . . . 1865

SHERIDAN, RICHARD BRINSLEY

Against Warren Hastings. (*Delivered in Westminster Hall, London, Feb., 1788*) . . . 1872

SHERMAN, JOHN   PAGE
    The Financial Situation. (*Delivered in the United
      States Senate, Dec. 31, 1895*) 1904

SPOONER, JOHN COIT
    On the Government of the Philippines. (*Delivered
      before the United States Senate, in 1900*) .   . 1913

SPRINGER, WILLIAM McKENDREE
    Retrenchment, Economy, and Reform. (*In the
      House of Representatives, 1876*)   .   .   . 1924

STEPHENS, ALEXANDER HAMILTON
    On Secession. (*Delivered in 1861*)   .   .   . 1932
    Corner-Stone Address. (*Delivered in the Athenæum,
      Savannah, Ga., 1861*) 1936

STEVENS, THADDEUS
    Against Webster and Northern Compromisers.
      (*Delivered in the House of Representatives, 1850*) 1943

SUMNER, CHARLES
    The Crime Against Kansas. (*Delivered in the United
      States Senate, May 20, 1856*)   .   .   . 1952

TECUMSEH
    Speech at Vincennes. (*Delivered on the Sale of Lands
      to Governor Harrison, at Vincennes, Aug. 12,
      1813*) 1970
    Speech to General Proctor. (*Delivered to General
      Proctor shortly before the battle of the Thames,
      Oct. 5, 1813*). 1971

THIERS, LOUIS ADOLPHE
    Mexico and Louis Napoleon's Policy. (*Delivered in
      the French Assembly, Jan. 2, 1865*) .   .   . 1974

THURMAN, ALLEN GRANBERY
    The Tilden-Hayes Election. (*Delivered in 1877*) . 1986

TILDEN, SAMUEL JONES
    Negro Suffrage. (*In the Democratic State Convention
      at Albany, March 11, 1868*) 1992

TOOMBS, ROBERT   PAGE
    Revolution or Secession. (*His Last Speech before
        retiring from the United States Senate, delivered
        Jan. 7, 1861*)   2003

VEST, GEORGE GRAHAM
    On Indian Schools. (*Delivered in the United States
        Senate, 1900*)   2013

VOORHEES, DANIEL WOLSEY
    On the Tilden Controversy. (*Delivered in 1876, on
        the disputed Presidential election*)   .   . 2021

WALPOLE, ROBERT
    On a Motion for his Removal. (*Delivered in the
        House of Commons, Feb., 1741*)   .   .   . 2025

WASHINGTON, GEORGE
    First Inaugural Address. (*Delivered in New York
        City, April 30, 1789*)   2032
    Farewell Address. (*Issued Sept. 19, 1796*)   .   . 2036

WEBSTER, DANIEL
    Reply to Hayne. (*Delivered in the Senate, Jan. 26,
        1830*)   2053
    Adams and Jefferson. (*Delivered in Faneuil Hall,
        Boston, Aug. 2, 1826*)   2082
    Bunker Hill. (*Delivered June 17, 1825*)   .   . 2090

WELLINGTON, THE DUKE OF
    On Catholic Emancipation. (*Delivered in the House
        of Lords, May 31, 1829*)   2107

WILBERFORCE, WILLIAM
    Horrors of the British Slave-Trade. (*Delivered in
        the House of Commons, May 10, 1789*)   .   . 2120

WILLIAM OF GERMANY, THE EMPEROR
    Moses and Amalek. (*Delivered on board his yacht,
        Aug., 1900*)   2129

WIRT, WILLIAM   PAGE
    Against Aaron Burr.   (*Delivered in the Circuit Court
        of the United States, Richmond, Va., May, 1807*)   2135

WISE, HENRY ALEXANDER
    Know-Nothingism.   (*Delivered in Alexandria, Va.,
        1854*)   2141

ILLUSTRATIONS

VOLUME XV

FACING
PAGE

GEORGE WASHINGTON . . . *Frontispiece*
    Photogravure after a painting by Gilbert Stuart

LORD SALISBURY 1812
    Photogravure after a photograph from life

WILLIAM HENRY SEWARD 1856
    Photogravure after a painting

CHARLES SUMNER 1954
    Photogravure after a painting

FRENCH CHAMBER OF DEPUTIES 1978
    Photogravure after a photograph

DANIEL WEBSTER 2082
    Photogravure after an etching by T. Johnson

KAISER WILHELM II 2132
    Photogravure after a painting

THEODORE ROOSEVELT

ADDRESS AT STATE FAIR OF MINNESOTA

[Theodore Roosevelt, President of the United States, was born in New York city in 1858. He graduated at Harvard in his twenty-second year, and almost at once interested himself in the political affairs of his native city as a member of the Republican party. He was elected to the State Legislature, and in 1886 was a candidate for the mayoralty of New York city, and three years later was appointed a civil service commissioner of the United States. When the "reform" administration of Mayor Strong assumed the government of New York city, Theodore Roosevelt was made president of the police board. President McKinley's administration having taken over the national government, young Roosevelt was selected as assistant secretary of the navy. But the war with Spain came on, and he resigned to go to the front with the regiment known officially as the First United States Cavalry Volunteers, but popularly as "Roosevelt's Rough Riders." The war over, he was elected governor of the state of New York. Before his term ended he was nominated by the Republican national convention as the party candidate for Vice-President of the United States. The assassination of McKinley in 1901 placed Theodore Roosevelt in the presidential chair—the youngest of all the successors of Washington. The first of the following addresses was made at Minneapolis, 1901; the second, before the Bible Society, 1901; the third, at Cincinnati, 1902.]

IN his admirable series of studies of twentieth-century problems, Dr. Lyman Abbott has pointed out that we are a nation of pioneers; that the first colonists to our shores were pioneers, and that pioneers selected out from among the descendants of these early pioneers, mingled with others selected afresh from the Old World, pushed westward into the wilderness, and laid the foundations for new commonwealths. They were men of hope and expectation, of enterprise and energy; for the men of dull content, or more, dull despair, had no part in the great movement into and across the New World. Our country has

2

been populated by pioneers, and therefore it has in it more energy, more enterprise, more expansive power, than any other in the wide world.

You whom I am now addressing stand, for the most part, but one generation removed from these pioneers. You are typical Americans, for you have done the great, the characteristic, the typical work of our American life. In making homes and carving out careers for yourselves and your children you have built up this state; throughout our history the success of the home-maker has been but another name for the upbuilding of the nation. The men who with ax in the forest and pick in the mountains and plow on the prairies pushed to completion the dominion of our people over the American wilderness have given the definite shape to our nation. They have shown the qualities of daring, endurance, and far-sightedness, of eager desire for victory and stubborn refusal to accept defeat, which go to make up the essential manliness of the American character. Above all, they have recognized in practical form the fundamental law of success in American life—the law of worthy work, the law of high, resolute endeavor. We have but little room among our people for the timid, the irresolute, and the idle, and it is no less true that there is scant room in the world at large for the nation with mighty thews that dares not to be great.

Surely, in speaking to the sons of men who actually did the rough and hard and infinitely glorious work of making the great Northwest what it now is, I need hardly insist upon the righteousness of this doctrine. In your own vigorous lives you show by every act how scant is your patience with those who do not see in the life of effort the life supremely worth living. Sometimes we hear those who do not work spoken of with envy. Surely the wilfully idle need arouse in the breast of a healthy man no emotion stronger than that of contempt—at the outside, no emotion stronger than angry contempt.

The feeling of envy would have in it an admission of inferiority on our part, to which the men who know not the sterner joys of life are not entitled. Poverty is a bitter thing, but it is not as bitter as the existence of restless vacuity and physical, moral, and intellectual flabbiness, to which those doom themselves who elect to spend all their years in that vainest of all vain pursuits—the pursuit of mere pleasure as a sufficient end in itself. The wilfully idle man, like the wilfully barren woman, has no place in a sane, healthy, and vigorous community. Moreover, the gross and hideous selfishness for which each stands defeats even its own miserable aims. Exactly as infinitely the happiest woman is she who has borne and brought up many healthy children, so infinitely the happiest man is he who has toiled hard and successfully in his life work. The work may be done in a thousand different ways—with the brain or the hands, in the study, the field, or the workshop; if it is honest work, honestly done and well worth doing, that is all we have a right to ask. Every father and mother here, if they are wise, will bring up their children not to shirk difficulties, but to meet them and overcome them; not to strive after a life of ignoble ease, but to strive to do their duty, first to themselves and their families, and then to the whole state; and this duty must inevitably take the shape of work in some form or other. You, the sons of pioneers, if you are true to your ancestry, must make your lives as worthy as they made theirs. They sought for true success, and therefore they did not seek ease. They knew that success comes only to those who lead the life of endeavor.

It seems to me that the simple acceptance of this fundamental fact of American life, this acknowledgment that the law of work is the fundamental law of our being, will help us to start aright in facing not a few of the problems that confront us from without and from within. As regards internal affairs, it should teach us the prime need of remembering that, after all has been said and done, the chief factor in any man's success or failure must be his own character; that is, the sum of his common sense, his courage, his virile energy and capacity. Nothing can take the place of this individual factor.

I do not for a moment mean that much cannot be done to supplement it. Besides each of us working individually, all of us have got to work together. We cannot possibly do our best work as a nation unless all of us know how to act in combination as well as how to act each individually

III

for himself. The acting in combination can take many forms, but of course its most effective form must be when it comes in the shape of law; that is, of action by the community as a whole through the law-making body.

But it is not possible ever to insure prosperity merely by law. Something for good can be done by law, and a bad law can do an infinity of mischief; but, after all, the best law can only prevent wrong and injustice, and give to the thrifty, the far-seeing, and the hard-working a chance to exercise to the best advantage their special and peculiar abilities. No hard-and-fast rule can be laid down as to where our legislation shall stop in interfering between man and man, between interest and interest. All that can be said is that it is highly undesirable, on the one hand, to weaken individual initiative, and, on the other hand, that in a constantly increasing number of cases we shall find it necessary in the future to shackle cunning as in the past we have shackled force.

It is not only highly desirable, but necessary, that there should be legislation which shall carefully shield the interests of wage-workers, and which shall discriminate in favor of the honest and humane employer by removing the disadvantages under which he stands when compared with unscrupulous competitors who have no conscience, and will do right only under fear of punishment.

Nor can legislation stop only with what are termed labor questions. The vast individual and corporate fortunes, the vast combinations of capital, which have marked the development of our industrial system, create new conditions and necessitate a change from the old attitude of the state and the nation toward property.

It is probably true that the large majority of the fortunes that now exist in this country have been amassed, not by injuring our people, but as an incident to the conferring of great benefits upon the community; and this no matter what may have been the conscious purpose of those amassing them. There is but the scantiest justification for most of the outcry against the men of wealth as such, and it ought to be unnecessary to state that any appeal which directly or indirectly leads to suspicion and hatred among ourselves, which tends to limit opportunity, and therefore to shut the door of success against poor men of talent, and finally, which entails the possibility of lawlessness and violence, is an attack upon the fundamental properties of American citizenship. Our interests are at bottom common; in the long run, we go up or go down together. Yet more and more it is evident that the state, and if necessary the nation, has got to possess the right of supervision and control as regards the great corporations, which are its creatures; particularly as regards the great business combinations which derive a portion of their importance from the existence of some monopolistic tendency. The right should be exercised with caution and self-restraint; but it should exist, so that it may be invoked if the need arise.

So much for our duties, each to himself and each to his neighbor, within the limits of our own country. But our country, as it strides forward with ever-increasing rapidity to a foremost place among the world powers, must necessarily find, more and more, that it has world duties also. There are excellent people who believe that we can shirk these duties and yet retain our self-respect; but these good people are in error. Other good people seek to deter us from treading the path of hard but lofty duty by bidding us remember that all nations that have achieved greatness, that have expanded and played their part as world powers, have in the end passed away. So they have, and so have all others.

The weak and the stationary have vanished as surely as, and more rapidly than, those whose citizens felt within them the life that impels generous souls to great and noble effort. This is another way of stating the universal law of death, which is itself part of the universal law of life. The man who works, the man who does great deeds, in the end dies as surely as the veriest idler who cumbers the earth's surface; but he leaves behind him the great fact that he has done his work well. So it is with nations. While the nation that has dared to be great, that has had the will and the power to change the destiny of the ages, in the end must die, yet no less surely the nation that has played the part of the weakling must also die; and whereas the nation that has done nothing leaves nothing behind it, the nation that has done a great work really continues, though in changed form, for evermore. The Roman has passed away, exactly as all nations of antiquity which did not expand when he expanded have passed away; but their very memory has vanished, while he himself is still a living force throughout the wide world in our entire civilization of to-day, and will so continue through countless generations, through untold ages.

It is because we believe with all our heart and soul in the greatness of this country, because we feel the thrill of hardy life in our veins, and are confident that to us is given the privilege of playing a leading part in the century that has just opened, that we hail with eager delight the opportunity to do whatever task Providence may allot us. We admit with all sincerity that our first duty is within our own household; that we must not merely talk, but act, in favor of cleanliness and decency and righteousness, in all political, social, and civic matters. No prosperity and no glory can save a nation that is rotten at heart. We must ever keep the core of our national being sound, and see to it that not only our citizens in private life, but above all, our statesmen in public life, practise the old commonplace virtues which from time immemorial have lain at the root of all true national well-being.

Yet, while this is our first duty, it is not our whole duty. Exactly as each man, while doing first his duty to his wife and the children within his home, must yet, if he hopes to amount to much, strive mightily in the world outside his home, so our nation, while first of all seeing to its own domestic well-being, must not shrink from playing its part among the great nations without.

Our duty may take many forms in the future, as it has taken many forms in the past. Nor is it possible to lay down a hard-and-fast rule for all cases. We must ever face the fact of our shifting national needs, of the always changing opportunities that present themselves. But we may be certain of one thing: whether we wish it or not, we cannot avoid hereafter having duties to do in the face of other nations. All that we can do is to settle whether we shall perform these duties well or ill.

Right here let me make as vigorous a plea as I know how in favor of saying nothing that we do not mean, and of acting without hesitation up to whatever we say. A good many of you are probably acquainted with the old proverb, "Speak softly and carry a big stick—you will go far." If a man continually blusters, if he lacks civility, a big stick will not save him from trouble; and neither will speaking softly avail, if back of the softness there does not lie strength, power. In private life there are few beings more obnoxious than the man who is always loudly boasting; and if the boaster is not prepared to back up his words, his position becomes absolutely contemptible. So it is with the nation. It is both foolish and undignified to indulge in undue self-glorification, and, above all, in loose-tongued denunciation of other peoples. Whenever on any point we come in contact with a foreign power, I hope that we shall always strive to speak courteously and respectfully of that foreign power. Let us make it evident that we intend to do justice. Then let us make it equally evident that we will not tolerate injustice being done us in return. Let us further make it evident that we use no words which we are not prepared to back up with deeds, and that, while our speech is always moderate, we are ready and willing to make it good. Such an attitude will be the surest possible guaranty of that self-respecting peace the attainment of which is and must ever be the prime aim of a self-governing people.

This is the attitude we should take as regards the Monroe doctrine. There is not the least need of blustering about it. Still less should it be used as a pretext for our own aggrandizement at the expense of any other American state. But, most emphatically, we must make it evident that we intend on this point ever to maintain the old American position. Indeed, it is hard to understand how any man can take any other position now that we are all looking forward to the building of the Isthmian Canal. The Monroe doctrine is not international law, but there is no necessity that it should be.

All that is needful is that it should continue to be a cardinal feature of American policy on this continent; and the Spanish-American states should, in their own interests, champion it as strongly as we do. We do not by this doctrine intend to sanction any policy of aggression by one

American commonwealth at the expense of any other, nor any policy of commercial discrimination against any foreign power whatsoever. Commercially, as far as this doctrine is concerned, all we wish is a fair field and no favor; but if we are wise we shall strenuously insist that under no pretext whatsoever shall there be any territorial aggrandizement on American soil by any European power, and this no matter what form the territorial aggrandizement may take.

We most earnestly hope and believe that the chance of our having any hostile military complication with any foreign power is very small. But that there will come a strain, a jar here and there, from commercial and agricultural—that is, from industrial—competition, is almost inevitable. Here again we have got to remember that our first duty is to our own people; and yet that we can best get justice by doing justice. We must continue the policy that has been so brilliantly successful in the past, and so shape our economic system as to give every advantage to the skill, energy, and intelligence of our farmers, merchants, manufacturers, and wage-workers; and yet we must also remember, in dealing with other nations, that benefits must be given where benefits are sought. It is not possible to dogmatize as to the exact way of attaining this end, for the exact conditions cannot be foretold. In the long run, one of our prime needs is stability and continuity of economic policy; and yet, through treaty or by direct legislation, it may, at least in certain cases, become advantageous to supplement our present policy by a system of reciprocal benefit and obligation.

Throughout a large part of our national career our history has been one of expansion, the expansion being of different kinds at different times. This explanation is not a matter of regret, but of pride. It is vain to tell a people as masterful as ours that the spirit of enterprise is not safe. The true American has never feared to run risks when the prize to be won was of sufficient value. No nation capable of self-government, and of developing by its own efforts a sane and orderly civilization, no matter how small it may be, has anything to fear from us.

Our dealings with Cuba illustrate this, and should be forever a subject of just national pride. We speak in no spirit of arrogance when we state as a simple historic fact that never in recent times has any great nation acted with such disinterestedness as we have shown in Cuba. We freed the island from the Spanish yoke. We then earnestly did our best to help the Cubans in the establishment of free education, of law and order, of material prosperity, of the cleanliness necessary to sanitary well-being in their great cities. We did all this at great expense of treasure, at some expense of life, and now we are establishing them in a free and independent commonwealth, and have asked in return nothing whatever save that at no time shall their independence be prostituted to the advantage of some foreign rival of ours, or so as to menace our well-being. To have failed to ask this would have amounted to national stultification on our part.

In the Philippines we have brought peace, and we are at this moment giving them such freedom and self-government as they could never under any conceivable conditions have obtained had we turned them loose to sink into a welter of blood and confusion, or to become the prey of some strong tyranny without or within. The bare recital of the facts is sufficient to show that we did our duty—and what prouder title to honor can a nation have than to have done its duty? We have done our duty to ourselves, and we have done the higher duty of promoting the civilization of mankind.

The first essential of civilization is law. Anarchy is simply the handmaiden and forerunner of tyranny and despotism. Law and order enforced by justice and by strength lie at the foundation of civilization. Law must be based upon justice, else it cannot stand, and it must be enforced with resolute firmness, because weakness in enforcing it means in the end that there is no justice and no law—nothing but the rule of disorderly and unscrupulous strength. Without the habit of orderly obedience to the law, without the stern enforcement of the laws at the expense of those who defiantly resist them, there can be no possible progress, moral or material, in civilization. There can be no weakening of the law-abiding spirit at home if we are permanently to succeed, and just as little can we afford to show weakness abroad. Lawlessness and anarchy were put down in the Philippines as a prerequisite to inducing the reign of justice.

Barbarism has and can have no place in a civilized world. It is our duty toward the people living in barbarism to see that they are freed from their chains, and we can only free them by destroying barbarism itself. The missionary, the merchant, and the soldier may each have to play a part in this destruction, and in the consequent uplifting of the people. Exactly as it is the duty of a civilized power scrupulously to respect the rights of all weaker civilized powers and gladly to help those who are struggling toward civilization, so it is its duty to put down savagery and barbarism. As in such a work human instruments must be used, and as human instruments are imperfect, this means that at times there will be injustices—that at times merchant or soldier, or even missionary, may do wrong.

Let us instantly condemn and rectify such wrong when it occurs, and, if possible, punish the wrong-doer. But, shame, thrice shame, to us if we are so foolish as to make such occasional wrong-doing an excuse for failing to perform a great and righteous task. Not only in our own land, but throughout the world, throughout all history, the advance of civilization has been of incalculable benefit to mankind, and those through whom it has advanced deserve the higher honor. All honor to the missionary, all honor to the soldier, all honor to the merchant, who now in our own day have done so much to bring light into the world's dark places.

Let me insist again, for fear of possible misconstruction, upon the fact that our duty is twofold, and that we must raise others while we are benefiting ourselves. In bringing order to the Philippines, our soldiers added a new page to the honor-roll of American history, and they incalculably benefited the islanders themselves. Under the wise administration of Governor Taft the islands now enjoy a peace and liberty of which they have hitherto never even dreamed. But this peace and liberty under the law must be supplemented by material, by industrial, development. Every encouragement should be given to their commercial development, to the introduction of American industries and products; not merely because this will be a good thing for our people, but infinitely more because it will be of incalculable benefit to the people of the Philippines.

We shall make mistakes; and if we let these mistakes frighten us from work, we shall show ourselves weaklings. Half a century ago, Minnesota and the two Dakotas were Indian hunting-grounds. We committed plenty of blunders, and now and then worse than blunders, in our dealings with the Indians. But who does not admit at the present day that we were right in wresting from barbarism and adding to civilization the territory out of which we have made these beautiful states? And now we are civilizing the Indian and putting him on a level to which he could never have attained under the old conditions.

In the Philippines, let us remember that the spirit and not the mere form of government is the essential matter. The Tagals have a hundredfold the freedom under us that they would have if we had abandoned the islands. We are not trying to subjugate a people; we are trying to develop them and make them a law-abiding, industrious, and educated people, and, we hope, ultimately, a self-governing people. In short, in the work we have done we are but carrying out the true principles of our democracy. We work in a spirit of self-respect for ourselves and of good-will toward others; in a spirit of love for and of infinite faith in mankind. We do not blindly refuse to face the evils that exist or the shortcomings inherent in humanity; but across blunderings and shirking, across selfishness and meanness of motive, across short-sightedness and cowardice, we gaze steadfastly toward the far horizon of golden triumph.

If you will study our past history as a nation, you will see we have made many blunders and have been guilty of many shortcomings, and yet that we have always in the end come out victorious, because we have refused to be daunted by blunders and defeats—have recognized them, but have persevered in spite of them. So it must be in the future. We gird up our loins as a nation with the stern purpose to play our part manfully in winning the ultimate triumph; and therefore we turn scornfully aside from the paths of mere ease and idleness, and with unfaltering steps tread the rough road of endeavor, smiting down the wrong and battling for the right as Greatheart smote and battled in Bunyan's immortal story.

ON READING THE BIBLE

Mr. President, Dr. Russell, and you my friends and neighbors here, and those who on behalf of my friends and neighbors I greet as guests to-night: I want to say first of all, sir, that you could not have enjoyed coming up as much as I enjoyed having you at my house. All I regret is that there were not more of you present.

I am glad to have the opportunity of saying a few words to you this evening, and in a sense my text has been furnished me by what Mr. Russell said when he spoke of the Bible as not only essential to Christianity but essential to good citizenship; that not only as Christians but as good citizens we have the right to challenge support for the work done by this and kindred societies.

As all of you know, there are certain truths which are so very true that we call them truisms; and yet I think we often half forget them in practise. Every thinking man, when he thinks, realizes what a very large number of people tend to forget that the teachings of the Bible are so interwoven and entwined with our whole civic and social life that it would be literally—I do not mean figuratively, I mean literally—impossible for us to figure to ourselves what that life would be if these teachings were removed. We would lose almost all the standards by which we now judge both public and private morals; all the standards toward which we, with more or less of resolution, strive to raise ourselves. Almost every man who has by his life-work added to the sum of human achievement of which the race is proud, of which our people are proud, almost every such man has based his life-work largely upon the teachings of the Bible. Sometimes it has been done unconsciously, more often consciously; and among the very greatest men a disproportionately large number have been diligent and close students of the Bible at first hand.

Lincoln—sad, patient, kindly Lincoln, who, after bearing upon his weary shoulders for four years a greater burden than that borne by any other man of the nineteenth century, laid down his life for the people whom living he had served so well—built up his entire reading upon his early study of the Bible. He had mastered it absolutely; mastered it as later he mastered only one or two other books, notably Shakespeare; mastered it so that he became almost "a man of one book," who knew that book, and who instinctively put into practise what he had been taught therein; and he left his life as part of the crowning work of the century that has just closed.

In this country we rightly pride ourselves upon our system of wide-spread popular education. We most emphatically do right to pride ourselves upon it. It is not merely of inestimable advantage to us; it lies at the root of our power of self-government. But it is not sufficient in itself. We must cultivate the mind; but it is not enough only to cultivate the mind. With education of the mind must go the spiritual teaching which will make us turn the trained intellect to good account. A man whose intellect has been educated, while at the same time his moral education has been neglected, is only the more dangerous to the community, because of the exceptional additional power which he has acquired. Surely what I am saying needs no proof; surely the mere statement of it is enough, that education must be education of the heart and conscience no less than of the mind.

It is an admirable thing, a most necessary thing, to have a sound body. It is an even better thing to have a sound mind. But infinitely better than either is it to have that for the lack of which neither sound mind nor a sound body can atone—character. Character is in the long run the decisive factor in the life of individuals and of nations alike.

Sometimes, in rightly putting the stress that we do upon intelligence, we forget the fact that there is something that counts more. It is a good thing to be clever, to be able and smart; but it is a better thing to have the qualities that find their expression in the Decalogue and the Golden Rule. It is a good and necessary thing to be intelligent; it is a better thing to be straight and decent and fearless. It was a Yale professor, Mr. Lounsberry, who remarked that his experience in the class room had taught him "the infinite capacity of the human mind to withstand the introduction of knowledge." Some of you preachers must often feel the same way about the ability of mankind to withstand the introduction of elementary decency and morality.

A man must be honest in the first place; but that by itself is not enough. No matter how good a man is, if he is timid he cannot accomplish much in the world. There is only a very circumscribed sphere of usefulness for the timid good man. So, besides being honest, a man has got to have courage, too. And these two together are not enough. No matter how brave and honest he is, if he is a natural born fool, you can do little with him. Remember the order in which I name them. Honesty first; then courage; then brains—*and all are indispensable*. We have no room in a healthy community for either the knave, the fool, the weakling, or the coward.

You may look through the Bible from cover to cover, and nowhere will you find a line that can be construed into an apology for the man of brains who sins against the light. On the contrary, in the Bible, taking that as a guide, you will find that because much has been given to you much will be expected from you; and a heavier condemnation is to be visited upon the able man who goes wrong than upon his weaker brother, who cannot do the harm that the other does, because it is not in him to do it.

So I plead, not merely for training of the mind, but for the moral and spiritual training of the home and the church; the moral and spiritual training that have always been found in, and that have ever accompanied the study of, this book; this book, which in almost every civilized tongue can be described as "The Book," with the certainty of all understanding you when you so describe it. One of the highest tributes of modern times to the worth of the Bible as an educational and moral influence of incalculable value to the whole community came from the great scientist Huxley, who said: "Consider the great historical fact that for three centuries this book has been woven into the life of all that is noblest and best in our history, and that it has become the national epic of our race; that it is written in the noblest and purest English, and abounds in exquisite beauties of mere literary form; and, finally, that it forbids the veriest hind, who never left his village, to be ignorant of the existence of other countries and other civilizations and of a great past, stretching back to the furthest limits of the oldest nations in the world.

"By the study of what other book could children be so much humanized and made to feel that each figure in that vast historical procession fills, like themselves, but a momentary space in the interval between the eternities?

"The Bible has been the Magna Charta of the poor and of the oppressed. Down to modern times, no state has had a constitution in which the interests of the people are so largely taken into account; in which the duties, so much more than the privileges, of rulers are insisted upon, as that drawn up for Israel in Deuteronomy and Leviticus. Nowhere is the fundamental truth that the welfare of the state, in the long run, depends upon the righteousness of the citizen, so strongly laid down. The Bible is the most democratic book in the world."

The teaching of the Bible to children is, of course, a matter of especial interest to those of us who have families —and, incidentally, I wish to express my profound belief in large families. Older folks often fail to realize how readily a child will grasp a little askew something they do not take the trouble to explain. We cannot be too careful in seeing that the biblical learning is not merely an affair of rote, so that the child may understand what it is being taught. And, by the way, I earnestly hope that you will never make your children learn parts of the Bible as punishment. Do you not know families where this is done? For instance: "You have been a bad child—learn a chapter of Isaiah." And the child learns it as a disagreeable task, and in his mind that splendid and lofty poem and prophecy is forever afterward associated with an uncomfortable feeling of disgrace. I hope you will not make your children learn the Bible in that way, for you can devise no surer method of making a child revolt against all the wonderful beauty and truth of Holy Writ.

Probably there is not a mother or a school teacher here who could not, out of her own experience, give instance after instance of the queer twists that the little minds give to what seem to us perfectly simple sentences. Now, I would make a very strong plea for each of us to try and see that the child understands what the words mean. I do not think that it is ordinarily necessary to explain the simple and beautiful stories of the Bible; children understand readily the lessons taught therein; but I do think it necessary to see that they really have a clear idea of what each sentence means, what the words mean.

Probably some of my hearers remember the old Madison Square Presbyterian Church in New York, when it was under the ministry of Dr. Adams, and those of you who remember the doctor will, I think, agree with me that he was one of those very rare men with whose name one instinctively tends to couple the adjective "saintly." I attended his church when I was a little boy. The good doctor had a small grandson, and it was accidentally discovered that the little fellow felt a great terror of entering the church when it was vacant. After vain attempts to find out exactly what his reasons were, it happened late one afternoon that the doctor went to the church with him on some errand. They walked down the aisle together, their steps echoing in the vacant building, the little boy clasping the doctor's hand and gazing anxiously about. When they reached the pulpit he said, "Grandpa, where is the zeal?" "The what?" asked Dr. Adams. "The zeal," repeated the little boy; "why, don't you know, 'the zeal of Thine house hath eaten me up'?" You can imagine the doctor's astonishment when he found that this sentence had sunk deep into his little grandson's mind as a description of some terrific monster which haunted the inside of churches.

The immense moral influence of the Bible, though of course infinitely the most important, is not the only power it has for good. In addition there is the unceasing influence it exerts on the side of good taste, of good literature, of proper sense of proportion, of simple and straightforward writing and thinking.

This is not a small matter in an age when there is a tendency to read much that even if not actually harmful on moral grounds is yet injurious because it represents slipshod, slovenly thought and work; not the kind of serious thought, of serious expression, which we like to see in anything that goes into the fiber of our character.

The Bible does not teach us to shirk difficulties, but to overcome them. That is a lesson that each one of us who has children is bound in honor to teach these children if he or she expects to see them become fitted to play the part of men and women in our world.

Again, I want you to think of your neighbors, of the people you know. Don't you, each one of you, know some man (I am sorry to say, perhaps more often, some woman) who gives life an unhealthy turn for children by trying to spare them in the present the very things which would train them to do strong work in the future? Such conduct is not kindness. It is short-sightedness and selfishness; it means merely that the man or woman shrinks from the little inconveniences, to himself or herself, of making the child fit itself to be a good and strong man or woman hereafter. There should be the deepest and truest love for their children in the hearts of all fathers and mothers. Without such love there is nothing but black despair for the family; but the love must respect both itself and the one beloved. It is not true love to invite future disaster by weak indulgence for the moment.

What is true affection for a boy? To bring him up so that nothing rough ever touches him, and at twenty-one turn him out into the world with a moral nature that turns black and blue in great bruises at the least shock from any one of the forces of evil with which he is bound to come in contact? Is that kindness? Indeed, it is not. Bring up your boys with both love and wisdom; and turn them out as men, strong-limbed, clear-eyed, stout-hearted, clean-minded, able to hold their own in this great world of work and strife and ceaseless effort.

If we read the Bible aright, we read a book which teaches us to go forth and do the work of the Lord; to do the work of the Lord in the world as we find it; to try to make things better in this world, even if only a little better, because we have lived in it. That kind of work can be done only by the man who is neither a weakling nor a coward; by the man who in the fullest sense of the word is a true Christian, like Greatheart, Bunyan's hero. We plead for a closer and wider and deeper study of the Bible, so that our people may be in fact as well as in theory "doers of the word and not hearers only."

TRUSTS AND THE TARIFF

To-day I wish to speak to you on the subject, or group of subjects, which we mean when we talk of the trusts. The word is used very loosely, and almost always with technical inaccuracy. But the average man when he speaks of the trusts means rather vaguely all of the very big corporations, the growth of which has been so signal a feature of our modern times, and especially those big corporations which, though organized in one state, do business in several states, and some of which have a tendency to monopoly. This whole subject of the trusts is of vital concern to us, because it presents one, and perhaps the most conspicuous, of the many problems forced upon our attention by the tremendous industrial development which has taken place during the last half-century in all civilized countries, and notably in our own. Many factors have concurred in bringing about these changed industrial conditions.

It matters very little whether or not we like these new conditions, the creation of these new opportunities. Many admirable qualities which were developed in the older, simpler, less progressive life, have to some degree atrophied under the conditions of our rather feverish, high-pressure, complex, and specialized life of to-day. But our likes and dislikes have very little to do with the matter. The new conditions are here. They have produced both good and evil. We cannot get rid of them—even if it were not undesirable to get rid of them—and our instant duty is to try to accommodate our social, economic, and legislative life to them, and to frame a system of law and conduct under which we shall get out of them the utmost possible benefit and the least amount of harm. It is foolish to pride ourselves on our marvelous progress and prosperity, upon our commanding position in the international world, and at the same time have nothing but denunciation for the men to whose commanding business ability we in part owe this very progress and prosperity, this commanding position.

Law can to a degree guide, protect, and control industrial development, but it can never cause it or play more than a subordinate part in its healthy development. Unfortunately, it is easy enough by bad laws to bring it to an almost complete stop. In dealing with the big corporations we intend to proceed not by revolution, but by evolution. We wish to face the facts, declining to have our vision blinded either by the folly of those who say there are no evils, or by the more dangerous folly of those who either see, or make believe that they see, nothing but evil in all the existing system, and who, if given their way, would destroy the evil by the simple process of bringing ruin and disaster to the entire country.

Corporations that are handled honestly and fairly, so far from being an evil, are a natural business evolution, and make for the general prosperity of our land. We do not wish to destroy corporations. We wish to make them subserve the public good. All individuals, rich or poor, private or corporate, must be subject to the law of the land, and the government will hold them to a rigid obedience thereto. The biggest corporation, like the humblest private citizen, must be held to strict compliance with the will of the people as expressed in the fundamental law. The rich man who does not see that this is in his interest is indeed short-sighted. When we make him obey the law we insure for him the absolute protection of the law. The savings banks show what can be done in the way of genuinely beneficent work by large corporations when intelligently administered and supervised. They now hold over twenty-six hundred millions of the people's money, and pay annually about one hundred millions of interest or profit to their depositors. There is no talk of danger from these corporations; yet they possess great power, holding over three times the amount of our present national debt; more than all the currency, gold, silver, greenbacks, etc., in circulation in the United States. The chief reason for there being no talk of danger from them is that they are on the whole faithfully administered for the benefit of all, under wise laws which require frequent and full publication of their condition, and which prescribe certain needful regulations with which they have to comply, while at the same time giving full scope for the best enterprise of their managers within these limits.

Now, of course, savings banks are as highly specialized a class of corporations as railroads, and we cannot force too far the analogy with other corporations; but there are certain conditions which I think we can lay down as indispensable to the proper treatment of all corporations which from their size have become important factors in the social development of the community.

Before speaking, however, of what can be done by way of remedy, let me say a word or two as to certain proposed remedies which, in my judgment, would be ineffective or mischievous. The first thing to remember is that, if we are to accomplish any good at all, it must be by resolutely keeping in mind the intention to do away with any evils in the conduct of big corporations, while steadfastly refusing to assent to indiscriminate assault upon all forms of corporate capital as such. The line of demarcation we draw must always be on conduct, not on wealth; our objection to any given corporation must be, not that it is big, but that it behaves badly.

Nor can we afford to tolerate any proposal which will strike at the so-called trusts only by striking at the general well-being. If we are forced to the alternative of choosing a system under which most of us prosper somewhat, though a few of us prosper too much, or else a system under which no one prospers enough, why, of course, we will choose the former. A remedy much advocated at the moment is to take off the tariff from all articles which are made by trusts. To do this it will be necessary first to define trusts. The language commonly used by the advocates of the method implies that they mean all articles made by large corporations, and that the changes in tariff are to be made with punitive intent toward these large corporations. Of course, if the tariff is to be changed in order to punish them, it should be changed so as to punish those that do ill, not merely those that are prosperous. It would neither be just nor expedient to punish the big corporations as big corporations; what we wish to do is to protect the people from any evil that may grow out of their existence or mal-administration.   Some of those corporations do well and others do ill.   If, in any case, the tariff is found to foster a monopoly which does ill, why, of course, no protectionist would object to a modification of the tariff sufficient to remedy the evil.

But in very few cases does the so-called trust really monopolize the market.   Take any very big corporation which controls, say, something over half the products of a given industry.   Surely, in rearranging the schedules affecting such a big corporation, it would be necessary to consider the interests of its smaller competitors, which control the remaining part, and which, being weaker, would suffer most from any tariff designed to punish all the producers; for, of course, the tariff must be made light or heavy for big and little producers alike.   Moreover, such a corporation necessarily employs very many thousands of workmen, and the minute we proceeded from denunciation to action it would be necessary to consider the interests of these workmen.   Furthermore, the products of many trusts are unprotected, and would be entirely unaffected by any change in the tariff, or, at most, very slightly so.   The Standard Oil Company offers a case in point, and the corporations which control the anthracite coal output offer another—for there is no duty whatever on anthracite coal.

I am not discussing the question of the tariff as such, whether from the standpoint of the fundamental difference between those who believe in a protective tariff and those who believe in free trade; or from the standpoint of those who, while they believe in a protective tariff, feel that there could be a rearrangement of our schedules, either by direct legislation or by reciprocity treaties which would result in enlarging our markets; nor yet from the standpoint of those who feel that stability of economic policy is at the moment our prime economic need, and that the benefits to be derived from any change in schedules would not compensate for the damage to business caused by the widespread agitation which would follow any attempted general revision of the tariff at this moment.

Without regard to the wisdom of any one of those three positions, it remains true that the real evils connected with the trusts cannot be remedied by any change in the tariff laws. The trusts can be damaged by depriving them of the benefits of a protective tariff only on condition of damaging all their smaller competitors and all the wage-workers employed in the industry.

This point is very important, and it is desirable to avoid any save wilful misunderstanding. I am not now considering whether or not, on grounds totally unconnected with the trusts, it would be well to lower the duties on various schedules, either by direct legislation or by legislation or treaties designed to secure as an effect reciprocal advantages from the nations with which we trade. My point is that changes in the tariff would have little appreciable effect on the trusts, save as they shared in the general harm or good proceeding from such changes. No tariff change would help one of our smaller corporations or one of our private individuals in business, still less one of our wage-workers, as against a large corporation in the same business; on the contrary, if it bore heavily on the large corporation, it would inevitably be felt still more by that corporation's weaker rivals, while any injurious result would of necessity be shared by both the employer and employed in the business concerned.

The immediate introduction of substantial free trade in all articles manufactured by trusts—that is, by the largest and most successful corporations—would not affect some of the most powerful of our business combinations in the least, save by the damage done to the general business welfare of the country; others would undoubtedly be seriously affected, but much less so than their weaker rivals, while the loss would be divided between the capitalists and the laborers, and after the years of panic and distress had been lived through, and some return to prosperity had occurred, even though all were on a lower plane of prosperity than before, the relative difference between the trusts and their rivals would remain as marked as ever. In other words, the trust, or big corporation, would have suffered relatively to and in the interest of its foreign competitors, but its relative position toward its American competitors would probably be improved; little would have been done toward cutting out or minimizing the evils in the trusts; nothing toward securing adequate control and regulation of the large modern corporations.   In other words, the question of regulating the trusts with a view to minimizing or abolishing the evils existent in them is separate and apart from the question of tariff revision.

You must face the fact that only harm will come from a proposition to attack the so-called trusts in a vindictive spirit by measures conceived solely with a desire of hurting them, without any regard as to whether or not discrimination should be made between the good and evil in them, and without even any regard as to whether a necessary sequence of the action would be the hurting of other interests.   The adoption of such a policy would mean temporary damage to the trusts, because it would mean temporary damage to all of our business interests; but the effect would be only temporary, for exactly as the damage affected all alike, good and bad, so the reaction would affect all alike, good and bad.

The necessary supervision and control, in which I firmly believe as the only method of eliminating the real evils of the trust, must come through wisely and cautiously framed legislation which shall aim, in the first place, to give definite control to some sovereign over the great corporations, and which shall be followed, when once this power has been conferred, by a system giving to the government the full knowledge which is the essential for satisfactory action. Then, when this knowledge, one of the essential features of which is proper publicity, has been granted, what further steps of any kind are necessary can be taken with the confidence born of the possession of power to deal with the subject and of a thorough knowledge of what ought to and can be done in the matter.

We need additional power, and we need knowledge. Our Constitution was formed when the economic conditions were so different that each state could wisely be left to handle the corporations within its limits as it saw fit.   Nowadays all the numerous corporations which I am considering do what is really an interstate business, and as the states have proceeded on very different lines in regulating them, they are often organized in a state in which they do little or no business, and do an enormous business in other states, to the spirit of whose laws they may be openly antagonistic.

It might be better if all the states could agree to work along the same lines in dealing with these corporations, but I see not the slightest prospect of such agreement. Therefore, I personally feel that ultimately the nation will have to assume the responsibility of regulating these very large corporations which do an interstate business. The states must combine to meet the problem caused by the great combinations of capital, and the easiest way for the states to combine is by action through the national government.

I am well aware that the process of constitutional amendment is necessarily a slow one, and one into which our people are reluctant to enter save for the best of reasons, but I am confident that in this instance the reasons exist. I am also aware that there will be difficulty in framing an amendment which will meet the objects of the case, and yet which will secure the necessary support. The very fact that there must be delay in securing the adoption of such an amendment insures full discussion and calm consideration of the whole subject, and will prevent any ill-considered action. I have no intention of trying to outline the proper phraseology of such an amendment, for I know it must come as a matter of agreement and discussion. But I firmly believe that all these obstacles can be met, if only we face them both with the determination to overcome them, and with the further determination to overcome them in ways which shall not do damage to the country as a whole, which, on the contrary, shall further our industrial development, and shall help, instead of hinder, all corporations which work out their success by means that are just and fair toward all men.

Without the adoption of a constitutional amendment, my belief is that a good deal can be done by law. It is difficult to say exactly how much, because experience has taught us that, in dealing with these subjects, where the lines dividing the rights and duties of the state and of the nation are in doubt, it has sometimes been difficult for Congress to forecast the action of the courts upon its legislation. Such legislation (whether obtainable now or obtainable only after a constitutional amendment) should provide for a reasonable supervision, the most prominent feature of which at first should be publicity—that is, the making public both to the governmental authorities and to the people at large the essential facts in which the public is concerned. This would give us exact knowledge of many points which are now not only in doubt, but the subject of fierce controversy. Moreover, the mere fact of the publication would cure some very grave evils, for the light of day is a deterrent to wrong-doing. It would doubtless disclose other evils, with which for the time being we could devise no way to grapple. Finally, it would disclose others that could be grappled with and cured by further legislative action.

I advocate action which the President only can advise, and which he has no power in himself to take. Under our present legislative and constitutional limitations, the national executive can work only between narrow lines in the field of action concerning great corporations. Between those lines I assure you that exact and even-handed justice will be dealt, and is being dealt, to all men, without regard to persons.

I wish to repeat with all emphasis that, desirable though it is that the nation should have the power I suggest, it is equally desirable that it should be used with wisdom and self-restraint. The mechanism of modern business is tremendous in its size and complexity, and ignorant intermeddling with it would be disastrous. We should not be made timid or daunted by the size of the problem; we should not fear to undertake it, but we should undertake it with, ever present in our minds, dread of the sinister spirits of rancor, ignorance, and vanity. We need to keep steadily in mind the fact that, besides the tangible property in each corporation, there lies behind it the spirit which brings it success, and in the case of each very successful corporation this is usually the spirit of some one man or set of men. Under exactly similar conditions one corporation will make a stupendous success where another makes a stupendous failure, simply because one is well managed and the other is not. While making it clear that we do not intend to allow wrong-doing by one of the captains of indus.try, any more than by the humblest private in the industrial ranks, we must also, in the interests of all of us, avoid cramping a strength which, if beneficently used, will be for the good of all of us.

The marvelous prosperity we have been enjoying for the last few years has been due primarily to the high average of honesty, thrift, and business capacity among our people as a whole; but some of it, also, has been due to the ability of the men who are the industrial leaders of the nation. In securing just and fair dealing by these men, let us remember to do them justice in return, and this not only because it is our duty, but because it is our interest, not only for their sakes, but for ours. We are neither the friend of the rich man as such nor the friend of the poor man as such; we are the friend of the honest man, rich or poor, and we intend that all men, rich and poor, shall obey the law alike, and receive its protection alike.

THE EARL OF ROSEBERY

QUESTIONS OF EMPIRE

[Archibald Philip Primrose, Earl of Rosebery, sometime premier
of Great Britain, was born in London in 1847. He was educated at
Eton and Oxford, and became a peer at twenty-one. He held office
under Gladstone in 1881 and again in 1886. His remarkable political ap-
titudes and the popular qualities of his oratory had by this time made
him prominent in the political world. His devotion to the principles
of the Liberal party as led by Gladstone could not be questioned,
and upon the retirement of "the grand old man" in 1894 the Queen
sent for Lord Rosebery, who thereupon became premier, but he went
out of power the following year. His subsequent course has made his
attitude toward his party anomalous. Throughout the South African
war he declined to act with a section of the Liberal party headed by
Sir Henry Campbell-Bannerman, some of the points of difference being
Irish Home Rule, which he repudiated, and imperialism, which he
interpreted in a vigorous sense. Subsequently, however, he showed a
more conciliatory disposition, and the movement to reunite the Liberal
party under his leadership has recently gathered considerable force.
The speech that follows was made before the University of Glasgow,
as Lord Rector, in 1900, and deals with the progress and increase of
the political power of Great Britain.]

I HAVE thought that I would best serve you, my young
constituents, by speaking to you of a subject which
affects us all, and with which I have had something, though
not much, to do—a concrete contemporary subject, which
fills all minds at times, which will increasingly fill yours.
I wish to say something to you of that British empire of
which we are the tenants in fee, of which we inherit the
responsibility and the glory. It is so vast a topic that
I can only touch a fringe, I can only deal with considerations which directly affect yourselves. It is in the strict
sense a political subject, but it is outside party politics, and
can and should be treated without affecting the most sensitive apprehension. But even here I must make a single

exception; for there are some to whom the very word is abhorrent, to whom at any rate the word is under suspicion. It bears to them some taint of disagreeable association. They affect to see in it danger of braggadocio or aggression. Personally I do not share their suspicions. Still, it is not the word, but the thing, that I value. I admit that the term has been constantly prostituted in Britain as well as elsewhere. And yet we cannot discard it, for there is no convenient synonym. If any other word can be invented which as adequately expresses a number of states of vast size under a single sovereign, I would gladly consider it. But at present there is none. And in the meantime the word "empire" represents to us our history, our tradition, our race. It is to us a matter of influence, of peace, of commerce, of civilization—above all, a question of faith.

But it is also a matter of business, a practical affair. You have received from your forefathers this great appanage; no one outside an asylum wishes to be rid of it. The question, then, at this time is simply how to do the best with it. That is a tremendous problem, so tremendous that you and I and all of us have to take our share of it. And all of us in this hall, rich or poor, young or old, clever or dull, can do something, each in his line of life, like bees in their cells, to make this empire surer, better, and happier, even if only by being honest, industrious citizens ourselves. Moreover, the empire never needed such loyal service so much as now. Never did it so urgently require the strenuous and united support of its subjects. For in the present state of the world an active vigilance is more than ever required. We have to make sure of our equipment. This we are apt to take for granted. On the contrary, I maintain that there is much to overhaul, to examine, and to reconsider; that what would have kept the empire together in the days when we had an unenvied monopoly of colonies and when armaments were both less vast and less menacing will not suffice now; that there is a disposition to challenge both our naval and commercial position, which requires our utmost vigilance; that we may have to test our training, our habits, our character, our capacity, for work by severer standards than have hitherto been applied; that we must be called upon for effort and sacrifice if we wish to maintain our place; that we must be prepared, in a word, to set our house in order and to consider whether what has sufficed in the past will suffice in the future.

What is this empire?

The last calculation seems to be this: that its area is between eleven and twelve millions of square miles, and that its subjects number in round figures some four hundred millions. The details in so spacious a summary matter little. It is already beyond comprehension. And yet one cannot but pause for a moment to reflect that but for a small incident—the very ordinary circumstance of the acceptance of a peerage—this empire might have been incalculably greater. Had the elder Pitt, when he became first minister, not left the House of Commons, he would probably have retained his sanity and his authority. He would have prevented, or suppressed, the reckless budget of Charles Townshend, have induced George III. to listen to reason, have introduced representatives from America into the Imperial Parliament, and preserved the thirteen American colonies to the British crown. Is it fanciful to dwell for a moment on what might have happened? The Reform bill which was passed in 1832 would probably have been passed much earlier, for the new blood of America would have burst the old vessels of the Constitution. It would have provided for some self-adjusting system of representation such as now prevails in the United States, by which increasing population is proportionately represented. And at last, when the Americans became the majority, the seat of empire would perhaps have been moved solemnly across the Atlantic, and Britain have become the historical shrine and the European outpost of the world empire.

What an extraordinary revolution it would have been had it been accomplished! The greatest known without bloodshed; the most sublime transference of power in the history of mankind. Our conceptions can scarcely picture the procession across the Atlantic—the greatest sovereign in the greatest fleet in the universe, ministers, government, Parliament, departing solemnly for the other hemisphere, not, as in the case of the Portuguese sovereigns, emigrating to Brazil under the spur of necessity, but under the vigorous embrace of the younger world. It is well to bridle the imagination, lest it become fantastic and extravagant.

Moreover, it is a result to which we can scarcely acclimatize ourselves, even in idea. But the other effects might have been scarcely less remarkable. America would have hung on the skirts of Britain and pulled her back out of European complications. She would have profoundly affected the foreign policy of the mother-country in the direction of peace. Her influence in our domestic policy would have been scarcely less potent. It might probably have appeased and even contented Ireland. The ancient Constitution of Great Britain would have been rendered more comprehensive and more elastic. On the other hand, the American yearning for liberty would have taken a different form; it would have blended with other traditions and flowed into other molds. And, above all, had there been no separation there would have been no War of Independence, no War of 1812, with all the bitter memories that these have left on American soil. To secure that priceless boon I could have been satisfied to see the British Federal Parliament sitting in Columbia Territory. It is difficult indeed to dam the flow of ideas in dealing with so pregnant a possibility. But I restrain myself, because I know that I am dreaming, and that an historical dream, though not a bad relaxation in itself, should not be allowed to become a nightmare. I acknowledge, too, that this is what is called an academical discussion. But where should one be academical if not in the ancient University of Glasgow?

Let us then return to earth, or at any rate to that large proportion of it which is covered by the Union Jack. I have, before wandering into the empire as it might have been, given you the broad aspect of the empire as it is. Now, for my purpose it is not important to consider whether this empire is greater or less than others, for it is impossible to compare states. Mere area, mere population, do not necessarily imply power; still less do they import the security and contentment of the inhabitants. But my main reason for discarding relative proportions is very different. We have to consider not others, but ourselves. It is not alien empires which should concern us, except when they menace or compete. Our first main necessary responsibility is to our own. It is so vast, so splendid, so pregnant, that we have to ask ourselves: Are we adequate to it? Can we discharge our responsibility to God and to man for so magnificent, so populous a proportion of the world?

Our answer, offhand, is ready and simple. We are adequate. We do discharge our responsibilities. We are a conquering and imperial race. All over the world we have displayed our mettle. We have discovered and annexed and governed vast territories. We have circled the globe with our commerce. We have penetrated the pagan races with our missionaries. We have inoculated the universe with our institutions. We are apt indeed to believe that our soldiers are braver, our sailors hardier, our captains, naval and military, skilfuller, our statesmen wiser, than those of other nations. As for our Constitution, there is no Briton at any hour of the day or night who will suffer it to be said that there is any that approaches it.

All this is in a measure true, I hope; at any rate, I am not here to dispute it. When, indeed, I remember some episodes during the past twelve months, I feel that it is hardly possible to exaggerate the courage and character of our nation: the brave boys at the front, the silent endurance at home—I cannot think of these without emotion, as well as with admiration and with pride. But our boasts, even if they be true, do not contain the whole truth. It would be well enough if we could lie on a bank of asphodel, basking in our history, our glory, and our past. That, however, is not possible. Never was it less possible than now. Fifty years ago we had to face a world that was comparatively inert. Europe was concerned with Europe, and little more. The armies of Europe were relatively small, and not wholly disproportionate to ours. The United States had no army. Ten or twelve years later a terrible convulsion rent the great Republic, and for a moment her hosts were numbered by the million. That baleful flame shot up to heaven and sank down when the agony was overpast, but its memory remained a portent. Twenty years later, a national war arose between France and Germany which produced a potent German empire, and converted all the nations of Europe into passive armies. We remained complacent in the confidence that these storms could not pass the channel. The channel has indeed done much for us. It has often protected us from the broils of the Continent. It has been our bulwark, though heedless speculators have sought to undermine it. But it cannot guard us from the peaceful attacks of trained and scientific rivalry in the arts of peace. It cannot protect us against the increasing subtlety and development of the arts of war.

There is a further and perhaps a mightier change in the conditions of the world during the past half-century. Fifty years ago the world looked lazily on while we discovered, developed, and annexed the waste or savage territories of the world. All that is now changed. The colonial microbe has penetrated almost every empire except that of Charles V., which has outlived it; and even here I must except his Netherland Provinces. France, in the last ten or fifteen years, has annexed perhaps a quarter of Africa, and has made a considerable irruption into Asia. Germany has shown no less a desire to become a colonizing nation. Russia pursues her secular path of unchecked absorption, constantly attracting fresh bodies into her prodigious orbit. Italy has been bitten by the same desire for expansion. The United States finds itself sitting like a startled hen on a brood of unnumbered islands in the Philippine group. All this is well and fair enough, but it changes our relation to the world. Every mile of unmapped country, every naked tribe of savages, is wrangled over as if it were situated in the center of Europe. The world has shrunk into a continent of ascertained boundaries. The illimitable and the unknown, the happy field of dreams, have disappeared. That is a blow to imagination, but it is not a fact of substantial importance to us, who do not desire to increase our territories. Indirectly, however, it raises a number of delicate and disputable points. Moreover, a colonial passion is apt to cause an ill-feeling, composed of envy, jealousy, and other hostile tendencies toward the ancient colonial empire. This again does not signify, provided we realize it, and do not deserve it, and are ready to deal with it.

Then, again, there is the question of trade. Foreign countries used to sneer at trade. It was considered below the dignity of warlike races. We were described as a nation of shopkeepers. Now every nation wishes to be a nation of shopkeepers. This new object is pursued with the intelligent purpose which was once applied to the balance of power. That is a great change. We once had a sort of monopoly; we now have to fight for existence.

I summarize these various circumstances, to show how greatly the conditions of our commonwealth and its relations to the outer world have become modified. Some of these changes have passed almost unperceived. I call attention to them, to demonstrate the necessity of our asking ourselves this vital and imperative question: Have our state machinery and methods been examined and remodeled in view of them? If not, no time should be lost.

After all, a state is in essence a great joint-stock company, with unlimited liability on the part of its shareholders. It is said, and said with truth, that, difficult as it is to make a great fortune, it is scarcely less difficult to keep it. With even more accuracy the same may be said of a business. A fortune without care is apt to disappear, as snow wastes away in a languid thaw. And a business depends on incessant vigilance, on method, on keeping abreast of the times. A business in these days can live but a short time on its past reputation, and what is true of a business is true of an empire. It is found out to be a sham: its aims, its government, its diplomacy, are seen to be out of date by watchful rivals; an excuse is found for a quarrel (and such excuses are easy)—the empire is tested, and fails, and succumbs.

As in a business, too, a periodical stock-taking is necessary in a state. So far as mere money is concerned, this is regularly done. We know, with some accuracy, our income, our expenditure, and our debts. But money, though a national necessity and a valuable international weapon, is not everything. A business house in these days looks over its managers and its agents, and considers whether they continue efficient. It surveys its methods and compares them with those of its rivals; it discards those which are obsolete and adopts all improvements. If it does not do this, it is doomed. This sort of stock-taking is unknown to the British Empire. The ordinary Briton thinks it is needless. He says comfortably that we have won Waterloo and Blenheim and Trafalgar, and have produced Nelson and Wellington and Roberts; we have plenty of trade and plenty of money; how on earth could we do better? And this fatal complacency is so ingrained that some despair of a remedy until we are awakened by a national disaster. For an empire, like a business, if neglected, may become obsolete.

Take the example of Prussia—for I know no other so striking—of the necessity of constant vigilance in the strict maintenance of a state. Though he began to reign over little but an inland spit of sand, her Great Frederick raised her to be the most formidable power in Europe. So he left her when he died in 1786. And yet, twenty years afterward, owing to the neglect and inadequacy of his successors, she had almost ceased to exist. She was wrecked, and dismembered, and prostrate; she ceased to have a voice among the nations. That interval was short, for the catastrophe brought out the real resources of the national character. You will see in Königsberg, which some of you perhaps venerate as the home of Kant, the little room—at the end of a long hall, chosen for that reason so that none might overhear—the little room where the heroic and saintly Queen Louise worked for the regeneration of the country. But here again, as in the most Teutonic transactions, her statesmen were not satisfied with stop-gap reform. They went to the root of the matter. They indeed effected a sane, simple, and momentous amendment in their army system. But they went much further. Stein and his compeers saw that a malady which had almost produced dissolution required a drastic remedy. They had the courage to face it. At great sacrifice, with natural grumblings and moanings, still audible to us, they cut the feudal system out of the body politic. The remedy was severe, but it saved the patient. In no other country but Prussia would such a course, even under such circumstances, have been possible. But the North German, when he sees that things go wrong, will at once return to first principles. So Prussia was saved, and emerged once more a first-rate power. Then there was another interval, on which it is not necessary to dwell. And again, with the aid of trained, able servants not afraid to face heroic measures, she emerged more puissant than before. Can there be a clearer instance of the building up of a power by vigilant care, of its quick destruction by neglect, and of its recovery by a return to the secret of its original success?

The first question, then, as I have said, which we must put to ourselves, and we cannot put a more momentous one, is: Are we worthy of this prodigious inheritance? Is the race which holds it capable of maintaining and developing it? Are we, like the Romans, not merely a brave, but also a persistent, businesslike, alert, governing people? And if we can answer this affirmatively, as I hope we can, we have these further questions to ask ourselves: Are we going the right way about our work, and are our methods abreast of our time?

I do not profess to ask these questions to-day, still less to answer them. But I suggest that you should ask them of yourselves, for they concern you all. You cannot, indeed, give a full or adequate answer; but the questions will recur to you as long as you live. At different periods of life you will give different answers, but no one can attempt a complete reply. Even if the nation chose to ask them of itself, I suppose it would only appoint a royal commission, which would produce a library of blue books when we were in our graves. And yet the nation might do worse. Suppose, when it decennially takes stock of its population, that it took stock of a little more. Suppose, when it numbered the people, that it tested their plight; that it inquired if their condition were better or worse than ten years before; and so as to the position of our industries, of our education, of our naval and military systems. Suppose that the state did at some such periods demand an account of each of its stewards. The general result would probably be satisfactory; but it may be predicted with much more certainty that weaknesses, and abuses, and stagnation would be discovered—an ill condition, which is apt when neglected to be contagious and dangerous.

The nation does, indeed, confess itself from time to time spasmodically through the newspapers. But that impulse, sincere though it be, is apt to disappear with the stress which inspired it. It is not sustained or businesslike. It evaporates in a committee, or in some new ecstasy. Dogged, unrelenting, unreserved self-examination there is none; perhaps none is possible. The churches, it is true, are always demanding it—all the more honor to them. But the adverb "always" contains the secret of their want of success, or of their only partial success. They are always, necessarily, doing it, so they necessarily deaden their effect; it is their business to do it, and so men pass on. The shadow of the future is as vain as all other shadows. Prosperity, while it endures, is the drug, the hashish, which blinds the patient to all but golden visions. And yet we are nearing an epoch of no common kind, short indeed in the lives of nations, but longer than the life of man, when we may well pause to take stock. Within six weeks we shall have closed the nineteenth century, and have entered on a new one for better or for worse. It is, of course, only an imaginary division of time, though it seems solemn enough, for we are on the pinnacle of the world's temple, where we can look forward or look back.

What will that twentieth century be? What will be its distinctive note? Of the nineteenth we may say generally that it has been an era of emancipation, considerable though not complete. Nations, as a rule, have been sorted into boundaries more consonant with their aspirations and traditions than was formerly the case. The tyranny of sects, in Britain at any rate, has partially abated. The undue pressure of government has diminished. Slavery has disappeared. All over the world there have been great strides toward freedom; and though inadequate, they have been so considerable as to produce for a moment an apathy of self-satisfaction. But the twentieth! What does it bear in its awful womb? Of one thing only can we be certain—that it will be a period of keen, intelligent, almost fierce international competition, more probably in the arts of peace even than in the arts of war. How, then, should we prepare for such an epoch and such a conflict?

It is a matter in which universities have a deep concern. For there is one fact, at any rate, to which we cannot be blind. The first need of our country is a want of men. We want men for all sorts of high positions—first-rate men, if possible; if not, as nearly first-rate as may be. The supply of such men is never excessive, but, as the empire has increased, so has the demand, and the supply seems to be much less elastic. In other words, the development and expansion of the empire have produced a corresponding demand for first-rate men, but the supply has remained, at best, stationary. Of course we do not employ all those that we have, for by the balance of our Constitution, while one half of our capable statesmen is in full work, the other half is, by that fact, standing idle in the market-place with no one to hire them. This used to be on a five years' shift, but all that is now altered. Anyhow, it is a terrible waste. But, putting that incident apart, even among the fixed eternal stars of the public service there is not a sufficient supply of men for the purposes of government. I could name a typical diplomatist, a typical soldier, a typical civil servant, and could say of each of them that could he be multiplied by forty the market would not be glutted. I am not gloomy about all this. I believe that the men, or something of the kind, are there; the difficulty is to find them. The processes of discovery and selection are apt to lead to jobbery, so we employ the slow ladder of a fixed service and of promotion by seniority. Now a senior is a very good thing, but I am sure that I shall have the unanimous approval of my constituents in saying that a junior is a better—wherever, at any rate, physical strength and activity are required. Our civil service is a noble one, perhaps matchless—certainly unsurpassed. Its zeal and capacity for its special work are admirable. Its members are loyal to all chiefs and strenuous to help them. But it does not give us what we want for the elastic needs of the empire. A service of that kind, however excellent, and perhaps because it is excellent, is apt to become a caste. Moreover, the admittance to it is by brain-work alone. Now brains, though necessary and desirable, are not everything; for administration under varying climes and circumstances, what I may call wild administration, you want much more. You want, for this purpose, force of character, quick decision, physical activity, and endurance of all kinds, besides, if possible, the indefinable qualities which sway mankind. You want men who will go anywhere at a moment's notice and do anything. These qualities cannot be tested by civil service examiners. And yet we have a good deal of dare-devil, adaptable raw material on hand. Some of the young generals who have come through the arduous experiences of this war will be fit for almost anything that they may be called on to do. But these have been seasoned by the severest of training, and we cannot often afford such an education.

This dearth of men, as I have said, concerns you directly, for you are part of the coming generation, and I hope that there may be among my constituents some of these necessary men. But this at any rate is clear, that it is the function of our universities to produce such men.

And this leads me to another question. Are we setting ourselves sufficiently to train such men? I doubt it. The most illustrious of our public schools has no modern side. Oxford and Cambridge still exact their dole of Latin and Greek. I cannot believe, from the imperial point of view, having regard to the changed conditions of the world, that this is necessary, or adequate, or wise. I concede Latin as a training instrument and a universal language. But how about Greek? It is, perhaps, the noblest of tongues: it enshrines, perhaps, the noblest of literatures. To learned men it is a necessity. But must it be a part of the necessary equipment of the ordinary youth of the nineteenth century, who has so much to learn in order to be equal to his age? Heine once remarked, with sardonic humor: "How fortunate were the Romans that they had not to learn the Latin grammar, for if so they would not have had time to conquer the world." Well, I pass the Latin grammar with a gloomy respect, but I will say that the Greek grammar, except in the learned professions, seems to me a heavy burden for our empire, subject as it is to eager and intelligent competition. I think that when our national ignorance of foreign languages has become not merely a byword, but almost a commercial disaster, we might reconsider part of our educational apparatus. This is no new question. Thirty-three years ago it was raised at Edinburgh by one who was not merely a remarkable statesman, but a brilliant scholar. He had been a famous classical tutor at Oxford, yet, nevertheless, he protested against our educational bondage to the dead languages. The same protest is being raised in Edinburgh again to-day, but this time by the voice of the mercantile community. The leading bodies of that calling lately appointed a committee to consider the subject of

commercial education.   Their report is well worth reading.
They speak of the ancient tongues with courtesy and respect, but they demand something more practically useful,
less divorced from every-day life.   For one thing, they urge
with earnestness the better teaching of modern languages.
There is required, they say, on the part of the educational
authorities, an admission that a man may be an educated,
and even a cultured gentleman, although he has not seriously studied Latin or Greek; and they further point out
that both France and Germany possess invaluable literatures, with the advantage that they are in languages which
are living, and not dead.   I agree with them in thinking
that for the purposes of the present age, especially for the
merchant and the politician, there is required a more modern education, more especially as regards languages.   I do
not pretend that a modern education will necessarily produce the men you need for all purposes of administration.
No; but it will help you to train them, it will give them
the weapons of life, it will give you citizens who are so far
capable of meeting the new requirements of the world.

I must not expatiate.   I will merely say that we want
good men for the public service; that the demand has grown
with the growth of the empire, and that the supply has
failed to keep pace with it.   I doubt, moreover, whether
we are going the right way to rear such a supply.   But that
is only a small part of the question of race.   In reality we
do not depend so much on our governments as would seem
to be the case.   Looking back over the past century, there
is one luminous fact—how little the Anglo-Saxon nations
depend on their governments, or owe to them.   The people
wield their own destinies; they walk their own paths.   The
governments are passing signs—as it were the cockades of
different colors which used to be worn, and which denoted
the parties to which the wearers belonged.   And this view
of the case incalculably enhances the importance of our
race problem.   Our people in the main govern themselves
—let them be worthy governors; mentally and physically,
let them be worthy of their high destiny.

But education, as I have said, is only a part of our race
problem.   An empire such as ours requires as its first condition an imperial race—a race vigorous and industrious

and intrepid. Are we rearing such a race? In the rural
districts I trust that we are. I meet the children near
Edinburgh returning from school, and I will match them
against any children in the world. But in the great cities,
in the rookeries and slums which still survive, an imperial
race cannot be reared. You can scarcely produce anything
in those foul nests of crime and disease but a progeny
doomed from its birth to misery and ignominy. That is
a rift in the corner-stone of your commonwealth, but it
brings some of you directly into its service. For many here
are reared to the service of medicine. They will be phy-
sicians, surgeons, medical officers, medical inspectors.
Remember, then, that where you promote health and arrest
disease, where you convert an unhealthy citizen into a
healthy one, where you exercise your authority to promote
sanitary conditions and suppress those which are the reverse,
you in doing your duty are also working for the empire.
"Sanitas sanitatum, omnia sanitas," said one of your dead
rectors, and he did not greatly exaggerate. Health of mind
and body exalt a nation in the competition of the universe.
The survival of the fittest is an absolute truth in the conditions of the modern world. Even if our schools and universities train the national mind efficiently, the national body
may not be neglected. Another of your dead rectors declared, in a phrase scarcely less famous than Lord Beaconsfield's, that the schoolmaster was abroad—meaning that he
was active. Let us hope that we may soon feel that the
medical officer is abroad with sufficient power in his arm,
power which he must derive from public opinion as well
as from his central or municipal employers.

And there are other relative questions which we cannot
ignore. How do we stand with regard to those healthy,
hardy, frugal virtues which mean so much, physically and
morally, to a people? Whether an insidious and excessive
luxury is not prevalent among us; whether the passion for
wealth, its influence, and the worship it receives, be not a
danger; whether, indeed, our land is not becoming the
playground and pleasance of the plutocrats of all nations,
in itself a symptom not wholly bad, but yet not wholly
good, for a plutocracy is one of the most detestable of all
dominations: these are grave questions with which we are

confronted. Against this apparent luxury we set the rough manliness of our sports, our cricket, our football, our hunting. That in itself is no adequate answer, for even healthy sport, like other good things, may be overdone. But, looking back at the past as a guide for the future, I ask myself what was the secret of the marvelous success of the Scottish people during the last century in Scotland itself, in England, and in the outer Britains? It was not achieved in purple and fine linen, in soft raiment, or in kings' houses. No! their poverty was equal to their patriotism; their energy to both. How did they succeed? By intense industry, by severe frugality, by constant adaptability to all circumstances and all conditions, however rigorous and novel they might be. And so it was that they raised Scotland to wealth and Scotsmen to power, and made both Scotland and her sons the objects of that jealousy and suspicion which are some of the sincerest testimonies to success.

I have spoken of their intense industry, and this leads me to another question. Do we work hard enough?—or rather, as I would put it, Are we thorough enough? That was a great word, "thorough," bequeathed to us by one of the most memorable of British statesmen: a great word, not as he used it, but a word in itself which should thrill through all mankind from the age of reason to the shadow of death. But fortune, success, and well-being are apt to make us forget it. I doubt if Jeshurun, in his proverbial prosperity, kicked thoroughly; it was probably a sort of elegant flourish. And now we cannot but observe that it is beginning to be hinted that we are a nation of amateurs. Is this true? If so, it is not merely a grave charge, but an obvious danger. Let us test it in passing. For example, we are warriors, and merchants, and statesmen. Are we as thorough masters of these crafts as we should be? Wars, for example, always find us unprepared. I dare say no more, but so much is incontrovertible. And yet, on the other hand, I cannot help suspecting that in the most consummate military administration which now exists, nothing is left to chance which can be guarded against by forethought. Then, again, in statesmanship (I speak, of course, of all our statesmen of all parties), do we conspicuously shine? Are we businesslike and thorough? Do we antici-

pate or follow events?   Are our ministries not overwhelmed
by the treble task of departmental administration, of preparing policies, and of oratorical combat, inside and outside
Parliament?   We have abroad the reputation of being
subtle, unscrupulous, and of corrupting the universe with
our gold.   But, as a matter of fact, we are never subtle,
seldom unscrupulous, and have no gold which Parliament
would allow to be used in corruption.   It is almost a
reproach to the honorable statesmanship of Great Britain
that, abstaining as it does, voluntarily or involuntarily, from
these successful qualities, it should have managed to earn
all the opprobrium attached to them.   Then is our policy
sufficiently persistent and continuous to insure success?   I
cannot give an answer to so broad a question on this occasion.   But, as in the military case, I will cite another power.
There is one signal quality which I specially admire in the
policy of Russia.   It is practically unaffected by the life of
man or the lapse of time—it moves on, as it were, by its
own impetus; it is silent, concentrated, perpetual, and unbroken; it is, therefore, successful.   But I must pass from
these arts, for such topics verge on that forbidden territory
which no rector can touch and survive.

Commerce, however, comes fairly within my limits as
a bond of empire, and affects our university, which stands
aloft in such a teeming mart.   Here, then, is, at any rate,
ample opportunity for taking stock and considering methods.
I cannot enter into the discussion whether there is cause for
alarm as to the future of our trade; there is no time for
that, nor is this the place.   But it may fairly be alleged that
there are disquieting symptoms.   Whether these symptoms
be truthful indications or not, they are, at any rate, worthy
of careful, incisive investigation.   In some quarters such
indications are never neglected.   I am greatly struck by a
passage in the report of the United States consul at Chem-
nitz, cited in the pamphlet in which our university sets
forth its requirements.   "If an industry in Germany lan-
guishes," he says, "immediately a commission inquires
into the causes, and recommends remedial measures, among
which usually is the advice to establish technical or industrial schools, devoted to the branch of business under consideration."   In a word, they go to the root, to the prin-

ciple, to the source. This is thoroughness, this is the scientific method applied to manufacture, and we see its success. The Americans, I gather, have hitherto applied themselves rather less to the principles than the applications of science. I do not pretend to say which are right. The Germans are alarmed at the development of American commerce, and we are alarmed at both. At any rate, both in Germany and the United States you see an expenditure and a systematic devotion to commercial, and technical, and scientific training. I know that much is done, too, in Great Britain. But I doubt if even that is carried out in the same methodical way; nor is there anything like the same lavish, though well-considered expenditure. It always seems to me as if in Germany nothing, and in Britain everything, is left to chance. "Nothing but a miracle can stop us," think the Germans, when they have completed their preparations. "We shall have our usual miracle," thinks the cheerful Briton, as he sets out a good deal in arrear. With the same intelligent persistence with which the German makes war, he has entered on the peaceful conflict of commerce, and therefore has achieved the same brilliant success. We need not envy that success, we do not grudge it; but it is well to observe it, and to note its causes.

Commerce, then, is a bond of empire which this university by its training may do much to strengthen. The mercantile committee at Edinburgh demand, indeed, that to our universities shall be added a commercial faculty which would stimulate the commercial side in our secondary schools, and which would be of substantial importance in attracting to the university men who are about to enter on a commercial life. They "believe that a university education would be of the greatest service to the men who are to occupy the chief positions in large commercial undertakings." Our university has not as yet seen its way, where so much has to be done, to take this new and important step. It has done much, it is doing much, but it is well aware of its weakness. It is now appealing for aid to place itself on a properly scientific footing, a footing adequate to its position in this great commercial community, which so greatly needs and which can so fruitfully utilize opportunities of technical and scientific training. It will not, I think, appeal to the second city of the empire in vain.

But the newest of our universities has advantages which are denied to the more ancient with regard to modern requirements. For the practical purposes of the present day a university which starts in the twentieth century has a great superiority over a university founded in the fifteenth, more especially when it is launched with keen intelligence of direction and ample funds, as is the new University of Birmingham. These practical universities are the universities of the future, for the average man who has to work for his livelihood cannot superadd the learning of the dead to the educational requirements of his life and his profession. There will always be universities, or at any rate colleges, for the scholar, the teacher, and the divine; but year by year the ancient universities will have to adapt themselves more and more to modern exigencies. And where so much has to be absolutely novel it is, perhaps, easier to begin than to remodel or adapt. So that the new universities which do not require for their utilitarian purposes hoary antiquity or ancient prescription will have an advantage over the venerable schools which have for centuries guarded and interpreted and transmitted the accumulated treasures of erudition.

There was a time, long years ago, when the spheres of action and of learning were separate and distinct; when laymen dealt hard blows and left letters to the priesthood. That was to some extent the case when our oldest universities were founded. But the separation daily narrows, if it has not already disappeared. It has been said that the true university of our days is a collection of books. What if a future philosopher shall say that the best university is a workshop? And yet the latter definition bids fair to be the sounder of the two. The training of our schools and colleges must daily become more and more the training for action, for practical purpose. The question will be asked of the product of our educational system: "Here is a young fellow of twenty; he has passed the best years of acquisition and impression; he has cost so much; what is his value? For what in all the manifold activities of the world is he fit?" And if the answer be not satisfactory, if the product

be only a sort of learned mummy, the system will be condemned. Are there not thousands of lads to-day plodding
away, or supposed to be plodding away, at the ancient
classics who will never make anything of those classics, and
who, at the first possible moment, will cast them into space,
never to reopen them? Think of the wasted time that that
implies; not all wasted, perhaps, for something may have
been gained in power of application, but entirely wasted so
far as available knowledge is concerned. And if you consider, as you will have to consider in the stress of competition, that the time and energy of her citizens is part of
the capital of the commonwealth, all those wasted years
represent a dead loss to the empire.

If, then, these recent events and the present conditions
of the world induce thinkers and leaders in this country to
test our strength and methods for the great—but, I hope,
peaceful—struggle before us, they must reckon the training
of man. On that, under Providence, depends the future,
and the immediate future, of the race; and what is empire
but the predominance of race?

How is that predominance to be secured? Remember
the conditions: nations all becoming more dense and numerous, and therefore more hungry and more difficult to satisfy; nations more and more educated and intelligent, more
observant of each other; nations more and more alive to
their substantial interests and capable of pursuing them;
nations, therefore, increasingly aware of the vital necessity
of a healthy, growing commerce, and fiercely determined to
obtain it; nations more and more civilized, and therefore
less and less anxious for the wager of battle, but still ready
even for that, if it be necessary for their new objects. After
all, when you have reduced all this to its last expression, it
comes to this—the keener and more developed intelligence
of humanity, stimulated by competition and enhanced by
training. It is with that intelligence that we have to struggle and to vie.

This conflict we have no reason to fear, if we choose to
rouse ourselves. We have, I believe, the best natural
material in the world. But I doubt if we are sufficiently
alive to the exigencies of the situation. It is, perhaps, well
to revel in a sunburst of prosperity and of high wages. It

may be well to owe much of that prosperity to an unbounded exportation of coal, of which we have a large but
limited supply, and which is vitally necessary to us as the
element of existence.   It is well in a time of stress to send
a host of spirited volunteers to the front, to admire their
hereditary valor, and to welcome them back.   It is well to
be convinced that we are the finest fellows on the earth,
and supreme on the seas.   If that be the truth, it is comfortable enough.   But the mere exhilarating impression is
scarcely sufficient.   If it were founded on hard, tested facts,
it would be eminently satisfactory.   But is it?

There is no disparagement implied in the criticism of
this attitude.   There is only a sense of the heedless self-
confidence of strength.   Our people do not realize the
actual closeness of competition, and the cold, elaborate,
vigilant science which that fact involves.   The calculating
tortoise in these days will always overtake the exuberant
hare; and yet even the tortoise will seek to improve his
pace.   Everything that survives becomes refined to an art.
Take your games as an instance.   Chess, I suppose, was in
its inception an artless diversion.   It now taxes the most
acute minds, and elicits new powers from the brain.   The
first cricketer, as I judge from portraits, played with an
elementary club which would now be wholly incompetent
to defend a wicket for an instant.   But football affords an
even stronger illustration.   I suppose it began in the childish propensity to play with a ball and the boyish anxiety
to kick anything.   But it has developed into a science.   I
know of no sport which affords such lessons for national
success as Association football.   I do not, indeed, understand the refinements of the game.   But the meanest intellect can grasp that it implies incessant watchfulness; that
its essence is an alert combination of all powers for one
object; that indolence or selfishness are fatal; that the
player, indeed, who does not do his best to coöperate or
who plays for his own hand must necessarily be outlawed.
So it is with nations.   If they desire to survive, they must
constantly sharpen their intelligence and equipment.   They
need the constant coöperation of the government with the
governed; of science and vigilance with commerce; of the
teachers with the taught, and with the age in which they teach.

Remember, too, this historical fact. We belong to a nation which has ever been ambitious. Under the great Edwards and Harries and the mighty reign of Elizabeth, ambition grew and swelled and has never had leisure to shrink. But ambition, though an exulting, is an exacting, virtue. It is made of stern stuff; it cannot endure apathy or even content. It exacts constant sacrifice and untiring endeavor. Planting a flag here and there, or demarcating regions with a red line on a map, are vain diversions if they do not imply an unswerving purpose to develop and to maintain. But maintenance requires that we shall be alive to all modern methods. Yet we are apt to forget this, and to imagine that our swaddling-clothes will suffice for our maturity.

I urge you then, gentlemen, to realize in your own persons and studies the responsibility which rests on yourselves. You are, after all, members of that company of adventurers (used in the Elizabethan and not the modern sense) which is embarked in the business of carrying this British Empire through the twentieth century. Each of you has his share in that glorious heritage, and each of you is answerable for that share. Be, then, practical partners, intelligent partners, industrious partners, and so you will be in the best sense practical, intelligent, industrious imperialists. Be inspired in your various callings with the thought of the service that you can do to your country in faithfully following your profession, so that in doing private you are doing public duty too. The church, the law, and medicine, those chaste and venerable sisters, will, I suppose, claim most of you, and in the service of each you have ample opportunities of rendering service to the Commonwealth. The law is the ladder to Parliament; and the tribunal of appeal is, and I hope will increasingly be, a constitutional bond of empire. The missions of the churches, and the churches themselves, apart from their sacred functions and home labors, which directly serve the state so far as they raise their flocks, have incalculably aided in the expansion, consolidation, and civilization of the empire. And medicine should tend and raise the race, on which all depends. For from my point of view there is not a close in the darkest quarters of Glasgow, or a crofter's cabin in the Hebrides, which is not a matter of imperial concern, quite as truly, in its proportion and degree, as those more glowing topics to which that adjective is too often limited.

And mark this: in all that I have said there is no word of war, not even the beat of a drum, or the distant singing of a bullet. To some the empire is little else, and that makes many hate the word. That is not my view. Our empire is not founded on the precedents associated with that name. It is not the realm of conquest which that term has been used to imply. It has often used the sword, it could not exist without the sword, but it does not live by the sword. Defense and readiness to fight are vital enough in their way, but not less vital is the civil and domestic side: the commerce, the education, the intelligence, the unceasing leaven of a high and the sour decadence of a low ideal. War and conquest can fill the lives of but a part of the nation: a sane and simple duty to the empire may well inspire the whole.

And when we work in that spirit, we should receive grace from the idea, from that glorious vision transformed into fact—the British Empire.

Remember how incomparably Shakespeare described it:—

> " This royal throne of kings, this sceptered isle,
> This earth of majesty, this seat of Mars,
> This other Eden, demi-paradise,
> This fortress built by Nature for herself
> Against infection and the hand of war,
> This happy breed of men—this little world,
> The precious stone set in the silver sea,
>
> .   .   .   .
>
> This blessed spot, this earth, this realm, this England."

And yet that was only the source and center of what we now behold, which has soared so far beyond whatever Shakespeare can have conceived.

How marvelous it all is! Built not by saints and angels, but the work of men's hands; cemented with men's honest blood and with a world of tears, welded by the best brains of centuries past; not without the taint and reproach incidental to all human work, but constructed on the whole with pure and splendid purpose. Human, and yet not wholly human, for the most heedless and the most cynical must see the finger of the Divine. Growing as trees grow, while others slept; fed by the faults of others as well as by the character of our fathers; reaching with the ripple of a resistless tide over tracts, and islands, and continents, until our little Britain woke up to find herself the foster-mother of nations and the source of united empires. Do we not hail in this less the energy and fortune of a race than the supreme direction of the Almighty? Shall we not, while we adore the blessing, acknowledge the responsibility? And while we see, far away in the rich horizons, growing generations fulfilling the promise, do we not own with resolution mingled with awe the honorable duty incumbent on ourselves? Shall we then falter or fail? The answer is not doubtful. We will rather pray that strength may be given us, adequate and abundant, to shrink from no sacrifice in the fulfilment of our mission; that we may be true to the high tradition of our forefathers; and that we may transmit their bequest to our children, aye, and, please God, to their remote descendants, enriched and undefiled, this blessed and splendid dominion.

LORD SALISBURY

ON THE ABANDONMENT OF GENERAL ("CHINESE") GORDON

[Robert Arthur Talbot Gascoigne Cecil, Marquis of Salisbury, a statesman and prime minister of England, was born at Hatfield, Hertfordshire, in 1830. He was educated at Eton and Christ Church, and at the age of twenty-three was elected to the House of Commons. In 1866 he joined Lord Derby's administration, but resigned in a year rather than support the Conservative suffrage reform bill. In 1868 his father died, and he left the Commons to enter the House of Lords, where after an interval of some years he became the recognized Conservative leader. When Disraeli became prime minister in 1874, Salisbury was made a member of the Cabinet, as Secretary of State for India. He now won a name for himself as a diplomatist, having, in 1878, become Minister for Foreign Affairs, and during the ensuing ten years negotiated many important treaties. In 1885 he became prime minister, but was forced to resign, though he was once more premier (1886–1892). In 1895 Salisbury was again called upon to form a ministry, and his last administration carried on the government until 1902, when the veteran statesman voluntarily withdrew to private life, having brought the Boer War to a successful conclusion and ushered in the great era of imperial federation. The first of the following speeches was made before the House of Lords in 1885, the second at a public meeting (the Middlesex Conservative Association) in London in 1875.]

THE motion which I have the honor to lay before your lordships has a double aspect—it passes judgment on the past, and expresses an opinion with regard to the policy of the future. Some people receive with considerable impatience the idea that, at the present crisis of our country's destiny, we should examine into the past, and spend our time in judging of that which cannot be recalled.

But I think that such objections are unreasonable. We depend in one of the greatest crises through which our country has ever passed on the wisdom and decision of those who guide our counsels, and we can only judge of what dependence is rightly to be placed by examining their conduct in the past, and seeing whether what they have done justifies us in continuing that confidence in the difficulties which are to come.

Now, whatever else may be said of the conduct of her Majesty's government, I think those who examine it carefully will find that it follows a certain rule and system, and that in that sense, if in no other, it is consistent. Their conduct at the beginning of the Egyptian affair has been analogous to their conduct at the end; throughout there has been an unwillingness to come to any requisite decision till the last moment.

There has been an absolute terror of fixing upon any settled course, and the result has been that, when the time came that external pressure forced a decision on some definite course, the moment for satisfactory action had already passed, and the measures that were taken were taken in haste, with little preparation, and often with little fitness for the emergencies with which they had to cope. The conduct of the government has been an alternation of periods of slumber and periods of rush. The rush, however vehement, has been too unprepared and too unintelligent to repair the damage which the period of slumber has effected.

I do not wish to go far back into the Egyptian question, but it is necessary to point out the uniformity of the character and conduct of the government. The first commencement of our trouble was the height to which Arabi's rebellion was allowed to go. The government knew very well the danger of Arabi while he was yet a small man and had little influence. They were perfectly aware of the mischief he was brewing, but they not only declined to act themselves, but, unless they have been greatly maligned, they prevented the local authorities from acting. They also prevented Arabi from being removed, as he should have been, from the confines of Egypt, by which, had it been done, all the evil would have been averted.

While this enterprise was going on, the government reposed in absolute security, and took no effective measure till the pressure of public opinion forced upon them the movement of the fleet into the harbor of Alexandria. That was a very fair illustration of the vice which characterized their policy. That movement was made suddenly, with no preparation, and forced us into what followed. The fleet was moved in; as a matter of course Arabi resisted, and the fleet, as was inevitable, suddenly replied; and then it was found that there were no forces to land and back up the action that was taken.

The result of that imprudence was that not only was the Khedive's throne shaken and the fidelity of his army utterly destroyed, but the town and fortifications of Alexandria were grievously injured, and that tremendous debt for the injury to Alexandria was incurred which still remains as a burden upon Egyptian finance, and a hindrance to all negotiations for the settlement of foreign claims. That was the first specimen of their period of slumber, followed by a sudden and unprepared rush.

Then came the question of the Sudan. It was no new question, for before the battle of Tel-el-Kebir the Mahdi was already in arms. It was a matter with which anybody who undertook to deal with the destiny of Egypt ought to have been familiar and ready with a decision. But none was at hand, and matters were allowed to drift. The government, plunged in absolute torpor, seemed to have but one care—that they should escape the nominal responsibility, though real responsibility must inevitably attach to their action. Their despatches, one after another, during that period, merely repeated the old burden, that the government had no responsibility.

The result was that the unhappy Hicks went into the Sudan wretchedly equipped, with an army beneath the number he ought to have had, and composed of men turned out as worthless from the Egyptian army. The inevitable result followed—a result at which her Majesty's government had no reason to be surprised, for they were warned of the danger by their own confidential agents, yet absolutely declined to interfere. They hoped by disclaiming responsibility to escape the consequences of their own neglect.

Hicks's army was totally destroyed, and not a man escaped to tell the tale, and then the government awoke from the period of slumber, and the period of rush began. They adopted two measures, both of them as inadequate and inapplicable to the circumstances as it was possible to conceive, and both big with future trouble.

In the first place, they announced suddenly to the world and to Egypt that Egypt must abandon the Sudan. It was impossible to have conceived a more stupendous political blunder. It was a proclamation to our enemies that they should enjoy impunity, and to our friends that they would be handed over without mercy to those who claimed to overcome them. But that announcement was made, and from that moment the fate of the garrisons scattered over the Sudan was sealed. The fate of the garrison of Khartum was brought home to them forcibly, but did they take any reasonable measures for its relief? Did they send any troops on which they could rely to defend the garrison?

No; they adopted the absurd and Quixotic plan of taking advantage of the chivalry and devotion of one of the noblest spirits our age has seen, by sending him forward on the impossible and hopeless errand of accomplishing by mere words and promises that which they had not the courage to do by force of arms. From that commencement, the abandonment of the Sudan to the mission of General Gordon, all our subsequent troubles arose.

But that was not all, for among those garrisons in the Sudan were those of Sinkat and Tokar, which, so far back as November 1883, were severely pressed by the Mahdi's lieutenants, and their danger was announced to the government as extreme. But for three months they took no notice of that danger. They allowed the matter to be left to General Baker and a body of Egyptians, whose worthlessness was denounced in every page of the correspondence that was laid before them. Of course General Baker with such a force was inevitably defeated; but it was not until April or May—I think not till a vote of censure was announced—that the government determined on making an effort to do that which they ought to have done, and which, if they had not been asleep, they would have done three months before—namely, to relieve the garrisons of Sinkat and Tokar. And when the resolution came at last—when the necessity dawned upon their minds—they plunged into it with their usual imprudence and want of plan. They sent men down to Suakin apparently with no idea as to what those men were to do, and before they could take effective measures Sinkat had fallen, and the garrison of Tokar, giving up in despair, had surrendered themselves.

Then the aimlessness of the government was revealed. Having landed their forces, they would not expose themselves to the ridicule of taking them away without doing anything, so they slaughtered six thousand Arabs, and then came away absolutely without any result for the blood of their friends and their enemies shed. They came away guilty of all this bloodshed, because they had plunged into the enterprise without any definite view or any fixed plan by which they proposed to guide themselves.

Now, my lords, these three things, the case of the bombardment of Alexandria, the abandonment of the Sudan, and the mission of General Graham's force—they are all on the same plan, and they all show that remarkable characteristic of torpor during the time that action was needed, and of impulsive, hasty, and ill-considered action when the moment for action had passed by.

Their future conduct was modeled on their conduct in the past. So far was it modeled that we were able to put it to the test which establishes a scientific law. The proof of scientific law is when you can prophesy from previous experience what will happen in the future. It is exactly what took place in the present instance. We had had these three instances of the mode of working of her Majesty's government before us. We knew the laws that guided their action, as astronomers, observing the motions of a comet, can discover by their observations the future path which that comet is to travel; and we prophesied what would happen in the case of General Gordon.

My right honorable friend Sir Stafford Northcote prophesied it in the House of Commons, and was met by a burst of fury from the prime minister such as that assembly has seldom seen. He was told that Egypt was of much less importance than, I think, Sutherland or Caithness, that everything wrong was the result of deficits imputed to him in the finances of some ten years ago, and he was generally denounced because he interfered with the beneficent legislation on the subject of capable citizens, and so forth, by introducing the subject of Egypt as many as seventeen

THE ABANDONMENT OF GENERAL GORDON   1813

times.   That did not prevent his prophecies being correct,
and I ventured to repeat them in this house.

I do not like to quote my own words; it is egotistical;
but as proof of what I call the accuracy of the scientific
law, I should like to refer to what I said on the fourth of
April, when we were discussing the prospect of the relief of
General Gordon.   The government were maintaining that
he was perfectly safe, and that it was very unreasonable for
us to raise the question in Parliament.   What I said was
this:

> "Are these circumstances encouraging to us, when we are asked to
> trust to the inspiration of the moment, that when the danger comes the
> government will find some means of relieving General Gordon?   I feel
> that the history of the past will be again repeated, and just again when
> it is too late the critical resolution will be taken.   The same news will
> come that the position of Gordon is forlorn and helpless, and then some
> desperate resolution of sending an expedition will be formed too late to
> achieve its object."

I quote these words to show that we had ascertained the
orbits of those eccentric comets who sit on the treasury
bench.   Now, the terrible responsibility and blame which
rests upon them does so because they were warned in March
and April of the danger of General Gordon; they had received every intimation which men could reasonably look
for that his danger would be extreme, and delayed it from
March and April right down to the fifteenth of August
before they took a single measure.

What were they doing all that time?   It is very difficult
to conceive.   Some people have said, but I think it is an
unreasonable supposition, that the cause of the tardiness of
her Majesty's government was the accession to the Cabinet
of the noble earl the secretary for the colonies [Earl of
Derby].   I have quoted, partly with the object of defending the noble lord from that charge, for I have quoted to
show that the government were almost as bad before he
joined them as they were after.   What happened during
these eventful months?

I suppose one day some memoirs will tell our grand-
children, but we shall never know.   Some people think
there were divisions in the Cabinet, and that, after division

and division, the decision was put off in order that the Cabinet should not be broken up. I am rather inclined to think that it was due to the peculiar position of the prime minister. He came in as the apostle of the Midlothian campaign, loaded with the doctrines and the follies of that pilgrimage. We have seen it on each occasion, after each one of these mishaps when the government has been forced by events and the common sense of the nation to take some more active steps. We have seen how his extreme supporters in that campaign have reproached him as he deserted their opinions and disappointed their ardent hopes. I think that he always felt the danger of that reproach and the debt he had incurred to those supporters, and felt a dread lest they should break away and put off again and again till the last practical moment any action which might bring him into open conflict with the doctrines by which his present eminence was gained.

At all events, this is clear, that throughout those six months the government knew perfectly well the danger in which General Gordon was placed. It has been said that General Gordon did not ask for troops. Well, I am surprised at that defense. One of the characteristics of General Gordon was the extreme abnegation of his nature. It was not to be expected that he should send home a telegram to say, "I am in great danger, therefore send me troops." He would probably have cut off his right hand before he would have sent such a telegram. But he did send a telegram that the people of Khartum were in danger, and that the Mahdi must win unless military succor was sent forward, and distinctly telling the government— and this is the main point—that unless they would consent to his views the supremacy of the Mahdi was assured.

This is what he said not later than the twenty-ninth of February, almost as soon as he first saw the nature of the problem with which he had been sent to deal. It is impossible that General Gordon could have spoken more clearly than he did, but Mr. Power, who was one of the three Englishmen in Khartum, and who was sent down with Stewart on that ill-fated journey, on the twenty-third of March sent a telegram saying: "We are daily expecting British troops; we cannot bring ourselves to believe that we are to be abandoned by the government.   Our existence depends on England.''

My lords, is it conceivable that after that—two months after that—in May, the prime minister should have said that the government were waiting to have reasonable proof that Gordon was in danger? By that time Khartum was surrounded, and the governor of Berber had announced that his case was desperate, which was too surely proved by the massacre which took place in June.

And yet in May Mr. Gladstone was waiting for reasonable proof that they were in danger. Apparently he did not get that proof till August.

I may note in passing that I think the interpretation which the government have placed upon the language of their trusted officers has been exceedingly ungenerous. They told us that they did not think it necessary to send an expedition to relieve Sinkat and Tokar because they could quote some language of hope from the despatches of General Baker, and in the same way they could quote some language of hope from the despatches of General Gordon.

But a general sent forward on a dangerous expedition does not like to go whining for assistance, unless he is pressed by absolute peril. All those great qualities which go to make men heroes are such as are absolutely incompatible with such a course, and lead them to shrink as from a great disgrace from any unnecessary appeal for exertion for their protection. It was the business of the government not to interpret General Gordon's telegrams as if they had been statutory declarations, but to judge for themselves of the circumstances of the case, and to see that those who were surrounded, who were the only three Englishmen among this vast body of Mohammedans, who were already cut off from all communication with the civilized world by the occupation of every important town upon the river, were in real danger.

I cannot understand what blindness fell over the eyes of some members of the government. Lord Hartington, on the thirteenth of May, gave utterance to this expression: ''I say it would be an indelible disgrace if we should neglect any means at the disposal of this country for saving General Gordon.''

And after that announcement by the minister chiefly responsible, three months elapsed before any step was taken for doing that which he admitted the government were bound to do under the penalty of indelible disgrace. It has been said that Gordon was destroyed by treachery, and that treachery would have happened at any time when the British army came near Khartum. What does that extraordinary theory mean?

It means that the Mahdi had agreed with Farag Bey that it was much more comfortable to go on besieging, and that until Lord Wolseley made it dangerous they would go on besieging. I think those who started that unreasonable theory could hardly have been aware of the straits to which the Mahdi had been put. His army was suffering from fever, from cholera, from smallpox; there was great danger of dealing with his men, who were constantly threatening mutiny and desertion. Never was a force more hardly put to it to maintain its position than was this; and depend upon it, if he could have shortened that period of trial by an hour he would certainly have done so. But, supposing it was true that treachery was certain to do its work, what does that prove? Does it not show that sending Gordon to Khartum was an act of extreme folly?

I do not know any other instance in which a man has been sent to maintain such a position without a certain number of British troops. If the British troops had been there, treachery would have been impossible; but sending Gordon by himself to rely on the fidelity of Africans and Egyptians was an act of extreme rashness, and if the government succeed in proving, which I do not think they can, that treachery was inevitable, they only pile up an additional reason for their condemnation. I confess it is very difficult to separate this question from the personal matters involved. It is very difficult to argue it on purely abstract grounds without turning for a moment to the character of the man who was engaged and the terrible position in which he was placed.

When we consider all that he underwent, all that he sacrificed in order to serve the government in a moment of extreme exigency, there is something infinitely pathetic in reflecting on his feelings, as day after day, week after week, month after month passed by—as he spared no exertions, no personal sacrifice, to perform the duties that were placed upon him—as he lengthened out the siege by inconceivable prodigies of ingenuity, of activity, of resource—and as, in spite of it all, in spite of the deep devotion to his country which had prompted him to this great risk and undertaking, the conviction gradually grew upon him that his country had abandoned him.

It is terrible to think what he must have suffered when at last, as a desperate measure to save those he loved, he parted with the only two Englishmen with whom during those long months he had had any converse, and sent Stewart and Power down the river to escape from the fate which had become inevitable to himself. It is very painful to think of the reproaches to his country and to his country's government that must have passed through the mind of that devoted man during those months of unmerited desertion. In Gordon's letter of the fourteenth of December he said: "All is up. I expect a catastrophe in ten days' time; it would not have been so if our people had kept me better informed as to their intentions."

They had no intentions to inform him of. They were merely acting from hand to mouth to avert the parliamentary censure with which they were threatened. They had no plan, they had no intentions to carry out. If they could have known their intentions, a great hero would have been saved to the British army, a great disgrace would not have fallen on the English government.

Now, by the light of this sad history, what are the prospects for the future? Was there ever a time when clearness of plan and distinctness of policy were more required than they are now? I am not going to say that the policy of the government is bad. It would be paying them an extravagant compliment if I said so. They have no policy. My right honorable friend Mr. Gibson epigrammatically described their policy when he said, "They were going to Khartum to please the Whigs, and were going to abandon Khartum to please the Radicals."

Is there not something strange that at such a crisis of our country's fate, in both Houses of Parliament, in the press, in society, and everywhere you hear people asking what is their policy, and can get no answer? Here and there you get a distant echo of policy, something vague and ill-defined, like a distant sound to which you can attach no definite meaning. You sometimes for a moment see the phantom of a policy, but if you try to grasp it, it escapes you.

We used to think the policy of the government was the evacuation of the Sudan as soon as the military operations were over—a very bad policy—but even that does not seem to be their policy. They do not know whether they are going to evacuate the Sudan or not. They don't know who is to hold the Sudan—it may be the Italians, it may be the Turks, or the Chinese.

On one point only do they put down their foot, and that is, the Egyptians shall not keep it. We were told that they were going to smash the Mahdi, but now we are to make peace with the smashed Mahdi. If you smash the Mahdi thoroughly, he will be of no use to you, and if you do not smash him thoroughly he may maintain at the bottom of his heart a certain resentment against the process of being smashed.

It is probable that the Mahdi, in fulfilment of the claims of the religious position he occupies, will decline to have any dealings with the infidel; and if you crush him so entirely by force of arms, he will have lost all his position in the minds of his countrymen; and you will in his assist-ance or support not find any solution of the terrible problem with which you have to deal.

In the same way with the railway. So far as I know, it is unprecedented to project a railway through an enemy's country, but it implies some views of policy. It appears that her Majesty's government are going to make a railway, and then leave it to the first comers to do what they like with it. Now, it appears to me that in this matter of our Egyptian policy, though I do not say we can lay down the precise steps by which our ends may be obtained—this must depend in a great measure on the judgment of the ministry—still, it is time when we should conceive to our-selves what the ends of our policy are to be, and clearly define it and follow it up with consistency and persistency.

Now, let us examine what are the interests of England

in this matter. With Mediterranean politics as such we have no great interest to concern ourselves; but Egypt stands in a peculiar position. It is the road to India. The condition of Egypt can never be indifferent to us, and, more than that, we have a duty to insist—that our influence shall be predominant there. I do not care by what technical arrangements that result is to be obtained; but, with all due regard to the rights of the suzerain, the influence of England in Egypt must be supreme.

Now, the influence of England in Egypt is threatened from two sides. It is threatened from the north diplomatically. I do not think it is necessary that the powers should have taken up the position they have done, and I believe that with decent steering it might have been avoided; but, unfortunately, we have to face inchoate schemes which will demand the utmost jealousy and vigilance of Parliament. I do not know what arrangement the government has arrived at, but I greatly fear that it may include a multiple control, and to that I believe this country will be persistently and resolutely hostile.

But we have to face a danger of another kind. We have forces of fanatical barbarians let loose upon the south of Egypt, and owing to the blunders that have been committed this danger has reached a terrible height. Unless we intend to give over Egypt to barbarism and anarchy, we must contrive to check this inroad of barbarian fanaticism, which is personified in the character and action of the Mahdi. General Gordon never said a truer thing than that you do this by simply drawing a military line. If the insurgent Mohammedans reach the north of Egypt, it will not be so much by their military force as by the moral power of their example. We have therefore to check this advance of the Mahdi's power.

Her Majesty's government in the glimpses of policy which they occasionally afford us have alluded to the possibility of setting up a good government in the Sudan. I quite agree that a good government is essential to us in the Sudan. It is the only dike we can really erect to keep out this inundation of barbarism and fanatical forces.

But her Majesty's government speak as if a good government were a Christmas present, which you can give a

country and then take away. A good government, like
any other organization, must pass through the stages of
infancy to maturity. There must be a long stage of infancy,
during which that government is unable to defend itself,
and it requires during that period protection and security,
which it can only derive from the action of an external
power. It is that protection and security which England
must give. She must not desert her task in the Sudan
until there is that government there which can protect
Egypt, in which the interests of this country are vital. I
do not say whether it shall be done from the Nile or from
Suakin.

I see a noble lord, one of the greatest ornaments of this
House, who has conducted an expedition, not of two hundred and fifty miles, but of four hundred miles, and that
with success, over the same burning country, and his opinion, given last year, was that Suakin and Berber are the
roads by which we should advance. In that opinion I do
not say I concur—that would be impertinent—but it is an
opinion to which I humbly subscribe. I believe that by
the Suakin and Berber route we may obtain a hold over
that portion of the Sudan which may enable us to perform
our primary duty—namely, to repress the forces of barbarism and fanaticism, to encourage that civilization which, if
protected, will find such abundant root in that fertile country, and, above all, to restrain, check, and ultimately to
destroy the slave-trade, which has been the curse of Africa.

All those advantages can be obtained if England will lay
down a definite policy and will adhere to it, but consistency
of policy is absolutely necessary. We have to assure our
friends that we shall stand by them; we have to assure our
enemies that we are permanently to be feared. The blunders of the last three years have placed us in the presence
of terrible problems and difficulties. We have great sacrifices to make. This railway will be an enormous benefit to
Africa, but do not let us conceal from ourselves that it is
a task of no small magnitude. If you are to carry this railway forward, you will not only have to smash the Mahdi,
but Osman Digma also.

All this will involve great sacrifices and the expenditure
not only of much money, but of more of the English blood

of which the noblest has already been poured forth.   And we are not so strong as we were.   At first all nations sympathized with us, but now they look on us coldly, and even with hostility.   Those who were our friends have become indifferent, those who were indifferent have become our adversaries; and if our misfortunes and disasters go on much longer we shall have Europe saying that they cannot trust us, that we are too weak, that our prestige is too low to justify us in undertaking this task.

My lords, those great dangers can only be faced by a consistent policy, which can only be conducted by a ministry capable of unity of counsel and decision of purpose. I have shown you that from this ministry we can expect no such results.   They can only produce after their kind. They will only do what they have already done.   You cannot look for unity of counsel from an administration that is hopelessly divided.   You cannot expect a resolute policy from those whose purpose is hopelessly halting.

It is for this reason, my lords, that I ask you to record your opinion that from a ministry in whom the first of all —the quality of decision of purpose—is wanting, you can hope no good in this crisis of our country's fate.   And if you continue to trust them, if for any party reasons Parliament continues to abandon to their care the affairs which they have hitherto so hopelessly mismanaged, you must expect to go on from bad to worse; you must expect to lose the little prestige which you retain; you must expect to find in other portions of the world the results of the lower consideration that you occupy in the eyes of mankind; you must expect to be drawn on, degree by degree, step by step, under the cover of plausible excuses, under the cover of highly philanthropic sentiments, to irreparable disasters, and to disgrace that it will be impossible to efface.

TAMPERING WITH THE CONSTITUTION

My Lord Mayor, Ladies and Gentlemen: I listened to the resolutions which were read one after another from the various deputations which constitute this very remarkable, significant, and representative meeting, and I could not help wondering why it was that the truths which seemed to be so obvious had not made their impression upon her Majesty's government. Why, having this great work to do, did they deliberately depart from the practise of all which had gone before them and raise up gratuitous difficulties in their way? It was not from any ignorance on their part of the importance of redistribution as an integral portion of reform. I need only quote that sentence of Mr. Bright's which has been quoted again and again, but which I should like to see prefixed as a sort of text to every conservative sermon.

"Repudiate without mercy any bill that any government whatever may introduce, whatever its seeming concessions may be, if it does not redistribute the seats that are obtained from the extinction of small boroughs amongst the large towns."

But their knowledge was not such ancient history as that. Mr. Bright seems to imagine that he has entirely explained away his utterance given publicly in 1859 by reciting a private note which he says he wrote to Lord Beaconsfield in 1867, and he concludes in the most self-satisfied way that he has entirely explained his previous declaration.

But his colleague on the platform was not less conscious of the necessity of a redistribution of seats. Only on Saturday Lord Hartington is reported to have said, "We admit the inconvenience which will arise if a dissolution should take place."

If a dissolution should take place, as if Mr. Chamberlain and the wire-pullers were not perfectly resolved on that matter!

"We admit the inconvenience which will arise if any dissolution should take place with the extended numbers of the existing constituencies. We know that that will be no fair representation of the people."

Well, at least Lord Hartington knew perfectly well what he was about. Then, what was the motive which induced them to undertake this eccentric and abnormal plan of reform? Well, we had some difficulty in measuring it at first. We were told that it was the extraordinary block in the House of Commons, as if blocks in the House of Commons had never existed before the year 1884.

But, fortunately, as the controversy went on candor increased. It is one of the advantages of the thorough discussion which I hope this question will receive between this and November that all false pretenses and all hollow pretexts will be dissipated, and the cause which logically and constitutionally is in the right will be triumphantly established.

You know that Mr. Gladstone at the Foreign Office told us that it was necessary that some pressure should be applied to the House of Commons, that he could not hope to pass his Redistribution bill unless it was put before them in such a manner that they were to understand that if they had no redistribution bill they should have to go to the existing constituencies with the new franchise.

That speech of Mr. Gladstone's at the Foreign Office has been apologized for and slurred over. People intimate that he was not exactly possessed of his usual presence of mind when he made it, and that indeed must have been the case, or otherwise how could he deliberately impute to me words which I never uttered, and not only impute them, but make them the basis of a long, and elaborate, and most injurious indictment? He could not have made that statement if his memory had been in its usual condition.

But now Lord Hartington comes forward and explains to us that it was not merely some spontaneous exuberance of Mr. Gladstone's indignation that produced this explanation. It was the deliberate purpose of the government to establish a machine for controlling and coercing the judgment of the House of Commons and of the House of Lords. Lord Hartington on Saturday said:—

" We know that the passing of any really rational or fair redistribution bill is an impossibility unless Parliament and all shades of political opinion are acting under some pressure and compulsion, and that compulsion to the House of Commons and to the House of Lords was to be applied by the creature of Parliament, the prime minister of the day."

Such a pretension has never before been made in our history. The most encroaching monarchs have never made it. It has never been pretended that any man, however high his pretensions and great his authority, should have the power given to him of applying pressure and compulsion to Parliament in the discharge of its legislative duties. Well, it is a tremendous claim.

Let us look what grounds have we for believing that such a power, so unexampled, so without parallel in English history, will be exercised with equity and with justice. Mr. Gladstone—I do not wish to use any harsh language in the matter, but this lies on the surface of current history— Mr. Gladstone has been preëminent among statesmen for the rigor with which he has used a victory when he has obtained it; for the determination with which he has pressed to the utmost limit any advantage he has obtained over those opposed to him.

It is not, therefore, to his hands that we should like to trust ourselves, without condition and without defense. And if we look to his past conduct, to the past conduct of the Liberal party, or to the professions which they now put forward in respect to this very question of redistribution, it does not exalt our confidence.

I should like to remind you of a little incident in the last redistribution that took place—the redistribution of 1868—which throws a flood of light on Mr. Bright's views of justice in this matter. There is a certain suburb of Birmingham which is named Aston. It runs in the counties of North Warwickshire and East Worcestershire. At the last redistribution the commissioners—impartially selected men—recommended that this, which was a suburb of Birmingham, and was in continuity with it, and was simply part of the town, should be made part of the borough of Birmingham.

The matter came before the House of Commons. The Liberal party, though the opposition, were in a majority. Distinctly because this suburb of Aston might have the effect of influencing in the direction which he wished the counties of North Warwickshire and East Worcestershire, distinctly because it belonged to a community in which the ideas that he admired prevailed, Mr. Bright insisted that the recommendation of the commissioners should be discarded, and that Aston—though it was really part of Birmingham—should be thrown into North Warwickshire and East Worcestershire, for the purpose of controlling, by a population which he hoped was devoted to him and imbued with his ideas, a population that he had reason to think was adverse to him.   He was supported by the Liberal party, and a majority reversed the decision of the commissioners.

Now, we do not often have a case which shows the precise spirit in which the leading statesman of the dominant party will approach a question of that kind; but that particular case of Aston might be multiplied a hundred times. It involves the whole question of the separation of interests in this country.   It involves the whole question of keeping alive those rural communities which have existed from the first beginning of our parliamentary system.   It involves, above all, the avoidance of arrangements devised to give exceptional power to populations which are impregnated with the political doctrines of the ministry of the day.

Now, we may be quite sure that if Parliament is to be under compulsion and pressure—that means to say, if they are forced to accept any redistribution scheme which the government offers them—this precedent and model of Aston will be followed in every county in the kingdom.

But we need not go to instances of the past.   Let us look to what we know of Mr. Gladstone's own professions upon this question of redistribution.   He has not told us much.   Most of his assertions of principle are very little better than platitudes.   But one thing he has told us, and that is that the communities which are at a distance from London are to be better represented than the communities which are close.

Now at first sight that seemed like one of those fantastic theories which sometimes cross the brain of a man of genius, but when you look a little closer there is method in the madness.   Let us first look at the distant counties which are to be enfranchised.   I will confine myself to this island. We get into hot water directly we get into Ireland.

But confining ourselves to this island only, there is Cornwall.   I suppose that is a distant county.   That has been uniformly Liberal since the Reform bill.   Then there are the Highlands of Scotland.   I suppose that Scotland is a distant county.   Well, in Scotland the increase of Liberalism, especially among the distant counties, has, to our misfortune, been very considerable. Twenty years ago we had fifteen Scotch county members. Now we have only six out of thirty-two. Wales, again, that is a distant county —one of the counties to be specially favored under this scheme. Well, in Wales twenty years ago we had a majority. Now we have only two out of thirty seats.

So that those places which Mr. Gladstone wished, by special exception from the numerical principle, to give a decided advantage to, were places in which his own particular politics were violently on the increase. Well, the circumference is to be favored, because it is Gladstonian.

Now, let us look at the center, which is to receive no favor. Twenty or thirty years ago we had not a single Conservative member in the metropolis. In 1874, dealing with the constituencies which existed then for the sake of comparison, we should have had—but for the minority seat which is an artificial arrangement in this city—we should have had half the members for the metropolis. So that you see what the center is which is to be treated with marked disfavor so far as the Gladstone scheme is concerned.

Do you think that is wholly accidental? I find it difficult to bring myself to such a conclusion. And it seems to me that that is a guiding line, and that that is a principle which will animate the people when they come to consider the ministerial redistribution scheme. I heard my right honorable friend say—and I cannot help stealing the phrase from him—that it would be a redistribution scheme by results. It will be favorable, so far as it can decently be done, to those parts of the country where Liberal principles obtain, and unfavorable to those parts where Conservatism is at present in the ascendant.

And to show you how embarrassing is this problem of redistribution, how strongly it presses on statesmen, how incomplete any measure of reform is without it, I should like to compare the representation of the communities represented in this room with the representation of that favored county where Mr. Gladstone lives, to which I have just referred—the principality of Wales.

Whereas the principality represents some 1,400,000 inhabitants, we in this room represent some 5,000,000. Is it possible, with that fact before you, to go forward with a reform bill that shall not include redistribution? Is it possible that, knowing that Mr. Gladstone has laid down a principle that will uplift Wales and depress the metropolis, we should feel confidence and allow him to draw up his own redistribution bill? And we have heard something of blank checks; but this is not merely a blank check—this is a blank disposal of all that we possess for all time, given into the hands of a man who, by the previous conduct of his party and by his own previous utterances, has given us every reason to mistrust him.

I meet with the statement that it is very unconstitutional for the House of Lords to indicate when her Majesty's government may, in their wisdom, please to dissolve Parliament. Well, I should have said, as a matter of constitutional law, that the person who dissolves Parliament is her Majesty the queen, and that that is one of the few cases in which, necessarily, by the hypothesis of the minister being in issue, or being supposed to be in issue with the people, it is precisely one of the cases in which the sovereign cannot abandon her will absolutely to the guidance of her advisers.

But now there is the question, how far is it legitimate for the House of Lords to press for a dissolution? Well, I think that any such claim on the part of the House of Lords simply would not be justified by the Constitution. But the House of Lords has a right to say this—"We do not approve of the measure you bring before us. If you like to accept its rejection, well and good; if you object to its rejection, your remedy is to appeal to the people." And we do not think that under the Constitution there is any other remedy than that.

But with respect to the right, not only in the House of Lords, but in all of us, of pressing for a dissolution of Parliament, I admit that if it was to be done in respect to ordinary measures of controversy, or the ordinary legislation on which we have to decide, it would be matter of considerable inconvenience if we were to interfere with the discretion which is ordinarily reposed in the advisers of the Crown. But the fallacy, the fundamental fallacy, of all the reasonings of ministerial arguers upon this point is that they ignore the fact that it is not a common question of legislation; it is a vital question, it is a question of the revision of the Constitution. And in neither of the other popularly governed countries is the revision of the Constitution treated even so lightly as we desire and are content to treat it.

Look at what they do in France. In France they have, curiously enough, the contemporaneous phenomenon of a Liberal minister who is trying to alter the constitution of the country in the hopes that it may affect agreeably the constitution of the next assembly that he has to meet. I presume that that is a characteristic of Liberal ministers all over the world. That whenever they don't know how to get a majority in any other way they try to revise the constitution; but it cannot be done by a simple bill in France as it can in England. There is an elaborate process of revision. A congress must be called under certain guaranties, and guarantees of a tolerably stringent character. It is not treated in an ordinary manner, and the very fullest recognition is given to the right of the second chamber to make its own opinions heard and felt in the conduct of that revision.

Well, but we pass from France, with which we have only a certain point of analogy, and go to our kith and kin on the other side of the Atlantic, who, full of English traditions, but cut off by circumstances from monarchy, set up a republic according to their own judgment for themselves. What did they do? They surrounded the question of the revision of the constitution with the most minute and elaborate guarantees. It can only be proposed, in the first instance, by a two-thirds majority in both of the houses of the legislature, and when it has been proposed that is not sufficient. It has to be submitted to each state of the country, and passed there by three-fourths of the states.

That is the amount of security which the Anglo-Saxon mind, by circumstances cast loose from tradition, has judged to be absolutely necessary in the conduct of a popular government. And now, because the House of Lords interposes, and says that by a vote of a House of Commons, in the fifth year of its existence, passed at the bidding of a dictatorial minister—and thrown into an unprecedented form—because the House of Lords demurs to such a measure passing into law without the people having been consulted, you are told that they have been guilty of some strange and intolerable arrogance.

Just consider for a moment what the authority of the House of Commons is. I wish to speak of the House of Commons with the highest respect, and there is no doubt that, for ordinary purposes, dealing with ordinary bills, its authority is full and unquestioned to the term of its natural career; but when it lays hands upon the Constitution for the purpose of revising it, a very different state of things arises, and then you cannot turn away your attention from the fact that it is a House of Commons on the decline —that it has already existed longer than the average of Parliaments which have been since the Reform bill of 1832 —the average is four years and two months, and we have passed that—and that its action is discredited and disavowed by every election that takes place in those constituencies which this bill is intended to affect.

You tell me that this bill has been passed by the representatives of the people. In a legal sense they are the representatives of the people—in a legal sense every Act of Parliament is submitted to the unfettered will of the sovereign, the House of Lords, and the House of Commons; but if you pass from a legal to an actual sense they are not the representatives of the people; they are the representatives of what the people were five years ago. And between that day and this there is an absolute gulf, so completely has the whole surface of the political world changed, so entirely different are all the objects of political controversy and interest, so utterly have passed away the burning questions upon which the last election was decided.

Now Mr. Bright tries to dispose of the House of Lords by saying that it is a Tory caucus. He tries to give you the impression that it was a Tory caucus under Lord Aberdeen and Lord Palmerston, for he mentions their names. But my memory, I think, is as fresh as Mr. Bright's. I can perfectly remember what took place in the House of Lords, for instance. We will not deal with Lord Aberdeen's government. We will deal with Lord Palmerston's. There were two great questions which shook the ministry and

closely divided the House of Commons.   They were two
of the most burning questions of the day.   They were the
questions of the Chinese war and the Danish war.

The decision of one of them forced Lord Palmerston to
dissolve.   The decision of the other in his favor was regarded as the great victory of his administration.   How
did the House of Lords, this Tory caucus, vote?   On both
occasions the lords assembled at Westminster voted in
favor of Lord Palmerston.

The truth is, that until Mr. Gladstone became a leading
figure—became the leader of the Liberal party—there was
no talk about this permanent majority in the House of
Lords, and my belief is that if ever Mr. Gladstone ceases to
be the leader of the Liberal party there will then be no
longer that decided Tory majority in the House of Lords.

For, whatever else you may say about his legislation, at
least there can be no doubt of this: that he has applied
principles to the rights of property of his fellow-subjects
which we never heard of in this England of ours before.
Whether they were right or wrong, they were absolutely
new, and they seemed to lead not only to gross injustice in
the present, but to an illimitable horizon of spoliation in
the future, and therefore it is that in the legislative body
which has special charge of those interests and those rights,
and to watch over the conservance and the protection of
those rights of our fellow-citizens—that in them that alarm
at Mr. Gladstone's proceedings has spread and increased
with every year.

I told you when Lord Palmerston was in office he was
able on great critical questions to obtain a majority of the
House of Lords.   Since that time fifty-one Liberal peers
have been created, against only thirty-one Conservatives,
and yet the normal majority is between fifty and seventy
against the government in the House of Lords.   Is it surprising that the lords have felt something of that apprehension which has spread to every class and interest and industry in this country?

Look around.   Where will you find men who count on
a secure and certain future in the history of trade?   Everywhere you will hear of industry languishing, of commerce
unable to find profitable channels, of the hearts of men of

business failing them for fear, of banks refusing to receive money on deposit because they do not know where to invest it—every sign of the presence over the community of a great apprehension, of the disappearance of that old security which made property in England seem as solid as the rocks upon which England herself was founded. That time has passed away. Men will not invest as they formerly would; men are not employed as they formerly were; capitalists do not gain profit, the working classes are ceasing in many places to gain livelihoods. Is it surprising that this apprehension, which has reached so many classes of their countrymen, should deeply infect the peers as well, and that the shadow of Mr. Gladstone's formidable individuality should be thrown alike upon the judgment and the apprehensions of English peers as upon the industry, the commerce, and the labor upon which this country depends?

Well, Mr. Bright tells us that he does not go into the question whether the House of Lords has done right or wrong; he seems to abuse the House of Lords, and to desire to prove that they are a very disreputable body of men, who hold a title which he wishes to discredit. But I venture to say, and I submit it to the judgment of those who wish to consider this controversy impartially, that the merits of the House of Lords have nothing whatever to do with the case. The question is, not what the House of Lords are, or how they got there, but whether they did right or wrong.

It would be no excuse for them, if they had not done their duty, to say they have some doubts about the validity of their title to be there. That distinguished assembly over which my right honorable friend the lord mayor presides in the city of London have at least this in common with the House of Lords, that they have been doomed by a distinguished statesman. The decree has gone forth from the lips of Sir William Harcourt that the one shall cease to exist as the decree has gone forth from the lips of Mr. Bright that the House of Lords shall cease to exist; and I think it is quite possible that both assemblies will continue to exist to do useful work for a very long time. If the corporation were to refuse to assemble to-morrow, and to perform their ordinary duties, would it be any excuse for them to say, "Oh, we are condemned by Sir William Harcourt, or by any other statesman, and it is perfectly impossible that we can go on performing our duties"?

Well, if the House of Lords had not performed what I think I have shown to you to be the elementary duty of a second chamber, to prevent the first chamber from using its power to filch a perpetuity of political predominance for one party in the state, if the House of Lords had refused to do its duty, on the ground that some radicals thought that the country had an objection to the principles on which it is formed, would it not have been guilty of the most cowardly and craven action that you can possibly conceive? It is a question which we shall be ready to argue when the time comes—the question as to the constitution of the second chamber, and what is the best way in which it shall be upheld, and whatever its present theoretical difficulties, you will not in practice much improve upon the House of Lords.

That has nothing to do with the question we have in hand. The question is, if the House of Lords does its duty, could it have acted otherwise than we have done? What is it, after all, that we have done? We have seen this strange and sinister spectacle of a minister claiming to resist by the compulsion of the House of Commons the action of the House of Lords. We have seen him applying that principle, not to ordinary principles of legislation, but to the most vital matter in which a deliberative assembly can be engaged—the reform of the Constitution. We have seen him tampering with the very springs of political power. We have seen him do that in a manner unexampled and without precedent, and the House of Lords said to him: "You shall not exercise this unprecedented power; you shall not claim this right of compulsion; you shall not model the Constitution according to your will and the interests of the dominant party of the day.

"We are prepared to resist your power unless you will be able to assure us and prove to us that the people, by whom alone you exist, by whose mandate you hold power, sanctions this strange exercise of power, and we utterly repudiate the idea that in assuming that attitude we shall be misconstrued by our countrymen."

I am sure that they will feel that in this, as in so many

other cases, liberty has had to fear chiefly from the hands of its professed friends.   We have been maintaining the essential conditions on which popular government reposes, and we have been upholding the true and ancient principles of English liberty.

CARL SCHURZ

THE POLICY OF IMPERIALISM

[Carl Schurz, an American statesman, was born in Germany in 1829. He received a university education in his native land, became imbued with liberal political ideas, was prominent in the reforming movement of 1848 and 1849, and was finally forced to leave Germany. He settled in the United States in 1852, became a lawyer, made himself a leader of the German element, and was in due time a prominent figure in the Republican party. President Lincoln made him minister to Spain, but he resigned that post to serve in the Civil War. He rose through the various grades to that of major-general of volunteers, having commands at Bull Run, Gettysburg, and Chattanooga. From 1869 to 1875 he was United States Senator from Missouri. President Hayes made him secretary of the interior. In 1881 he became editor-in-chief of the New York Evening Post, retiring from that place in 1883. In the presidential campaign of 1884 he supported Cleveland, and, when the issue of imperialism was raised after the war with Spain, he opposed the policy of the McKinley administration. His ideas on the annexation of the Philippines and Hawaii find expression in the following speech, delivered at the Anti-Imperialist Conference at Chicago in 1899.]

MORE than eight months ago I had the honor of addressing the citizens of Chicago on the subject of American imperialism, meaning the policy of annexing to this Republic distant countries and alien populations that will not fit into our democratic system of government. I discussed at that time mainly the baneful effect the pursuit of an imperialistic policy would produce upon our political institutions.

After long silence, during which I have carefully reviewed my own opinions as well as those of others in the light of the best information I could obtain, I shall now approach the same subject from another point of view.

We all know that the popular mind is much disturbed by the Philippine war, and that, however highly we admire the bravery of our soldiers, nobody professes to be proud of the war itself. There are few Americans who do not frankly admit their regret that this war should ever have happened.

In April, 1898, we went to war with Spain for the avowed purpose of liberating the people of Cuba, who had long been struggling for freedom and independence. Our object in that war was clearly and emphatically proclaimed by a solemn resolution of Congress repudiating all intention of annexation on our part and declaring that the Cuban people "are, and of right ought to be, free and independent." This solemn declaration was made to do justice to the spirit of the American people, who were indeed willing to wage a war of liberation, but would not have consented to a war of conquest. It was also to propitiate the opinion of mankind for our action. President McKinley also declared with equal solemnity that annexation by force could not be thought of, because, according to our code of morals, it would be "criminal aggression."

Can it justly be pretended that these declarations referred only to the island of Cuba? What would the American people, what would the world have said, if Congress had resolved that the Cuban people were indeed rightfully entitled to freedom and independence, but that as to the people of other Spanish colonies we recognized no such right; and if President McKinley had declared that the forcible annexation of Cuba would be criminal, but that the forcible annexation of other Spanish colonies would be a righteous act? A general outburst of protest from our own people, and of derision and contempt from the whole world, would have been the answer. No; there can be no cavil. The war was proclaimed to all mankind to be a war of liberation, and not of conquest, and even now our very imperialists are still boasting that the war was prompted by the most unselfish and generous purposes, and that those insult us who do not believe it.

In the course of that war Commodore Dewey, by a brilliant feat of arms, destroyed the Spanish fleet in the harbor of Manila. This did not change the heralded character of the war—certainly not in Dewey's own opinion. The Filipinos, constituting the strongest and foremost tribe of the population of the archipelago, had long been fighting for freedom and independence, just as the Cubans had. The great mass of the other islanders sympathized with them. They fought for the same cause as the Cubans, and they fought against the same enemy—the same enemy against whom we were waging our war of humanity and liberation. They had the same title to freedom and independence which we recognized as "of right" in the Cubans —nay, more; for, as Admiral Dewey telegraphed to our government, "They are far superior in their intelligence, and more capable of self-government than the natives of Cuba." The admiral adds, "I am familiar with both races, and further intercourse with them has confirmed me in this opinion."

Indeed, the mendacious stories spread by our imperialists which represent those people as barbarians, their doings as mere "savagery," and their chiefs as no better than "cut-throats," have been refuted by such a mass of authoritative testimony, coming in part from men who are themselves imperialists, that their authors should hide their heads in shame; for surely it is not the part of really brave men to calumniate their victims before sacrificing them. We need not praise the Filipinos as in every way the equals of the "embattled farmers" of Lexington and Concord, and Aguinaldo as the peer of Washington; but there is an overwhelming abundance of testimony, some of it unwilling, that the Filipinos are fully the equals, and even the superiors, of the Cubans and the Mexicans. As to Aguinaldo, Admiral Dewey is credited with saying that he is controlled by men abler than himself. The same could be said of more than one of our Presidents. Moreover, it would prove that those are greatly mistaken who predict that the Filipino uprising would collapse were Aguinaldo captured or killed. The old slander that Aguinaldo had sold out the revolutionary movement for a bribe of $400,000 has been so thoroughly exploded by the best authority that it required uncommon audacity to repeat it.

Now let us see what has happened. Two months before the beginning of our Spanish war our consul at Manila reported to the State Department: "Conditions here and in Cuba are practically alike. War exists; battles are

almost of daily occurrence.   The crown forces (Spanish)
have not been able to dislodge a rebel army within ten
miles of Manila.   A republic is organized here as in Cuba.''
When two months later our war of liberation and humanity
began, Commodore Dewey was at Hong-kong with his
ships.   He received orders to attack and destroy the Spanish fleet in those waters.   It was then that our consul-
general at Singapore informed our State Department that he
had conferred with General Aguinaldo, then at Singapore,
as to the coöperation of the Philippine insurgents, and that
he had telegraphed to Commodore Dewey that Aguinaldo
was willing to come to Hong-kong to arrange with Dewey
for "general coöperation if desired;" whereupon Dewey
promptly answered: "Tell Aguinaldo come soon as possible."   The meeting was had.   Dewey sailed to Manila to
destroy the Spanish fleet, and Aguinaldo was taken to the
seat of war on a vessel of the United States.   His forces
received a supply of arms through Commodore Dewey, and
did faithfully and effectively coöperate with our forces
against the Spaniards, so effectively, indeed, that soon
afterward, by their efforts, the Spaniards had lost the whole
country except a few garrisons in which they were practically blockaded.

Now, what were the relations between the Philippine
insurgents and this Republic?   There is some dispute as to
certain agreements, including a promise of Philippine independence, said to have been made between Aguinaldo and
our consul-general at Singapore, before Aguinaldo proceeded
to coöperate with Dewey.   But I lay no stress upon this
point.   I will let only the record of facts speak.   Of these
facts the first, of highest importance, is that Aguinaldo
was "desired"—that is, invited—by officers of the United
States to coöperate with our forces.   The second is that the
Filipino junta in Hong-kong immediately after these confer-
ences appealed to their countrymen to receive the American
fleet about to sail for Manila as friends, by a proclamation
which had these words:—

"Compatriots, divine Providence is about to place independence
within our reach.   The Americans, not from any mercenary motives,
but for the sake of humanity, have considered it opportune to extend

their protecting mantle to our beloved country. Where you see the American flag flying assemble in mass. They are our redeemers."

With this faith his followers gave Aguinaldo a rapturous greeting upon his arrival at Cavité, where he proclaimed his government and organized his army under Dewey's eyes.

The arrival of our land forces did not at first change these relations. Brigadier-General Thomas M. Anderson, commanding, wrote to Aguinaldo, July 4, as follows: "General, I have the honor to inform you that the United States of America, whose land forces I have the honor to command in this vicinity, being at war with the kingdom of Spain, has entire sympathy and most friendly sentiments for the native people of the Philippine Islands. For these reasons I desire to have the most amicable relations with you, and to have you and your people coöperate with us in military operations against the Spanish forces," etc. Aguinaldo responded cordially, and an extended correspondence followed, special services being asked for by the party of the first part, being rendered by the second, and duly acknowledged by the first. All this went on pleasantly until the capture of Manila, in which Aguinaldo effectively coöperated by fighting the Spaniards outside, taking many prisoners from them, and hemming them in. The services they rendered by taking thousands of Spanish prisoners, by harassing the Spaniards in the trenches, and by completely blockading Manila on the land side, were amply testified to by our own officers. Aguinaldo was also active on the sea. He had ships, which our commanders permitted to pass in and out of Manila Bay, under the flag of the Philippine republic, on their expeditions against other provinces.

Now, whether or not there was any formal compact of alliance signed and sealed, no candid man who has studied the official documents will deny that in point of fact the Filipinos, having been desired and invited to do so, were, before the capture of Manila, acting, and were practically recognized as our allies, and that as such they did effective service, which we accepted and profited by. This is an indisputable fact, proved by the record.

It is an equally indisputable fact that during that period the Filipino government constantly and publicly, so that nobody could plead ignorance of it or misunderstand it, informed the world that their object was the achievement of national independence, and that they believed the Americans had come in good faith to help them accomplish that end, as in the case of Cuba. It was weeks after various proclamations and other public utterances of Aguinaldo to that effect that the correspondence between him and General Anderson, which I have quoted, took place, and that the useful services of the Filipinos as our practical allies were accepted. It is, further, an indisputable fact that during this period our government did not inform the Filipinos that their fond expectations as to our recognition of their independence were mistaken.

Our secretary of state did, indeed, on June 16 write to Mr. Pratt, our consul-general at Singapore, that our government knew the Philippine insurgents, not indeed as patriots struggling for liberty, and who, like the Cubans, "are and of right ought to be free and independent," but merely as "discontented and rebellious subjects of Spain," who, if we occupied their country in consequence of the war, would have to yield us due "obedience." And other officers of our government were instructed not to make any promises to the Filipinos as to the future. But the Filipinos themselves were not so informed. They were left to believe that, while fighting in coöperation with the American forces, they were fighting for their own independence. They could not imagine that the government of the great American Republic, while boasting of having gone to war with Spain under the banner of liberation and humanity in behalf of Cuba, was capable of secretly plotting to turn that war into one for the conquest and subjugation of the Philippines.

Thus the Filipinos went faithfully and bravely on doing for us the services of allies, of brothers-in-arms, far from dreaming that the same troops with whom they had been asked to coöperate would soon be employed by the great apostle of liberation and humanity to slaughter them, for no other reason than that they, the Filipinos, continued to stand up for their own freedom and independence.

But just that was to happen. As soon as Manila was taken, and we had no further use for our Filipino allies, they were ordered to fall back and back from the city and its suburbs. Our military commanders treated the Filipinos' country as if it were our own. When Aguinaldo sent one of his aides-de-camp to General Merritt with a request for an interview, General Merritt was "too busy." When our peace negotiations with Spain began, and representatives of the Filipinos asked for audience to solicit consideration of the rights and wishes of their people, the doors were slammed in their faces, in Washington as well as in Paris.

And behind those doors the scheme was hatched to deprive the Philippine Islanders of independence from foreign rule and to make them the subjects of another foreign ruler, and that foreign ruler their late ally, this great Republic, which had grandly proclaimed to the world that its war against Spain was not a war of conquest, but a war of liberation and humanity.

Behind those doors which were tightly closed to the people of the Philippines a treaty was made with Spain, by the direction of President McKinley, which provided for the cession of the Philippine Islands by Spain to the United States for a consideration of $20,000,000. It has been said that this sum was not purchase money, but a compensation for improvements made by Spain, or a solatium to sweeten the pill of cession, or what not; but, stripped of all cloudy verbiage, it was really purchase money, the sale being made by Spain under duress. Thus Spain sold, and the United States bought, what was called the sovereignty of Spain over the Philippine Islands and their people.

Now look at the circumstances under which that "cession" was made. Spain had lost the possession of the country, except a few isolated and helpless little garrisons, most of which were effectively blockaded by the Filipinos. The American forces occupied Cavité and the harbor and city of Manila, and nothing more. The bulk of the country was occupied and possessed by the people thereof, over whom Spain had, in point of fact, ceased to exercise any sovereignty, the Spanish power having been driven out or destroyed by the Filipino insurrection, while the United States had not acquired, beyond Cavité and Manila, any authority of whatever name by military occupation, nor by recognition on the part of the people. Aguinaldo's army surrounded Manila on the land side, and his government claimed organized control over fifteen provinces. That government was established at Malolos, not far from Manila, and a very respectable government it was. According to Mr. Barrett, our late minister in Siam, himself an ardent imperialist, who had seen it, it had a well-organized executive, divided into several departments, ably conducted, and a popular assembly, a congress, which would favorably compare with the parliament of Japan—an infinitely better government than the insurrectionary government of Cuba ever was.

It is said that Aguinaldo's government was in operation among only a part of the people of the islands. This is true. But it is also certain that it was recognized and supported by an immeasurably larger part of the people than Spanish sovereignty, which had practically ceased to exist, and than American rule, which was confined to a harbor and a city and which was carried on by the exercise of military force under what was substantially martial law over a people that constituted about one-twentieth of the whole population of the islands. Thus, having brought but a very small fraction of the country and its people under our military control, we bought by that treaty the sovereignty over the whole from a power which had practically lost that sovereignty, and therefore did no longer possess it; and we contemptuously disdained to consult the existing native government, which actually did control a large part of the country and the people, and which had been our ally in the war with Spain. The sovereignty we thus acquired may well be defined as Abraham Lincoln once defined the "popular sovereignty" of Senator Douglas's doctrine—as being like a soup made by boiling the shadow of the breastbone of a pigeon that had been starved to death.

No wonder that treaty found opposition in the Senate. Virulent abuse was heaped upon the "statesman who would oppose the ratification of a peace treaty." A peace treaty? This was no peace treaty at all. It was a treaty with half a dozen bloody wars in its belly. It was, in the first place, an open and brutal declaration of war against our allies, the Filipinos, who struggled for freedom and independence from foreign rule. Every man not totally blind could see that. For such a treaty the true friends of peace could, of course, not vote.

But more. Even before that treaty had been assented to by the Senate—that is, even before that ghastly shadow of our Philippine sovereignty had obtained any legal sanction—President McKinley assumed of his own motion the sovereignty of the Philippine Islands by his famous "benevolent assimilation" order of December 21, 1898, through which our military commander at Manila was directed forthwith to extend the military government of the United States over the whole archipelago, and by which the Filipinos were notified that if they refused to submit, they would be compelled by force of arms. Having bravely fought for their freedom and independence from one foreign rule, they did refuse to submit to another foreign rule, and then the slaughter of our late allies began—the slaughter by American arms of a once friendly and confiding people. And this slaughter has been going on ever since.

This is a grim story. Two years ago the prediction of such a possibility would have been regarded as a hideous nightmare, as the offspring of a diseased imagination. But to-day it is a true tale—a plain recital of facts taken from the official records. These things have actually been done in these last two years by and under the administration of William McKinley. This is our Philippine war as it stands. Is it a wonder that the American people should be troubled in their consciences?

I am not here as a partizan, but as an American citizen anxious for the future of the Republic. And I cannot too earnestly admonish the American people, if they value the fundamental principles of their government and their own security and that of their children, for a moment to throw aside all partizan bias and soberly to consider what kind of a precedent they would set if they consented to, and by consenting approved, the President's management of the Philippine business merely "because we are in it."

We cannot expect all our future Presidents to be models of public virtue and wisdom, as George Washington was. Imagine now in the presidential office a man well-meaning, but, it may be, short-sighted and pliable, and under the influence of so-called "friends" who are greedy and reckless speculators, and who would not scruple to push him into warlike complications in order to get great opportunities for profit; or a man of that inordinate ambition which intoxicates the mind and befogs the conscience; or a man of extreme partizan spirit, who honestly believes the victory of his party to be necessary for the salvation of the universe, and may think that a foreign broil would serve the chances of his party; or a man of an uncontrollable combativeness of temperament which might run away with his sense of responsibility—and that we shall have such men in the presidential chair is by no means unlikely with our loose way of selecting candidates for the Presidency.

Imagine, then, a future President belonging to either of these classes to have before him the precedent of Mr. McKinley's management of the Philippine business, sanctioned by the approval or only the acquiescence of the people, and to feel himself permitted—nay, even encouraged—to say to himself that, as this precedent shows, he may plunge the country into warlike conflicts of his own motion, without asking leave of Congress, with only some legal technicalities to cover his usurpation, or even without such, and that he may, by a machinery of deception called a war censorship, keep the people in the dark about what is going on; and that, into however bad a mess he may have got the country, he may count upon the people, as soon as a drop of blood has been shed, to uphold the usurpation and to cry down everybody who opposes it as a "traitor," and all this because "we are in it!" Can you conceive a more baneful precedent, a more prolific source of danger to the peace and security of the country? Can any sane man deny that it will be all the more prolific of evil if in this way we drift into a foreign policy full of temptation for dangerous adventure?

I say, therefore, that if we have the future of the Republic at heart we must not only not uphold the administration in its course because "we are in it," but, just because we are in it, have been got into it in such a way, the American people should stamp the administration's proceedings with a verdict of disapproval so clear and emphatic and "get out of it" in such a fashion that this will be a solemn warning to future Presidents instead of a seductive precedent.

What, then, to accomplish this end, is to be done? Of course we, as we are here, can only advise. But by calling forth expressions of the popular will by various means of public demonstration and, if need be, at the polls, we can make that advice so strong that those in power will hardly disregard it. We have often been taunted with having no positive policy to propose. But such a policy has more than once been proposed, and I can only repeat it.

In the first place, let it be well understood that those are egregiously mistaken who think that if by a strong military effort the Philippine war be stopped, everything will be right, and no more question about it. No; the American trouble of conscience will not be appeased, and the question will be as big and virulent as ever, unless the close of the war be promptly followed by an assurance to the islanders of their freedom and independence, which assurance, if given now, would surely end the war without more fighting.

We propose, therefore, that it be given now. Let the Philippine Islanders at the same time be told that the American people will be glad to see them establish an independent government, and to aid them in that task as far as may be necessary, and even, if required, lend our good offices to bring it about; and that meanwhile we shall deem it our duty to protect them against interference from other foreign powers—in other words, that with regard to them we mean honestly to live up to the righteous principles with the profession of which we recommended to the world our Spanish war.

And then let us have in the Philippines, to carry out this program, not a small politician, nor a meddlesome martinet, but a statesman of large mind and genuine sympathy, who will not merely deal in sanctimonious cant and oily promises with a string to them, but who will prove by his acts that he and we are honest; who will keep in mind that their government is not merely to suit us, but to suit them; that it should not be measured by standards which we ourselves have not been able to reach, but be a government of their own, adapted to their own conditions and notions—whether it be a true republic, like ours, or a dictatorship like that of Porfirio Diaz, in Mexico, or an oligarchy like the one maintained by us in Hawaii, or even something like the boss rule we are tolerating in New York and Pennsylvania.

Those who talk so much about "fitting a people for self-government" often forget that no people were ever made "fit" for self-government by being kept in the leading strings of a foreign power. You learn to walk by doing your own crawling and stumbling. Self-government is learned only by exercising it upon one's own responsibility. Of course there will be mistakes and troubles and disorders. We have had and now have these, too—at the beginning our persecution of the Tories, our flounderings before the Constitution was formed, our Shay's rebellion, our whisky war, and various failures and disturbances, among them a Civil war that cost us a loss of life and treasure horrible to think of, and the murder of two Presidents. But who will say that on account of these things some foreign power should have kept the American people in leading strings to teach them to govern themselves? If the Philippine Islanders do as well as the Mexicans, who have worked their way, since we let them alone after our War of 1847, through many disorders, to an orderly government, who will have a right to find fault with the result? Those who seek to impose upon them an unreasonable standard of excellence in self-government do not seriously wish to let them govern themselves at all. You may take it as a general rule that he who wants to reign over others is solemnly convinced that they are quite unable to govern themselves.

Now, what objection is there to the policy dictated by our fundamental principles and our good-faith? I hear the angry cry: "What? Surrender to Aguinaldo? Will not the world ridicule and despise us for such a confession of our incompetency to deal with so feeble a foe? What will become of our prestige?" No, we shall not surrender to Aguinaldo. In giving up a criminal aggression we shall surrender only to our own consciences, to our own sense of right and justice, to our own understanding of our own true interests, and to the vital principles of our own Republic. Nobody will laugh at us whose good opinion we have reason to cherish. There will, of course, be an outcry of disappointment in England. But from whom will it come? From such men as James Bryce or John Morley or any one of those true friends of this Republic who understand and admire and wish to perpetuate and spread the fundamental principles of its vitality? No, not from them.

But the outcry will come from those in England who long to see us entangled in complications apt to make this American Republic dependent upon British aid, and thus subservient to British interests. They, indeed, will be quite angry. But the less we mind their displeasure as well as their flattery, the better for the safety as well as the honor of our country.

The true friends of this Republic in England, and, indeed, all over the world, who are now grieving to see us go astray, will rejoice, and their true hearts will be uplifted with new confidence in our honesty, in our wisdom, and in the virtue of democratic institutions when they behold the American people throwing aside all the puerilities of false pride and returning to the path of their true duty. . . .

Who are the true patriots in America to-day—those who drag our Republic, once so proud of its high principles and ideals, through the mire of broken pledges, vulgar ambitions and vanities and criminal aggressions; those who do violence to their own moral sense by insisting that, like the Dreyfus iniquity, a criminal course once begun must be persisted in, or those who, fearless of the demagogue clamor, strive to make the flag of the Republic once more what it was once—the flag of justice, liberty, and true civilization —and to lift up the American people among the nations of the earth to the proud position of the people that have a conscience and obey it?

The country has these days highly and deservedly honored Admiral Dewey as a national hero. Who are his true friends—those who would desecrate Dewey's splendid achievement at Manila by making it the starting-point of criminal aggression, and thus the opening of a most disgraceful and inevitably disastrous chapter of American history, to be remembered with sorrow, or those who strive so to shape the results of that brilliant feat of arms that it may stand in history not as a part of a treacherous conquest, but as a true victory of American good-faith in an honest war of liberation and humanity—to be proud of for all time, as Dewey himself, no doubt, meant it to be?

I know the imperialists will say that I have been pleading here for Aguinaldo and his Filipinos against our Republic. No, not for the Filipinos merely, although, as one of those who have grown gray in the struggle for free and honest government, I would never be ashamed to plead for the cause of freedom and independence, even when its banner is carried by dusky and feeble hands. But I am pleading for more. I am pleading for the cause of American honor and self-respect, American interests, American democracy; aye, for the cause of the American people against an administration of our public affairs which has wantonly plunged this country into an iniquitous war; which has disgraced the Republic by a scandalous breach of faith to a people struggling for their freedom whom we had used as allies; which has been systematically seeking to deceive and mislead the public mind by the manufacture of false news; which has struck at the very foundation of our Constitutional government by an executive usurpation of the war-power; which makes sport of the great principles and high ideals that have been and should ever remain the guiding star of our course, and which, unless stopped in time, will transform this government of the people, for the people, and by the people into an imperial government cynically calling itself republican—a government in which the noisy worship of arrogant might will drown the voice of right; which will impose upon the people a burdensome and demoralizing militarism, and which will be driven into a policy of wild and rapacious adventure by the unscrupulous greed of the exploiter—a policy always fatal to democracy.

I plead the cause of the American people against all this, and I here declare my profound conviction that if this administration of our affairs were submitted for judgment to a popular vote on a clear issue, it would be condemned by an overwhelming majority.

I confidently trust that the American people will prove themselves too clear-headed not to appreciate the vital difference between the expansion of the Republic and its free institutions over contiguous territory and kindred populations, which we all gladly welcome if accomplished peaceably or honorably, and imperialism which reaches out for distant lands to be ruled as subject provinces; too intelligent not to perceive that our very first step on the road of imperialism has been a betrayal of the fundamental principles of democracy, followed by disaster and disgrace; too enlightened not to understand that a monarchy may do such things and still remain a strong monarchy, while a democracy cannot do them and still remain a democracy; too wise not to detect the false pride, or the dangerous ambitions, or the selfish schemes which so often hide themselves under that deceptive cry of mock patriotism: "Our country, right or wrong!" They will not fail to recognize that our dignity, our free institutions, and the peace and welfare of this and coming generations of Americans will be secure only as we cling to the watchword of true patriotism: "Our country—when right to be kept right; when wrong to be put right."

WILLIAM HENRY SEWARD

THE IRREPRESSIBLE CONFLICT

[William Henry Seward, statesman and orator, was born at Florida, N. Y., in 1801. Entering Union College, Schenectady, at the age of 15, he left at the end of the third year and taught school in the South. He returned to take his degree in 1820, and then studied law, and was admitted to the bar at Utica. Upon entering politics he allied himself with the Democratic party; but with the election of Jackson as President he severed his connection with that party, and in 1830 went to the State Senate as a representative of the Anti-Masons. He held his seat by repeated elections for four years. In 1834 he failed of election as Whig candidate for the governorship of New York; but four years later took his place in the gubernatorial chair. In 1849 he was elected to the United States Senate, where he sat for twelve years. At the national republican convention held in Chicago in 1860, Mr. Seward's name led on the first two ballots for the presidency. The nomination and election going to Abraham Lincoln, Mr. Seward became the secretary of state and retained that office for eight years, the exacting period of the Civil War and Reconstruction. On the night of the assassination of Lincoln an unsuccessful attempt was made upon Seward's life also. In 1869 Mr. Seward retired from public affairs, visited the West and Mexico, and in 1870 started on a tour around the world. He returned to his home at Auburn, N. Y., in October 1871, and began the composition of his autobiography, which, however, was left unfinished at the time of his death, October 10, 1872. The ensuing speech was delivered at Rochester, N. Y., 1858, and conveyed a warning of the danger in the situation between North and South.]

FELLOW-CITIZENS: The unmistakable outbreaks of zeal which occur all around me show that you are earnest men—and such a man am I. Let us, therefore, at least for the time, pass by all secondary and collateral questions, whether of a personal or of a general nature, and consider the main subject of the present canvass. The Democratic party, or, to speak more accurately, the party which wears that attractive name, is in possession of the Federal Government. The Republicans propose to dislodge that party and dismiss it from its high trust.

The main subject, then, is whether the Democratic party deserves to retain the confidence of the American people. In attempting to prove it unworthy, I think that I am not actuated by prejudices against that party, or by prepossessions in favor of its adversary; for I have learned, by some experience, that virtue and patriotism, vice and selfishness, are found in all parties, and that they differ less in their motives than in the policies they pursue.

Our country is a theater, which exhibits in full operation two radically different political systems, the one resting on the basis of servile or slave labor, the other on the basis of voluntary labor of freemen.

The laborers who are enslaved are all negroes, or persons more or less purely of African derivation. But this is only accidental. The principle of the system is, that labor in every society, by whomsoever performed, is necessarily unintellectual, groveling, and base; and that the laborer, equally for his own good and for the welfare of the state, ought to be enslaved. The white laboring man, whether native or foreigner, is not enslaved, only because he cannot, as yet, be reduced to bondage.

You need not be told now that the slave system is the older of the two, and that once it was universal.

The emancipation of our own ancestors, Caucasians and Europeans as they were, hardly dates beyond a period of five hundred years. The great melioration of human society which modern times exhibit is mainly due to the incomplete substitution of the system of voluntary labor for the old one of servile labor, which has already taken place. This African slave system is one which, in its origin and in its growth, has been altogether foreign from the habits of the races which colonized these States, and established civilization here. It was introduced on this new continent as an engine of conquest, and for the establishment of monarchical power, by the Portuguese and the Spaniards, and was rapidly extended by them all over South America, Central America, Louisiana, and Mexico. Its legitimate fruits are seen in the poverty, imbecility, and anarchy which now pervade all Portuguese and Spanish America. The free labor system is of German extraction, and it was established in our country by emigrants from Sweden, Holland, Germany, Great Britain, and Ireland. We justly ascribe to its influences the strength, wealth, greatness, intelligence, and freedom which the whole American people now enjoy. One of the chief elements of the value of human life is freedom in the pursuit of happiness. The slave system is not only intolerant, unjust, and inhuman toward the laborer, whom, only because he is a laborer, it loads down with chains and converts into merchandise, but is scarcely less severe upon the freeman, to whom, only because he is a laborer from necessity, it denies facilities for employment, and whom it expels from the community because it cannot enslave and convert him into merchandise also. It is necessarily improvident and ruinous, because, as a general truth, communities prosper and flourish, or droop and decline, in just the degree that they practise or neglect to practise the primary duties of justice and humanity. The free-labor system conforms to the divine law of equality, which is written in the hearts and consciences of men, and therefore is always and everywhere beneficent.

The slave system is one of constant danger, distrust, suspicion, and watchfulness. It debases those whose toil alone can produce wealth and resources of defense, to the lowest degree of which human nature is capable, to guard against mutiny and insurrection, and thus wastes energies which otherwise might be employed in national development and aggrandizement.

The free-labor system educates all alike, and, by opening all the fields of industrial employment, and all the departments of authority, to the unchecked and equal rivalry of all classes of men, at once secures universal contentment, and brings into the highest possible activity all the physical, moral, and social energies of the whole state. In states where the slave system prevails, the masters, directly or indirectly, secure all political power, and constitute a ruling aristocracy. In states where the free-labor system prevails, universal suffrage necessarily obtains, and the state inevitably becomes, sooner or later, a republic or a democracy.

Russia yet maintains slavery, and is a despotism. Most of the other European states have abolished slavery, and adopted the system of free labor. It was the antagonistic political tendencies of the two systems which the first Napoleon was contemplating when he predicted that Europe would ultimately be either all Cossack or all republican. Never did human sagacity utter a more pregnant truth. The two systems are at once perceived to be incongruous. But they are more than incongruous; they are incompatible. They never have permanently existed together in one country, and they never can. It would be easy to demonstrate this impossibility, from the irreconcilable contrast between their great principles and characteristics. But the experience of mankind has conclusively established it. Slavery, as I have already intimated, existed in every state in Europe. Free labor has supplanted it everywhere except in Russia and Turkey. State necessities developed in modern times are now obliging even those two nations to encourage and employ free labor; and already, despotic as they are, we find them engaged in abolishing slavery. In the United States slavery came into collision with free labor at the close of the last century, and fell before it in New England, New York, New Jersey, and Pennsylvania, but triumphed over it effectually, and excluded it for a period yet undetermined from Virginia, the Carolinas, and Georgia. Indeed, so incompatible are the two systems, that every new state which is organized within our ever-extending domain makes its first political act a choice of the one and an exclusion of the other, even at the cost of civil war if necessary. The Slave states, without law, at the last national election successfully forbade, within their own limits, even the casting of votes for a candidate for President of the United States supposed to be favorable to the establishment of the free-labor system in new states.

Hitherto, the two systems have existed in different states, but side by side within the American Union. This has happened because the Union is a confederation of states. But in another aspect the United States constitute only one nation. Increase of population, which is filling the states out to their very borders, together with a new and extended network of railroads and other avenues, and an

internal commerce which daily becomes more intimate, is
rapidly bringing the states into a higher and more perfect
social unity or consolidation.   Thus, these antagonistic systems are continually coming into closer contact, and collision results.

Shall I tell you what this collision means?   They who
think that it is accidental, unnecessary, the work of interested or fanatical agitators, and therefore ephemeral, mistake the case altogether.   It is an irrepressible conflict
between opposing and enduring forces, and it means that
the United States must and will, sooner or later, become
either entirely a slaveholding nation, or entirely a free-labor
nation.   Either the cotton and rice-fields of South Carolina
and the sugar plantations of Louisiana will ultimately be
tilled by free labor, and Charleston and New Orleans become marts for legitimate merchandise alone, or else the
rye-fields and wheat-fields of Massachusetts and New York
must again be surrendered by their farmers to slave culture
and to the production of slaves, and Boston and New York
become once more markets for trade in the bodies and souls
of men.   It is the failure to apprehend this great truth that
induces so many unsuccessful attempts at final compromise
between the Slave and Free states, and it is the existence of
this great fact that renders all such pretended compromises,
when made, vain and ephemeral.   Startling as this saying
may appear to you, fellow-citizens, it is by no means an
original or even a modern one.   Our forefathers knew it to
be true, and unanimously acted upon it when they framed
the Constitution of the United States.   They regarded the
existence of the servile system in so many of the states with
sorrow and shame, which they openly confessed, and they
looked upon the collision between them, which was then
just revealing itself, and which we are now accustomed to
deplore, with favor and hope.   They knew that either the
one or the other system must exclusively prevail.

Unlike too many of those who in modern times invoke
their authority, they had a choice between the two.   They
preferred the system of free labor, and they determined to
organize the government and so to direct its activity that
that system should surely and certainly prevail.   For this
purpose, and no other, they based the whole structure of

government broadly on the principle that all men are created equal, and therefore free—little dreaming that, within the short period of one hundred years, their descendants would bear to be told by any orator, however popular, that the utterance of that principle was merely a rhetorical rhapsody; or by any judge, however venerated, that it was attended by mental reservations which rendered it hypocritical and false. By the Ordinance of 1787 they dedicated all of the national domain not yet polluted by slavery to free labor immediately, thenceforth, and forever; while by the new Constitution and laws they invited foreign free labor from all lands under the sun, and interdicted the importation of African slave labor, at all times, in all places, and under all circumstances whatsoever. It is true that they necessarily and wisely modified this policy of freedom by leaving it to the several states, affected as they were by differing circumstances, to abolish slavery in their own way and at their own pleasure, instead of confiding that duty to Congress, and that they secured to the slave states, while yet retaining the system of slavery, a three-fifths representation of slaves in the Federal Government, until they should find themselves able to relinquish it with safety. But the very nature of these modifications fortifies my position that the fathers knew that the two systems could not endure within the Union, and expected that within a short period slavery would disappear forever. Moreover, in order that these modifications might not altogether defeat their grand design of a republic maintaining universal equality, they provided that two-thirds of the states might amend the Constitution.

It remains to say on this point only one word to guard against misapprehension. If these states are again to become universally slaveholding, I do not pretend to say with what violations of the Constitution that end shall be accomplished. On the other hand, while I do confidently believe and hope that my country will yet become a land of universal freedom, I do not expect that it will be made so otherwise than through the action of the several states coöperating with the Federal Government, and all acting in strict conformity with their respective constitutions.

The strife and contentions concerning slavery, which gently disposed persons so habitually deprecate, are nothing more than the ripening of the conflict which the fathers themselves not only thus regarded with favor, but which they may be said to have instituted.

It is not to be denied, however, that thus far the course of that contest has not been according to their humane anticipations and wishes. In the field of federal politics, slavery, deriving unlooked-for advantages from commercial changes, and energies unforeseen from the facilities of combination between members of the slaveholding class and between that class and other property classes, early rallied, and has at length made a stand, not merely to retain its original defensive position, but to extend its sway throughout the whole Union. It is certain that the slaveholding class of American citizens indulge this high ambition, and that they derive encouragement for it from the rapid and effective political successes which they have already obtained. The plan of operation is this: By continued appliances of patronage and threats of disunion, they will keep a majority favorable to these designs in the Senate, where each state has an equal representation. Through that majority they will defeat, as they best can, the admission of free states, and secure the admission of slave-states. Under the protection of the judiciary, they will, on the principle of the Dred Scott case, carry slavery into all the territories of the United States now existing, and hereafter to be organized. By the action of the President and the Senate, using the treaty-making power, they will annex foreign slaveholding states. In a favorable conjuncture they will induce Congress to repeal the Act of 1808, which prohibits the foreign slave-trade, and so they will import from Africa, at the cost of only twenty dollars a head, slaves enough to fill up the interior of the Continent. Thus relatively increasing the number of slave states, they will allow no amendment to the Constitution prejudicial to their interests; and so, having permanently established their power, they expect the federal judiciary to nullify all state laws which shall interfere with internal or foreign commerce in slaves. When the free states shall be sufficiently demoralized to tolerate these designs, they reasonably conclude that slavery will be accepted by those states themselves. I shall not stop to show how speedy or how complete would be the ruin which the accomplishment of these slaveholding schemes would bring upon the country. For one, I should not remain in the country to test the sad experiment. Having spent my manhood, though not my whole life, in a free state, no aristocracy of any kind, much less an aristocracy of slaveholders, shall ever make the laws of the land in which I shall be content to live. Having seen the society around me universally engaged in agriculture, manufactures, and trade, which were innocent and beneficent, I shall never be a denizen of a state where men and women are reared as cattle, and bought and sold as merchandise. When that evil day shall come, and all further effort at resistance shall be impossible, then, if there shall be no better hope for redemption than I can now foresee, I shall say with Franklin, while looking abroad over the whole earth for a new and congenial home, "Where liberty dwells, there is my country."

You will tell me that these fears are extravagant and chimerical. I answer, they are so; but they are so only because the designs of the slaveholders must and can be defeated. But it is only the possibility of defeat that renders them so. They cannot be defeated by inactivity. There is no escape from them, compatible with non-resistance. How, then, and in what way, shall the necessary resistance be made? There is only one way. The Democratic party must be permanently dislodged from the government. The reason is, that the Democratic party is inextricably committed to the designs of the slaveholders, which I have described. Let me be well understood. I do not charge that the Democratic candidates for public office now before the people are pledged to, much less that the Democratic masses who support them really adopt, those atrocious and dangerous designs. Candidates may, and generally do, mean to act justly, wisely, and patriotically, when they shall be elected; but they become the ministers and servants, not the dictators, of the power which elects them. The policy which a party shall pursue at a future period is only gradually developed, depending on the occurrence of events never fully foreknown. The motives of men, whether acting as electors, or in any other capacity, are generally pure. Nevertheless, it is not more true that "Hell is paved with good intentions" than it is that earth

WILLIAM HENRY SEWARD
Photogravure after a painting

is covered with wrecks resulting from innocent and amiable motives.

The very constitution of the Democratic party commits it to execute all the designs of the slaveholders, whatever they may be. It is not a party of the whole Union, of all the free states, and of all the slave states; nor yet is it a party of the free states in the North and in the Northwest; but it is a sectional and local party, having practically its seat within the slave states, and counting its constituency chiefly and almost exclusively there. Of all its representatives in Congress and in the Electoral College, two-thirds uniformly come from these states. Its great element of strength lies in the vote of the slaveholders, augmented by the representation of three-fifths of the slaves. Deprive the Democratic party of this strength, and it would be a helpless and hopeless minority, incapable of continued organization. The Democratic party, being thus local and sectional, acquires new strength from the admission of every new slave state, and loses relatively by the admission of every new free state in the Union.

A party is, in one sense, a joint-stock association, in which those who contribute most direct the action and management of the concern. The slaveholders contributing in an overwhelming proportion to the capital strength of the Democratic party, they necessarily dictate and prescribe its policy. The inevitable caucus system enables them to do so with a show of fairness and justice. If it were possible to conceive for a moment that the Democratic party should disobey the behests of the slaveholders, we should then see a withdrawal of the slaveholders, which would leave the party to perish. The portion of the party which is found in the free states is a mere appendage, convenient to modify its sectional character, without impairing its sectional constitution, and is less effective in regulating its movement than the nebulous tail of the comet is in determining the appointed though apparently eccentric course of the fiery sphere from which it emanates.

To expect the Democratic party to resist slavery and favor freedom is as unreasonable as to look for Protestant missionaries to the Catholic Propaganda of Rome. The history of the Democratic party commits it to the policy of slavery. It has been the Democratic party, and no other agency, which has carried that policy up to its present alarming culmination. Without stopping to ascertain critically the origin of the present Democratic party, we may concede its claim to date from the era of good-feeling which occurred under the administration of President Monroe. At that time, in this state, and about that time in many others of the free states, the Democratic party deliberately disfranchised the free colored, or African citizen, and it has pertinaciously continued this disfranchisement ever since. This was an effective aid to slavery; for while the slaveholder votes for his slaves against freedom, the freed slave in the free states is prohibited from voting against slavery.

In 1824 the Democracy resisted the election of John Quincy Adams—himself before that time an acceptable Democrat—and in 1828 it expelled him from the Presidency, and put a slaveholder in his place, although the office had been filled by slaveholders thirty-two out of forty years.

In 1836 Martin Van Buren—the first non-slaveholding citizen of a free state to whose election the Democratic party ever consented—signalized his inauguration into the Presidency by a gratuitous announcement that under no circumstances would he ever approve a bill for the abolition of slavery in the District of Columbia. From 1838 to 1844, the subject of abolishing slavery in the District of Columbia and in the national dockyards and arsenals was brought before Congress by repeated popular appeals. The Democratic party thereupon promptly denied the right of petition, and effectually suppressed the freedom of speech in Congress, so far as the institution of slavery was concerned.

From 1840 to 1843, good and wise men counseled that Texas should remain outside of the Union until she should consent to relinquish her self-instituted slavery; but the Democratic party precipitated her admission into the Union, not only without that condition, but even with a covenant that the state might be divided and reorganized so as to constitute four slave states instead of one.

In 1846, when the United States became involved in a war with Mexico, and it was apparent that the struggle would end in the dismemberment of that republic, which was a non-slaveholding power, the Democratic party rejected a declaration that slavery should not be established within the territory to be acquired.   When, in 1850, governments were to be instituted in the territories of California and New Mexico, the fruits of that war, the Democratic party refused to admit New Mexico as a free state, and only consented to admit California as a free state on the condition, as it has since explained the transaction, of leaving all of New Mexico and Utah open to slavery, to which was also added the concession of perpetual slavery in the District of Columbia and the passage of an unconstitutional, cruel, and humiliating law for the recapture of fugitive slaves, with a further stipulation that the subject of slavery should never again be agitated in either chamber of Congress.   When in 1854 the slaveholders were contentedly reposing on these great advantages, then so recently won, the Democratic party, unnecessarily, officiously, and with superserviceable liberality, awakened them from their slumber, to offer and force on their acceptance the abrogation of the law which declared that neither slavery nor involuntary servitude should ever exist within that part of the ancient territory of Louisiana which lay outside of the State of Missouri, and north of the parallel of 36° 30′ north latitude—a law which, with the exception of one other, was the only statute of freedom then remaining in the federal code.

In 1856, when the people of Kansas had organized a new state within the region thus abandoned to slavery, and applied to be admitted as a free state into the Union, the Democratic party contemptuously rejected their petition and drove them with menaces and intimidations from the halls of Congress, and armed the President with military power to enforce their submission to a slave code, established over them by fraud and usurpation.   At every subsequent stage of the long contest which has since raged in Kansas, the Democratic party has lent its sympathies, its aid, and all the powers of the government which it controlled, to enforce slavery upon that unwilling and injured people.   And now, even at this day, while it mocks us with the assurance that Kansas is free, the Democratic party keeps the state excluded from her just and proper place in the Union, under the hope that she may be dragooned into the acceptance of slavery.

The Democratic party, finally, has procured from a supreme judiciary, fixed in its interest, a decree that slavery exists by force of the Constitution in every territory of the United States, paramount to all legislative authority either within the territory or residing in Congress.

Such is the Democratic party. It has no policy, state or federal, for finance, or trade, or manufacture, or commerce, or education, or internal improvements, or for the protection or even the security of civil or religious liberty. It is positive and uncompromising in the interest of slavery—negative, compromising, and vacillating, in regard to everything else. It boasts its love of equality and wastes its strength, and even its life, in fortifying the only aristocracy known in the land. It professes fraternity, and, so often as slavery requires, allies itself with proscription. It magnifies itself for conquests in foreign lands, but it sends the national eagle forth always with chains, and not the olive branch, in his fangs.

This dark record shows you, fellow-citizens, what I was unwilling to announce at an earlier stage of this argument, that of the whole nefarious schedule of slaveholding designs which I have submitted to you, the Democratic party has left only one yet to be consummated—the abrogation of the law which forbids the African slave trade.

Now, I know very well that the Democratic party has at every stage of these proceedings disavowed the motive and the policy of fortifying and extending slavery, and has excused them on entirely different and more plausible grounds. But the inconsistency and frivolity of these pleas prove still more conclusively the guilt I charge upon that party. It must, indeed, try to excuse such guilt before mankind, and even to the consciences of its own adherents. There is an instinctive abhorrence of slavery, and an inborn and inhering love of freedom in the human heart, which renders palliation of such gross misconduct indispensable. It disfranchised the free African on the ground of a fear that, if left to enjoy the right of suffrage, he might seduce the free white citizen into amalgamation with his wronged and despised race. The Democratic party condemned and deposed

John Quincy Adams because he expended $12,000,000 a year, while it justifies his favored successor in spending $70,000,000, $80,000,000, and even $100,000,000 a year. It denies emancipation in the District of Columbia, even with compensation to masters and the consent of the people, on the ground of an implied constitutional inhibition, although the Constitution expressly confers upon Congress sovereign legislative power in that district, and although the Democratic party is tenacious of the principle of strict construction. It violated the express provisions of the Constitution in suppressing petition and debate on the subject of slavery, through fear of disturbance of the public harmony, although it claims that the electors have a right to instruct their representatives, and even demand their resignation in cases of contumacy. It extended slavery over Texas, and connived at the attempt to spread it across the Mexican territories, even to the shores of the Pacific Ocean, under a plea of enlarging the area of freedom. It abrogated the Mexican slave law and the Missouri Compromise prohibition of slavery in Kansas, not to open the new territories to slavery, but to try therein the new and fascinating theories of non-intervention and popular sovereignty; and, finally, it overthrew both these new and elegant systems by the English Lecompton bill and the Dred Scott decision, on the ground that the free states ought not to enter the Union without a population equal to the representative basis of one member of Congress, although slave states might come in without inspection as to their numbers.

Will any member of the Democratic party now here claim that the authorities chosen by the suffrages of the party transcended their partisan platforms, and so misrepresented the party in the various transactions I have recited? Then I ask him to name one Democratic statesman or legislator, from Van Buren to Walker, who either timidly or cautiously like them, or boldly or defiantly like Douglas, ever refused to execute a behest of the slaveholders, and was not therefor, and for no other cause, immediately denounced, and deposed from his trust, and repudiated by the Democratic party for that contumacy.

I think, fellow-citizens, that I have shown you that it is high time for the friends of freedom to rush to the rescue of the Constitution, and that their very first duty is to dismiss the Democratic party from the administration of the Government.

Why shall it not be done? All agree that it ought to be done. What, then, shall prevent its being done? Nothing but timidity or division of the opponents of the Democratic party.

Some of these opponents start one objection, and some another. Let us notice these objections briefly. One class say that they cannot trust the Republican party; that it has not avowed its hostility to slavery boldly enough, or its affection for freedom earnestly enough.

I ask in reply: Is there any other party which can be more safely trusted? Every one knows that it is the Republican party or none, that shall displace the Democratic party. But I answer further, that the character and fidelity of any party are determined, necessarily, not by its pledges, programs, and platforms, but by the public exigencies, and the temper of the people when they call it into activity. Subserviency to slavery is a law written, not only on the forehead of the Democratic party, but also in its very soul—so resistance to slavery, and devotion to freedom, the popular elements now actively working for the Republican party among the people, must and will be the resources for its ever-renewing strength and constant invigoration.

Others cannot support the Republican party, because it has not sufficiently exposed its platform, and determined what it will do, and what it will not do, when triumphant. It may prove too progressive for some, and too conservative for others. As if any party ever foresaw so clearly the course of future events as to plan a universal scheme for future action, adapted to all possible emergencies. Who would ever have joined even the Whig party of the Revolution, if it had been obliged to answer, in 1775, whether it would declare for Independence in 1776, and for this noble Federal Constitution of ours in 1787, and not a year earlier or later?

The people of the United States will be as wise next year, and the year afterward, and even ten years hence, as we are now. They will oblige the Republican party to act as the public welfare and the interests of justice and human-

ity shall require, through all the stages of its career, whether
of trial or triumph.

Others will not venture an effort, because they feel that
the Union would not endure the change. Will such ob-
jectors tell me how long a constitution can bear a strain
directly along the fibres of which it is composed? This is
a Constitution of freedom. It is being converted into a
Constitution of slavery. It is a republican Constitution.
It is being made an aristocratic one. Others wish to wait
until some collateral questions concerning temperance, or
the exercise of the elective franchise, are properly settled.
Let me ask all such persons whether time enough has not
been wasted on these points already, without gaining any
other than this single advantage, namely, the discovery that
only one thing can be effectually done at one time, and that
the one thing which must and will be done at any one time
is just that thing which is most urgent, and will no longer
admit of postponement or delay. Finally, we are told by
faint-hearted men that they despond; the Democratic
party, they say, is unconquerable, and the dominion of
slavery is consequently inevitable. I reply to them, that
the complete and universal dominion of slavery would be
intolerable enough when it should have come after the last
possible effort to escape should have been made. There
would, in that case, be left to us the consoling reflection of
fidelity to duty.

But I reply, further, that I know—few, I think, know
better than I—the resources and energies of the Democratic
party, which is identical with the slave-power. I do ample
justice to its traditional popularity. I know further—few,
I think, know better than I—the difficulties and disadvantages of organizing a new political force like the Republican
party, and the obstacles it must encounter in laboring without prestige and without patronage. But, notwithstanding
all this, I know that the Democratic party must go down,
and that the Republican party must rise into its place. The
Democratic party derived its strength, originally, from its
adoption of the principles of equal and exact justice to all
men. So long as it practised this principle faithfully, it
was invulnerable. It became vulnerable when it renounced
the principle, and since that time it has maintained itself,

not by virtue of its own strength, or even of its traditional merits, but because there as yet had appeared in the political field no other party that had the conscience and the courage to take up, and avow, and practise the life-inspiring principles which the Democratic party had surrendered. At last, the Republican party has appeared. It avows now, as the Republican party of 1800 did, in one word, its faith and its works: "Equal and exact justice to all men." Even when it first entered the field, only half-organized, it struck a blow which only just failed to secure complete and triumphant victory. In this, its second campaign, it has already won advantages which render that triumph now both easy and certain.

The secret of its assured success lies in that very characteristic which, in the mouth of scoffers, constitutes its great and lasting imbecility and reproach. It lies in the fact that it is a party of one idea; but that idea is a noble one—an idea that fills and expands all generous souls; the idea of equality—the equality of all men before human tribunals and human laws, as they are all equal before the Divine tribunal and Divine laws.

I know, and you know, that a revolution has begun. I know, and all the world knows, that revolutions never go backward. Twenty senators and a hundred representatives proclaim boldly in Congress to-day sentiments and opinions and principles of freedom which hardly so many men, even in this free state, dared to utter in their own homes twenty years ago. While the Government of the United States, under the conduct of the Democratic party, has been all that time surrendering one plain and castle after another to slavery, the people of the United States have been no less steadily and perseveringly gathering together the forces with which to recover back again all the fields and all the castles which have been lost, and to confound and overthrow, by one decisive blow, the betrayers of the Constitution and freedom forever.

RICHARD LALOR SHEIL

IRELAND'S PART IN ENGLISH ACHIEVEMENT

[Richard Lalor Sheil, an Irish patriotic orator, was born in Tipperary, Ireland, in 1791. He received his education at a Jesuit college in England and at Trinity College, Dublin. He settled in the Irish capital as a barrister, devoting himself also to literature with success. But it was as an orator that he was destined to achieve an enduring renown. The agitation for Roman Catholic Emancipation, headed by Daniel O'Connell, had assumed formidable proportions. Sheil came vigorously to the support of O'Connell and was himself elected to Parliament. His speeches lifted him far above any Irish patriot of his time, with the single exception of the great liberator himself. He subsequently filled important posts under the government. His death occurred in Italy in 1851, while acting as British Minister at Florence. The following speech, characteristically Irish in its fervid eloquence and stanch patriotism, was delivered in the House of Commons in 1837.]

WHEREVER we turn our eyes, we see the national power dilating, expanding, and ascending; never did a liberated nation spring on in the career that freedom throws open towards improvement with such a bound as we have; in wealth, in intelligence, in high feeling, in all the great constituents of a state, we have made in a few years an astonishing progress. The character of our country is completely changed: we are free, and we feel as if we never had been slaves. Ireland stands as erect as if she had never stooped; although she once bowed her forehead to the earth, every mark and trace of her prostration have been effaced. But these are generalities; these are vague and abstract vauntings, without detail. Well, if you stand in need of specification, it shall be rapidly, but not inconclusively, given. But hold: I was going to point to the first law offices in the country, filled by Roman Catholics; I was going to point to the second judicial office in Ireland, filled by a Roman Catholic; I was going to point to the crowds of Roman Catholics, who, in every profession and walk of life, are winning their way to eminence in the walks that lead to affluence or to honor. But one single fact suffices for my purpose; emancipation was followed by reform, and reform has thrown sixty men, devoted to the interests of Ireland, into the House of Commons. If the Clare election was a great incident; if the Clare election afforded evidence that emancipation could not be resisted, look at sixty of us (what are Longford and Carlow but a realization of the splendid intimations that Clare held out?), look, I say, at sixty of us—the majority, the great majority, of the representatives of Ireland—leagued and confederated by an obligation and a pledge as sacred as any with which men, associated for the interests of their country, were ever bound together. Thank God, we are here! I remember the time when the body to which I belong was excluded from all participation in the great legislative rights of which we are now in the possession. I remember to have felt humiliated at the tone in which I heard the cause of Ireland pleaded, when I was occasionally admitted under the gallery of the House of Commons. I felt pain at hearing us represented as humble suppliants for liberty, and as asking freedom as if it were alms that we were soliciting. Perhaps that tone was unavoidable: thank God, it is no longer necessary or appropriate. Here we are, in all regards your equals, and demanding our rights as the representatives of Britons would demand their own. We have less eloquence, less skill, less astuteness than the great men to whom, of old, the interests of Ireland were confided; but we make up for these imperfections by the moral port and national bearing that become us. In mastery of diction we may be defective; in resources of argument we may be wanting; we may not be gifted with the accomplishments by which persuasion is produced; but in energy, in strenuousness, in union, in fidelity to our country and to each other, and, above all, in the undaunted and dauntless determination to enforce equality for Ireland, we stand unsurpassed. This, then, is the power with which the noble lord courts an encounter, foretells his own victories, and triumphs in their anticipation in the House of Commons. Where are his

means of discomfiting us? To what resources does he look
for the accomplishment of the wonders which he is to perform? Does he rely upon the excitement of the religious
and national prejudices of England; and does he find it in
his heart to resort to the "no Popery" cry? Instead of
telling him what he is doing, I'll tell the country what,
thirty years ago, was done. In 1807 the Whigs were in
possession of Downing Street, and the Tories were in possession of St. James's Palace, but, without the people, the
possession of St. James's was of no avail. The Whigs proposed that Roman Catholics should be admitted to the
higher grades in the army and navy. The Tories saw that
their opportunity was come, and the "no Popery" cry was
raised. There existed, at that time, a great mass of prejudice in England. You had conquered Ireland and enslaved
her; you hated her for the wrongs that you had done her,
and despised her, and perhaps justly, for her endurance:
the victim of oppression naturally becomes the object of
scorn; you loathed our country, and you abhorred our
creed. Of this feeling the Tories took advantage; the
tocsin of fanaticism was rung; the war-whoop of religious
discord, the savage yell of infuriated ignorance, resounded
through the country.

Events that ought to have been allowed to remain buried
in the oblivion of centuries were disinterred; every misdeed
of Catholics, when Catholics and Protestants imbrued their
hands alternately in blood, was recalled; the ashes of the
Smithfield fires were stirred for sparks with which the
popular passions might be ignited. The reëstablishment
of Popery; the downfall of every Protestant institution;
the annihilation of all liberty, civil or religious; these were
the topics with which crafty men, without remorse of conscience, worked on the popular delusion. At public assemblies, senators, more remarkable for Protestant piety than
Christian charity, delivered themselves of ferocious effusions
amidst credulous and enthusiastic multitudes. Then came
public abuses, at which libations to the worst passions of
human nature were prodigally poured out. "Rally round
the king, rally round the church, rally round the religion of
your forefathers," these were the invocations with which
the English people were wrought into frenzy; and having,

by these expedients, driven their antagonists from office, the Tories passed, themselves, the very measure for which they made their competitors the objects of their denunciation. Are you playing the same game? If you are, then shame, shame upon you! I won't pronounce upon your motives: let the facts be their interpreters. What is the reason that a new edition of Fox's "Martyrs," with hundreds of subscribers, and with the name of the Duke of Cumberland at their head, has been announced? Wherefore, from one extremity of the country to the other, in every city, town, and hamlet, is a perverse ingenuity employed, in order to inspire the people of this country with a detestation of the religion of millions of their fellow-citizens? Why is Popery, with her racks, her tortures, and her fagots, conjured up in order to appal the imagination of the English people? Why is perjury to our God, treason to our sovereign, a disregard of every obligation, divine and human, attributed to us? I leave you to answer those questions, and to give your answers, not only to the interrogatories which thus vehemently, and, I will own, indignantly I put to you, but to reply to those which must be administered to you, in your moments of meditation, by your own hearts. But, whatever be your purpose in the religious excitement which you are endeavoring to get up in this country, of this I am convinced, that the result of your expedients will correspond with their deserts, and that as we have prevailed over you before, we shall again and again discomfit you. Yes, we, the Irish millions, led on by men like those that plead the cause of those millions in this House, must (it is impossible that we should not) prevail; and I am convinced that the people of England, so far from being disposed to array themselves against us, despite any remains of the prejudices which are fast passing away in this country, feel that we are entitled to the same privileges, and extend to us their sympathies in this good and glorious cause.

What is that cause? I shall rapidly tell you. You took away our Parliament—you took from us that Parliament which, like the House of Commons of this country, must have been under the control of the great majority of the people of Ireland, and would not, and could not, have withheld what you so long refused us.   Is there a man here who doubts that if the Union had not been conceded, we should have extorted emancipation and reform from our own House of Commons?   That House of Commons you bought, and paid for your bargain in gold; aye, and paid for it in the most palpable and sordid form in which gold can be paid down.   But, while this transaction was pending, you told us that all distinctions should be abolished between us, and that we should become like unto yourselves.   The great minister of the time, by whom that unexampled sale of our legislature was negotiated, held out equality with England as the splendid equivalent for the loss of our national representation; and, with classical references, elucidated the nobleness of the compact into which we had persuaded the depositants of the rights of their countrymen to enter.   The Act of Union was passed, and twenty-nine years elapsed before any effectual measure was taken to carry its real and substantial terms into effect.   At last, our enfranchisement was won by our own energy and determination; and, when it was in progress, we received assurances that, in every respect, we should be placed on a footing with our fellow-citizens; and it was more specially announced to us, that to corporations, and to all offices connected with them, we should be at once admissible.

Pending this engagement, a bill is passed for the reform of the corporations of this country; and in every important municipal locality in England councilors are selected by the people as their representatives.   This important measure having been carried here, the Irish people claim an extension of the same advantages, and ground their title on the Union, on emancipation, on reform, and on the great principle of perfect equality between the two countries, on which the security of one country and the prosperity of both must depend.   This demand on the part of Ireland is rejected; and that which to England no one was bold enough to deny, from Ireland you are determined, and you announce it, to withhold.   Is this justice?   You will say that it is, and I should be surprised if you did not say so. I should be surprised, indeed, if, while you are doing us wrong, you did not profess your solicitude to do us justice. From the day on which Strongbow set his foot on the shores of Ireland, Englishmen were never wanting in protestations of their deep anxiety to do us justice—even Strafford, the deserter of the people's cause—the renegade Wentworth, who gave evidence in Ireland of the spirit of instinctive tyranny which predominated in his character— even Strafford, while he trampled upon our rights, and trod upon the heart of the country, protested his solicitude to do justice to Ireland. What marvel is it, then, that gentlemen opposite should deal in such vehement protestations? There is, however, one man of great abilities, not a member of this House, but whose talents and whose boldness have placed him in the topmost place in his party—who, disdaining all imposture, and thinking it the best course to appeal directly to the religious and national antipathies of the people of this country—abandoning all reserve, and flinging off the slender veil by which his political associates affect to cover, although they cannot hide, their motives— distinctly and audaciously tells the Irish people that they are not entitled to the same privileges as Englishmen; and pronounces them, in any particular which could enter his minute enumeration of the circumstances by which fellow-citizenship is created, in race, identity, and religion—to be aliens—to be aliens in race, to be aliens in country, to be aliens in religion. Aliens! good God! was Arthur, Duke of Wellington, in the House of Lords, and did he not start up and exclaim: "Hold! I have seen the aliens do their duty"? The Duke of Wellington is not a man of an excitable temperament. His mind is of a cast too martial to be easily moved; but, notwithstanding his habitual inflexibility, I cannot help thinking that when he heard his Roman Catholic countrymen (for we are his countrymen) designated by a phrase as offensive as the abundant vocabulary of his eloquent confederate could supply—I cannot help thinking that he ought to have recollected the many fields of fight in which we have been contributors to his renown. "The battles, sieges, fortunes that he has passed" ought to have come back upon him. He ought to have remembered that, from the earliest achievement in which he displayed that military genius which has placed him foremost in the annals of modern warfare, down to that last and surpassing combat which has made his name imperishable—from Assaye

to Waterloo—the Irish soldiers, with whom your armies
are filled, were the inseparable auxiliaries to the glory with
which his unparalleled successes have been crowned. Whose
were the arms that drove your bayonets at Vimiera through
the phalanxes that had never before reeled in the shock of
war? What desperate valor climbed the steeps and filled
the moats at Badajos? All his victories should have rushed
and crowded back upon his memory—Vimiera, Badajos,
Salamanca, Albuera, Toulouse, and, last of all, the greatest—. Tell me, for you were there—I appeal to the gallant soldier before me [Sir Henry Hardinge] from whose
opinions I differ, but who bears, I know, a generous heart
in an intrepid breast—tell me, for you must needs remember—on that day when the destinies of mankind were trembling in the balance—while death fell in showers—when the
artillery of France was leveled with a precision of the
most deadly science—when her legions, incited by the voice,
and inspired by the example of their mighty leader, rushed
again and again to the onset—tell me if, for an instant,
when to hesitate for an instant was to be lost, the "aliens"
blenched? And when at length the moment for the last
and decisive movement had arrived, and the valor which
had so long been wisely checked was at last let loose—
when, with words familiar, but immortal, the great captain
commanded the great assault—tell me, if Catholic Ireland,
with less heroic valor than the natives of this your own
glorious country, precipitated herself upon the foe? The
blood of England, Scotland, and of Ireland flowed in the
same stream, and drenched the same field. When the chill
morning dawned, their dead lay cold and stark together;
in the same deep pit their bodies were deposited—the green
corn of Spring is now breaking from their commingled dust
—the dew falls from heaven upon their union in the grave.
Partakers in every peril—in the glory shall we not be permitted to participate; and shall we be told, as a requital,
that we are estranged from the noble country for whose
salvation our life-blood was poured out?

RICHARD BRINSLEY SHERIDAN

AGAINST WARREN HASTINGS

[Richard Brinsley Sheridan, a dramatist and public man, distinguished for his wit and eloquence, was born in Dublin in 1751. He received a good but unsystematic education and took to literature, writing "The Rivals," a brilliant comedy, before he was twenty-five. He produced other plays, including "The School for Scandal," and gained a large income from an interest he acquired in Drury Lane Theater. He entered Parliament in 1780, earning unprecedented applause by his speeches, especially by one in which he urged the impeachment of Warren Hastings. He remained a member of the House of Commons, with slight intermission, until 1812. He advocated freedom of the press, reform, and milder game laws. He opposed the legislative union of England and Ireland and indorsed the French Revolution. His death occurred at London in 1816, and his burial took place in the great Abbey of Westminster. His famous impeachment of Warren Hastings for so-called infamous actions in India was delivered in Westminster Hall (the "Hall of Rufus"), adjoining the English Houses of Parliament, in 1788, during Hastings's historic trial.]

IF, my lords, a stranger had at this time entered the province of Oude, ignorant of what had happened since the death of Sujah Dowlah—that prince who with a savage heart had still great lines of character, and who, with all his ferocity in war, had, with a cultivating hand, preserved to his country the wealth which it derived from benignant skies and a prolific soil—if, observing the wide and general devastation of fields unclothed and brown; of vegetation burned up and extinguished; of villages depopulated and in ruin; of temples unroofed and perishing; of reservoirs broken down and dry, this stranger should ask, "what has thus laid waste this beautiful and opulent land; what monstrous madness has ravaged with wide-spread war; what desolating foreign foe; what civil discords; what disputed succession; what religious zeal; what fabled monster has stalked abroad, and, with malice and mortal enmity to man, withered by the grasp of death every growth of nature and

humanity, all means of delight, and each original, simple
principle of bare existence?" the answer would have been,
not one of these causes! No wars have ravaged these lands
and depopulated these villages! No desolating foreign
foe! No domestic broils! No disputed succession! No
religious, superserviceable zeal! No poisonous monster!
No affliction of Providence, which, while it scourged us,
cut off the sources of resuscitation! No! This damp of
death is the mere effusion of British amity! We sink under
the pressure of their support! We writhe under their perfidious gripe! They have embraced us with their protecting arms, and lo! these are the fruits of their alliance!

What then, my lords, shall we bear to be told that,
under such circumstances, the exasperated feelings of a
whole people, thus spurred on to clamor and resistance,
were excited by the poor and feeble influence of the Begums? After hearing the description given by an eye-
witness [Colonel Naylor, successor of Hannay] of the par-
oxysm of fever and delirium into which despair threw the
natives when on the banks of the polluted Ganges, panting
for breath, they tore more widely open the lips of their
gaping wounds, to accelerate their dissolution; and while
their blood was issuing, presented their ghastly eyes to
heaven, breathing their last and fervent prayer that the dry
earth might not be suffered to drink their blood, but that
it might rise up to the throne of God, and rouse the eternal
Providence to avenge the wrongs of their country—will it
be said that all this was brought about by the incantations
of these Begums in their secluded Zenana; or that they
could inspire this enthusiasm and this despair into the
breasts of a people who felt no grievance, and had suffered no
torture? What motive, then, could have such influence in
their bosom? What motive! That which nature, the common parent, plants in the bosom of man; and which, though
it may be less active in the Indian than in the Englishman,
is still congenial with, and makes a part of, his being. That
feeling which tells him that man was never made to be the
property of man; but that, when in the pride and insolence
of power, one human creature dares to tyrannize over
another, it is a power usurped, and resistance is a duty.
That principle which tells him that resistance to power

usurped is not merely a duty which he owes to himself and to his neighbor, but a duty which he owes to his God, in asserting and maintaining the rank which he gave him in his creation. That principle which neither the rudeness of ignorance can stifle, nor the enervation of refinement extinguish! That principle which makes it base for a man to suffer when he ought to act; which, tending to preserve to the species the original designations of Providence, spurns at the arrogant distinctions of man, and indicates the independent quality of his race.

I trust, now, that your lordships can feel no hesitation in acquitting the unfortunate princesses of this allegation. But though the innocence of the Begums may be confessed, it does not necessarily follow, I am ready to allow, that the prisoner must be guilty. There is a possibility that he might have been deluded by others, and incautiously led into a false conclusion. If this be proved, my lords, I will cheerfully abandon the present charge. But if, on the other hand, it shall appear, as I am confident it will, that in his subsequent conduct there was a mysterious conceal-ment denoting conscious guilt; if all his narrations of the business be found marked with inconsistency and contradic-tion, there can be, I think, a doubt no longer entertained of his criminality.

It will be easy, my lords, to prove that such conceal-ment was actually practised. From the month of Septem-ber, in which the seizure of the treasures took place, till the succeeding January, no intimation whatever was given of it by Mr. Hastings to the council at Calcutta. But, my lords, look at the mode in which this concealment is attempted to be evaded. The first pretext is, the want of leisure! Contemptible falsehood! He could amuse his fancy at this juncture with the composition of Eastern tales, but to give an account of a rebellion which convulsed an empire, or of his acquiring so large an amount of treas-ure, he had no time!

The second pretext is, that all communication between Calcutta and Fyzabad was cut off. This is no less untrue. By comparing dates, it will be seen that letters, now in our possession, passed at this period between Mr. Middleton and the prisoner. Even Sir Elijah Impey has unguardedly declared that the road leading from the one city to the other was as clear from interruption as that between London and any of the neighboring villages. So satisfied am I, indeed, on this point, that I am willing to lay aside every other topic of criminality against the prisoner, and to rest this prosecution alone on the question of the validity of the reasons assigned for the concealment we have alleged. Let those, my lords, who still retain any doubts on the subject, turn to the prisoner's narrative of his journey to Benares. They will there detect, amid a motley mixture of cant and mystery, of rhapsody and enigma, the most studious concealment.

It may, perhaps, be asked why did Mr. Hastings use all these efforts to veil this business? Though it is not strictly incumbent on me to give an answer to the question, yet I will say that he had obviously a reason for it. Looking to the natural effect of deep injuries on the human mind, he thought that oppression must beget resistance. The attempt which the Begums might be driven to make in their own defense, though really the effect, he was determined to represent as the cause of his proceedings. He was here only repeating the experiment which he so successfully performed in the case of Cheyte Sing. Even when disappointed in those views by the natural meekness and submission of the princesses, he could not relinquish the scheme; and hence, in his letter to the court of Directors January 5, 1782, he represents the subsequent disturbances in Oude as the cause of the violent measures he had adopted two months previous to the existence of these disturbances! He there congratulates his masters on the seizure of the treasures which he declares, by the law of Mohammed, were the property of Asaph-ul-Dowlah.

My lords, the prisoner more than once assured the House of Commons that the inhabitants of Asia believed him to be a preternatural being, gifted with good fortune or the peculiar favorite of Heaven; and that Providence never failed to take up and carry, by wise, but hidden means, every project of his to its destined end. Thus, in his blasphemous and vulgar puritanical jargon, did Mr. Hastings libel the course of Providence. Thus, according to him, when his corruptions and briberies were on the eve of exposure, Providence inspired the heart of Nuncomar to commit a low, base crime, in order to save him from ruin. Thus, also, in his attempts on Cheyte Sing, and his plunder of the Begums, Providence stepped forth, and inspired the one with resistance and the other with rebellion, to forward his purposes! Thus, my lords, did he arrogantly represent himself as a man not only the favorite of Providence, but as one for whose sake Providence departed from the eternal course of its own wise dispensations, to assist his administration by the elaboration of all that is deleterious and ill; heaven-born forgeries—inspired treasons—providential rebellions! arraigning that Providence

"Whose works are goodness, and whose ways are right."

It does undoubtedly, my lords, bear a strange appearance, that a man of reputed ability, like the prisoner, even when acting wrongly, should have recourse to so many bungling artifices, and spread so thin a veil over his deceptions. But those who are really surprised at this circumstance must have attended very little to the demeanor of Mr. Hastings. Through the whole of his defense upon this charge, sensible that truth would undo him, he rests his hopes on falsehood. Observing this rule, he has drawn together a set of falsehoods without consistency and without connection; not knowing, or not remembering, that there is nothing which requires so much care in the fabrication as a system of lies. The series must be regular and unbroken; but his falsehoods are eternally at variance, and demolish one another. Indeed, in all his conduct, he seems to be actuated but by one principle: to do things contrary to the established form. This architect militates against the first principles of the art. He begins with the frieze and the capital, and lays the base of the column at the top. Thus turning his edifice upside down, he plumes himself upon the novelty of his idea, till it comes tumbling about his ears. Rising from these ruins, he is soon found rearing a similar structure. He delights in difficulties, and disdains a plain and secure foundation. He loves, on the contrary, to build on a precipice, and to encamp on a mine. Inured to falls, he fears not danger. Frequent defeats have given him a hardihood, without impressing a sense of disgrace.

It was once, my lords, a maxim, as much admitted in the practise of common life as in the schools of philosophy, that where Heaven is inclined to destroy, it begins with frenzying the intellect. "Quem Deus vult perdere prius dementat." This doctrine the right honorable manager [Mr. Burke], who opened generally to your lordships the articles of impeachment, still further extended. He declared that the coexistence of vice and prudence was incompatible; that the vicious man, being deprived of his best energies, and curtailed in his proportion of understanding, was left with such a short-sighted penetration as could lay no claim to prudence. This is the sentiment of my noble and exalted friend, whose name I can never mention but with respect and admiration due to his virtue and talents; whose proud disdain of vice can only be equaled by the ability with which he exposes and controls it; to whom I look up with homage; whose genius is commensurate with philanthropy; whose memory will stretch itself beyond the fleeting objects of any little partial shuffling—through the whole wide range of human knowledge and honorable aspiration after good—as large as the system which forms life—as lasting as those objects which adorn it; but in this sentiment, so honorable to my friend, I cannot implicitly agree. If the true definition of prudence be the successful management and conduct of a purpose to its end, I can at once bring instances into view where this species of prudence belonged to minds distinguished by the atrocity of their actions. When I survey the history of a Philip of Macedon, of a Cæsar, of a Cromwell, I perceive great guilt successfully conducted, if not by legitimate discretion, at least by a consummate craft, or by an all-commanding sagacity, productive of precisely the same effects. These, however, I confess, were isolated characters, who left the vice they dared to follow either in the state of dependent vassalage, or involved it in destruction. Such is the perpetual law of nature, that virtue, whether placed in a circle more contracted or enlarged, moves with sweet concert. There is no dissonance to jar; no asperity to divide; and that harmony which makes its felicity at the same time constitutes its protection. Of vice, on the contrary, the parts are disunited, and each in barbarous language clamors for its preëminence. It is a scene where, though one domineering passion may have sway, the others still press forward with their dissonant claims; and, in the moral world, effects waiting on their causes, the discord which results, of course, insures defeat.

In this way, my lords, I believe the failure of Mr. Hastings is to be explained, and such, I trust, will be the fate of all who shall emulate his character or his conduct. The doctrine of my friend, from what I have said, can, therefore, hold only in those minds which cannot be satisfied with the indulgence of a single crime; where, instead of one base master passion having the complete sway, to which all the faculties are subject, and on which alone the mind is bent, there is a combustion and rivalry among a number of passions yet baser, when pride, vanity, avarice, lust of power, cruelty, all at once actuate the human soul and distract its functions; all of them at once filling their several spaces, some in their larger, some in their more contracted orbits; all of them struggling for preëminence, and each counteracting the other. In such a mind, undoubtedly, great crimes can never be accompanied by prudence. There is a fortunate disability, occasioned by the contention, that rescues the human species from the villainy of the intention. Such is the original denunciation of nature. Not so with the nobler passions. In the breast where they reside, the harmony is never interrupted by the number. A perfect and substantial agreement gives an accession of vigor to each, and, spreading their influence in every direction, like the divine intelligence and benignity from which they flow, they ascertain it to the individual by which they are possessed, and communicate it to the society of which he is a member.

My lords, I shall now revert again to the claims made on the Princesses of Oude. The counsel for the prisoner have labored to impress on the court the idea that the nabob was a prince sovereignly independent, and in no degree subject to the control of Mr. Hastings; but, after the numberless proofs we have adduced of his being, on the contrary, a mere cipher in the hands of the governor-general, your lordships will require of them, to create such a conviction on your minds, much more conclusive evidence than any which they have hitherto presented. I believe, both as regards the resumption of the jaghires, and especially the seizure of the treasures, they will find it very difficult to show the independence of the prince.

It has, my lords, been strenuously contended on our parts, that the measure of seizing the treasures originated with the prisoner, and in maintenance of the position we have brought forward a chain of testimony clear, and, we think, satisfactory; but the counsel for the prisoner, on the other hand, assert with equal earnestness, that the proposition for seizing the treasures came originally from the nabob. It is therefore incumbent on them to support their assertion by proof, as we have done. Certainly the best evidence of the fact would be the exhibition of the letter of the nabob to Mr. Hastings, in which they allege the proposition was made. Why, then, is not this document, whch must at once settle all disputation on the subject, produced? The truth is, there is no such letter. I peremptorily deny it, and challenge the prisoner and his counsel to produce a letter or paper containing any proposition of the kind coming immediately from the prince.

My lords, the seizure of the treasures and the jaghires was the effect of a dark conspiracy, in which six persons were concerned. Three of the conspirators were of a higher order. These were Mr. Hastings, who may be considered as the principal and leader in this black affair; Mr. Middleton, the English resident at Lucknow; and Sir Elijah Impey. The three inferior or subordinate conspirators were Hyder Beg Khan, the nominal minister of the nabob, but in reality the creature of Mr. Hastings, Colonel Hannay, and Ali Ibrahim Khan.

Sir Elijah Impey was intrusted by Mr. Hastings to carry his orders to Mr. Middleton, and to concert with him the means of carrying them into execution. The chief-justice, my lords, being a principal actor in the whole of this iniquitous business, it will be necessary to take notice of some parts of the evidence which he has delivered upon oath at your lordships' bar.

When asked what became of the Persian affidavit, sworn before him, after he had delivered them to Mr. Hastings, he replied that he really did not know! He was also asked if he had them translated, or knew of their having been translated, or had any conversation with Mr. Hastings on the subject of the affidavits. He replied "that he knew nothing at all of their having been translated, and that he had no conversation whatever with Mr. Hastings on the subject of the affidavits after he had delivered them to him." He was next asked whether he did not think it a little singular that he should not have held any conversation with the governor-general on a subject of so much moment as that of the affidavits which he had taken. His answer was, that he did not think it singular, because he left Chunar the very day after he delivered the affidavits to Mr. Hastings. By this answer the witness certainly meant it should be understood that when he quitted Chunar he left the governor-general behind him; but it appears from letters written by the witness himself, and which we have already laid before the court, that he arrived at Chunar on the first of December, 1781; that he then began to take the affidavits, and, when completed, he and Mr. Hastings left Chunar in company, and set out on the road to Benares; and that, after being together from the first to the sixth of the month, the former took leave of the latter, and proceeded on his journey to Calcutta. Here, then, my lords, we detect a subterfuge artfully contrived to draw you into a false conclusion! There is also another part of the witness's evidence which is entitled to as little credit. He has sworn that he knew nothing of the Persian affidavits having been translated. Now, my lords, we formerly produced a letter from Major William Davy, the confidential secretary and Persian translator to the governor-general, in which he states that he made an affidavit before Sir Elijah Impey at Buxar, on the twelfth of December, just six days after Sir Elijah parted from Mr. Hastings, swearing that the papers annexed to the affidavits were faithful translations of the Persian affidavits! What shall we say, my lords, of such testimony? I will make only one remark upon it, which I shall borrow from an illustrious man: "that no one could tell where to look for truth, if it could not be found on the judgment seat, or know what to credit, if the affirmation of a judge was not to be trusted."

I have, my lords, before observed, that the chief-justice was intrusted by the prisoner to concert with Mr. Middleton the means of carrying into execution the order of which he was the bearer from the governor-general to the resident. These orders do not appear anywhere in writing, but your lordships are acquainted with their purport. The court must recollect that Mr. Middleton was instructed by them to persuade the nabob to propose, as from himself to Mr. Hastings, the seizure of the Begums' treasures. That this was really so, appears undeniably as well from the tenor of Mr. Middleton's letter on the subject, as from the prisoner's account of the business in his defense. Evidently, Mr. Hastings was on this occasion hobbled by difficulties which put all his ingenuity into requisition. He was aware that it must seem extraordinary, that at the very moment he was confiscating the property of the Begums, on the plea of their treasonable machinations, he should stipulate that an annual allowance equal almost to the produce of that property should be secured to them. Though he had accused the princesses of rebellion, by which, of course, their treasures were forfeited to the state, yet he was reluctant to appear as the principal in seizing them.

Do not, my lords, these embarrassments prove that the prisoner was sensible of the injustice of his proceedings? If the princesses were in rebellion, there could be no ground for his demurring to seize their property. The consciousness of their innocence could alone, therefore, make him timid and irresolute. To get rid at once of his difficulties, he resorts to the expedient which I have before stated, namely, of giving directions to Sir Elijah Impey that Mr. Middleton should urge the nabob to propose, as from himself, the seizure of the treasures. My lords, the unhappy prince, without a will of his own, consented to make the proposal, as an alternative for the resumption of the jaghires; a measure to which he had the most unconquerable reluctance. Mr. Hastings, as it were to indulge the nabob, agreed to the proposal; rejoicing, at the same time, that his scheme had proved so far successful; for he thought this proposal, coming from the nabob, would free him from the odium of so unpopular a plundering. But the artifice was too shallow; and your lordships are now able to trace the measure to its source. The court will see from the evidence that Mr. Hastings suggested it to Sir Elijah Impey, that Sir Elijah Impey might suggest it to Middleton, that Middleton might suggest it to the nabob, that his highness might suggest it to Mr. Hastings; and thus the suggestion returned to the place from which it had originally set out!

One single passage of a letter, written by Middleton to Mr. Hastings on the second of December, 1781, will make this point as clear as day. He informs the governor-general that "the nabob, wishing to evade the measure of resuming the jaghires, had sent him a message to the following purport: that if the measure proposed was intended to procure the payment of the balance due to the company, he could better and more expeditiously effect that object by taking from his mother the treasures of his father, which he asserted to be in her hands, and to which he claimed a right, founded on the laws of the Koran; and that it would be sufficient that he [Mr. Hastings] would hint his opinion upon it, without giving a formal sanction to the measure proposed." Mr. Middleton added, "the resumption of the jaghires it is necessary to suspend till I have your answer to this letter."

In the first place, it is clear from this letter that, though the nabob consented to make the desired proposal for seizing the treasures, it was only as an alternative; for it never entered into his head both to seize the treasures and resume the jaghires. The former measure he wished to substitute in the room of the latter, and by no means to couple them together. But Mr. Hastings was too nice a reasoner for the prince. He insisted that one measure should be carried into execution, because the nabob had proposed upon it; and the other, because he himself determined upon it.

It also appears that the nabob was taught to plead his right to the treasures, as founded upon the laws of the Koran. Not a word was said about the guarantee and treaty which had barred that right, whatever it might have been! But, my lords, if all Mr. Hastings would have the world believe is true, he [the nabob] had still a much better title—one against which the treaty and guarantee could not be raised, and this was the treason of the Begums, by which they forfeited all their property to the state, and every claim upon English protection. On this right by forfeiture, the nabob, however, was silent. Being a stranger to the rebellion, and to the treason of his parents, he was reduced to the necessity of reviving a right under the laws of the Koran, which the treaty and guarantee had forever extinguished.

This letter, moreover, contains this remarkable expression, namely, " that it would be sufficient to hint his [Mr. Hastings'] opinion upon it, without giving a formal sanction to the measure proposed." Why this caution? If the Begums were guilty of treason, why should he be fearful of declaring to the world that it was not the practise of the English to protect rebellious subjects, and prevent their injured sovereigns from proceeding against them according to law?—that he considered the treaty and guarantee, by which the Begums held their property, as no longer binding upon the English government, who consequently could have no farther right to interfere between the nabob and his rebellious parents, but must leave him at liberty to punish or forgive them as he should think fit? But, my lords, instead of holding this language, which manliness and conscious integrity would have dictated, had he been convinced of the guilt of the Begums, Mr. Hastings wished to derive all possible advantage from active measures against them, and at the same time so far to save appearances, as that he might be thought to be passive in the affair.

My lords, in another part of the same letter Mr. Middleton informs the governor-general "that he sent him, at the same time, a letter from the nabob on the subject of seizing the treasures." This letter has been suppressed. I challenge the counsel for the prisoner to produce it, or to account satisfactorily to your lordships for its not having been entered upon the company's records. Nor is this, my lords, the only suppression of which we have reason to complain. The affidavit of Goulass Roy, who lived at Fyzabad, the residence of the Begums, and who was known to be their enemy, is also suppressed. No person could be so well informed of their guilt, if they had been guilty, as Goulass Roy, who resided upon the spot where levies were said to have been made for Cheyte Sing by their order. If, therefore, his testimony had not destroyed the charge of a rebellion on the part of the Begums, there is no doubt but it would have been carefully preserved. The information of Mr. Scott has, moreover, been withheld from us. This gentleman lived unmolested at Taunda, where Sumshire Khan commanded for the Begums, and where he carried on an extensive manufacture without the least hindrance from this supposed disaffected governor. Mr. Scott was at Taunda too when it was said that the governor pointed the guns of the fort upon Captain Gordon's party. If this circumstance, my lords, did really happen, Mr. Scott must have heard of it, as he was himself at the time under the protection of those very guns. Why, then, is not the examination of this gentleman produced? I believe your lordships are satisfied that, if it had supported the allegations against Sumshire Khan, it would have been canceled.

It is not clear to me, my lords, that, as servile a tool as Mr. Middleton was, the prisoner intrusted him with every part of his intentions throughout the business of the Begums. He certainly mistrusted, or pretended to mistrust him, in his proceedings relative to the resumption of the jaghires. When it began to be rumored abroad that terms so favorable to the nabob as he obtained in the treaty of Chunar—by which Mr. Hastings consented to withdraw the temporary brigade, and to remove the English gentlemen from Oude—would never have been granted, if the nabob had not bribed the parties concerned in the negotiation to betray the interests of the company, Mr. Hastings confirmed the report by actually charging Mr. Middleton and his assistant resident, Mr. Johnson, with having accepted of bribes. They both joined in the most solemn assurances of their innocence, and called God to witness the truth of their declarations. Mr. Hastings, after this, appeared satisfied; possibly the consciousness that he had in his own pocket the only bribe which was given on the occasion, the £100,000, might have made him the less earnest in prosecuting any farther inquiry into the business.

A passage in a letter from Mr. Hastings shows that he did not think proper to commit to writing all the orders which he wished Mr. Middleton to execute; for there Mr.

Hastings expresses his doubts of the resident's " firmness and activity; and, above all, of his recollection of his instructions and their importance; and said that if he, Mr. Middleton, could not rely on his own power, and the means he possessed for performing those services, he would free him from the charge, and proceed to Lucknow and undertake it himself." My lords, you must presume that the instructions here alluded to were verbal; for had they been written, there could be no danger of their being forgot. I call upon the counsel to state the nature of those instructions, which were deemed of so much importance, that the governor was so greatly afraid Mr. Middleton would not recollect them, and which, nevertheless, he did not dare to commit to writing.

To make your lordships understand some other expressions in the above passage, I must recall to your memory that it has appeared in evidence that Mr. Middleton had a strong objection to the resumption of the jaghires; which he thought a service of so much danger, that he removed Mrs. Middleton and his family when he was about to enter upon it; for he expected resistance not only from the Begums, but from the nabob's own aumeels [agents]; who, knowing that the prince was a reluctant instrument in the hands of the English, thought they would please him by opposing a measure to which he had given his authority against his will. Middleton undoubtedly expected the whole country would unanimously rise against him; and therefore it was, my lords, that he suspended the execution of the order of resumption, until he should find whether the seizure of the treasures, proposed as an alternative, would be accepted as such. The prisoner pressed him to execute the order for resuming the jaghires, and offered to go himself upon that service if he should decline it. Middleton at last, having received a thundering letter from Mr. Hastings, by which he left him to act under " a dreadful responsibility," set out for Fyzabad.

My lords, for all the cruelties and barbarities that were executed there, the governor-general in his narrative says, he does not hold himself answerable, because he commanded Middleton to be personally present during the whole of the transaction, until he should complete the seizing of the treasures and resuming the jaghires. But for what purpose did he order Middleton to be present? I will show, by quoting the orders verbatim: "You yourself must be personally present; you must not allow any negotiation or forbearance, but must prosecute both services, until the Begums are at the entire mercy of the nabob." These peremptory orders, given under "a dreadful responsibility," were not issued, my lords, as you see, for purposes of humanity; not that the presence of the resident might restrain the violence of the soldier; but that he might be a watch upon the nabob, to steel his heart against the feelings of returning nature in his breast, and prevent the possibility of his relenting, or granting any terms to his mother and grandmother. This, truly, was the abominable motive which induced the prisoner to command the personal attendance of Middleton, and yet, my lords, he dares to say that he is not responsible for the horrid scene which ensued. [Here Mr. Sheridan was taken ill, and retired for a while to try if in the fresh air he could recover, so as that he might conclude all he had to say upon the evidence on the second charge. Some time after, Mr. Fox informed their lordships that Mr. Sheridan was much better, but that he felt he was not sufficiently so to be able to do justice to the subject he had in hand. The managers therefore hoped their lordships would be pleased to appoint a future day, on which Mr. Sheridan would finish his observations on the evidence.

Upon this, their lordships returned to their own House, and adjourned the court.]

My lords, permit me to remind you that, when I had last the honor of addressing you, I concluded with submitting to the court the whole of the correspondence, as far as it could be obtained, between the principal and agents in the nefarious plot carried on against the nabob vizier and the Begums of Oude. These letters demand of the court the most grave and deliberate attention, as containing not only a narrative of that foul and unmanly conspiracy, but also a detail of the motives and ends for which it was formed, and an exposition of the trick and quibble, the prevarication and the untruth with which it was then acted, and is now attempted to be defended. It will here be naturally inquired, with some degree of surprise, how the private correspondence which thus establishes the guilt of its authors came to light? This was owing to a mutual resentment which broke out about the middle of December, 1782, between the parties. Mr. Middleton, on the one hand, became jealous of the abatement of Mr. Hastings's confidence; and the governor-general was incensed at the tardiness with which the resident proceeded.

From this moment, shyness and suspicion between the principal and the agent took place. Middleton hesitated about the expediency of resuming the jaghires, and began to doubt whether the advantage would be equal to the risk. Mr. Hastings, whether he apprehended that Middleton was retarded by any return of humanity or sentiments of justice, by any secret combination with the Begum and her son, or a wish to take the lion's share of the plunder to himself, was exasperated at the delay. Middleton represented the unwillingness of the nabob to execute the measure—the low state of his finances—that his troops were mutinous for want of pay—that his life had been in danger from an insurrection among them—and that in this moment of distress he had offered one hundred thousand pounds, in addition to a like sum paid before, as an equivalent for the resumption which was demanded of him. Of this offer, however, it now appears, the nabob knew nothing! In conferring an obligation, my lords, it is sometimes contrived, from motives of delicacy, that the name of the donor shall be concealed from the person obliged; but here it was reserved for Middleton to refine this sentiment of delicacy, so as to leave the person giving utterly ignorant of the favor he bestowed!

But notwithstanding these little differences and suspicions, Mr. Hastings and Mr. Middleton, on the return of the latter to Calcutta in October 1782, lived in the same style of friendly collusion and fraudulent familiarity as formerly. After, however, an intimacy of about six months, the governor-general very unexpectedly arraigns his friend before the board at Calcutta. It was on this occasion that the prisoner, rashly for himself, but happily for the purposes of justice, produced these letters. Whatever, my lords, was the meaning of this proceeding—whether it was a juggle to elude inquiry, or whether it was intended to make an impression at Fyzabad—whether Mr. Hastings drew up the charge, and instructed Mr. Middleton how to prepare the defense; or whether the accused composed the charge, and the accuser the defense, there is discernible in the transaction the same habitual collusion in which the parties lived, and the prosecution ended, as we have seen, in a rhapsody, a repartee, and a poetical quotation by the prosecutor!

The private letters, my lords, are the only part of the correspondence thus providentially disclosed, which is deserving of attention. They were written in the confidence of private communication, without any motives to palliate and color facts, or to mislead. The counsel for the prisoner have, however, chosen to rely on the public correspondence, prepared, as appears on the very face of it, for the concealment of fraud and the purpose of deception. They, for example, dwelt on a letter from Mr. Middleton, dated December 1781, which intimates some supposed contumacy of the Begums; and this they thought countenanced the proceedings which afterward took place, and particularly the resumption of the jaghires; but, my lords, you cannot have forgotten, that both Sir Elijah Impey and Mr. Middleton declared, in their examination at your bar, that the letter was totally false. Another letter, which mentions "the determination of the nabob to resume the jaghires," was also dwelt upon with great emphasis; but it is in evidence that the Nabob, on the contrary, could not, by any means, be induced to sanction the measure; that it was not, indeed, till Mr. Middleton had actually issued his own Perwannas [warrants] for the collection of the rents, that the prince, to avoid a state of the lowest degradation, consented to give it the appearance of his act.

In the same letter, the resistance of the Begums to the seizure of their treasures is noticed as an instance of female levity, as if their defense of the property assigned for their subsistence was a matter of censure, or that they merited a reproof for feminine lightness, because they urged an objection to being starved!

The opposition, in short, my lords, which was expected from the princesses, was looked to as a justification of the proceedings which afterward happened. There is not, in the private letters, the slightest intimation of the anterior rebellion, which by prudent after-thought was so greatly magnified. There is not a syllable of those dangerous machinations which were to dethrone the nabob, nor of those sanguinary artifices by which the English were to be extirpated. It is indeed said, that if such measures were rigorously pursued, as had been set on foot, the people might be driven from murmurs to resistance, and rise up in arms against their oppressors.

Where, then, my lords, is the proof of this mighty rebellion? It is contained alone, where it is natural to expect it, in the fabricated correspondence between Middleton and Hastings, and in the affidavits collected by Sir Elijah Impey.

The gravity of the business on which the chief-justice was employed on this occasion, contrasted with the vivacity, the rapidity, and celerity of his movements, is exceedingly curious. At one moment he appeared in Oude, at another in Chunar, at a third in Benares, procuring testimony, and in every quarter exclaiming, like Hamlet's Ghost, "SWEAR!" To him might also have been applied the words of Hamlet to the Ghost, "What, Truepenny! are you there?" But the similitude goes no farther. He was never heard to give the injunction,

> " Taint not thy mind, nor let thy soul contrive
> Against thy mother aught ! "

It is, my lords, in some degree worthy of your observation, that not one of the private letters of Mr. Hastings has at any time been disclosed. Even Middleton, when all confidence was broken between them by the production of his private corespondence at Calcutta, either feeling for his own safety, or sunk under the fascinating influence of his master, did not dare attempt a retaliation! The letters of Middleton, however, are sufficient to prove the situation of the nabob, when pressed to the resumption of the jaghires. He is there described as being sometimes lost in sullen melancholy—at others, agitated beyond expression, exhibiting every mark of agonized sensibility. Even Middleton was moved by his distresses to interfere for a temporary respite, in which he might become more reconciled to the measure. "I am fully of opinion," said he, "that the despair of the nabob must impel him to violence. I know, also, that the violence must be fatal to himself; but yet I think that, with his present feelings, he will disregard all consequences."

Mr. Johnson, the assistant-resident, also wrote to the same purpose. The words of his letter are memorable. "He thought it would require a campaign to execute the orders for the resumption of the jaghires!" A campaign against whom? Against the nabob, our friend and ally, who had voluntarily given the order! This measure, then, which we have heard contended was for his good and the good of his country, could truly be only enforced by a campaign! Such is British justice! Such is British humanity! Mr. Hastings guarantees to the allies of the company their prosperity and his protection. The former he secures by sending an army to plunder them of their wealth and to desolate their soil. The latter produces the misery and the ruin of the protected. His is the protection which the vulture gives to the lamb, which covers while it devours its prey; which, stretching its baleful pinions and hovering in mid-air, disperses the kites and lesser birds of prey, and saves the innocent and helpless victim from all talons but its own.

It is curious, my lords, to remark that, in the correspondence of these creatures of Mr. Hastings, and in their earnest endeavors to dissuade him from the resumption of the jaghires, not a word is mentioned of the measure being contrary to honor—to faith; derogatory to national character; unmanly, or unprincipled. Knowing the man to whom they were writing, their only arguments were that it was contrary to policy and to expediency. Not one word do they mention of the just claims which the nabob had to the gratitude and friendship of the English. Not one syllable of the treaty by which we were bound to protect him. Not one syllable of the relation which subsisted between him and the princesses they were about to plunder. Not one syllable is hinted of justice or mercy. All which they addressed to him was the apprehension that the money to be procured would not be worth the danger and labor with which it must be attended. There is nothing, my lords, to be found in the history of human turpitude; nothing in the nervous delineations and penetrating brevity of Tacitus; nothing in the luminous and luxuriant pages of Gibbon, or of any other historian, dead or living, who, searching into measures and characters with the rigor of truth, presents to our abhorrence depravity in its blackest shapes, which can equal, in the grossness of the guilt, or in the hardness of heart with which it was conducted, or in low and groveling motives, the acts and character of the prisoner. It was he who, in the base desire of stripping two helpless women, could stir the son to rise up in vengeance against them; who, when that son had certain touches of nature in his breast, certain feelings of an awakened conscience, could accuse him of entertaining peevish objections to the plunder and sacrifice of his mother; who, having finally divested him of all thought, all reflection, all memory, all conscience, all tenderness and duty as a son, all dignity as a monarch; having destroyed his character and depopulated his country, at length brought him to violate the dearest ties of nature, in countenancing the destruction of his parents. This crime, I say, has no parallel or prototype in the Old World or the New, from the day of original sin to the present hour. The victims of his oppression were confessedly destitute of all power to resist their oppressors. But their debility, which from other bosoms would have claimed some compassion, at least with respect to the mode of suffering, with him only excited the ingenuity of torture. Even when every feeling of the nabob was subdued; when, as we have seen, my lords, nature made a last, lingering, feeble stand within his breast; even then, that cold spirit of malignity, with which his doom was fixed, returned with double rigor and sharper acrimony to its purpose, and compelled the child to inflict on the parent that destruction of which he was himself reserved to be the final victim.

Great as is this climax, in which, my lords, I thought the pinnacle of guilt was attained, there is yet something still more transcendently flagitious. I particularly allude to his [Hastings'] infamous letter, falsely dated the fifteenth of February, 1782, in which, at the very moment that he had given the order for the entire destruction of the Begums, and for the resumption of the jaghires, he expresses to the nabob the warm and lively interest which he took in his welfare; the sincerity and ardor of his friendship; and that, though his presence was eminently wanted at Calcutta, he could not refrain from coming to his assistance, and that in the meantime he had sent four regiments to his aid; so deliberate and cool, so hypocritical and insinuating, is the villainy of this man! What heart is not exasperated by the malignity of a treachery so barefaced and dispassionate? At length, however, the nabob was on his guard. He could not be deceived by this mask. The offer of the four regiments developed to him the object of Mr. Hastings. He perceived the dagger bunglingly concealed in the hand which was treacherously extended as if to his assistance. From this moment the last faint ray of hope expired in his bosom. We accordingly find no further confidence of the nabob in the prisoner. Mr. Middleton now swayed his iron scepter without control. The jaghires were seized. Every measure was carried. The nabob, mortified, humbled, and degraded, sank into insignificance and contempt. This letter was sent at the very time when the troops surrounded the walls of Fyzabad; and then began a scene of horrors which, if I wished to inflame your lordships' feelings, I should only have occasion minutely to describe—to state the violence committed on that palace which the piety of the kingdom had raised for the retreat and seclusion of the objects of its pride and veneration! It was in these shades, rendered sacred by superstition, that innocence reposed. Here venerable age and helpless infancy found an asylum! If we look, my lords, into the whole of this most wicked transaction, from the time when this treachery was first conceived, to that when, by a series of artifices the most execrable, it was brought to a completion, the prisoner will be seen standing aloof, indeed, but not inactive. He will be discovered reviewing his agents, rebuking at one time the pale conscience of Middleton, at another relying on the stouter villainy of Hyder Beg Cawn. With all the calmness of veteran delinquency, his eye will be seen ranging through the busy prospect, piercing the darkness of subordinate guilt, and disciplining with congenial adroitness the agents of his crimes and the instruments of his cruelty.

The feelings, my lords, of the several parties at the time will be most properly judged of by their respective correspondence. When the Bow [younger] Begum, despairing of redress from the nabob, addressed herself to Mr. Middleton, and reminded him of the guarantee which he had signed, she was instantly promised that the amount of her jaghire should be made good, though he said he could not interfere with the sovereign decision of the nabob respecting the lands. The deluded and unfortunate woman "thanked God that Mr. Middleton was at hand for her relief." At this very instant he was directing every effort to her destruction; for he had actually written the orders which were to take the collection out of the hands of her agents! But let it not be forgotten, my lords, when the Begum was undeceived—when she found that British faith was no protection—when she found that she should leave the country, and prayed to the God of nations not to grant His peace to those who remained behind—there was still no charge of rebellion, no recrimination made to all her reproaches for the broken faith of the English; that, when stung to madness, she asked "how long would be her reign," there was no mention of her disaffection. The stress is therefore idle, which the counsel for the prisoner have strove to lay on these expressions of an injured and enraged woman. When at last, irritated beyond bearing, she denounced infamy on the heads of her oppressors, who is there that will not say that she spoke in a prophetic spirit; and that what she then predicted has not, even to its last letter, been accomplished? But did Mr. Middleton, even to this violence, retort any particle of accusation? No! he sent a jocose reply, stating that he had received such a letter under her seal, but that, from its contents, he could not suspect it to come from her; and begged, therefore, that she would endeavor to detect the forgery! Thus did he add to foul injuries the vile aggravation of a brutal jest. Like the tiger, he showed the savageness of his nature by grinning at his prey, and fawning over the last agonies of his unfortunate victim!

The letters, my lords, were then inclosed to the nabob,

who, no more than the rest, made any attempt to justify himself by imputing any criminality to the Begums. He only
sighed a hope that his conduct to his parents had drawn no
shame upon his head; and declared his intention to punish,
not any disaffection in the Begums, but some officious servants
who had dared to foment the misunderstanding between
them and himself. A letter was finally sent to Mr. Hastings, about six days before the seizure of the treasures from
the Begums, declaring their innocence, and referring the
governor-general, in proof of it, to Captain Gordon, whose
life they had protected, and whose safety should have been
their justification. This inquiry was never made. It was
looked on as unnecessary, because the conviction of their
innocence was too deeply impressed already.

The counsel, my lords, in recommending an attention
to the public in reference to the private letters, remarked
particularly that one of the latter should not be taken in
evidence, because it was evidently and abstractedly private,
relating the anxieties of Mr. Middleton on account of the
illness of his son. This is a singular argument, indeed.
The circumstance, however, undoubtedly merits strict observation, though not in the view in which it was placed by
the counsel. It goes to show that some, at least, of the
persons concerned in these transactions felt the force of
those ties which their efforts were directed to tear asunder;
that those who could ridicule the respective attachment of
a mother and a son; who could prohibit the reverence of
the son to the mother; who could deny to maternal debility
the protection which filial tenderness should afford, were
yet sensible of the straining of those chords by which they
are connected. There is something in the present business,
with all that is horrible to create aversion, so vilely loathsome as to excite disgust. It is, my lords, surely superfluous to dwell on the sacredness of the ties which those
aliens to feeling, those apostates to humanity, thus divided.
In such an assembly as the one before which I speak, there
is not an eye but must look reproof to this conduct, not
a heart but must anticipate its condemnation. Filial piety!
It is the primal bond of society. It is that instinctive principle which, panting for its proper good, soothes, unbidden,
each sense and sensibility of man. It now quivers on every

lip. It now beams from every eye. It is that gratitude which, softening under the sense of recollected good, is eager to own the vast, countless debt it never, alas! can pay, for so many long years of unceasing solicitudes, honorable self-denials, life-preserving cares. It is that part of our practise where duty drops its awe, where reverence refines into love. It asks no aid of memory. It needs not the deductions of reason. Preëxisting, paramount over all, whether moral law or human rule, few arguments can increase, and none can diminish it. It is the sacrament of our nature; not only the duty, but the indulgence of man. It is his first great privilege. It is among his last most endearing delights. It causes the bosom to glow with reverberated love. It requites the visitations of nature, and returns the blessings that have been received. It fires emotion into vital principle. It changes what was instinct into a master passion; sways all the sweetest energies of man; hangs over each vicissitude of all that must pass away; and aids the melancholy virtues in their last sad tasks of life, to cheer the languors of decrepitude and age; and

" Explore the thought, explain the aching eye ! "

But, my lords, I am ashamed to consume so much of your lordships' time in attempting to give a cold picture of this sacred impulse, when I behold so many breathing testimonies of its influence around me; when every countenance in this assembly is beaming, and erecting itself into the recognition of this universal principle!

The expressions contained in the letter of Mr. Middleton, of tender solicitude for his son, have been also mentioned as a proof of the amiableness of his affections.   I confess that they do not tend to raise his character in my estimation.   Is it not rather an aggravation of his guilt, that he, who thus felt the anxieties of a parent, and who, consequently, must be sensible of the reciprocal feelings of a child, could be brought to tear asunder, and violate in others, all those dear and sacred bonds? Does it not enhance the turpitude of the transaction, that it was not the result of idiotic ignorance or brutal indifference? I aver that his guilt is increased and magnified by these consider-ations. His criminality would have been less had he been insensible to tenderness—less, if he had not been so thor-oughly acquainted with the true quality of parental love and filial duty.

The jaghires being seized, my lords, the Begums were left without the smallest share of that pecuniary compensa-tion promised by Mr. Middleton as an equivalent for the resumption. And as tyranny and injustice, when they take the field, are always attended by their camp-followers, pal-try pilfering and petty insult, so in this instance, the goods taken from the princesses were sold at a mock sale at an inferior value. Even gold and jewels, to use the language of the Begums, instantly lost their value when it was known that they came from them. Their ministers were impris-oned, to extort the deficiency which this fraud occasioned; and every mean art was employed to justify a continuance of cruelty toward them. Yet this was small to the frauds of Mr. Hastings. After extorting upward of £600,000, he forbade Mr. Middleton to come to a conclusive settlement with the princesses. He knew that the treasons of our allies in India had their origin solely in the wants of the Company. He could not, therefore, say that the Begums were entirely innocent, until he had consulted the General Record of Crimes, the cash account of Calcutta! His prudence was fully justified by the event; for there was actually found a balance of twenty-six lacs more against the Begums, which £260,000 worth of treason had never been dreamed of before. "Talk not to us," said the governor general, 'of their guilt or innocence, but as it suits the Com-pany's credit! We will not try them by the Code of Jus-tinian, nor the Institutes of Timur. We will not judge them either by British laws, or their local customs! No! we will try them by the multiplication table; we will find the guilty by the rule of three; and we will condemn them according to the unerring rules of—Cocker's Arithmetic!"

My lords, the prisoner has said in his defense, that the cruelties exercised toward the Begums were not of his order. But in another part of it he avows, "that whatever were their distresses, and whoever was the agent in the measure, it was, in his opinion, reconcilable to justice, honor, and sound policy." By the testimony of Major Scott, it appears that, though the defense of the prisoner was not drawn up by himself, yet that this paragraph he wrote with his own proper hand. Middleton, it seems, had confessed his share in these transactions with some degree of compunction, and solicitude as to the consequences. The prisoner, observing it, cries out to him, "Give me the pen, I will defend the measure as just and necessary. I will take something upon myself. Whatever part of the load you cannot bear, my unburdened character shall assume! Your conduct I will crown with my irresistible approbation. Do you find memory and I will find character, and thus twin-warriors we will go into the field, each in his proper sphere of action, and assault, repulse, and contumely shall all be set at defiance."

If I could not prove, my lords, that those acts of Mr. Middleton were in reality the acts of Mr. Hastings, I should not trouble your lordships by combating them; but as this part of his criminality can be incontestably ascertained, I appeal to the assembled legislators of this realm to say whether these acts were justifiable on the score of policy. I appeal to all the august presidents in the courts of British justice, and to all the learned ornaments of the profession, to decide whether these acts were reconcilable to justice. I appeal to the reverend assemblage of prelates feeling for the general interests of humanity and for the honor of the religion to which they belong, to determine whether these acts of Mr. Hastings and Mr. Middleton were such as a Christian ought to perform, or a man to avow.

My lords, with the ministers of the nabob [Bahar Ally Cawn and Jewar Ally Cawn] was confined in the same prison that arch-rebel Sumshire Cawn, against whom so much criminality has been charged by the counsel for the prisoner. We hear, however, of no inquiry having been made concerning his treason, though so many were held respecting the treasures of the others. With all his guilt, he was not so far noticed as to be deprived of his food, to be complimented with fetters, or even to have the satisfaction of being scourged, but was cruelly liberated from a dungeon, and ignominiously let loose on his parole!

[Here Mr. Sheridan read the following order from Mr.

Middleton to Lieutenant Rutledge in relation to the Begums' ministers, dated January 28, 1782:

"Sir,—When this note is delivered to you by Hoolas Roy, I have to desire that you order the two prisoners to be put in irons, keeping them from all food, etc., agreeably to my instructions of yesterday.
"Nath. Middleton."]

The Begums' ministers, on the contrary, to extort from them the disclosure of the place which concealed the treasures, were, according to the evidence of Mr. Holt, after being fettered and imprisoned, led out on a scaffold, and this array of terrors proving unavailing, the meek-tempered Middleton, as a *dernier resort*, menaced them with a confinement in the fortress of Churnargar. Thus, my lords, was a British garrison made the climax of cruelties! To English arms, to English officers, around whose banners humanity has ever entwined her most glorious wreath, how will this sound? It was in this fort, where the British flag was flying, that these helpless prisoners were doomed to deeper dungeons, heavier chains, and severer punishments. Where that flag was displayed which was wont to cheer the depressed, and to dilate the subdued heart of misery, these venerable but unfortunate men were fated to encounter every aggravation of horror and distress. It, moreover, appears that they were both cruelly flogged, though one was above seventy years of age. Being charged with disaffection, they vindicated their innocence—"Tell us where are the remaining treasures," was the reply. "It is only treachery to your immediate sovereigns, and you will then be fit associates for the representatives of British faith and British justice in India!" O Faith! O Justice! I conjure you by your sacred names to depart for a moment from this place, though it be your peculiar residence; nor hear your names profaned by such a sacrilegious combination as that which I am now compelled to repeat—where all the fair forms of nature and art, truth and peace, policy and honor, shrink back aghast from the deleterious shade—where all existences, nefarious and vile, have sway—where, amid the black agents on one side and Middleton with Impey on the other, the great figure of the piece—characteristic in his place, aloof and independent from the puny profligacy in his train, but far from idle and inactive, turning a malignant eye on all mischief that awaits him; the multiplied apparatus of temporizing expedients and intimidating instruments, now cringing on his prey, and fawning on his vengeance—now quickening the limping pace of craft, and forcing every stand that retiring nature can make to the heart; the attachments and the decorums of life; each emotion of tenderness and honor; and all the distinctions of national pride; with a long catalogue of crimes and aggravations beyond the reach of thought for human malignity to perpetrate or human vengeance to punish; lower than perdition—blacker than despair!

It might, my lords, have been hoped, for the honor of the human heart, that the Begums were themselves exempted from a share in these sufferings, and that they had been wounded only through the sides of their ministers. The reverse of this, however, is the fact. Their palace was surrounded by a guard, which was withdrawn by Major Gilpin to avoid the growing resentments of the people, and replaced by Mr. Middleton, through his fears of that "dreadful responsibility" which was imposed upon him by Mr. Hastings. The women, also, of the Khord Mahal, who were not involved in the Begums' supposed crimes; who had raised no sub-rebellion of their own; and who, it has been proved, lived in a distinct dwelling, were causelessly implicated, nevertheless, in the same punishment. Their residence surrounded with guards, they were driven to despair by famine, and when they poured forth in sad procession, were beaten with bludgeons, and forced back by the soldiery to the scene of madness which they had quitted. These are acts, my lords, which, when told, need no comment. I will not offer a single syllable to awaken your lordships' feelings; but leave it to the facts which have been stated to make their own impression.

The inquiry which now only remains, my lords, is, whether Mr. Hastings is to be answerable for the crimes committed by his agents? It has been fully proved that Mr. Middleton signed the treaty with the superior Begum in October 1778. He also acknowledged signing some others of a different date, but could not recollect the authority by which he did it! These treaties were recognized by Mr. Hastings, as appears by the evidence of Mr. Purling, in the year 1780. In that of October 1778, the jaghire was secured, which was allotted for the support of the women in the Khord Mahal. But still the prisoner pleads that he is not accountable for the cruelties which were exercised. His is the plea which tyranny, aided by its prime-minister, treachery, is always sure to set up. Mr. Middleton has attempted to strengthen this ground by endeavoring to claim the whole infamy in those transactions, and to monopolize the guilt! He dared even to aver that he had been condemned by Mr. Hastings for the ignominious part he had acted. He dared to avow this, because Mr. Hastings was on his trial, and he thought he never would be arraigned; but in the face of this court, and before he left the bar, he was compelled to confess that it was for the lenience, and not the severity, of his proceedings, that he had been reproved by the prisoner.

It will not, I trust, be concluded, that, because Mr. Hastings has not marked every passing shade of guilt, and because he has only given the bold outline of cruelty, he is therefore to be acquitted. It is laid down by the law of England, that law which is the perfection of reason, that a person ordering an act to be done by his agent is answerable for that act with all its consequences: "quod facit per alium, facit per se." Middleton was appointed, in 1777, the confidential agent, the second self of Mr. Hastings. The governor-general ordered the measure. Even if he never saw, nor heard afterward of its consequences, he was therefore answerable for every pang that was inflicted, and for all the blood that was shed. But he did hear, and that instantly, of the whole. He wrote to accuse Middleton of forbearance and of neglect! He commanded him to work upon the hopes and fears of the princesses, and to leave no means untried, until, to speak his own language, which was better suited to the banditti of a cavern, "he obtained possession of the secret hoards of the old ladies." He would not allow even of a delay of two days to smooth the compelled approaches of a son to his mother, on this occasion! His orders were peremptory. After this, my lords, can it be said that the prisoner was ignorant of the acts, or not culpable for their consequences? It is true, he did not direct the guards, the famine, and the bludgeons; he did not weigh the fetters, nor number the lashes to be inflicted on his victims; but yet he is just as guilty as if he had borne an active and personal share in each transaction. It is as if he had commanded that the heart should be torn from the bosom, and enjoined that no blood should follow. He is in the same degree accountable to the law, to his country, to his conscience, and to his God!

The prisoner has endeavored also to get rid of a part of his guilt, by observing that he was but one of the supreme council, and that all the rest had sanctioned those transactions with their approbation. Even if it were true that others did participate in the guilt, it cannot tend to diminish his criminality. But the fact is, that the council erred in nothing so much as in a reprehensible credulity given to the declarations of the governor-general. They knew not a word of those transactions until they were finally concluded. It was not until the January following that they saw the mass of falsehood which had been published under the title of "Mr. Hastings' Narrative." They were, then, unaccountably duped to permit a letter to pass, dated the twenty-ninth of November, intended to seduce the directors into a belief that they had received intelligence at that time, which was not the fact. These observations, my lords, are not meant to cast any obloquy on the council; they undoubtedly were deceived; and the deceit practised on them is a decided proof of his consciousness of guilt. When tired of corporeal infliction, Mr. Hastings was gratified by insulting the understanding. The coolness and reflection with which this act was managed and concerted raises its enormity and blackens its turpitude. It proves the prisoner to be that monster in nature, a deliberate and reasoning tyrant! Other tyrants of whom we read, such as a Nero, or a Caligula, were urged to their crimes by the impetuosity of passion. High rank disqualified them from advice, and perhaps equally prevented reflection. But in the prisoner we have a man born in a state of mediocrity; bred to mercantile life; used to system, and accustomed to regularity; who was accountable to his masters, and therefore was compelled to think and to deliberate on every part of his conduct. It is this cool deliberation, I say, which renders his crimes more horrible, and his character more atrocious.

When, my lords, the Board of Directors received the advices which Mr. Hastings thought proper to transmit, though unfurnished with any other materials to form their judgment, they expressed very strongly their doubts, and properly ordered an inquiry into the circumstances of the alleged disaffection of the Begums, declaring it, at the same time, to be a debt which was due to the honor and justice of the British nation. This inquiry, however, Mr. Hastings thought it absolutely necessary to elude. He stated to the council, in answer, "that it would revive those animosities that subsisted between the Begums and the nabob [Asuph Dowlah], which had then subsided. If the former were inclined to appeal to a foreign jurisdiction, they were the best judges of their own feeling, and should be left to make their own complaint." All this, however, my lords, is nothing to the magnificent paragraph which concludes this communication. "Besides," says he, "I hope it will not be a departure from official language to say, that the majesty of justice ought not to be approached without solicitation. She ought not to descend to inflame or provoke, but to withhold her judgment until she is called on to determine." What is still more astonishing, is, that Sir John Macpherson, who, though a man of sense and honor, is rather Oriental in his imagination, and not learned in the "Sublime and Beautiful" from the immortal leader of this prosecution, was caught by this bold, bombastic quibble, and joined in the same words, "that the majesty of justice ought not to be approached without solicitation." But, my lords, do you, the judges of this land, and the expounders of its rightful laws, do you approve of this mockery, and call it the character of justice, which takes the form of right to excite wrong? No, my lords, justice is not this halt and miserable object; it is not the ineffective bauble of an Indian pagod; it is not the portentous phantom of despair; it is not like any fabled monster, formed in the eclipse of reason, and found in some unhallowed grove of superstitious darkness and political dismay! No, my lords. In the happy reverse of all this, I turn from the disgusting caricature to the real image! Justice I have now before me august and pure! The abstract idea of all that would be perfect in the spirits and the aspirings of men!—where the mind rises; where the heart expands; where the countenance is ever placid and benign; where her favorite attitude is to stoop to the unfortunate; to hear their cry and to help them; to rescue and relieve, to succor and save; majestic, from her mercy; venerable, from her utility; uplifted, without pride; firm, without obduracy; beneficent in each preference; lovely, though in her frown!

On that justice I rely: deliberate and sure, abstracted from all party purpose and political speculation; not on words, but on facts. You, my lords, who hear me, I conjure, by those rights which it is your best privilege to preserve; by that fame which it is your best pleasure to inherit; by all those feelings which refer to the first term in the series of existence, the original compact of our nature, our controlling rank in the creation. This is the call on all to administer to truth and equity, as they would satisfy the laws and satisfy themselves, with the most exalted bliss possible or conceivable for our nature; the self-approving consciousness of virtue, when the condemnation we look for will be one of the most ample mercies accomplished for mankind since the creation of the world! My lords, I have done.

JOHN SHERMAN

THE FINANCIAL SITUATION

[John Sherman, orator, financier, and lawyer, was born at Lancaster, Ohio, in 1823. He received an academic education, studied law, and was admitted to the bar at twenty-one. He early joined the Whig party, and was a delegate to the national Whig conventions in 1848 and 1852. He took part in the organization of the Republican party, and presided over the first Ohio Republican convention. He was a representative in Congress from 1855–61, and a candidate for speaker in 1859–60. He held a seat in the Federal Senate in 1861, in 1866, and 1872. Under President Hayes he was secretary of the treasury from 1877 to 1881. Entering the Senate again in 1881 he was reëlected in 1886 and in 1892. In several Republican conventions he was a prominent candidate for President. He was secretary of state in 1897, but failing health compelled him to resign in 1898, after fifty years of public service. It was due to him that the resumption of specie payment was effected in 1879, and the national credit thus maintained. He died in Washington in 1900. The speech that follows is an expression of his views regarding President Cleveland's financial policy, and was delivered in the United States Senate in 1895.]

THE President, in his annual message to Congress, confined himself to two important subjects, one our foreign relations and the other the condition of our national finances.

While Congress has heartily, perhaps too hastily, but with entire unanimity, supported him in maintaining the interests and honor of our country in the field of diplomacy, it has not and will not approve his recommendations on the more important subject of our financial policy and especially of our currency. He proposes a line of public policy that will produce a sharp contraction of our currency, add greatly to the burden of existing debts, and arrest the progress of almost every American industry which now competes with foreign productions.

The President is supported in these views by Mr. Carlisle, his able secretary of the treasury, in his report to Congress. It is with diffidence I undertake to controvert their opinions; but my conviction that they are in error is so strong that I hope the strength of the facts I will submit to the Senate will convince it that the true line of public policy is to supply the government with ample means to meet current expenditures and to pay each year a portion of the public debt. The gold reserve provided for the redemption of United States notes can then be easily maintained without cost except the loss of interest on the gold in the treasury, but with a saving of interest on United States notes and treasury notes of five times the interest lost by the gold held in reserve. A vastly greater benefit than saving interest is secured to our people by a national paper currency at par with coin supported by the credit of the United States and redeemed on demand in coin at the treasury in the principal city of the United States.

The only difficulty in the way of an easy maintenance of our notes at par with coin is the fact that during this administration the revenues of the government have not been sufficient to meet the expenditures authorized by Congress. If Congress had provided necessary revenue, or if the President and Mr. Carlisle had refused to expend appropriations not mandatory in form, but permissive, so as to confine expenditures within receipts, they would have had no difficulty with the reserve. This would have been a stalwart act in harmony with the President's character and plainly within his power.

All appropriations which are not provided to carry into effect existing law are permissive, but not mandatory, and his refusal to expend money in excess of the revenues of the government would not only be justified by public policy, but would have been heartily approved by the people of the United States. He knew as well as any one that since the close of the Civil war to the date of his inauguration the expenditures of the government had been less than its receipts. I have here a table which shows the receipts and expenditures each year from 1866 to 1893.

From this official statement it appears that each and every year during that long period there was a surplus, which was applied to the reduction of the public debt bearing interest.

The President, in his recent annual message, complains that the law of October 6, 1890, known as the McKinley Act, was "inefficient for the purposes of revenue." That law, though it largely reduced taxation by placing many articles on the free list and granted a bounty for the production of sugar, yet did not reduce revenues below expenditures, but provided a surplus of $37,239,762.57 June 30, 1891, and $9,914,453.66 June 30, 1892, and $2,341,674.29 on the thirtieth of June, 1893, when Mr. Cleveland was President and a Democratic majority in both Houses of Congress had been elected, all pledged to repeal the McKinley Act and to reduce duties. That the McKinley Act did not produce more revenue in 1893 and 1894 is not a matter of surprise. Any tariff law denounced by the party in power, with a promise to repeal it and to reduce duties, would prevent importations under the old law and thus lower the revenue. Early in December 1893, at the first regular session of Congress during Mr. Cleveland's term, a bill was formulated, and as soon as practicable passed the House of Representatives.

That bill met the hearty approval of the President. If it had become a law as originally presented, the deficiency in revenue would have been much greater than now; but conservative Democratic senators, with the aid of Republican senators, greatly improved the House bill, added other duties, and changed the scope of the measure. With these amendments it became a law. The President refused to sign it, expressing his opposition to the Senate amendments, and yet now supports it when deficiencies have been greatly increased, when the public debt is increasing, and doubts are expressed as to the ability of the government to maintain its notes at par with coin. The President makes no mention in his message of these deficiencies; no mention of the issue of interest-bearing bonds to meet them. The secretary of the treasury is more frank in his statement. He reports a deficiency of $69,803,260.58 during the fiscal year ended June 30, 1894, and for the year ended June 30, 1895, $42,805,223.18, and for the six months prior to December 1, 1895, $17,613,539.24; in all, $130,221,023.

No complaint was made that the McKinley law "was inefficient for the purposes of revenue" when the Wilson bill was pending. The objection to the McKinley law was that it was a "protective tariff," and the Wilson bill was a "revenue tariff." I have a statement showing the receipts and expenditures under each law each month—the McKinley law from its passage to the election of Cleveland, and the Wilson law from its passage to December 1, 1895. During the twenty-five months of the McKinley law the average monthly surplus was $1,129,821. During the existence of the Wilson law the average monthly deficiency was $4,699,-603. If the McKinley law was, in the opinion of the President, inefficient for revenue, he should have said of the Wilson law that it was bounteous in deficiencies.

I could pursue the analysis of these two laws further, but I have said enough to explain the preference by the President of the Wilson bill. He believes in large importations at the lowest cost, without regard to the industries and labor of our countrymen, while I believe in a careful discrimination and the imposition of such duties on articles that compete with home productions as will diversify our employments and protect and foster impartially all industries, whether of the farm, the workshop, the mine, the forest, or the sea. I have not been satisfied with any tariff law made during my public life, though I have shared in framing many. I prefer a law that will impartially protect and encourage all home industries, and regard the McKinley law as infinitely better than the Wilson law, which I believe is the cause of all the evils which we now encounter by adverse balance of trade, by exportation of gold and derangement of our monetary system. The Wilson law has produced a deficiency in every hour and day that it has been on the statute book, while the McKinley law has always produced a surplus until after the incoming of this administration, and if administered since that time by friendly agents would have furnished the government all the revenue needed.

The deficiency of revenue was the primary cause of the demand for gold for United States notes. The gold hoarded for resumption purposes was not separated from the money received for current revenue, and this revenue being insufficient to meet expenses, the gold accumulated for redemption purposes was drawn upon to make good deficiencies. This created a doubt of the ability of the government to maintain the parity of United States notes with coin, and led to their presentation for redemption in coin. The draft on the treasury for coin during this administration has been greater than the amount of deficiency of revenue during the same period. In every aspect in which the subject presents itself to my mind I come to no other conclusion than that the deficiency of revenue and the consequent encroachment upon the redemption fund is the cause of our present financial condition and that the only remedies are either a radical reduction of expenditures or an increase of taxation, and perhaps both. I do not believe that the condition requires a suspension of public works or a postponement of measures now in progress to strengthen the army and navy.

Such a deficiency is discreditable to the United States, with its vast wealth and resources. There is no difficulty in collecting for taxation all and more money than is necessary for its expenditures. It is humiliating to read in the newspapers of the day that our government is negotiating for money from associated bankers, and, like a distressed debtor in view of bankruptcy, is offered by a friendly power its accumulated gold to relieve us from our supposed financial distress. The true remedy is to supply additional revenue by taxation in some form, and, until this can be effected, to borrow from the people of the United States enough money to cover past and future deficiencies. This done, gold will readily be exchanged for United States notes, as was done from January 1879 to the election of Mr. Cleveland.

The President complains that the notes are presented and paid, reissued, and paid again and again, making a continuous circuit. When did this circuit commence? The only answer is, when this administration, supported by the last Congress, created a deficiency. Why does the circuit continue? It is because the deficiency continues. The government resorts to the financial policy of Micawber. It gives its bonds and thinks the debt paid. But the circuit continues. The money received for current revenue is paid to cover deficiencies and is returned for gold, and then more bonds. The secretary hopes that in two or three years there will be no deficiency. What is the ground for this hope? It is that a new administration will provide more revenue, and then the circuit will be broken. Why not apply the remedy now?

If deficiencies occur, Congress should immediately supply the means to meet them, and Congress, and not the administration, must be the judge of the mode and manner of relief. The invasion and misapplication of the resumption fund is of infinitely greater injury to our people than the imposition of ten times the amount of taxation.

It is said that the law for their continued reissue is mandatory. That is not a fair construction of the law. The plain meaning of it is the redemption of the notes shall not cause their cancelation. They are placed on the footing of bank notes. What solvent bank would reissue its notes when there was a run upon it? It would hold them until the demand ceased. The government ought to exercise the same prudence. The President is of the opinion that the United States notes and treasury notes should be retired and give place to bank notes. This is a question for Congress to decide. It is certainly not of that opinion now, nor was the last Congress of that opinion. Outside of a few large cities where banking facilities are abundant and business is conducted by checks and commercial paper, there is no desire for the retirement of national paper money. It is not right for the executive authorities to discredit this money by using it for current deficiencies. It was the use and dispersion of the redemption fund that created the circle of which he complains.

I believe that under existing law the aggregate sum of United States notes and treasury notes issued under the Act of 1890, amounting to about $460,000,000, can be easily maintained at par with coin if the two amendments I have mentioned are adopted by Congress. These notes are a legal tender for all debts, public or private. They are a debt of the United States without interest and without other material cost to the government than the interest on the cost of the coin or bullion held in the treasury to redeem them. They are preferred by the people to any other form of paper money that has been devised. They have all the sanctions of law and all the security that has been or can be given to our bonds. They have the pledge of the public faith that they will be redeemed in coin. The substitution of these notes for state-bank paper money was one of the greatest benefits that has resulted from the Civil war. These notes have all the sanction, protection, and security that has been or can be given to our national bank notes, with the added benefit that the large saving derived from them inures to the people of the United States instead of to the bankers.

Another reason, founded upon belief, is that the national banking system could not long endure if the United States notes were withdrawn. I will not on this occasion discuss this, nor any other of the numerous financial questions involved, such as the policy of requiring the duties on imports to be paid in gold. Imports are purchased with gold, are paid for in gold, and we may require gold for duties. The disposition of silver certificates is a much more serious problem. They are in express terms redeemable in silver dollars. Ought they not to be redeemed by silver dollars? While the silver dollars are maintained at par with gold it would seem that there was no injustice in paying the silver dollars for silver certificates. Then comes up the question of free coinage of silver, which I regard as the most dangerous policy.

All these are vital questions I do not wish to mingle with the pressing recommendation of the President in his last annual message "that authority be given the secretary of the treasury to issue bonds of the United States bearing a low rate of interest payable by their terms in gold for the purpose of maintaining a sufficient gold reserve and also for the redemption and cancelation of outstanding United States notes and the treasury notes issued for the purchase of silver under the law of 1890." He recommends the exchange of gold interest-bearing bonds for the legal-tender notes of the United States, and the substitution of national bank notes as our only currency.

He is supported in this by large and influential classes of our fellow-citizens, most of them engaged in banking or classed as capitalists. Their arguments mainly rest upon the difficulties encountered by this administration in maintaining a reserve in coin to redeem United States notes. They forget that during a period of fourteen years, when the revenues of the government exceeded expenditures and when the public debt was being reduced with unexampled rapidity, there was no difficulty in maintaining our notes at par with coin. There is scarcely a doubt but that in all conditions of trade or finance, except the contingency of war, the whole mass of United States notes and treasury notes now in circulation can be maintained at par with coin if it is supported by a reserve of gold coin or bullion or silver bullion at market value in due proportions equal to one-third or one-fourth of the amount of such notes.

A careful study of the systems of banking, currency, and coinage adopted by the principal nations of Europe convinces me that our system, when cured of a few defects developed by time, founded upon the bimetallic coinage of gold and silver maintained at par with each other, with free national banks established in every city and town of importance in the United States, issuing their notes secured beyond doubt by United States bonds or some equivalent security, redeemable on demand in United States notes, and the issue of an amount of United States notes and treasury notes equal to the amount now outstanding, with provision for a ratable increase with the increase of population, always redeemable in coin and supported by an ample reserve of coin in the treasury, not to be invaded by deficiencies of revenue, and separated by the sub-treasury system from all connection with the receipts and expenditures of the government—such a system would make our money current in commercial circles in every land and clime, better than the best that now exists in Europe, better than that of Great Britain, which now holds the purse-string of the world.

It is not given to man to foresee with certainty the future; but if we may judge the future by the past, the growth and progress of our country will continue, the diversity and extent of our industries will expand, the vast plains of our broad territory will be teeming with population. The rapid growth of our cities, unexampled in the history of mankind, will continue. A century spans the life of this Republic; what will the next century do? I have seen great changes in my life, but those who come after us will see greater changes still. I may on some proper occasion hereafter give the reasons for my faith in our present financial system. All I ask now is that you will not disturb it with your deficiencies, you will not rob it of its safeguards, you will not return to the days of wildcat money, you will not lessen the savings of prudent labor or the accumulations of the rich. Time makes all things even. Let us give to the executive authorities ample means to meet the appropriations you have made, but let us strengthen rather than weaken our monetary system, which lies at the foundation of our prosperity and progress.

JOHN COIT SPOONER

ON THE GOVERNMENT OF THE PHILIPPINES

[John Coit Spooner, an American political leader, noted as a Republican campaign speaker, was born in Indiana in 1843. Settling as a lad in Wisconsin, he graduated at the University of that State, and at once enlisted in the army as a private, for the Civil War was then raging. He rose through various grades in the volunteer service, and attained the brevet rank of major. When the conflict ended, he took up the study of law, was admitted to the bar, and entered political life as a Republican. He served as assistant attorney-general of Wisconsin, was elected to the State legislature, and in 1885 to the United States Senate. Upon the expiration of his term he resumed the practice of law, but was sent back to the upper house of Congress for a full term of six years in 1897. The speech given here is on the important and interesting subject of the new government in the Philippines. It was delivered in the United States Senate in 1900.]

MR. PRESIDENT: I am impelled to address the Senate upon this measure, which is the unfinished business, partly because I took the responsibility of introducing it, and owe it to myself to state with frankness the reasons which led me to do so.

The Senator from Massachusetts [Mr. Lodge] has addressed the Senate upon it in a speech that was very masterful and very eloquent and beautiful, with most of which I agree. I wish to consider the subject upon somewhat different and in some respects less radical lines.

I suppose, Mr. President, it will be admitted that had there been no war with Spain and she had tendered to us "without money and without price" a cession of the Philippine archipelago, and a treaty accepting that cession had been transmitted to the Senate for its action, it would have received hardly a vote in this body, and would have proved entirely unattractive to the great body of our people. The suggestion in advocacy of it that we are "trustees" to lead the nations of the earth in the work of civilization would not have been at all persuasive.

The quick and sufficient answer to that, would have been that, while this is a missionary people, this is not and cannot become a missionary government, and that it is not our function, philanthropic as we may be and as this people may be, that their government shall police the world, seeking for people oppressed, living in the darkness of ignorance and half civilization, in order to uplift them.

It would have been said that we have problems of our own to solve, some of them complicated, all of them important, and that the first duty of this government, trustee of our people, is to subserve the interests of our people, to develop the illimitable resources of this continent, to spread the blessings of education among the people, to give to the country equal laws, and to lift up as far as possible all here who are oppressed. If it had been said that the islands are full of mineral wealth, of untold richness in soil, and of unspeakable beauty, that would have produced no effect on this chamber.

Our people would not have harbored the thought of going into distant seas and taking archipelagoes of alien people because of the richness of the islands. I can conceive of no argument in favor of the acceptance of such a proposition which would have found much, if any, favor here or in the country.

There would have been found no lust of empire among us; nor is there now, in my opinion, in the sense in which that term is now used in this body and in the country by certain distinguished gentlemen.

But, Mr. President, when the Treaty of Paris was sent to the Senate, containing, as it did, a cession of the Philippine archipelago to us, it came, not as a simple proposition of purchase in time of peace, but it came to us environed by the complications of war and as one of the fruits of war. The debate did not ignore that. We have gone to war with Spain, a war the like of which in its inspiration the whole world never before saw.

No people ever can give to the world higher evidence, Mr. President, of devotion to liberty than the people of the

United States gave when they demanded the withdrawal of Spain from Cuba, and resorted to war to enforce that demand. Admiral Dewey, long before that treaty of cession came to us, had destroyed the Spanish fleet in Manila Bay, and made for himself a fame which can never fade. Our troops in Cuba, bearing themselves with the utmost heroism, had forced the capitulation of Santiago, and Sampson and Schley had sent to the bottom the prize fleet of Spain under command of Cervera.

Something more had happened, Mr. President. Admiral Dewey had called for troops to be sent to Manila, and they had been sent. They were not sent to defend the fleet, and every one knew it. Admiral Dewey could have forced in a day the surrender of Manila, but he had not the troops with which to hold it. There are men who have regretted that troops were sent to Manila. Was any voice raised in this chamber or in this country against the sending of soldiers to Manila? I remember very well some criticism of the President that they were not sent with sufficient alacrity; but I never heard a lisp of objection to their being sent to Manila. When the Paris Treaty came before us for ratification, Manila had been captured with 13,000 Spanish troops and their arms, and the soldiers of the United States held that city and its suburbs.

I did not myself take at all kindly to the acquisition under its provisions of the Philippine archipelago. There was a time when, if it had come to a vote, I would not have been willing to vote for it.

I stated to the Senate while that treaty was pending, and I restate it now in a word, that, facing each of the alternatives which presented themselves to the President, I could not see how he could have done any other thing than demand the incorporation in that treaty of a cession to us of the Philippine archipelago. Several alternatives were open to us. I shall not spend much time upon this. One was to leave the Philippine Islands with Spain; to omit it from the treaty. I felt obliged to reject that alternative.

I could not see then, nor have I ever been able to see since, how the President could have concluded, under the circumstances, a treaty of peace with Spain which did not contain a cession of the Philippine archipelago. All with whom I have spoken upon this subject have said to me—and it was the sentiment of our country, and it had no lust of empire in it—whatever else is done about the Philippine archipelago, that people must not be left under the tyranny of Spain. That sentiment pervaded the entire people. Am I wrong about that?

Mr. President, our people had been inexpressibly shocked by the unspeakable cruelties perpetrated by Spain in Cuba. No one will soon forget the black days of the reconcentrado period. No one will soon forget the stories, not overtold —impossible to overtell—of the tyranny, the wickedness, and the awful savagery of Spain in Cuba. Our people, not choosing to consider a cause of war existing in their own behalf, sustained the Congress and sustained the President in going into a war to snatch the island of Cuba and her people from that thraldom.

It was hardly to be expected, Mr. President, after our navy had broken the power of Spain in both seas, and after Spain had applied for a suspension of hostilities with a view to a treaty of peace, that a people who, without a cause of war which it chose to enforce on its own behalf, had poured out its treasure and the blood of its sons for the liberty of another people alien to them, because of cruelty and oppression which could not longer be tolerated, would be willing that in the end of that struggle another people, vastly greater in number, who had also been subject to the same tyranny, should be left in the hands of Spain. By the fortunes of war we were there.

It would have seemed to the world, many of us thought, that we had carried our flag of liberty to a mountain top, where all the world could see it, and then, afraid to meet responsibility, shuddering from duty, had incontinently run with it into the valley below, where no man could see it or would wish to see it.

It has been thought if all mention of the Philippines had been omitted from the treaty, Spain never could have retaken those islands. Mr. President, I have never believed that. I have had no doubt myself that Spain would have resumed her sway in the Philippine archipelago. I have never seen any reason to doubt it. First, it must be remembered that we had sent back to Spain 142,000 soldiers, with their arms. Spain, no longer involved in Cuba or Porto Rico; Spain, vanquished by us, but proud and haughty, would not have been willing to abandon the last of her possessions—that one in the Pacific seas.

We would have been obliged to march our troops out of Manila, and to allow the troops of Spain, in such numbers as she chose, to occupy the city. Spain then had a navy free. Many of the nations of the world sympathized with her. They all would have preferred her retention of the Philippines to strife among themselves for their possession, as there would have been.

The holders of Spanish bonds all over Europe, based upon a hypothecation of the revenues of Cuba, Porto Rico, and possibly the Philippines, would have been eager to furnish the money, for obvious reasons, to enable Spain to retain her great Pacific possessions, and with her fleet and her troops, she would have resumed her sway in the Philippines.

We could not do that, we thought; and there was not a man in the Senate then, nor is there one here now, I take it, who would have been willing that all mention of the Philippines should have been omitted from the treaty.

Even Aguinaldo contemplated the possibility that the treaty might leave the Philippines with Spain, and the certainty that Spain would attempt to resume her sovereignty there. In his letter of August 21, 1898, to the commanding officer of our forces, in reply to the demand that he withdraw his forces from Manila, he stated thus one of the conditions of such withdrawal:

They also [referring to the Filipinos] desired that if, in consequence of the treaty of peace which may be concluded between the United States of America and Spain, the *Philippines should continue under the domination of the latter*, the American forces should give up all the suburbs to the Filipinos, in consideration of the coöperation lent by the latter in the capture of Manila.

In reply to this he was informed that in the event of the United States withdrawing from these islands care should be taken to leave him in as advantageous a position as he was found by the forces of the government.

It has been said that we should have demanded of Spain that she relinquish sovereignty over the Philippines as she did over Cuba. That could not be expected of her. It would have been a demand to which Spain, even in her overthrow and in her poverty, could not have yielded.

Spain might very well say to us, "We relinquish our title to Cuba; that was the cause of the war; that was your demand at the outset, coupled with a declaration that you would not acquire Cuba; we will cede to you Porto Rico; and while we will, if it is exacted, cede to you the Philippines,—you have no right to demand of us,—you not taking them, you not willing to take the burden of them, you not willing to safeguard them,—that we quitclaim them to the world, purely in the interests of your philanthropy and of your vaunted love of liberty."

She would have said to us, "You have no interest in the Philippines; you have never been in the Philippines except during this war; the Philippines or their people had no relation to the inception of the war; you are there only by the accident of war; you have no property interests there; you allege no violated treaties with reference to the Philippines, and you have no foundation upon which a nation, victorious in war, dealing justly with a defeated antagonist, can demand, simply for reasons of sentimentality, our relinquishment of title and sovereignty over this great possession, as we agreed in the protocol and agree in the treaty to do as to Cuba."

Mr. President, it was thought by many, too, that that would have left them, if Spain had been willing to relinquish the Philippines, we not taking them, to a strife among the nations for their possession; and, more than that, to an internecine strife among the many tribes of different characteristics, of different grades of civilization, which would have shocked the world.

So I thought that the treaty ought to be ratified. I voted for its ratification, containing, as it did, the cession of Porto Rico and of the Philippine archipelago to the United States. I said at the time, Mr. President, that, in my judgment, if it committed the country to permanent dominion in the Philippines, I would not vote for its ratification.

Mr. President, it was, and is still, insisted and eloquently argued that the treaty should have been so amended that by its terms we should sustain the same relation to the Philippines which we do as to Cuba. If Spain could have been brought to consent to it, which there is no good reason to believe, subsequent events have made plain the absolute impossibility of our successfully sustaining the same relation to the Filipinos that we sustain as to Cuba.

Cuba is near at hand, with a small population, comparatively, who knew us, who believed in us, and were grateful to us. Spain had surrendered Cuba and her cities to us, and we were military occupants.

The Philippines are 7,000 miles away, with a population of eight or ten millions of many tribes, strangers to us, easily prejudiced against us, with an alleged government really hostile to us, as I will show. Even under cession of title and sovereignty we have been unable to avert attack and hostility begun before ratification of the treaty.

It is idle now to suppose that Aguinaldo would have consented to our doing in the Philippines what we are doing and will do in Cuba in the way of establishing a stable government. With no cession of the archipelago, and with the hostility of the Tagalos, we should have been obliged to use force, without even claim of title or sovereignty; remain only in Manila or withdraw from the islands. What many of us thought then has been abundantly demonstrated since.

We had taken Manila. That was a complication not to be overlooked. The Spaniards had gone back to the mother country, and when we drove the Spaniards out of Manila, when our soldiers marched into that city and the flag of the United States floated over it, what did it mean? It meant that we had driven out the power that protected the inhabitants of that city, and had taken upon ourselves the duty of protecting its inhabitants; and there never has been a day since the thirteenth of August, when Manila was captured—and I say it without fear of successful contradiction—when the United States, without cowardice and absolute dishonor, could have withdrawn her troops from Manila and sailed away.

Many of us thought so when we voted on the treaty.

We know it now, Mr. President. The Senator from Massachusetts [Mr. Lodge] referred to it in his speech. Aguinaldo's secretary of the interior, who was also a member of his staff, issued a proclamation or order calling on the Filipinos in Manila and elsewhere to join in the massacre of every foreigner. It was dated February 15, 1899.

Here is the second clause of the order, Mr. President. Men who talk about civilization over there, who draw parallels between the greatest leaders for liberty in history and some of the half-caste leaders in the Philippines, who have seemed to exult sometimes in coupling with the name of Aguinaldo the name of Washington, can find no comfort in this production:

> Philippine families *only* will be respected. They should not be molested ; but *all other individuals of whatever race they may be* will be exterminated without any compassion after the *extermination* of the army of occupation.

That is not simply the father. It is the mother, the wife, the sons, and the daughters. It is those of mature years and the little ones—the family.

Was ever anything worse than that? And who made this order? Teodoro Sandico. Who was he? One of the men closest to Aguinaldo; a member of the junta in Hongkong, present at the meeting of the junta on May 5, and largely governing its deliberations by his ability and his will; one of the thirteen chosen by Aguinaldo to accompany him to Manila; secretary of the interior, and a staff officer; one of the three men whom one of our consuls mentioned in his correspondence—Aguinaldo, Agoncillo, and Sandico—as men of great ability who would be leaders anywhere, in any affair.

And when Senators introduce the proposition to withdraw our army now from Manila, with Englishmen there, with Germans there, with Spaniards there, with Hollanders there, with Frenchmen there, and Americans there, with their wives, and their children, and their property, and with friendly Filipinos there, against whom vengeance has been sworn, Mr. President, they make a proposition which in the end they themselves would hesitate to adopt.

If the Spanish fleet had not happened to be in Manila

Harbor, but had been found by Dewey on the open sea, the Spaniards might not have been in Havana, and yet the Spaniards would have remained in the Philippines. That the Spanish fleet was destroyed in Manila Harbor, that it happened to be there, was one of the fortunes or accidents of war.

The suggestion that the liberation of the Philippine archipelago from Spain was wrought by Aguinaldo is stated in this book by him, but it ought not to be stated here. In the Philippines, as in Cuba, the lion in the pathway of Spain was not the insurrectionists. It was the United States; but when the Spaniards evacuated Iloilo they did it because we, having conquered Spain, having destroyed the power of Spain practically in the Philippines, she surrendered them to us. It was because of our power, not Aguinaldo's; and after the Spaniards had marched out Aguinaldo marched in. That is all there was of it. There was no conquest about it.

Men talk about our waging a war of conquest against the Philippine republic or people. We have done no such thing. We did not obtain the Philippines, to such I think we have a perfect title, by any conquest of the so-called Philippine republic, by any conquest of the Philippine people; but by the conquest of Spain.

Mr. President, we accepted that cession; we ratified the treaty; we acquired, so far as the treaty could give it to us, the Philippine archipelago; Congress appropriated $20,000,-000; there was fighting and has continued to be fighting in the Philippines; our troops were involved in contest with the Filipinos, and Congress knowing that fact passed a military bill providing for a fast increase of the army.

It was perfectly understood that a large part of that force, so much as the President might deem necessary, was to be sent to the Philippines. That very law mentions the Philippines as a place in which troops were to serve. What was the President to do but to send troops to the Philippines, Mr. President, and to enforce there the authority of the United States? Could he hesitate, under his oath, upon the assumption that there was any doubt as to our title?

One of the strange phases of this matter now is that men who voted to furnish troops for the President to send to the Philippines, criticize him for sending them, criticize him for using them. He was obliged to take it as settled that we had acquired the Philippine archipelago; that it was his duty to extend the authority of the United States over that archipelago; and he has done so. He notified Congress by his annual message that until Congress indicated a purpose otherwise he should continue to use the troops of the United States in enforcing the authority of this government in the Philippines. Had he not done so, Mr. President, all things considered, criticism could have been made of him which would have been unanswerable.

Some one asked the other day why the President did not bring about a cessation of hostilities. Upon what basis could he have brought about a cessation of hostilities? Should he have asked Aguinaldo for an armistice? If so, upon what basis should he have requested it? What should he say to him? "Please stop this fighting?" "What for," Aguinaldo would say, "do you propose to retire?" "No." "Do you propose to grant us independence?" "No, not now." "Well, why, then, an armistice?" The President would doubtless be expected to reply: "Some distinguished gentlemen in the United States, members of the United States Senate, and others, have discovered a doubt about our right to be here at all, some doubt whether we have acquired the Philippines, some question as to whether we have correctly read the Declaration of Independence; and I want an armistice until we can consult and determine finally whether we have acquired the Philippines or not, whether we are violating the Declaration of Independence or not, whether we are trampling upon the Constitution or not." That is practically the proposition.

No, Mr. President, men may say in criticism of the President what they choose. He has been grossly insulted in this chamber, and it appears upon the record. He has gone his way patiently, exercising the utmost forbearance, all his acts characterized by a desire to do precisely what the Congress had placed upon him by its ratification of the treaty and its increase of the army. He has done it in a way to impress upon the Filipinos, so far as language and action could do it, his desire and the desire of our people to do them good, to give them the largest possible measure of liberty, civil, religious, and individual, and it gave them, as rapidly as may be, participation in the government out there.

He has done it all in disregard of hostile criticism, embarrassment, and complication of the situation vastly intensified and enhanced here at home; but he has done what under his oath he was obliged to do.   He has gone forward with the army of the United States and the flag of the United States to enforce the authority of the United States and obedience to it over territory of the United States.   Any President of any party, if faithful to his trust, could not have done otherwise.

WILLIAM McKENDREE SPRINGER

RETRENCHMENT, ECONOMY, AND REFORM

[William McKendree Springer was born in Indiana in 1836. His family removed to Illinois in 1848, and after a careful education in the public schools and the Indiana University, where he graduated in 1858, he became a newspaper man. He received a degree of A.M. in 1861, was admitted to the bar in 1859, and married the same year. In 1871 he became a member of the Illinois State legislature, went to Congress in 1875, and was repeatedly reëlected until 1895. In 1886 he received the degree of LL.D. from the Illinois College, Jacksonville, Ill. While in Congress he was chairman of many important committees, a Democratic leader of ability, and the author of many notable bills. From 1895 to 1899 he was United States Judge, Northern District, I. T., and Chief Justice of the United States Court of Appeals, I. T. In 1900 he resumed the practice of law in Washington, D. C., but died there December 4, 1903. The following satirical speech, regarding unnecessary expending of public money, was delivered in the House of Representatives in 1876.]

THE reductions in the salaries of diplomatic officers are such as are demanded by the nature of their service and by the absolute necessity at this time for a rigid economy in every department of government. Does any one suppose that any one of our foreign ministers will resign on account of the reduction of their salaries as proposed? Will Schenck do it, or Bancroft Davis, or Boker, or Godlove Orth, or Cramer, or Horace Maynard resign and come home in disgust? I trust not. It would be a great calamity to them, if not to the country. The annual salaries of ministers to the four great powers were $17,500 each, in gold. This bill reduces them to $14,000. Will any of our constituents complain of this? They will rather suggest that, in view of the general stagnation of business and the necessity for individual economy on the part of the rich and poor, it is not unreasonable to ask our foreign diplomats to give fewer entertainments and live in less splendor than formerly. We do not ask them to deny themselves the necessities of life. We pay our cabinet ministers $8,000 per annum, and I assert, without fear of successful contradiction, that every member of the President's cabinet is called upon to make more pecuniary outlays, in order to live in a manner befitting his position, than is required of any of our ministers at foreign courts. President Grant has no difficulty in finding gentlemen to fill his cabinet offices on account of inadequate salaries.

The salaries of our ministers are not the only expenses we have to meet in connection with our diplomatic services. I call the attention of the committee to George H. Boker's account for contingent expenses. The large amount of such expenses in the Turkish mission needs explanation. Upon examination of the accounts and vouchers on file in the fifth auditor's office, it appeared that Mr. Boker concluded a treaty with Turkey just before his departure for Russia in April, 1875. He presented a bill for "presents purchased for officials of the Turkish government, on the conclusion of treaties, as per instructions of secretary of state. This account amounted to $10,607.56, in gold, and was promptly paid. The items of this bill are quite suggestive, and I may be pardoned for particularizing.

[Mr. Springer here read out the items of the account.]

This is a most remarkable list of presents. We have diamonds, rubies, and emeralds in rich profusion. Imagine the festive youth, the son of the minister of Foreign Affairs, promenading upon the avenues of Constantinople or dancing with princesses in the palace of the sublime porte, wearing upon his shirt-bosom an $800 breastpin, paid for by the taxpayers of America.

Mr. Chairman, the time was, many years ago, when the people were so sensitive about these expenditures that, because a few gold spoons had been purchased for the executive mansion, the people of this country became indignant and overthrew the administration. Here we have one minister in a foreign court expending over $10,000, in gold, for presents to Turkish officials on one occasion. It has been thought that such favors were reciprocal. I do not know whether that be so or not; but it seems to me the Turkish officials have never said "turkey" to us once. At least

Mr. Boker has not asked Congress to allow him to receive presents from the Turkish government, as he ought to have done had any been made him. What this treaty was I do not know; it has not been transmitted to us with the President's message. The people will be anxious to know whether it, like the Indian's gem, "has cost more than it has come to."

The bill under consideration makes no provision for the Greek mission. This will be unfortunate to no one except to John Meredith Read, our minister-resident at that court. The despatches sent by him to this government, and submitted in the reports made to Congress, are of such a character as to demonstrate conclusively the perfectly useless character of that mission. My friend from Indiana [Mr. Holman] has been kind enough to refer to one of them to show its great importance. But here is another which he has overlooked, which shows not only the nature of the correspondence, but the great learning and erudition of our minister. I shall have to get my learned friend Mr. Seelye to translate all this Greek, for Mr. Read is actually sending the despatch partly in English and partly in Greek, and we common people in the West never can know what it is, unless we can get it translated by some one. What is this all about? Greece is a great country; it is a sweet morsel in the mouth of our minister, this Greece to which he is accredited. They have wonderful people there. And he reports the subjects of taxation by that government. Enumerated among those subjects are bees, pigs, potatoes, onions, garlic, mulberries, and fig-trees. This is indeed a very great country, to have such fruitful subjects of taxation.

But that is not all. Mr. Read tells us what manner of country it is. He describes it as being one of those semi-barbarous countries in which it is very unsafe for any gentleman to be outside of the corporate limits of the city. I am assured of that fact. It is very unsafe, perhaps the most unsafe of any country claiming to be civilized in the world! And "a minister to Greece" is a great misnomer, for he is a minister to Athens only. He dare not go a mile outside of the corporate limits of the city without military protection. But there are other things in his correspondence. I have one here under date of March 8, 1875:

"SIR : A magnificent ball took place at the palace on the 3d instant. On that occasion the American minister had the honor to be selected to lead a contra-dance with the queen."

Now that must have been delightful. Just imagine the minister-resident of the United States leading a contra-dance with the Queen of Greece. He was so elated over it that he had to despatch the news as soon as possible to this country, it was so very important. He goes on further:

"The spacious salons were filled at half-past nine, and the festivities continued until half-past five in the morning."

At that time, we presume, our minister departed for his residence. I can imagine the scene, as he wended his way through the ancient city, at that unseemly hour of the night, inspired, as he wrote in the letter read yesterday by Mr. Holman, by the view of—

"The majestic outlines of the Acropolis and its immortal ruins, illuminated by the calm, silvery rays of the same fair moon which looked down upon the labors, ceremonies, and sacrifices of Phidias and Pericles, 2,000 years ago,"

singing that American refrain—which must have sounded to the inhabitants there as Greek would to us—

"We won't go home till morning,
Till daylight doth appear."

Yes; as my colleague suggests—wearing a spike-tailed coat, and a white cravat, of course. He then goes on:

"The arrangements throughout were of the most admirable character. An elaborate supper for eight hundred guests was laid in the royal *salle à manger* and in the two large adjoining rooms, while the ministers of state and the diplomatic corps "—

John Meredith Read—of course—for that is what that means—

"were entertained by the king and queen in the beautiful private apartments of their majesties."

No common people could enter these private apartments of their majesties, none but diplomatic representatives and ministers of state. If the people of this country could have looked upon that group, which might be fitly described in the touching language of John Hay, narrating the finding of Little Breeches in the sheep-fold, they would have

> "Seen them huddled there
> So warm and so sleepy, and white!"

How did our minister get there? It is simply amazing. It must have been by some providential interference, as was the case with Little Breeches, whose advent into the sheep-fold was caused by the interposition of the angels—

> "They just scooped down and toted him
> To whar it was safe and warm."

Mr. Read goes on further and says:

"The palace is well adapted for social assemblages upon a grand scale."

Well, I am very glad to hear that; I was afraid they would be crowded, there were so many present.

"The crimson carpets bring in relief the white marble floor."

I do not understand how the floor could be seen when the carpet covered it; but perhaps he could "see as through a glass darkly."

"On either hand a double row of attendants displayed the splendors of the national costumes. The two principal ballrooms are of vast size."

Now that is very important, because it is very annoying when ladies wear long trains to be crowded into small dancing-rooms. I am glad the apartments were spacious. It is very important, too, for us to know this, because we are paying money for it.

"Their highly decorated walls and lofty ceilings stand revealed in the soft rays of two thousand wax candles."

I thought they had gas in that city; but it seems not. It took 2,000 wax candles to illuminate on that great occasion.   And then our minister proceeds to say that it was very refreshing to see—

"not only the descendants of heroes, but heroes themselves walking along through those halls."

No doubt he imagined that he was one of those heroes! But he goes on in this state paper to give us some information to which I call the attention of the learned members of this House, because I confess it is a little mysterious to me.   I never knew before the important information here transmitted; and I am willing to pay a small amount for it.

" The names of Mavrocordato, Kolokotronis, Botzaris, Capo d'Istria, and many more which long ago became household words in America, have now in Greece living illustrations in the second and third generations."

Now, whoever heard before that Mavrocordato or Kolokotronis were household words in this country?   What little "contraband" walking up and down through the cotton-fields of the sunny South bears the euphonious name of Mavrocordato or Kolokotronis?   If any representative has such a constituent let him speak now; "for him have I offended."   "I pause for a reply."   "Then none have I offended."   There is no such person in this country, and Mavrocordato and Kolokotronis, as household words, exist only in the fertile imagination of our resident-minister to Greece.

Now, what must have been the delightful sensations of the State department when they received this despatch from Mr. Read, stating that he was dancing a contra-dance with the queen?   We can hardly imagine the sensations that must have crept over the amiable gentleman that presides in the palace on the other side of the Executive Mansion. I know some one must have sent a despatch in reply, saying:

" On with the dance ! let joy be unconfined !
No sleep till morn, when youth and pleasure meet
To chase the glowing hours with flying feet.
" Enviously yours," etc.

Of course they all wanted to dance a set with the queen on that occasion, but they could not.   John Meredith Read was so fortunate as to have all this great pleasure to himself. But I can imagine the sensation that will come over J. Meredith Read when he hears that this bill has passed both Houses, been approved by the President, and that "Othello's occupation's gone." He will doubtless cast one wistful look at the palace of the queen, and exclaim in the language of Byron:

> " Maid of Athens, ere we part,
>   Give, oh, give me back my heart !"

After J. Meredith Read has embarked upon a stately ship in the harbor at Piræus, and sees the queen standing on the shore, he will doubtless continue the beautiful song—

> " Maid of Athens, I am gone :
>   Think of me, sweet, when alone;
>   Though I fly to Istamboul ——"

I suppose that in Greek means Philadelphia—

> " Athens holds my heart and soul :
>   Can I cease to love thee ? No !"

I will not weary the House further. I have gone over the subject very hastily. I thank the House for the attention it has paid me. I believe that after gentlemen have explained carefully the consular service they will agree with me that it needs reform as well as all the other departments of the government, and if those on this side of the House intend to keep faith with the people who have sent them here they will not let up on this bill by reason of the alarm that has been expressed by the gentlemen from New York, who have supposed that our commerce with foreign countries was in some way unfavorably affected by it.

We must meet this measure and every measure alike. This bill is not an exception in its efforts toward economy. It illustrates a rule that we are going to apply to all appropriation bills. We are going to cut down the expenses in all the different branches of the government; and the President will find that we have divided his salary by two, as well as the appropriation for contingent expenses of foreign intercourse. But it is to be regretted that the President's salary cannot be reached during the present term.   Other officials who have been receiving large salaries and doing little or no work will find that their services will soon be dispensed with.   And this House will not have finished its work until it shall have cut off all manner of official extravagance, abolished all sinecures, exposed corruption and peculation, reduced the public expenses $30,000,000, and thus have carried out the pledges made to the people when we were elected to establish in all the branches and departments of the government retrenchment, economy, and reform.

ALEXANDER HAMILTON STEPHENS

ON SECESSION

[Alexander H. Stephens, vice-president of the Southern Confederacy, was born near Crawfordsville in Georgia, February 11, 1812. When a boy, he had the best educational advantages of the State, and graduated from the State University in 1832. Two years later he was admitted to the bar. In 1836 he was elected to the State Assembly, and was returned for subsequent sessions until 1841. Then, after two years had passed, he entered the Senate. He served in Congress until 1859, and then proposed retirement from active politics; but in 1860 he supported Douglas for President, still urging upon the South the abandonment of secession. He submitted to the will of the majority, and at the "Constitutional Convention" which met at Montgomery, Ala., February 4, 1861, was made vice-president of the Confederacy. As the war was nearing an end and the Southern cause seemed beyond recovery, he made efforts to open negotiations looking to peace with the national government. After Lee's surrender he was arrested at his home in Crawfordsville, and was confined for five months at Fort Warren in Boston Harbor, after which time he was released on parole. From 1874 to 1882 he was again in Congress, and in 1883 became governor of Georgia. He died at Atlanta, Ga., on March 4, 1883, in his seventy-second year. The first of the following speeches was delivered in Convention at Montgomery, Ala., in 1861, shortly before the Civil War began; the second in Savannah, Ga., also in 1861.]

MR. PRESIDENT: This step of secession, once taken, can never be recalled; and all the baleful and withering consequences that must follow, will rest on the convention for all coming time. When we and our posterity shall see our lovely South desolated by the demon of war, which this act of yours will inevitably invite and call forth; when our green fields of waving harvest shall be trodden down by the murderous soldiery and fiery car of war sweeping over our land; our temples of justice laid in ashes; all the

horrors and desolations of war upon us; who but this convention will be held responsible for it? And who but him
who shall have given his vote for this unwise and ill-timed
measure, as I honestly think and believe, shall be held to
strict account for this suicidal act by the present generation,
and probably cursed and execrated by posterity for all coming time, for the wide and desolating ruin that will inevitably follow this act you now propose to perpetrate? Pause,
I entreat you, and consider for a moment what reasons you
can give, that will even satisfy yourselves in calmer moments
—what reason you can give to your fellow-sufferers in the
calamity that it will bring upon us. What reasons can you
give to the nations of the earth to justify it? They will be
the calm and deliberate judges in the case; and what cause
or one overt act can you name or point, on which to rest
the plea of justification? What right has the North assailed? What interest of the South has been invaded?
What justice has been denied? And what claim founded
in justice and right has been withheld? Can either of you,
to-day, name one governmental act of wrong, deliberately
and purposely done by the government of Washington, of
which the South has a right to complain? I challenge the
answer. While on the other hand, let me show the facts
(and believe me, gentlemen, I am not here the advocate of
the North; but I am here the friend, the firm friend, and
lover of the South, and her institutions, and for this reason
I speak thus plainly and faithfully for yours, mine, and
every other man's interest, the words of truth and sober-
ness), of which I wish you to judge, and I will only state
facts which are clear and undeniable, and which now stand
as records authentic in the history of our country. When
we of the South demanded the slave-trade, or the importation of Africans for the cultivation of our lands, did they
not yield the right for twenty years? When we asked a
three-fifths representation in Congress for our slaves, was it
not granted? When we asked and demanded the return of
any fugitive from justice, or the recovery of those persons
owing labor or allegiance, was it not incorporated in the
Constitution, and again ratified and strengthened by the Fugitive Slave law of 1850? But do you reply that in many instances they have violated this compact, and have not been

faithful to their engagements? As individual and local communities, they may have done so; but not by the sanction of government; for that has always been true to Southern interests. Again, gentlemen, look at another act; when we have asked that more territory should be added, that we might spread the institution of slavery, have they not yielded to our demands in giving us Louisiana, Florida, and Texas, out of which four states have been carved, and ample territory for four more to be added in due time, if you, by this unwise and impolitic act, do not destroy this hope, and, perhaps, by it lose all, and have your last slave wrenched from you by stern military rule, as South America and Mexico were; or by the vindicative decree of a universal emancipation, which may reasonably be expected to follow.

But, again, gentlemen, what have we to gain by this proposed change of our relation to the general government? We have always had the control of it, and can yet, if we remain in it, and are as united as we have been. We have had a majority of the Presidents chosen from the South, as well as the control and management of most of those chosen from the North. We have had sixty years of Southern Presidents to their twenty-four, thus controlling the executive department. So of the judges of the Supreme Court, we have had eighteen from the South, and but eleven from the North; although nearly four-fifths of the judicial business has arisen in the free states, yet a majority of the Court has always been from the South. This we have required so as to guard against any interpretation of the Constitution unfavorable to us. In like manner we have been equally watchful to guard our interests in the legislative branch of government. In choosing the presiding presidents (pro tem.) of the Senate, we have had twenty-four to their eleven. Speakers of the House we have had twenty-three, and they twelve. While the majority of the representatives, from their greater population, have always been from the North, yet we have so generally secured the Speaker, because he, or to a great extent, shapes and controls the legislation of the country. Nor have we had less control in every other department of the general government. Attorney-generals we have had fourteen, while the

North have had but five. Foreign ministers we have had eighty-six, and they but fifty-four. While three-fourths of the business which demands diplomatic agents abroad is clearly from the free states, from their greater commercial interest, yet we have had the principal embassies, so as to secure the world-markets for our cotton, tobacco, and sugar on the best possible terms. We have had a vast majority of the higher offices of both army and navy, while a larger proportion of the soldiers and sailors were drawn from the North. Equally so of clerks, auditors, and comptrollers filling the executive department; the records show, for the last fifty years, that of the three thousand thus employed, we have had more than two-thirds of the same, while we have but one-third of the white population of the Republic.

Again, look at another item, and one, be assured, in which we have a great and vital interest; it is that of revenue, or means of supporting government. From official documents, we learn that a fraction over three-fourths of the revenue collected for the support of the government has uniformly been raised from the North.

Pause now while you can, gentlemen, and contemplate carefully and candidly these important items. Look at another necessary branch of government, and learn from stern statistical facts how matters stand in that department. I mean the mail and post-office privileges that we now enjoy under the general government as it has been for years past. The expense for the transportation of the mail in the free states was, by the report of the postmaster-general for the year 1860, a little over $13,000,000, while the income was $19,000,000. But in the slave states the transportation of the mail was $14,716,000, while the revenue from the same was $8,001,026, leaving a deficit of $6,704,974, to be supplied by the North, for our accommodation, and, without it, we must have been entirely cut off from this most essential branch of government.

Leaving out of view, for the present, the countless millions of dollars you must expend in a war with the North; with tens of thousands of your sons and brothers slain in battle, and offered up as sacrifices upon the altar of your ambition—and for what, we ask again? Is it for the overthrow of the American government, established by our common ancestry, cemented and built up by their sweat and blood, and founded on the broad principles of right, justice and humanity? And as such, I must declare here, as I have often done before, and which has been repeated by the greatest and wisest of statesmen and patriots, in this and other lands, that it is the best and freest government—the most equal in its rights, the most just in its decisions, the most lenient in its measures, and the most aspiring in its principles, to elevate the race of men, that the sun of heaven ever shone upon. Now, for you to attempt to overthrow such a government as this, under which we have lived for more than three-quarters of a century—in which we have gained our wealth, our standing as a nation, our domestic safety, while the elements of peril are around us, with peace and tranquility accompanied with unbounded prosperity and rights unassailed—is the height of madness, folly, and wickedness, to which I neither lend my sanction nor my vote.

THE "CORNER-STONE" ADDRESS

We are in the midst of one of the greatest epochs in our history. The last ninety days will mark one of the most interesting eras in the history of modern civilization. Seven States have in the last three months thrown off an old government and formed a new. This revolution has been signally marked, up to this time, by the fact of its having been accomplished without the loss of a single drop of blood. This new constitution, or form of government, constitutes the subject to which your attention will be partly invited.

In reference to it, I make this first general remark: it amply secures all our ancient rights, franchises, and liberties. All the great principles of Magna Charta are retained in it. No citizen is deprived of life, liberty, or property, but by the judgment of his peers under the laws of the land. The great principle of religious liberty, which was the honor and pride of the old Constitution, is still maintained and secured. All the essentials of the old Constitution, which have endeared it to the hearts of the American

people, have been preserved and perpetuated. Some
changes have been made. Some of these I should prefer
not to have seen made; but other important changes do
meet my cordial approbation. They form great improvements upon the old Constitution. So, taking the whole
new constitution, I have no hesitancy in giving it as my
judgment that it is decidedly better than the old.

Allow me briefly to allude to some of these improvements. The question of building up class interests, or
fostering one branch of industry to the prejudice of another
under the exercise of the revenue power, which gave us so
much trouble under the old Constitution, is put at rest
forever under the new. We allow the imposition of no
duty with a view of giving advantage to one class of persons, in any trade or business, over those of another. All,
under our system, stand upon the same broad principles of
perfect equality. Honest labor and enterprise are left free
and unrestricted in whatever pursuit they may be engaged.
This old thorn of the tariff, which was the cause of so much
irritation in the old body politic, is removed forever from
the new.

· Again, the subject of internal improvements, under the
power of Congress to regulate commerce, is put at rest
under our system. The power, claimed by construction
under the old Constitution, was at least a doubtful one; it
rested solely upon construction. We of the South, generally apart from considerations of constitutional principles,
opposed its exercise upon grounds of its inexpediency and
injustice. Our opposition sprang from no hostility to commerce, or to all necessary aids for facilitating it. With us
it was simply a question upon whom the burden should
fall. In Georgia, for instance, we have done as much for
the cause of internal improvements as any other portion of
the country, according to population and means. We have
stretched out lines of railroad from the seaboard to the
mountains; dug down the hills, and filled up the valleys,
at a cost of $25,000,000. No state was in greater need of
such facilities than Georgia, but we did not ask that these
works should be made by appropriations out of the common
treasury. The cost of the grading, the superstructure, and
the equipment of our roads was borne by those who had

entered into the enterprise. Nay, more, not only the cost of the iron—no small item in the general cost—was borne in the same way, but we were compelled to pay into the common treasury several millions of dollars for the privilege of importing the iron, after the price was paid for it abroad. What justice was there in taking this money, which our people paid into the common treasury on the importation of our iron, and applying it to the improvement of rivers and harbors elsewhere? The true principle is to subject the commerce of every locality to whatever burdens may be necessary to facilitate it. If Charleston harbor needs improvement, let the commerce of Charleston bear the burden. This, again, is the broad principle of perfect equality and justice; and it is especially set forth and established in our new constitution.

Another feature to which I will allude is that the new constitution provides that cabinet ministers and heads of departments may have the privilege of seats upon the floor of the Senate and House of Representatives, may have the right to participate in the debates and discussions upon the various subjects of administration. I should have preferred that this provision should have gone further, and required the President to select his constitutional advisers from the Senate and House of Representatives. That would have conformed entirely to the practise in the British Parliament, which, in my judgment, is one of the wisest provisions in the British Constitution. It is the only feature that saves that government. It is that which gives it stability in its facility to change its administration. Ours, as it is, is a great approximation to the right principle.

Another change in the constitution relates to the length of the tenure of the presidential office. In the new constitution it is six years instead of four, and the President is rendered ineligible for a reëlection. This is certainly a decidedly conservative change. It will remove from the incumbent all temptation to use his office or exert the powers confided to him for any objects of personal ambition. The only incentive to that higher ambition which should move and actuate one holding such high trusts in his hands will be the good of the people, the advancement, happiness, safety, honor, and true glory of the Confederacy.

But, not to be tedious in enumerating the numerous changes for the better, allow me to allude to one other— though last, not least. The new constitution has put at rest forever all the agitating questions relating to our peculiar institution, African slavery, as it exists amongst us, the proper status of the negro in our form of civilization. This was the immediate cause of the late rupture and present revolution. Jefferson, in his forecast, had anticipated this as the "rock upon which the old Union would split." He was right. What was conjecture with him is now a realized fact. But whether he fully comprehended the great truth upon which that rock stood and stands may be doubted. The prevailing ideas entertained by him and most of the leading statesmen at the time of the formation of the old Constitution were that the enslavement of the African was in violation of the laws of nature; that it was wrong in principle, socially, morally, and politically. It was an evil they knew not well how to deal with; but the general opinion of the men of that day was that, somehow or other, in the order of Providence, the institution would be evanescent and pass away. This idea, though not incorporated in the Constitution, was the prevailing idea at that time. The Constitution, it is true, secured every essential guaranty to the institution while it should last, and hence no argument can be justly urged against the constitutional guaranties thus secured, because of the common sentiment of the day. Those ideas, however, were fundamentally wrong. They rested upon the assumption of the equality of races. This was an error. It was a sandy foundation, and the government built upon it fell when "the storm came and the wind blew."

Our new government is founded upon exactly the opposite idea; its foundations are laid, its corner-stone rests, upon the great truth that the negro is not equal to the white man, that slavery—subordination to the superior race —is his natural and normal condition.

This, our new government, is the first in the history of the world based upon this great physical, philosophical, and moral truth. This truth has been slow in the process of its development, like all other truths in the various departments of science. It has been so even amongst us. Many who hear me, perhaps, can recollect well that this truth was not generally admitted, even within their day. The errors of the past generation still clung to many as late as twenty years ago. Those at the North who still cling to these errors, with a zeal above knowledge, we justly denominate fanatics. All fanaticism springs from an aberration of the mind, from a defect in reasoning. It is a species of insanity. One of the most striking characteristics of insanity, in many instances, is forming correct conclusions from fancied or erroneous premises. So with the antislavery fanatics; their conclusions are right, if their premises were. They assume that the negro is equal, and hence conclude that he is entitled to equal rights and privileges with the white man. If their premises were correct, their conclusions would be logical and just; but, their premise being wrong, their whole argument fails. I recollect once hearing a gentleman from one of the Northern States, of great power and ability, announce in the House of Representatives, with imposing effect, that we of the South would be compelled ultimately to yield upon this subject of slavery, that it was as impossible to war successfully against a principle in politics as it was in physics or mechanics; that the principle would ultimately prevail; that we, in maintaining slavery as it exists with us, were warring against a principle, founded in nature, the principle of the equality of men. The reply I made to him was that upon his own grounds we should ultimately succeed, and that he and his associates in this crusade against our institutions would ultimately fail. The truth announced, that it was as impossible to war successfully against a principle in politics as it was in physics and mechanics, I admitted; but told him that it was he, and those acting with him, who were warring against a principle. They were attempting to make things equal which the Creator had made unequal.

In the conflict, thus far, success has been on our side, complete throughout the length and breadth of the Confederate States. It is upon this, as I have stated, our social fabric is firmly planted; and I cannot permit myself to doubt the ultimate success of a full recognition of this principle throughout the civilized and enlightened world.

As I have stated, the truth of this principle may be slow

in development, as all truths are and ever have been, in the various branches of science. It was so with the principles announced by Galileo. It was so with Adam Smith and his principles of political economy. It was so with Harvey and his theory of the circulation of the blood; it is stated that not a single one of the medical profession, living at the time of the announcement of the truths made by him, admitted them. Now they are universally acknowledged. May we not, therefore, look with confidence to the ultimate universal acknowledgment of the truths upon which our system rests? It is the first government ever instituted upon the principles in strict conformity to nature and the ordination of Providence in furnishing the materials of human society. Many governments have been founded upon the principle of the subordination and serfdom of certain classes of the same race; such were and are in violation of the laws of nature. Our system commits no such violation of nature's laws. With us, all the white race, however high or low, rich or poor, are equal in the eye of the law. Not so with the negro; subordination is his place. He, by nature or by the curse against Canaan, is fitted for that condition which he occupies in our system. The architect, in the construction of buildings, lays the foundation with the proper material—the granite; then comes the brick or the marble. The substratum of our society is made of the material fitted by nature for it; and by experience we know that it is best not only for the superior race, but for the inferior race, that it should be so. It is, indeed, in conformity with the ordinance of the Creator. It is not for us to inquire into the wisdom of His ordinances, or to question them. For His own purposes he has made one race to differ from another, as He has made "one star to differ from another star in glory." The great objects of humanity are best attained when there is conformity to His laws and decrees, in the formation of governments as well as in all things else. Our confederacy is founded upon principles in strict conformity with these views. This stone, which was rejected by the first builders, "is become the chief of the corner," the real "corner-stone" in our new edifice.

Mr. Jefferson said in his inaugural, in 1801, after the heated contest preceding his election, that there might be differences of opinion without differences of principle, and that all, to some extent, had been Federalists, and all Republicans. So it may now be said of us that, whatever differences of opinion as to the best policy in having a coöperation with our border sister slave states, if the worst came to the worst, as we were all coöperationists, we are all now for independence, whether they come or not.

We are a young republic, just entering upon the arena of nations; we will be the architects of our own fortunes. Our destiny, under Providence, is in our own hands. With wisdom, prudence, and statesmanship on the part of our public men, and intelligence, virtue, and patriotism on the part of the people, success to the full measure of our most sanguine hopes may be looked for. But if unwise counsels prevail, if we become divided, if schisms arise, if dissensions spring up, if factions are engendered, if party spirit, nourished by unholy personal ambition, shall rear its hydra head, I have no good to prophesy for you. Without intelligence, virtue, integrity, and patriotism on the part of the people, no republic or representative government can be durable or stable.

THADDEUS STEVENS

AGAINST WEBSTER AND NORTHERN COMPROMISERS

[Thaddeus Stevens, an American statesman, and in his time Republican leader in the House of Representatives, was born in Vermont in 1792. He graduated at Dartmouth and settled in Pennsylvania, where he taught school at first, and then became a lawyer. He was politically an opponent of Andrew Jackson, and made himself a power in Pennsylvania politics. As a member of the legislature of that State he introduced the public school system by means of a series of bills. He watched its development with keen solicitude and delivered a speech in behalf of the free American public school that made him a famous man. In 1848 he was elected to Congress, and he served in that body with slight intermission until his death. The oratory of Thaddeus Stevens was of a highly original description, deriving its greatest force from the personality of the man. He was fine looking, tall, and erect, his features nobly chiseled, and his glance keen and piercing. His oratorical tone was vigorous, his language terse and accurate, and his style interesting. He died at Washington in 1868, just after taking an active part in the prosecution and impeachment of President Johnson. The following speech, directed against Webster and others regarding the Compromise of 1850, was delivered in the House of Representatives, 1850.]

DANTE, by actual observation, makes hell consist of nine circles, the punishments of each increasing in intensity over the preceding. Those doomed to the first circle are much less afflicted than those in the ninth, where are tortured Lucifer and Judas Iscariot—and I trust, in the next edition, will be added, the traitors to liberty. But notwithstanding this difference in degree, all, from the first circle to the ninth, inclusive, is hell—cruel, desolate, abhorred, horrible hell! If I might venture to make a suggestion, I would advise these reverend perverters of Scripture to devote their subtlety to what they have probably more interest in—to ascertaining and demonstrating (perhaps an accompanying map might be useful) the exact spot and location where the most comfort might be enjoyed—the coolest corner in the lake that burns with fire and brimstone!

But not only by honorable gentlemen in this House, and right honorable gentlemen in the other, but throughout the country, the friends of liberty are reproached as "transcendentalists and fanatics." Sir, I do not understand the terms in such connection. There can be no fanatics in the cause of genuine liberty. Fanaticism is excessive zeal. There may be, and have been, fanatics in false religion; in the bloody religion of the heathen. There are fanatics in superstition. But there can be no fanatics, however warm their zeal, in true religion, even although you sell your goods, and bestow your money on the poor, and go and follow your Master. There may be, and every hour shows around me, fanatics in the cause of false liberty—that infamous liberty which justifies human bondage; that liberty whose corner-stone is slavery. But there can be no fanaticism, however high the enthusiasm, in the cause of rational, universal liberty—the liberty of the Declaration of Independence.

This is the same censure which the Egyptian tyrant cast upon those old abolitionists, Moses and Aaron, when they "agitated" for freedom, and, in obedience to the command of God, bade him let the people go.

But we are told by these pretended advocates of liberty in both branches of Congress, that those who preach freedom here and elsewhere are the slave's worst enemies; that it makes the slaveholder increase their burdens and tighten their chains; that more cruel laws are enacted since this agitation began in 1835. Sir, I am not satisfied that this is the fact. I will send to the clerk, and ask him to read a law of Virginia enacted more than fifty years before this agitation began. It is to be found in the sixth volume of "Hening's Statutes at Large of Virginia," published in 1819, "pursuant to an Act of the General Assembly of Virginia, passed on the fifth day of February, 1808."

"SECTION xxiv. And that when any slave shall be notoriously guilty of going abroad in the night, or running away and laying out, and cannot be reclaimed from such disorderly courses by common methods of punishment, it shall be lawful for the county court, upon complaint and proof thereof to them made by the owner of such slave, to order and direct such punishment by dismembering, or any other way, not touching life, as the court shall think fit. And if such slave shall die by means of such dismembering, no forfeiture or punishment shall be thereby incurred."

I have had that law read to see if any gentleman can turn me to any more cruel laws passed since the "agitation." I did not read it myself, though found on the pages of Old Virginia's law books, lest it should make the modest gentleman from Virginia [Mr. Millson], and the gentleman from North Carolina [Mr. Stanly], and his gray-headed negro, blush!

[Mr. Bayly, of Virginia—That law is repealed, or not now in force. Mr. Stevens—Then I am glad that the agitation has produced some amelioration of your laws, although I still find it on your statute book.]

But suppose it were true that the masters had become more severe; has it not been so with tyrants in every age? The nearer the oppressed is to freedom, and the more hopeful his struggles, the tighter the master rivets his chains. Moses and Aaron urged the emancipation of the enslaved Jews. Their master hardened his heart. Those fanatical abolitionists, guided by Heaven, agitated anew. Pharaoh increased the burden of the slaves. He required the same quantity of brick from them without straw, as when the straw had been found them. They were seen dispersed and wandering to gather stubble to make out their task. They failed, and were beaten with stripes. Moses was their worst enemy, according to these philanthropic gentlemen. Did the Lord think so, and command him to desist, lest he should injure them? No; he directed him to agitate again, and demand the abolition of slavery from the king himself. That great slaveholder still hardened his heart, and refused. The Lord visited him with successive plagues—lice, frogs, locusts, thick darkness—until, as the agitation grew higher, and the chains were tighter drawn, he smote the firstborn of every house in Egypt; nor did the slaveholder relax the grasp on his victims, until there was wailing throughout the whole land, over one dead in every family, from the king that sat on the throne to the captive in the dungeon. So I fear it will be in this land of wicked slavery. You have already among you what is equivalent to the lice and the locusts, that wither up every green thing where the foot of slavery treads. Beware of the final plague. And you, in the midst of slavery, who are willing to do justice to the people, take care that your works testify to the purity of your intentions, even at some cost. Take care that your door-posts are sprinkled with the blood of sacrifice, that when the destroying angel goes forth, as go forth he will, he may pass you by.

Aside from the principle of Eternal Right, I will never consent to the admission of another Slave state into the Union (unless bound to do so by some constitutional compact, and I know of none such), on account of the injustice of slave representation. By the Constitution, not only the states now in the Union, but all that may hereafter be admitted, are entitled to have their slaves represented in Congress, five slaves being counted equal to three white freemen. This is unjust to the free states, unless you allow them a representation in the compound ratio of persons and property. There are twenty-five gentlemen on this floor who are virtually the representatives of slaves alone, having not one free constituent. This is an outrage on every representative principle, which supposes that representatives have constituents, whose will they are bound to obey and whose interest they protect.   .   .   .

I shall not now particularly refer to the features of the most extraordinary conspiracy against liberty in the Senate, called the Compromise bill. If it should survive its puerperal fever, we shall have another opportunity of knocking the monster in the head. I pass over what is familiarly known as the "ten-million bribe," which was evidently inserted for no other purpose than to create public opinion on 'change, and carry the bill.

But it is proposed to propitiate Virginia by giving her two hundred million dollars out of the public treasury, the proceeds of the public lands. If this sum were to be given for the purpose of purchasing the freedom of her slaves, large as it is, it should have my hearty support. It is, I think, at least fifty millions more than would pay for them all at a fair market price. But it is designed for no purpose of emancipation. The cool-headed, cool-hearted, philosophic author had no such "transcendental" object. It is to be specifically appropriated to exile her free people of color, and transport them from the land of their birth to the land of the stranger! Sir, this is a proposition not "fit to be made."

[Mr. Averett, of Virginia, here asked : Did not New England sell slaves ? Mr. Stevens—Yes, she sold, she imported slaves ; she was very wicked ; she has long since repented. Go ye and do likewise.

It is my purpose nowhere in these remarks to make personal reproaches; I entertain no ill-will toward any human being, nor any brute, that I know of, not even the skunk across the way, to which I referred. Least of all would I reproach the South. I honor her courage and fidelity. Even in a bad, a wicked cause, she shows a united front. All her sons are faithful to the cause of human bondage, because it is their cause. But the North—the poor, timid, mercenary, driveling North—has no such united defenders of her cause, although it is the cause of human liberty. None of the bright lights of the nation shine upon her section. Even her own great men have turned her accusers. She is the victim of low ambition—an ambition which prefers self to country, personal aggrandizement to the high cause of human liberty. She is offered up a sacrifice to propitiate Southern tyranny—to conciliate Southern treason.

We are told that she has not done her duty in restoring fugitive slaves, and that more stringent laws must be passed to secure that object. A distinguished senator from Kentucky [Mr. Clay] says it is the duty, not only of officers in the free states, but of all the people who happen to be present, to give active aid to the slave-owner to run down, arrest, and restore the man who is fleeing from slavery. An equally distinguished senator from Massachusetts [Mr. Webster] unites with him in denouncing the aggressions of the North in this particular; and they both declare their determination to vote for the bill, with its amendments, now on file, and which has become a part of the "Compromise."

It may be well to look a little at the law as it now stands

on the subject, and then at the one which has enlisted such powerful support. By the Constitution alone, without any legislation, the slaveholder may go into a free state, take with him such force as he pleases, and take his slave and carry him back. If the fact of his slavery be disputed, either by the alleged slave or any one for him, the claimant may issue his writ de homine repligiando, and unless the defendant give ample bail for his forthcoming on the final issue, and for the payment of all costs and damages (which include the value of his services in the meantime), the plaintiff may take him into his possession, and retain him until final trial by a court and jury. Is not this sufficient? It is all the right which he would have if he claim property in a horse, or other property which he might allege had strayed over the line. Why should he have any greater right when he claims property in man? Is a man of so much less value than a horse, that he should be deprived of the ordinary protection of the law? Sir, in my judgment, the remedy ought to be left where the Constitution places it, without any legislation. The odious law of 1793 ought to be repealed.

By that law, the slaveholder may not only seize his slave and drag him back, but he may command the aid of all the officers of the United States Court; take his alleged slave before the judge, and after summary examination, without trial by jury, may obtain a certificate of property; which, for the purpose of removal, is conclusive of his slavery, takes away the writ of habeas corpus, and the right of trial by jury, and sends the victim to hopeless bondage. If an inhabitant of a free state see a wretched fugitive, who he learns is fleeing from bondage, and gives him a meal of victuals to keep him from starving, and allows him to sleep in his outhouse, although his master is not in pursuit of him, he is liable to the penalty of five hundred dollars. A judge in Pennsylvania lately held that a worthy citizen of Indiana County incurred such penalty by giving a cup of water and a crust of bread to a famishing man whom he knew to be fleeing from bondage. A slave family escaped from Maryland, went into Cumberland County, Pennsylvania, and obtained the reluctant consent of a worthy farmer to sleep in his hay-loft. Their owner did not pursue them for a week afterward. It was held by a State court that the farmer was liable for the full value of the slaves, besides the five hundred dollars penalty, and a jury returned a verdict for two thousand dollars and costs. Such are some of the provisions of the law of 1793 now in force, which these great expounders of constitutional freedom hold to be too mild! And more stringent laws are to be passed to punish Northern men who have hearts!

The distinguished senator from Kentucky [Mr. Clay] wishes further to make it the duty of all bystanders to aid in the capture of fugitives; to join the chase and run down the prey. This is asking more than my constituents will ever grant. They will strictly abide by the Constitution. The slaveholder may pursue his slave among them with his own foreign myrmidons, unmolested, except by their frowning scorn. But no law that tyranny can pass will ever induce them to join the hue and cry after the trembling wretch who has escaped from unjust bondage. Their fair land, made by nature and their own honest toil as fertile and as lovely as the vale of Tempe, shall never become the hunting-ground on which the bloodhounds of slavery shall course their prey, and command them to join in the hunt.

Sir, this tribunal would be more odious than the Star Chamber—these officers more hateful than the familiars of the Inquisition.

Can the free North stand this? Can New England stand it? Can Massachusetts stand it? If she can, she has but one step further to take in degradation, and that is to deliver her own sons in chains to Southern masters! What would the bold barons of Runnymede have said to such defenders of liberty? What would the advocates of English freedom, at any time, have said to those who would strike down the writ of habeas corpus and the right of trial by jury, those vital principles of Magna Charta and the Bill of Rights? They would have driven them forth as enemies in disguise.

Sir, I am aware of the temerity of these remarks. I know how little effect they will have, coming from so obscure a quarter, and being opposed by the mighty influences that create public opinion. I was struck with the sound sense of the remark made to-day by the gentleman from Tennessee [Mr. Gentry]. He said that the "Compromise" bill was winning favor with the people, most of whom had never read it, merely because it is advocated by great names in whom they are accustomed to confide.

Late events have convinced me that it were better in republican, representative governments, where the people are to judge and decide on every measure, if there were no great, overshadowing names, to give factitious force to their views, and lead the public mind captive. If the people were to put faith in no man's argument, they would examine every question for themselves, and decide according to their intrinsic merit. The errors of the small do but little harm; those of the great are fatal. Had Lucifer been but a common angel, instead of the chief of the morning stars, he had not taken with him to perdition the third of the heavenly hosts, and spread disunion and discord in celestial, and sin and misery in earthly, places.

Sir, so long as man is vain and fallible; so long as great men have like passions with others, and, as in republics, are surrounded with stronger temptations, it were better for themselves if their fame acquired no inordinate height, until the grave had precluded error. The errors of obscure men die with them, and cast no shame on their posterity. How different with the great!

How much better had it been for Lord Bacon, that greatest of human intellects, had he never, during his life, acquired glory, and risen to high honors in the state, than to be degraded from them by the judgment of his peers. How much better for him and his, had he lived and died unknown, than to be branded through all future time as the—

"Wisest, brightest, meanest of mankind."

So now, in this crisis of the fate of liberty, if any of the renowned men of this nation should betray her cause, it were better that they had been unknown to fame. It need not be hoped that the brightness of their past glory will dazzle the eyes of posterity, or illumine the pages of impartial history. A few of its rays may still linger on a fading sky; but they will soon be whelmed in the blackness of darkness. For, unless progressive civilization, and the increasing love of freedom throughout the Christian and civilized world, are fallacious, the sun of liberty, of universal liberty, is already above the horizon, and fast coursing to his meridian splendor, when no advocate of slavery, no apologist of slavery, can look upon his face and live.

CHARLES SUMNER

THE CRIME AGAINST KANSAS

[Charles Sumner, eminent American statesman, orator and author, and the greatest advocate of the anti-slavery cause in Congress, was born in Boston, January 6, 1811. Distinguished at school and college, he took his Harvard degree in 1830, and adopted the career of the law. He was better adapted for the literary side of legal practice, and employed much time in writing for legal papers and editing "The Jurist." In 1837 he went to Europe to study the judicial practice of foreign countries. On July 4, 1845, he delivered the annual oration before the civil authorities of Boston on "The True Grandeur of Nations," in which the impending war with Mexico was strongly condemned and the slave-power as the inciting cause of the war vigorously arraigned. Four months later he made in Faneuil Hall his first speech as an anti-slavery advocate. He took his seat in the upper house of the national Congress December 1, 1851, and became known as the champion of the anti-slavery sentiment in Congress. In February, 1854, he addressed the Senate on the Kansas-Nebraska Bill, and on the nineteenth and twentieth of May, 1856, delivered his speech, "The Crime Against Kansas," arousing opposition, to which he replied contemptuously, especially singling out Senators Butler and Douglas. The result was a personal attack in the Senate chamber, made by Preston S. Brooks, a nephew of Butler. Sumner seemed never to recover fully from this atrocious assault. He died at Washington in 1874. His style of oratory was classic and elegant, and he was a master in the use of polished yet piercing satire.]

MR. PRESIDENT, you are now called to redress a great transgression. Seldom in the history of nations has such a question been presented. Tariffs, army bills, navy bills, land bills, are important, and justly occupy your care; but these all belong to the course of ordinary legislation. As means and instruments only, they are necessarily subordinate to the conservation of government itself. Grant them or deny them, in greater or less degree, and you will inflict no shock. The machinery of government will continue to move. The State will not cease to exist. Far otherwise is it with the eminent question now before you, involving, as it does, liberty in a broad territory, and also involving the peace of the whole country, with our good name in history for evermore.

Take down your map, sir, and you will find that the Territory of Kansas, more than any other region, occupies the middle spot of North America, equally distant from the Atlantic on the east, and the Pacific on the west; from the frozen waters of Hudson's Bay on the north, and the tepid Gulf stream on the south, constituting the precise territorial center of the whole vast continent. To such advantages of situation, on the very highway between two oceans, are added a soil of unsurpassed richness, and a fascinating, undulating beauty of surface, with a health-giving climate, calculated to nurture a powerful and generous people, worthy to be a central pivot of American institutions. A few short months only have passed since this spacious and mediterranean country was open only to the savage who ran wild in its woods and prairies; and now it has already drawn to its bosom a population of freemen larger than Athens crowded within her historic gates, when her sons, under Miltiades, won liberty for mankind on the field of Marathon; more than Sparta contained when she ruled Greece, and sent forth her devoted children, quickened by a mother's benediction, to return with their shields, or on them; more than Rome gathered on her seven hills, when, under her kings, she commenced that sovereign sway, which afterward embraced the whole earth; more than London held, when, on the fields of Crecy and Agincourt, the English banner was carried victoriously over the chivalrous hosts of France.

Against this territory, thus fortunate in position and population, a crime has been committed, which is without example in the records of the past. Not in plundered provinces or in the cruelties of selfish governors will you find its parallel; and yet there is an ancient instance, which may show at least the path of justice. In the terrible impeachment by which the great Roman orator has blasted through all time the name of Verres, amid charges of robbery and sacrilege, the enormity which most aroused the indignant voice of his accuser, and which still stands forth with strongest distinctness, arresting the sympathetic indignation of all who read the story, is, that away in Sicily he had scourged a citizen of Rome—that the cry, "I am a Roman citizen," had been interposed in vain against the lash of the tyrant governor. Other charges were that he had carried away productions of art, and that he had violated the sacred shrines. It was in the presence of the Roman senate that this arraignment proceeded; in a temple of the forum; amid crowds—such as no orator had ever before drawn together —thronging the porticos and colonnades, even clinging to the housetops and neighboring slopes—and under the anxious gaze of witnesses summoned from the scene of crime. But an audience grander far—of higher dignity—of more various people, and of wider intelligence—the countless multitude of succeeding generations, in every land, where eloquence has been studied, or where the Roman name has been recognized—has listened to the accusation, and throbbed with condemnation of the criminal. Sir, speaking in an age of light, and a land of constitutional liberty, where the safeguards of elections are justly placed among the highest triumphs of civilization, I fearlessly assert that the wrongs of much-abused Sicily, thus memorable in history, were small by the side of the wrongs of Kansas, where the very shrines of popular institutions, more sacred than any heathen altar, have been desecrated; where the ballot-box, more precious than any work, in ivory or marble, from the cunning hand of art, has been plundered; and where the cry, "I am an American citizen," has been interposed in vain against outrage of every kind, even upon life itself. Are you against sacrilege? I present it for your execration. Are you against robbery? I hold it up to your scorn. Are you for the protection of American citizens? I show you how their dearest rights have been cloven down, while a tyrannical usurpation has sought to install itself on their very necks!

But the wickedness which I now begin to expose is immeasurably aggravated by the motive which prompted it. Not in any common lust for power did this uncommon tragedy have its origin. It is the rape of a virgin territory, compelling it to the hateful embrace of slavery; and it may be clearly traced to a depraved longing for a new Slave state,

CHARLES SUMNER

Photogravure after a painting

the hideous offspring of such a crime, in the hope of adding to the power of slavery in the national government. Yes, sir, when the whole world, alike Christian and Turk, is rising up to condemn this wrong, and to make it a hissing to the nations, here in our Republic, force—aye, sir, FORCE—has been openly employed in compelling Kansas to this pollution, and all for the sake of political power. There is the simple fact, which you will in vain attempt to deny, but which in itself presents an essential wickedness that makes other public crimes seem like public virtues.

But this enormity, vast beyond comparison, swells to dimensions of wickedness which the imagination toils in vain to grasp, when it is understood that for this purpose are hazarded the horrors of intestine feud, not only in this distant territory, but everywhere throughout the country. Already the muster has begun. The strife is no longer local, but national. Even now, while I speak, portents hang on all the arches of the horizon threatening to darken the broad land, which already yawns with the mutterings of civil war. The fury of the propagandists of slavery, and the calm determination of their opponents, are now diffused from the distant territory over widespread communities, and the whole country, in all its extent—marshaling hostile divisions, and foreshadowing a strife which, unless happily averted by the triumph of freedom, will become war—fratricidal, parricidal war—with an accumulated wickedness beyond the wickedness of any war in human annals, justly provoking the avenging judgment of Providence and the avenging pen of history, and constituting a strife, in the language of the ancient writer, more than foreign, more than social, more than civil; but something compounded of all these strifes, and in itself more than war; sed potius commune quoddam ex omnibus, et plus quam bellum.

Such is the crime which you are to judge. But the criminal also must be dragged into day, that you may see and measure the power by which all this wrong is sustained. From no common source could it proceed. In its perpetration was needed a spirit of vaulting ambition which would hesitate at nothing; a hardihood of purpose which was insensible to the judgment of mankind; a madness for slavery which would disregard the Constitution, the laws, and all the great examples of our history; also a consciousness of power such as comes from the habit of power; a combination of energies found only in a hundred arms directed by a hundred eyes; a control of public opinion through venal pens and a prostituted press; an ability to subsidize crowds in every vocation of life—the politician with his local importance, the lawyer with his subtle tongue, and even the authority of the judge on the bench; and a familiar use of men in places high and low, so that none, from the President to the lowest border postmaster, should decline to be its tool; all these things and more were needed, and they were found in the Slave-power of our Republic. There, sir, stands the criminal, all unmasked before you—heartless, grasping, and tyrannical—with an audacity beyond that of Verres, a subtlety beyond that of Machiavelli, a meanness beyond that of Bacon, and an ability beyond that of Hastings. Justice to Kansas can be secured only by the prostration of this influence; for this the power behind—greater than any President—which succors and sustains the crime. Nay, the proceedings I now arraign derive their fearful consequences only from this connection.

In now opening this great matter, I am not insensible to the austere demands of the occasion; but the dependence of the crime against Kansas upon the slave-power is so peculiar and important, that I trust to be pardoned while I impress it with an illustration, which to some may seem trivial. It is related in northern mythology that the god of Force, visiting an enchanted region, was challenged by his royal entertainer to what seemed a humble feat of strength—merely, sir, to lift a cat from the ground. The god smiled at the challenge, and, calmly placing his hand under the belly of the animal, with superhuman strength strove, while the back of the feline monster arched far upward, even beyond reach, and one paw actually forsook the earth, until at last the discomfited divinity desisted; but he was little surprised at his defeat when he learned that this creature, which seemed to be a cat, and nothing more, was not merely a cat, but that it belonged to and was a part of the great terrestrial serpent, which, in its innumerable folds, encircled the whole globe. Even so the creature, whose paws are now fastened upon Kansas, whatever it may seem to be, constitutes in reality a part of the Slave-power, which, in its loathsome folds, is now coiled about the whole land.   Thus do I expose the extent of the present contest, where we encounter not merely local resistance, but also the unconquered sustaining arm behind. But out of the vastness of the crime attempted, with all its woe and shame, I derive a well-founded assurance of a commensurate vastness of effort against it by the aroused masses of the country, determined not only to vindicate right against wrong, but to redeem the Republic from the thraldom of that oligarchy which prompts, directs, and concentrates the distant wrong.

Such is the crime, and such is the criminal, which it is my duty in this debate to expose, and, by the blessing of God, this duty shall be done completely to the end.

But, before entering upon the argument, I must say something of a general character, particularly in response to what has fallen from senators who have raised themselves to eminence on this floor in championship of human wrongs.   I mean the Senator from South Carolina [Mr. Butler] and the Senator from Illinois [Mr. Douglas], who, though unlike as Don Quixote and Sancho Panza, yet, like this couple, sally forth together in the same adventure.   I regret much to miss the elder senator from his seat; but the cause, against which he has run full tilt, with such activity of animosity, demands that the opportunity of exposing him should not be lost; and it is for the cause that I speak.   The Senator from South Carolina has read many books of chivalry, and believes himself a chivalrous knight, with sentiments of honor and courage.   Of course he has chosen a mistress to whom he has made his vows, and who, though ugly to others, is always lovely to him; though polluted in the sight of the world, is chaste in his sight—I mean the harlot, Slavery.   For her, his tongue is always profuse in words.   Let her be impeached in character, or any proposition made to shut her out from the extension of her wantonness, and no extravagance of manner or hardihood of assertion is then too great for this senator.   The frenzy of Don Quixote, in behalf of his wench, Dulcinea del Toboso, is all surpassed.   The asserted rights of slavery, which shock equality of all kinds, are cloaked by a fantastic claim of equality. If the Slave-states cannot enjoy what, in mockery of the great fathers of the republic, he misnames equality under the Constitution—in other words, the full power in the national territories to compel fellow-men to unpaid toil, to separate husband and wife, and to sell little children at the auction block—then, sir, the chivalric senator will conduct the State of South Carolina out of the Union! Heroic knight! Exalted senator! A second Moses come for a second exodus!

But not content with this poor menace, which we have been twice told was "measured," the senator, in the unrestrained chivalry of his nature, has undertaken to apply opprobrious words to those who differ from him on this floor. He calls them "sectional and fanatical"; and opposition to the usurpation in Kansas he denounces as "an uncalculating fanaticism." To be sure, these charges lack all grace of originality, and all sentiment of truth; but the adventurous senator does not hesitate. He is the uncompromising, unblushing representative on this floor of a flagrant sectionalism, which now domineers over the Republic, and yet with a ludicrous ignorance of his own position —unable to see himself as others see him—or with an effrontery which even his white head ought not to protect from rebuke, he applies to those here who resist his sectionalism the very epithet which designates himself. The men who strive to bring back the government to its original policy, when freedom and not slavery was sectional, he arraigns as sectional. This will not do. It involves too great a perversion of terms. I tell that senator that it is to himself, and to the "organization" of which he is the "committed advocate," that this epithet belongs. I now fasten it upon them. For myself, I care little for names; but since the question has been raised here, I affirm that the Republican party of the Union is in no just sense sectional, but, more than any other party, national; and that it now goes forth to dislodge from the high places of the government the tyrannical sectionalism of which the senator from South Carolina is one of the maddest zealots.

As the Senator from South Carolina is the Don Quixote, the Senator from Illinois [Mr. Douglas] is the squire of slavery, its very Sancho Panza, ready to do all its humiliating offices. This senator, in his labored address, vindicating his labored report—piling one mass of elaborate error upon another mass—constrained himself, as you will remember, to unfamiliar decencies of speech. Of that address I have nothing to say at this moment, though before I sit down I shall show something of its fallacies. But I go back now to an earlier occasion, when, true to his native impulses, he threw into this discussion, "for a charm of powerful trouble," personalities most discreditable to this body. I will not stop to repel the imputations which he cast upon myself; but I mention them to remind you of the "sweltered venom sleeping not," which, with other poisoned ingredients, he cast into the caldron of this debate. Of other things I speak. Standing on this floor, the senator issued his rescript, requiring submission to the usurped power of Kansas; and this was accompanied by a manner —all his own—such as befits the tyrannical threat. Very well. Let the senator try. I tell him now that he cannot enforce any such submission. The senator, with the slave-power at his back, is strong; but he is not strong enough for this purpose. He is bold. He shrinks from nothing. Like Danton he may cry, "l'audace! l'audace! toujours l'audace!" but even his audacity cannot compass this work. The senator copies the British officer who, with boastful swagger, said that with the hilt of his sword he would cram the "stamps" down the throats of the American people, and he will meet a similar failure. He may convulse this country with a civil feud. Like the ancient madman, he may set fire to this temple of constitutional liberty, grander than the Ephesian dome; but he cannot enforce obedience to that tyrannical usurpation.

The senator dreams that he can subdue the North. He disclaims the open threat, but his conduct still implies it. How little that senator knows himself or the strength of the cause which he persecutes! He is but a mortal man; against him is an immortal principle. With finite power he wrestles with the infinite, and he must fall. Against him are stronger battalions than any marshaled by mortal arm—the inborn, ineradicable, invincible sentiments of the human heart; against him is nature in all her subtle forces; against him is God. Let him try to subdue these.

With regret, I come again upon the Senator from South Carolina [Mr. Butler], who, omnipresent in this debate, overflowed with rage at the simple suggestion that Kansas had applied for admission as a state; and, with incoherent phrases, discharged the loose expectoration of his speech, now upon her representative, and then upon her people. There was no extravagance of the ancient parliamentary debate which he did not repeat; nor was there any possible deviation from truth which he did not make, with so much of passion, I am glad to add, as to save him from the suspicion of intentional aberration. But the senator touches nothing which he does not disfigure—with error, sometimes of principle, sometimes of fact. He shows an incapacity of accuracy, whether in stating the Constitution or in stating the law; whether in the details of statistics or the diversions of scholarship. He cannot ope his mouth, but out there flies a blunder. Surely he ought to be familiar with the life of Franklin; and yet he referred to this household character, while acting as agent of our fathers in England, as above suspicion; and this was done that he might give point to a false contrast with the agent of Kansas—not knowing that, however they may differ in genius and fame, in this experience they are alike; that Franklin, when entrusted with the petition of Massachusetts Bay, was assaulted by a foul-mouthed speaker, where he could not be heard in defense, and denounced as a "thief," even as the agent of Kansas has been assaulted on this floor, and denounced as a "forger." And let not the vanity of the senator be inspired by the parallel with the British statesman of that day; for it is only in hostility to freedom that any parallel can be recognized.

But it is against the people of Kansas that the sensibilities of the senator are particularly aroused. Coming, as he announces, "from a state"—aye, sir, from South Carolina —he turns with lordly disgust from this newly-formed community, which he will not recognize even as a "body politic." Pray, sir, by what title does he indulge in this egotism? Has he read the history of "the state" which he represents? He cannot surely have forgotten its shameful imbecility from slavery, confessed throughout the Revolution, followed by its more shameful assumptions for slavery since. He cannot have forgotten its wretched persistence in the Slave-trade as the very apple of its eye, and the condition of its participation in the Union. He cannot have forgotten its Constitution, which is republican only in name, confirming power in the hands of the few, and founding the qualifications of its legislators on "a settled freehold estate and ten negroes." And yet the senator, to whom that "state" has in part committed the guardianship of its good name, instead of moving, with backward-treading steps, to cover its nakedness, rushes forward in the very ecstasy of madness, to expose it by provoking a comparison with Kansas. South Carolina is old; Kansas is young. South Carolina counts by centuries, where Kansas counts by years. But a beneficent example may be born in a day; and I venture to say, that against the two centuries of the older "state," may be already set the two years of trial, evolving corresponding virtue, in the younger community. In the one, is the long wail of slavery; in the other, the hymns of freedom. And if we glance at special achievements, it will be difficult to find anything in the history of South Carolina which presents so much of heroic spirit in a heroic cause as appears in that repulse of the Missouri invaders by the beleaguered town of Lawrence, where even the women gave their effective efforts to freedom. The matrons of Rome, who poured their jewels into the treasury for the public defense—the wives of Prussia, who, with delicate fingers, clothed their defenders against French invasion—the mothers of our own Revolution, who sent forth their sons, covered with prayers and blessings, to combat for human rights, did nothing of self-sacrifice truer than did these women on this occasion. Were the whole history of South Carolina blotted out of existence, from its very beginning down to the day of the last election of the senator to his present seat on this floor, civilization might lose—I do not say how little; but surely less than it has already gained by the example of Kansas, in its valiant struggle against oppression, and in the development of a new science of emigration. Already, in Lawrence alone, there are newspapers and schools, including a high school, and throughout this infant territory there is more mature scholarship far, in proportion to its inhabitants, than in all South Carolina. Ah.

sir, I tell the senator that Kansas, welcomed as a free state, will be a "ministering angel" to the Republic, when South Carolina, in the cloak of darkness which she hugs, "lies howling."

The Senator from Illinois [Mr. Douglas] naturally joins the Senator from South Carolina in this warfare, and gives to it the superior intensity of his nature. He thinks that the national government has not completely proved its power, as it has never hanged a traitor; but, if the occasion requires, he hopes there will be no hesitation; and this threat is directed at Kansas, and even at the friends of Kansas throughout the country. Again occurs the parallel with the struggle of our fathers, and I borrow the language of Patrick Henry, when, to the cry from the senator, of "Treason! treason!" I reply, "If this be treason, make the most of it." Sir, it is easy to call names; but I beg to tell the senator that if the word "traitor" is in any way applicable to those who refuse submission to a tyrannical usurpation, whether in Kansas or elsewhere, then must some new word, of deeper color, be invented, to designate those mad spirits who could endanger and degrade the Republic, while they betray all the cherished sentiments of the fathers and the spirit of the Constitution, in order to give new spread to slavery. Let the senator proceed. It will not be the first time in history that a scaffold erected for punishment has become a pedestal of honor. Out of death comes life, and the "traitor" whom he blindly executes will live immortal in the cause.

> " For humanity sweeps onward ; where to-day the martyr stands,
> On the morrow crouches Judas, with the silver in his hands ;
> While the hooting mob of yesterday in silent awe return,
> To glean up the scattered ashes into History's golden urn."

Among these hostile senators, there is yet another, with all the prejudices of the senator from South Carolina, but without his generous impulses, who, on account of his character before the country, and the rancor of his opposition, deserves to be named. I mean the Senator from Virginia [Mr. Mason], who, as the author of the Fugitive Slave bill, has associated himself with a special act of inhumanity and tyranny. Of him I shall say little, for he has said little in this debate, though within that little was compressed the bitterness of a life absorbed in the support of slavery. He holds the commission of Virginia; but he does not represent that early Virginia, so dear to our hearts, which gave to us the pen of Jefferson, by which the equality of men was declared, and the sword of Washington, by which independence was secured; but he represents that other Virginia, from which Washington and Jefferson now avert their faces, where human beings are bred as cattle for the shambles, and where a dungeon rewards the pious matron who teaches little children to relieve their bondage by reading the Book of Life. It is proper that such a Senator, representing such a State, should rail against free Kansas.

Senators such as these are the natural enemies of Kansas, and I introduce them with reluctance, simply that the country may understand the character of the hostility which must be overcome. Arrayed with them, of course, are all who unite, under any pretext or apology, in the propagandism of human slavery. To such, indeed, the time-honored safeguards of popular rights can be a name only, and nothing more. What are trial by jury, habeas corpus, the ballot-box, the right of petition, the liberty of Kansas, your liberty, sir, or mine, to one who lends himself, not merely to the support at home, but to the propagandism abroad, of that preposterous wrong, which denies even the right of a man to himself! Such a cause can be maintained only by a practical subversion of all rights. It is, therefore, merely according to reason that its partisans should uphold the usurpation in Kansas.

To overthrow this usurpation is now the special, importunate duty of Congress, admitting of no hesitation or postponement. To this end it must lift itself from the cabals of candidates, the machinations of party, and the low level of vulgar strife. It must turn from that slave oligarchy which now controls the Republic, and refuse to be its tool. Let its power be stretched forth toward this distant territory, not to bind, but to unbind; not for the oppression of the weak, but for the subversion of the tyrannical; not for the prop and maintenance of a revolting usurpation, but for the confirmation of liberty.

"These are imperial arts and worthy thee!"

Let it now take its stand between the living and dead, and cause this plague to be stayed. All this it can do; and if the interests of slavery did not oppose, all this it would do at once, in reverent regard for justice, law, and order, driving away all the alarms of war; nor would it dare to brave the shame and punishment of this great refusal. But the Slave-power dares anything; and it can be conquered only by the united masses of the people. From Congress to the people I appeal.

The contest, which, beginning in Kansas, has reached us, will soon be transferred from Congress to a broader stage, where every citizen will be not only spectator, but actor; and to their judgment I confidently appeal. To the people, now on the eve of exercising the electoral franchise, in choosing a Chief Magistrate of the Republic, I appeal, to vindicate the electoral franchise in Kansas. Let the ballot-box of the Union, with multitudinous might, protect the ballot-box in that territory. Let the voters everywhere, while rejoicing in their own rights, help to guard the equal rights of distant fellow-citizens; that the shrines of popular institutions, now desecrated, may be sanctified anew; that the ballot-box, now plundered, may be restored; and that the cry, "I am an American citizen," may not be sent forth in vain against outrage of every kind. In just regard for free labor in that territory, which it is sought to blast by unwelcome association with Slave-labor; in Christian sympathy with the slave, whom it is proposed to task and sell there; in stern condemnation of the crime which has been consummated on that beautiful soil; in rescue of fellow-citizens now subjugated to a tyrannical usurpation; in dutiful respect for the early fathers, whose aspirations are now ignobly thwarted; in the name of the Constitution, which has been outraged—of the laws trampled down—of justice banished—of humanity degraded—of peace destroyed—of freedom crushed to earth; and in the name of the Heavenly Father, whose service is perfect freedom, I make this last appeal.

[This portion of Mr. Sumner's speech was concluded on May 19, 1856. On the following day Mr. Douglas replied, Mr. Sumner in turn replying to the Senator from Illinois.]

Mr. Douglas.—I shall not detain the Senate by a de-

tailed reply to the speech of the Senator from Massachusetts.   Indeed, I should not deem it necessary to say one
word, but for the personalities in which he has indulged,
evincing a depth of malignity that issued from every sentence, making it a matter of self-respect with me to repel
the assaults which have been made.

As to the argument, we have heard it all before.   Not
a position, not a fact, not an argument has he used, which
has not been employed on the same side of the Chamber,
and replied to by me twice.   I shall not follow him, therefore, because it would only be repeating the same answer
which I have twice before given to each of his positions.
He seems to get up a speech as in Yankee-land they get up
a bed-quilt.   They take all the old calico dresses of various
colors, that have been in the house from the days of their
grandmothers, and invite the young ladies of the neighborhood in the afternoon, and the young men to meet them at
a dance in the evening.   They cut up these pieces of old
dresses and make pretty figures, and boast of what beautiful ornamental work they have made, although there was not
a new piece of material in the whole quilt.   Thus it is with
the speech which we have had rehashed here to-day, in regard
to matters of fact, matters of law, and matters of argument
—everything but the personal assaults and the malignity.

His endeavor seems to be an attempt to whistle to keep
up his courage by defiant assaults upon us all.   I am in
doubt as to what can be his object.   He has not hesitated
to charge three-fourths of the Senate with fraud, with swin-
dling, with crime, with infamy, at least one hundred times
over in his speech.   Is it his object to provoke some of us
to kick him as we would a dog in the street, that he may
get sympathy upon the just chastisement?   What is the
object of this denunciation against the body of which we
are members?   A hundred times he has called the Nebraska
bill a "swindle," an act of crime, an act of infamy, and
each time went on to illustrate the complicity of each man
who voted for it in perpetrating the crime.   He has brought
it home as a personal charge to those who passed the
Nebraska bill, that they were guilty of a crime which de-
served the just indignation of heaven, and should make
them infamous among men.

Who are the senators thus arraigned? He does me the honor to make me the chief. It was my good luck to have such a position in this body as to enable me to be the author of a great, wise measure, which the Senate has approved, and the country will endorse. That measure was sustained by about three-fourths of all the members of the Senate. It was sustained by a majority of the Democrats and a majority of the Whigs in this body. It was sustained by a majority of senators from the slaveholding states, and a majority of senators from the free states. The senator, by his charge of crime, then, stultifies three-fourths of the whole body, a majority of the North, nearly the whole South, a majority of Whigs, and a majority of Democrats here. He says they are infamous. If he so believed, who could suppose that he would ever show his face among such a body of men? How dare he approach one of those gentlemen to give him his hand after that act? If he felt the courtesies between men he would not do it. He would deserve to have himself spit in the face for doing so.

The attack of the Senator from Massachusetts now is not on me alone. Even the courteous and the accomplished Senator from South Carolina [Mr. Butler] could not be passed by in his absence.

Mr. Mason.—Advantage was taken of it.

Mr. Douglas.—It is suggested that advantage is taken of his absence. I think that this is a mistake. I think the speech was written and practised, and the gestures fixed; and if that part had been stricken out the senator would not have known how to repeat the speech. All that tirade of abuse must be brought down on the head of the venerable, the courteous, and the distinguished Senator from South Carolina. I shall not defend that gentleman here. Every senator who knows him loves him. The Senator from Massachusetts may take every charge made against him in his speech, and may verify by his oath, and by the oath of every one of his confederates, and there is not an honest man in this Chamber who will not repel it as a slander. Your oaths cannot make a senator feel that it was not an outrage to assail the honorable gentleman in the terms in which he has been attacked. He, however, will be here in due time to speak for himself, and to act for himself, too. I know what will happen. The Senator from Massachusetts will go to him, whisper a secret apology in his ear, and ask him to accept that as satisfaction for a public outrage on his character! I know the Senator from Massachusetts is in the habit of doing those things. I have had some experience of his skill in that respect.

Why these attacks on individuals by name, and two-thirds of the Senate collectively? Is it the object to drive men here to dissolve social relations with political opponents? Is it to turn the Senate into a bear-garden, where senators cannot associate on terms which ought to prevail between gentlemen? These attacks are heaped upon me by man after man. When I repel them, it is intimated that I show some feeling on the subject. Sir, God grant that when I denounce an act of infamy I shall do it with feeling, and do it under the sudden impulses of feeling, instead of sitting up at night writing out my denunciation of a man whom I hate, copying it, having it printed, punctuating the proof-sheets, and repeating it before the glass, in order to give refinement to insult, which is only pardonable when it is the outburst of a just indignation.

Mr. President, I shall not occupy the time of the Senate. I dislike to be forced to repel these attacks upon myself, which seem to be repeated on every occasion. It appears that gentlemen on the other side of the Chamber think they would not be doing justice to their cause if they did not make myself a personal object of bitter denunciation and malignity. I hope that the debate on this bill may be brought to a close at as early a day as possible. I shall do no more in these side discussions than vindicate myself and repel unjust attacks, but I shall ask the Senate to permit me to close the debate, when it shall close, in a calm, kind summary of the whole question, avoiding personalities.

Mr. Sumner.—Mr. President: To the Senator from Illinois, I should willingly leave the privilege of the common scold—the last word; but I will not leave to him, in any discussion with me, the last argument, or the last semblance of it. He has crowned the audacity of this debate by venturing to rise here and calumniate me. He said that I came here, took an oath to support the Constitution, and yet determined not to support a particular clause in that

Constitution. To that statement I give, to his face, the flattest denial. When it was made on a former occasion on this floor by the absent Senator from South Carolina [Mr. Butler], I then repelled it. I will read from the debate of the twenty-eighth of June, 1854, as published in the "Globe," to show what I said in response to that calumny when pressed at that hour. Here is what I said to the Senator from South Carolina:

"This senator was disturbed when to his inquiry, personally, pointedly, and vehemently addressed to me, whether I would join in returning a fellow-man to slavery, I exclaimed, 'Is thy servant a dog, that he should do this thing?'"

You will observe that the inquiry of the Senator from South Carolina was whether I would join in returning a fellow-man to slavery. It was not whether I would support any clause of the Constitution of the United States—far from that.

Sir, this is the Senate of the United States, an important body, under the Constitution, with great powers. Its members are justly supposed, from age, to be above the intemperance of youth, and from character to be above the lusts of vulgarity. They are supposed to have something of wisdom, and something of that candor which is the handmaid of wisdom. Let the senator bear these things in mind, and let him remember hereafter that the bowie-knife and bludgeon are not the proper emblems of senatorial debate. Let him remember that the swagger of Bob Acres and the ferocity of the Malay cannot add dignity to this body. The senator has gone on to infuse into his speech the venom which has been sweltering for months—ay, for years; and he has alleged facts that are entirely without foundation, in order to heap upon me some personal obloquy. I will not go into the details which have flowed out so naturally from his tongue. I only brand them to his face as false. I say, also, to that senator, and I wish him to bear in mind, that no person with the upright form of man can be allowed—[Hesitation.]

Mr. Douglas.—Say it.

Mr. Sumner.—I will say it—no person with the upright form of man can be allowed, without violation to all decency, to switch out from his tongue the perpetual stench of offensive personality. Sir, that is not a proper weapon of debate, at least, on this floor. The noisome, squat, and nameless animal, to which I now refer, is not a proper model for an American senator. Will the Senator from Illinois take notice?

Mr. Douglas.—I will; and therefore will not imitate you, sir.

Mr. Sumner.—I did not hear the Senator.

Mr. Douglas.—I said if that be the case I would certainly never imitate you in that capacity, recognizing the force of the illustration.

Mr. Sumner.—Mr. President, again the Senator has switched his tongue, and again he fills the Senate with his offensive odor.

Mr. Douglas.—I am not going to pursue this subject further. I will only say that a man who has been branded by me in the Senate, and convicted by the Senate of falsehood, cannot use language requiring a reply, and therefore I have nothing more to say.

124

TECUMSEH

SPEECH AT VINCENNES

[Tecumseh, the Shawanee warrior and orator, was born near the Scioto River about the year 1768. His first recorded exploit was an attack at Hacker's Creek in May 1792, upon the family of John Waggoner, whom he carried into captivity. From that time he engaged in many incursions upon the white settlements and interfered with traffic upon the Ohio River. It is said that in 1806 he formed the project of a general rising of the Indians against the Americans. He became an ally of the British in the War of 1812, and was ranked a brigadier-general. He fought with distinction at the battle of Brownstown and Maguaga in August 1812. In the battle of the Thames, on October 5, 1813, he fought under the British General Proctor and made a gallant stand against the American troops, but met his death before the end of the engagement. The first of the ensuing speeches was made at Vincennes, Ind., in 1810, on the sale of lands to Governor Harrison; the second was addressed to General Proctor in 1813, shortly before the battle of the Thames.]

IT is true I am a Shawanee. My forefathers were warriors. Their son is a warrior. From them I only take my existence; from my tribe I take nothing. I am the maker of my own fortune; and oh! that I could make that of my red people, and of my country, as great as the conceptions of my mind, when I think of the Spirit that rules the universe. I would not then come to Governor Harrison, to ask him to tear the treaty and to obliterate the landmark; but I would say to him: Sir, you have liberty to return to your own country. The being within, communing with past ages, tells me that once, nor until lately, there was no white man on this continent. That it then all belonged to red men, children of the same parents, placed on it by the Great Spirit that made them, to keep it, to traverse it, to enjoy its productions, and to fill it with the same race. Once a happy race. Since made miserable by the white people, who are never contented, but always encroaching.   The way, and the only way, to check and to stop this evil, is for all the red men to unite in claiming a common and equal right in the land, as it was at first, and should be yet; for it never was divided, but belongs to all for the use of each.   That no part has a right to sell, even to each other, much less to strangers; those who want all, and will not do with less.

The white people have no right to take the land from the Indians, because they had it first; it is theirs.   They may sell, but all must join.   Any sale not made by all is not valid.   The late sale is bad.   It was made by a part only.   Part do not know how to sell.   It requires all to make a bargain for all.   All red men have equal rights to the unoccupied land.   The right of occupancy is as good in one place as in another.   There cannot be two occupa- tions in the same place.   The first excludes all others.   It is not so in hunting or traveling; for there the same ground will serve many, as they may follow each other all day; but the camp is stationary, and that is occupancy.   It belongs to the first who sits down on his blanket or skins which he has thrown upon the ground; and till he leaves it no other has a right.

[Having thus explained his reasons against the validity of the purchase, Tecumseh took his seat amidst his war- riors.]

SPEECH TO GENERAL PROCTOR

FATHER: Listen to your children! you have them now all before you.   The war before this our British father gave the hatchet to his red children, when old chiefs were alive.   They are now dead.   In that war our father was thrown on his back by the Americans, and our father took them by the hand without our knowledge; and we are afraid that our father will do so again at this time.

Summer before last, when I came forward with my red brethren, and was ready to take up the hatchet, in favor of our British father, we were told not to be in a hurry, that he had not yet determined to fight the Americans.

Listen! When war was declared, our father stood up

and gave us the tomahawk, and told us that he was ready to strike the Americans; that he wanted our assistance, and that he would certainly get us our lands back, which the Americans had taken from us.

Listen! You told us, at that time, to bring forward our families to this place, and we did so; and you promised to take care of them, and that they should want for nothing, while the men would go and fight the enemy. That we need not trouble ourselves about the enemy's garrisons; that we knew nothing about them, and that our father would attend to that part of the business. You also told your red children that you would take good care of your garrison here, which made our hearts glad.

Listen! When we were last at the Rapids, it is true we gave you little assistance. It is hard to fight people who live like ground-hogs.

Father, listen! Our fleet has gone out; we know they have fought; we have heard the great guns, but know nothing of what has happened to our father with one arm. Our ships have gone one way, and we are much astonished to see our father tying up everything and preparing to run away the other, without letting his red children know what his intentions are. You always told us to remain here and take care of our lands. It made our hearts glad to hear that was your wish. Our great father, the king, is the head, and you represent him. You always told us that you would never draw your foot off British ground; but now, father, we see you are drawing back, and we are sorry to see our father doing so without seeing the enemy. We must compare our father's conduct to a fat animal that carries its tail upon its back, but when affrighted, it drops it between its legs and runs off.

Listen, Father! The Americans have not yet defeated us by land; neither are we sure that they have done so by water—we therefore wish to remain here and fight our enemy, should they make their appearance. If they defeat us, we will then retreat with our father.

At the battle of the Rapids, last war, the Americans certainly defeated us; and when we retreated to our father's fort in that place, the gates were shut against us. We were afraid that it would now be the case, but instead of that, we now see our British father preparing to march out of his garrison.

Father! You have got the arms and ammunition which our great father sent for his red children. If you have an idea of going away, give them to us, and you may go and welcome, for us. Our lives are in the hands of the Great Spirit. We are determined to defend our lands, and if it is his will, we wish to leave our bones upon them.

LOUIS ADOLPHE THIERS

MEXICO AND LOUIS NAPOLEON'S POLICY

[Louis Adolphe Thiers, a French historical writer and statesman, distinguished also for his eloquence, was born in Marseilles in 1797. He received an excellent education and, after studying law, entered journalism in Paris. His success made him a man to be reckoned with, especially after the appearance of his "History of the French Revolution," which he supplemented in later years with a "History of the Consulate and Empire." Meanwhile he had entered political life, leaped to distinction as an orator, served in the Cabinet and as premier, and been elected to the French Academy. He was a Liberal with Republican leanings, and suffered banishment for a time under the second empire, which he accused of loss of prestige abroad. Made head of the provisional government after the disaster of 1870, he became president of the French Republic upon the adoption of the Constitution. He held the office two years and died in 1877. The ensuing speech was delivered in the French Assembly in 1865, criticising the vast outlay of money on public improvements instituted by Napoleon III.]

GENTLEMEN: When I last year had the honor of addressing you for the first time on the state of our finances, I endeavored to give a retrospective view of them for the last twenty years, and to show from what causes our expenditure had risen in the last few years from about 1,500 millions to nearly 2,300 millions. To me the causes are evident enough; and had there been any doubt, the propositions now made to us would suffice to remove it. Within the last fortnight 360 millions have been demanded for France in general, and 250 for Paris; in all, 610 millions. It is said that a law is now under consideration in the Council of State demanding 100 or 200 millions more, making 700 or 800 millions in the space of a few weeks. I need not dwell on the causes of the increase of our budgets; I will only make a concise statement concerning them. I will afterward show the financial situation which those causes have produced; in short, I will attempt to present a balance sheet of our finances. I believe you will agree with me in thinking that the causes are these: Since our new institutions have diminished the share which our nation took in managing its own affairs, it was feared that the activity of mind with which I am reproached might be dangerous, unless means should be found to occupy the attention of the country. These means, sometimes dangerous, always odious, have been wars abroad, and enormous expenditure and great speculations at home. After great wars came small ones—small, if we consider the number of men engaged, but large if we consider their distance and the serious complications they may cause. The war in Mexico has already cost us more than the Italian war, to say nothing of the complications it may entail. The war expenditure has, of course, been met by loans, and the public debt has consequently been considerably increased. Next come our great public works, an excellent employment for the country's savings in time of peace, as every sensible man will acknowledge; but we ought to proceed prudently. It is a mistake to suppose, as some do, that there need be no limit to the application of our savings to public works; agriculture and manufactures ought to have their share, and if only a portion should be employed by the state in improving roads, canals, and other means of communication, still less should be devoted to the mere embellishment of towns. It is certainly necessary to widen the streets and improve the salubrity of cities, but there is no necessity for such vast changes as have been operated in Paris, where, as I think, all reasonable limits have been exceeded. The contagion of example is to be feared. The proverb says that he who commits one folly is wise. If Paris only were to be rebuilt, I should not have much to say against it, but you know what La Fontaine wittily says :—

> *"Tout bourgeois veut bâtir comme le grand seigneur,*
> *Tout petit prince a des ambassadeurs,*
> *Tout marquis veut avoir des pages."*

The glory of the prefect of the Seine has troubled the repose of all the prefects. The prefect of the Seine has rebuilt the Tuileries, and the prefect of the Bouches-du-Rhône wants to have his Tuileries also. Last year the minister of state answered me that only a trifling expenditure was intended, not more than six millions; but it appears from the debates of the council-general that the expense will be twelve or fourteen millions, and some persons say as much as twenty millions. I know that the prefect of the Bouches-du-Rhône is a senator; but if it takes twelve millions to build him a residence, that is a large sum. All the other prefects will be eager to follow his example, as the prefect of Lisle has already. The sub-prefects, also, will want new residences and new furniture. Where would all this lead to? The minister of public works, full of glory, must have more consideration for the cares of the minister of finance. But here we have a new minister of public works with a new glory to make, and demands for millions multiply. The minister of finance defends himself as best he can, but appears to be conquered; he might resist by resigning, certainly; but that is a means borrowed from past days. A compromise is at last effected. To spare the treasury, one hundred millions are to be obtained by selling part of the state forests. For this, however, your consent is necessary; but the matter is settled in principle, and the public domain will supply the funds which the treasury refuses. By whom is this torrent of expenditure to be arrested? By yourselves, gentlemen; your wisdom, patriotism, and courage can alone achieve the task. Your responsibility is great, especially in financial matters; in politics, your powers may be contested to a certain extent; but in questions of finance they are undisputed. In finances, you, therefore, are responsible for everything. It is time to halt in this course of expenditure, and not to imitate those sinners who are always talking of reforming and after all die in final impenitence.

We are often told that financial science is obscure; but the assertion is untrue. Sciences are never obscure, except through the dulness of those who expound them, or the charlatanism of those who assume a false air of profundity. I will take my examples from private life. Let us suppose two fathers, one methodical, strict, and somewhat morose; the other easy and good-natured. The former will regulate

his expenditure according to his income, and fix limits which
he will not pass; during the year this may cause some un-
pleasantness to himself and his family, but when settling
day comes he has neither anxiety nor embarrassment. The
latter takes no such precautions; he passes quietly through
the year, restricting neither his own expenditure nor that of
his family; but when he settles his accounts he finds that
he has exceeded his income, and is obliged to encroach on
his capital to pay his debts; and thus goes on from year to
year with ever increasing embarrassment till ruin stares him
in the face. The stern father, meanwhile, has preserved or
even increased his estate, and taught his children that which
will be useful to them through life. As in private life, so
it is in public affairs. Statesmen have the same passions as
other men, and it is only by resisting these passions that
they can save the state. I will now apply these reflections
to our finances. What is the principle which governs their
administration? You have five budgets, and I will show
the consequences of this multiplicity. First, there is the
ordinary one, which ranges from 1,370 to 1,780 millions;
this year it is 1,700 millions. Then there is a special budget
for the departments and communes, varying from 230 to 240
millions. Next comes the extraordinary budget, from 120 to
140 millions. But that is not all. As the budget is voted a
year beforehand, all expenses have not been foreseen, and at
the end of the year a rectificative budget of one hundred millions is required: so that the total budget exceeds 2,200
millions. Then, when the final settlement comes, it is found
that certain expenses have exceeded the credits voted, while
other credits have not been employed; the latter are made set-
offs against the former, but there is always a balance required
of from twenty to eighty millions which has to be voted by
special laws. The budget is thus raised to 2,200 millions
or more; in 1863 it was 2,292 millions. Such is the figure
we reach with our five budgets; and then, like the father
above mentioned, we have to strike the final balance. This
is done by the Court of Accounts, and when the result is
submitted to the chamber, if there be an excess of expenditure, the floating debt is increased by so much. Last year
you made a loan of 360 millions, and it will be exhausted
next year. This is how the budget has risen to between

2,200 and 2,300 millions. Last year M. de Vuitry, president of the council of state, told me that it would be a childish expedient to divide the budgets for the purpose of deceiving the chamber as to their total amount, seeing that the general situation might be ascertained by adding together a few figures. I replied that it took me two months to make those additions, and, if I mistake not, the reporter has found three months to be necessary this year, though he had numerous documents at his disposal, which those who are not members of the committee have never seen. Your reporter, indeed, has had confidential communications from the Ministry of Finance, which inform him of things he cannot repeat to us. We have not the information we ought to have, and yet the reporter required three months to work the little sum in addition, to which the president of the council of state alluded. It has been said: "Calumniate! Calumniate! some of your calumnies are sure to remain!" We may say: " Dissimulate! Dissimulate! something is sure to remain!" We will now see whether the plan of dividing the budget is not a means of creating illusions as to the true amount of the expenditure. The Honorable M. Gouin yesterday said that the budget was really 1,571 millions. When the law of accounts comes before us, that budget will be 2,300 millions. Were there any good reason for thus dividing the budget I would not object to it. Why should there be one budget for the state and another for the departments and communes, when all the expenditure is paid from the same treasury and made under the same responsibility? Separate budgets may be reasonable enough in Austria, which contains distinct kingdoms and provinces, but there is nothing to justify them in France. Then, there is another illusion, that of the ordinary and extraordinary budgets. When thousands of millions were concerned, as in the first establishment of railways, there was some reason for an extraordinary budget; but when the expenditure is only for ameliorations which may be effected gradually, it can only tend to dissimulate real expenses. The extraordinary budget contains the expenditure for repairs, which must always be a permanent item; why should it, then, not be put in the ordinary budget? I also see in it sums of five and six millions for the Ministry of War, which ought cer-

FRENCH CHAMBER OF DEPUTIES

Photogravure after a photograph

tainly to be considered ordinary expenditure. In the extraordinary budget of the Marine I see a sum of twelve and one-half millions for the arsenals, which ought certainly to be considered an ordinary item. But we are told that it was required for the transformation of our navy into ironclads. I have seen three of these transformations in the course of forty years, and therefore see no reason for calling it an extraordinary expenditure.

In the Ministry of Public Works I find five millions for improving the high-roads, but all such outlay has hitherto been considered ordinary expenditure. Then comes the large sum of thirty-three millions for payment to railways as guaranty of interest, but some parts of these payments will last eighty years, other parts twenty and forty years, and therefore ought to be in the ordinary budget. The only use of the extraordinary budget seems to be to make the ordinary budget appear less, and give it a more favorable appearance when compared with the ordinary revenue. M. Gouin says that our ordinary budget being 1,900 millions and our revenue of the same amount, there is an equilibrium. But even when viewed in that light, there is still a deficit of thirty millions. The division into ordinary and extraordinary budgets serves to put the real receipts in comparison with what are called ordinary expenses. As to the other expenses, they are met by instalments or other means. The rectificative budget also serves to diminish the apparent amount of the ordinary budget. The system of rectificative budgets is justified by alleging the impossibility of providing for all necessary expenditure a year in advance. I admit the necessity of supplementary credits; but even to justify them the expenditure to which they correspond ought to be really expenses in some degree expected. An eminent member of the old chamber, M. Le Pelletier d'Aulnay, was a severe critic of supplementary credits. But I repeat that the grand principle of such credits is the unforeseen. We have the rectificative budget of 1865. Well, gentlemen, read it; and see if it is composed of expenses impossible to foresee. Out of eighty millions there are sixty for the occupation of Rome, for Cochin China, and for Mexico. Can it be said that last year nobody foresaw that we should have to pay all this in the present year? And, doubtless, the minister of finance last year never anticipated that he should have to remove the postoffice to the Rue de Rivoli, for which he is now obliged to ask six millions. Was I not, therefore, right in calling the rectificative budget an extraordinary budget deferred? The expenses of this budget are met by augmentations of receipts—sometimes, but not always, realized; by the Mexican securities, the great resource of the moment; and, lastly, by annulments. Then comes the liquidation, when fresh expenses are discovered, ordinarily discharged by annulments, but these last are found to be exhausted. That is the way in which a budget of 1,900 millions is swelled to one of 2,200 or 2,300 millions. The form in which a budget is presented is of great importance; the present system enables people to say that we are nearly in equilibrium when we are very far removed from it. Let us take as an example the last three years. The budget of 1862, voted in 1861, was composed of 1,777 millions for state expenses, and 125 millions for communal and departmental outlay— 1,902 millions in all for the ordinary budget; the extraordinary was sixty-seven millions—in all 1,969 millions. In 1862 there came the rectificative budget, which added 193 millions, accounted for by the great cost of the Mexican expedition, and of the check at Puebla, so gloriously repaired.

The liquidation arrived in 1863; and it was found necessary to add from forty-nine to fifty millions, carrying the whole expenditure to 2,212 millions. The budget of 1863, voted in 1862, was composed of 1,721 millions for state expenses, and 217 millions for communal and departmental, besides 121 millions for the extraordinary budget—total, 2,061 millions; and the rectificative budget and liquidation raised that amount to 2,292 millions—the highest figure we have yet known. The budget of 1864, showed 2,105 millions as ordinary, and 135 as rectificative—total, 2,240 millions, swelled by the liquidation to 2,260 or 2,270 millions. The budget for 1865 was last year voted at a figure of 2,100 millions; the rectificative budget, which we are now discussing, has added eighty-eight millions, thus raising the figure to 2,188 millions, and leading to the belief that the total will exceed 2,200 millions. The budget of 1865 will be smaller than the preceding, for the reason that the Mexican expenses have diminished. I am aware that the minister of finance would gladly see a reduction in our expenditure, but the minister of public works is fond of renown, and it is always difficult to find the minister who pays and the one who spends in perfect accord. In the present case they seem to have arranged matters at the expense of a third party, purely passive—I mean the sinking fund. Allow me to say a few words on that topic. When the state borrows one hundred millions there is an annual expense of five millions incurred to pay the interest, and one million more is added to redeem the whole debt. At this rate such a debt could only be extinguished in one hundred years, and that would be bankruptcy.

When I was studying finance under the auspices of that great financier, Baron Louis, I came to the conclusion that to defer for a period beyond thirty years the extinction of a debt was tantamount to deferring it indefinitely. But how can a debt be extinguished in a little over thirty years? By leaving in the possession of the sinking fund the million of redeemed rentes: the next year it can redeem 1,050,000f. rentes, and thus by force of compound interest the object may be attained in somewhat over thirty years. Our laws have made the extinction of the public debt by a sinking fund obligatory. The dotation for that purpose has become a sacred thing; but not so the redeemed rentes—they can be annulled. And as the spirit of the law implies redemption when the prices are high, it is scarcely just to the holder of rentes purchased, perhaps, at eighty-four, to reimburse him at sixty-seven. But what is the budget that has been made by annulling the sixty-five millions of redeemed rentes? The advantages of the measure has not been complete; for out of that sum it was necessary to allot six or seven millions to the sinking fund and seven to the ordinary budget, so that fifty millions only remained to establish the budget of 1,700 millions; then there were 236 for departmental expenses—in all, 1,936 millions for the ordinary budget. Then comes the extraordinary one. The minister of public works is not content with the 119 millions which he got last year, but asks for 144, and the committee makes it 152; but 1,936 millions for the ordinary budget and 152 for the extraordinary make 2,086. Such is the budget of 1866, without counting the rectificative budget, which will infallibly come. Now, I will ask you, have you 2,086 millions of receipt in prospect? I maintain that you have not; that there is a deficit of at least two hundred millions. We are told, indeed, that the sum total of expenses can be reduced; I only hope it may. I cannot, however, agree with M. Garnier Pagès as to the facile suppression of a variety of taxes. There appear to me but four chapters in which savings can be realized—Mexico, if you evacuate it; public works, if you restrict them within bounds; the army, if it really can be reduced; and the sinking fund, if the principle of it, as some say, is really an effete and antiquated theory. The evacuation of Mexico will perhaps wound the susceptibilities of the government. But let me remind the chamber of the admirable language held by M. de Caulaincourt, Duke of Vicenza, to Napoleon I., at Dresden, in 1813. "Sire," said he, "conclude this peace; your amour propre may suffer, but not your glory; for your glory is that of France, and it is in no way tarnished by the proposals that have been made to you." I wish, then, to hold the same language to you. Let us imitate Spain in her conduct regarding San Domingo, since her amour propre did not hinder her from desisting from a fault which would cost her blood and treasure without any chance of success. By evacuating Mexico, you may save about fifty millions per annum. Again, by a judicious restriction of public works you may realize savings to an extent of twenty, thirty, and in time of fifty, millions annually. But with respect to economizing in the army and in the sinking fund I feel considerable doubts. Can there be any notable reduction of our army expenditure? I think not. In 1830 my friends on the left of the chamber demanded such a reduction, but without success, as the army was not diminished, but increased from 280,000 to 350,000 men. Personally, I share the opinion of Marshal Soult, who thought an effective force of from 360,000 to 380,000 men absolutely necessary. The figure was, indeed, reduced for a moment to 320,000, and what happened in 1840? That it was suddenly raised to 500,000 men, and at an enormous cost. The year 1848 arrived, and the effective was carried to 420,000, and continued so for two years. I come now to the empire. Believe me, I am far from wishing to put the august prince who now occupies the throne in contradiction with himself, but desire merely to cite facts. Prince Louis Napoleon had often in his works applauded the Prussian system, and affirmed that an army of 200,000 men with a strong reserve was quite sufficient for France. Since he has become emperor we are every day told that France cannot do with less than 400,000 soldiers. Thus it is that every one talks of reductions in the army before attaining to power, but power once gained nobody carries them out. Gentlemen, I do not hold this language for the sake of making myself popular with the French people. The real fact is that promises are often made of which circumstances prevent the fulfilment. For the different foreign services you will always have 100,000 men out of the country, and if you then take the figure of the non-effectives at 50,000, out of the 400,000 you will have 250,000 for our immense territory at home. What is the state of neighboring countries? In Prussia the crown accepts a fearful conflict with the parliament in order to maintain an effective force of 200,000 men; Austria has 400,000; Russia from 600,000 to 700,000. Those only who have not studied the subject are capable of calling for reduction. A soldier under arms costs about 430f. a year; suppress 50,000 men, and what will be the economy realized? About twenty-one millions. Such an economy is certainly not to be condemned; but nothing on a large scale can be realized without inducing, by negotiation, all the great powers to modify their military systems. Nor do I think there is any chance of success so long as Austria continues restless about Venetia, so long as Prussia aims at dominating all the small German states, and so long as Russia shall choose to retain Poland and foster her designs upon the East. I conclude, then, that any serious reduction of the army is impossible.

I must now say a few words on the sinking fund. There is a certain school which affirms that public debts are not disquieting, but even advantageous, and that England is happy in having so large a debt, as so many creditors are interested in her prosperity. Such may be the reasoning of merchants at Rotterdam or Marseilles at the sight of their quays covered with merchandise. "Oh, what splendid commerce!" they might exclaim; but if the bales contained goods which they could not pay for, they would change their note. A good financial market ought to be filled with goods representing the debts of other people. It is good here to cite the example of the United States. They redeemed the whole of their debt; and well it was for them, for they were thus enabled to find 20,000 million francs to pay for the reëstablishment of the American Union. I do not, however, wish you to redeem all your debt, but to diminish it. Public debts are like the lakes at the foot of great mountains; nature does not empty them; but, after the snows and rains of winter and spring, she diminishes gradually the mass of water by the dry heats of summer. Debts must be paid off in peace, so that we may be able to borrow when war comes. The government ought to buy up a part of the debt, were it only to afford the state creditors a certainty of finding a market for their securities, which they cannot unless the state maintains its credit. The English government, after long neglecting the sinking fund, has now decided to buy up every year seventy-five millions (of francs) of the public debt, but yet Mr. Gladstone tells the parliament that he does not think that sum sufficient, and apologized for not having done more. But you, who have done nothing in that way for ten years, now tell us that you have fulfilled your duties. When we are told that the sinking fund, after being entered as expenditure, is then entered as receipts, the result is the same as if a private individual, after laying aside 1,000*f.* to pay his creditors, should spend them before the year was out. I have now gone through the several means of economy proposed; but, with regard to the sinking fund, I must say that not to have effected any reduction of the debt for ten years, and to continue fifteen years longer in the same course as proposed, is, if I may be allowed the expression, walking blindfold on to bankruptcy. I know you do not intend to do so; but it would be prudent not to incur the risk. As to any great economy in the army, I do not see how it is to be accomplished. In fact, the only means of realizing any economy are, in my opinion, the evacuation of Mexico and the restriction of public works. Now, to draw the balance, have you the 2,086 millions required for your three budgets? If you have, go on; if not, begin at once to economize. All your resources amount to only 1,904 millions, so that you still want 182 millions. Against that sum you set 127 millions from the sinking fund, eighteen millions of supposed surplus on the budget of 1865, in which the committee has no faith; with 27,400,000f. from the Mexican indemnity, seven or eight millions from Cochin China, and other receipts of small amount. This is all you have toward the 182 millions. But shall you get the 27,400,000f. from Mexico? You inserted in the budget of 1864 fifty-four millions of Mexican securities, which were calculated at sixty-three, but are now worth only forty-four. Will you sell them at that price? This resource having failed in the budget of 1864, how can you expect to be paid the twenty-seven millions of 1865? The minister of finance has also taken twenty-two millions from the Army Dotation Fund, but that cannot be regarded as receipts. In fine, you have only 1,904 millions of receipts, and your expenditure amounts habitually to between 2,200 and 2,300 millions, and this deficit you cover only by means of the sinking fund and chimerical receipts. It will never do for the state thus to represent the finances to be flourishing when they are not like the directors of certain joint-stock companies, who distribute dividends which the state of their affairs does not justify. Be sure of one thing: when you engage in unlimited expenditure, apparently unaware of the course you are taking, it is our duty to tell you that you are on the road to ruin. You will be obliged either to fail in the engagements you have contracted in the name of France, or to have recourse to excessive taxation. I ask your pardon for speaking so warmly, but it is impossible to treat a graver or more interesting subject. I repeat that you are running toward the double rock, either of failing in your engagements, or of rendering inevitable the imposition of onerous taxes which may give rise to deplorable divisions. I adjure you to reflect most seriously on this state of affairs. You are on the brink of a financial gulf if you persist in the present course. I ask pardon for distressing you, but it is my duty to tell you the truth, and I tell it, whatever the result may be.

ALLEN GRANBERY THURMAN

THE TILDEN-HAYES ELECTION

[Allen Granbery Thurman, an American statesman and jurist, was born in Virginia in 1813. He settled in Ohio in early youth, received an academic education, became a lawyer, and practised with great success. He was elected to Congress in 1845. Some years later he was chosen to the Supreme Court of Ohio and was for a time chief-justice of the State. In 1867 he was defeated for the governorship, but two years later was elected to the United States Senate, serving two terms in that body as a Democrat. His name was mentioned in connection with the presidential nomination of his party at the national convention of 1876. In 1888 he was a candidate for Vice-President of the United States. He died in 1895. The following speech was delivered in the U. S. Senate in 1877, in reference to the disputed election to the Presidency between Hayes and Tilden.]

WHEN your committee got together, after a free and friendly conversation and discussion of the subject, and the reading of no small amount of history, it was soon discovered that to frame a bill upon the idea of defining by law what the Constitution means, settling that by law, would be a simple impossibility, and that no such bill could pass; for you could not frame a bill according to the one theory or the other opposite theory without its being supposed that it gave advantage to one party or to the other party. In the present circumstances of our country, and as the majorities of the two houses are of different politics, it was perfectly clear that any bill that gave the least advantage, aye, the weight of the dust in the balance, to either party, could not become the law of the land. Therefore it was that we did not attempt to do what the senator from Massachusetts thinks is so easy to do, namely, to interpret the Constitution in a statute. It would have been the most idle work that ever sane men attempted had we tried to do any such thing.   All that we could do was to constitute a tribunal as honest and impartial and fair as we could make it, as likely to be intelligent and learned and honest as we could find, and as likely to command the respect of the country as any we could frame, and submit to that as we submit to our supreme judicial tribunal, the Supreme Court of the United States, the constitutional questions that are involved in this subject.   Is there anything strange or novel in that?   Is there a constitutional question or can there be one that we do not submit to the final arbitrament of the Supreme Court of the United States?   In a case like this, where there is no opportunity of any such submission, where such a submission would be of doubtful constitutionality in view of the power conferred by implication at least upon Congress, is there anything strange in getting the aid, the advice, the judgment of a tribunal so carefully framed to make it honest, to make it able, to make it learned, to make it command the respect of the country, as the tribunal provided for in this bill?   Is there anything strange in that, and especially is there anything strange in it when the two houses of Congress, being charged with this great duty, reserve the power to overrule the decision of that tribunal and to decide otherwise, if the two houses consider its decision to be wrong?   I should like to know where there is anything that is justly subject to censure in a proposition like that.

But I said that I would state some of the conflicting opinions upon the interpretation of the Constitution to show with what your committee had to grapple, and to show what would be the field of inquiry upon which we should have to enter if we were to take the suggestion of the senator from Massachusetts and proceed to interpret the Constitution by statutory provisions.   Let us see what they are.   One proposition is that both houses must concur to count the vote.   That is a proposition very strongly and very logically supported by able men.   On the other hand, it is said that the true interpretation is that both houses must concur to reject a vote.   Right upon that fundamental question, so important, there is a direct antagonism of opinion.   That is number one.

Let us go to number two.   It is said that the two houses

act as one body, as a joint convention, in counting the vote, and the opposite opinion is that they act as separate organized bodies. The first opinion had the sanction of the great name of Mr. Jefferson and nearly all his supporters in 1800. The second proposition, directly antagonistic to the first, had the support of the more practical men of later times, and, indeed, it had the opinion of the party in the majority in 1800 in the government. There is the second case of directly antagonistic opinions.

Let us proceed to a third, that the House of Representatives is the sole judge whether there has been an election, and the opposite opinion is that the House is not the sole judge, but that the Senate has an equal right to decide. What more important question than that was or could be mooted? What question more fundamental in its character could be considered? And yet here are the most antagonistic opinions upon it. Writer after writer, men who have been chief justices of the supreme courts of their States, men who have held positions in the highest judicial tribunals of the land, are out in elaborate opinions on one side or the other side of that great question. How are you to decide that in a bill, and expect it to pass both Houses of Congress?

That is the third. Let us proceed to the fourth; that touches the amendment. It is that it is competent to go behind the certificate of the governor, and the directly opposite opinion that it is not competent to go behind the certificate of the governor.

The fifth is that it is competent to go behind the decision of a canvassing or returning board, and in opposition that it is not competent to do so. Are you going to decide that question, and are you going to decide that in a bill? The senator from Massachusetts intimates that if his amendment be put in the bill there are certain senators here who will not vote for it. He is quite right. He knows he is right. He knows it would not get one vote on this side of the chamber and it would not get one vote of a particular party in the other end of the Capitol, and yet he urges it, and still he talks about being in favor of the bill. Why, sir, upon that question and upon other questions we are obliged to submit in the first instance to this tribunal, composed as it is, to decide, reserving to ourselves power to reverse its decision if the two houses can agree to reverse it.

This question of going behind a returning board has a great many points in it. The Senator from Massachusetts seems to think that the only point in going behind a returning board is whether we can go clear to the bottom and find out how seven millions of people vote. If he says that he is opposed to that, I say, So am I. But that is one thing. Going behind the decision of a returning board is quite another thing. And that brings me to notice this point of difference. It is held by some that the decision of a returning board may be impeached for want of jurisdiction and by another set that it cannot be. I commend that to my friend from Massachusetts, who is a lawyer. On the one side it is said that every act done by any tribunal, from the highest court in the country to that of a single individual, if it is beyond his jurisdiction, is utterly null and void, and that returning boards are no exception to this rule, and if they, beyond their jurisdiction, ultra vires, undertake to disfranchise people, every act of disfranchisement is utterly null and void. On the other hand, this proposition is denied. Let me submit to my friend from Massachusetts that the decision of the proposition the one way or the other does not take him down to the seven millions of voters who cast their votes at the last presidential election, nor one step toward it. Furthermore, let me tell him that that does not even touch the integrity of the returning board, for, if these returning boards had been composed of the eleven Apostles after Judas Iscariot had hanged himself, and were they as pure as human tribunals could be, yet if they went beyond their jurisdiction, in the opinion of some men their acts would be utterly void.

Take this honest, learned, impartial tribunal, says the bill; let them examine the case and give us their judgment upon it. When that judgment comes from a tribunal of this character in favor of one of these returns, it creates a presumption in its favor that ought not to be overthrown except by the concurrent voice of the two houses. It creates a presumption in its favor as strong, if not stronger, than that which existed in favor of a single return; and that is the philosophy of this bill. It is the presumption in favor of a return, so as not to deprive any state of its vote; that presumption which exists where there is but one return, or that presumption which is created by the decision of this tribunal, which shall not be overthrown except by the concurrent voice of the two houses. But it is said: "Well, now, that is practically to leave it to the tribunal. Nay, further, that is practically to leave it to one man." Why, Mr. President, suppose it were left to this Senate alone, might not the vote be thirty-five against thirty-six, and then would it not be the thirty-sixth man that settled it? Suppose you were to leave it to five hundred and one men and there were two hundred and fifty on one side and two hundred and fifty-one on the other, might you not just as well say it is the one-man power? Why, sir, there is nothing in that at all.

Nor does it militate against the constitutionality of this bill one particle that in the present state of affairs—that is to say, with two houses having different political majorities —practically the decision of that tribunal may settle the question. That does not militate against the constitutionality of this bill in the slightest degree. You might just as well say that it would militate against the constitutionality of a law if you were to provide that a case involving a constitutional question might be appealed from the Court of Claims up to the Supreme Court.

It might be said: "Why, the practical effect will be that, as the judges of the Supreme Court are six Republicans certain and two Democrats, and one that cannot be counted—therefore, as a matter of course, the judgment will be in favor of the Republican interpretation of the Constitution." Would that be any argument against a bill conferring jurisdiction on that court? Where do you find in the Constitution anything about the politics of the members of the Supreme Court? Where do you find in the Constitution anything about the politics of senators on this floor? Where do you find in the Constitution anything about the politics of members of the House of Representatives? And can you say that a bill is unconstitutional because it may so happen that the court that is to decide the case, be it the Supreme Court of the United States, or a circuit court, or a State court, or a congressional tribunal, will happen to be composed of more members of one political party than the other? That is not constitutional reasoning. That is politicians' reasoning; that is office-holders' reasoning; that is office-seekers' reasoning; but that is not constitutional reasoning. This is the act of the two houses, and this bill contemplates nothing else; and it is just as much in a constitutional sense the act of the two houses and the decision of the two houses as if both houses were of the same political complexion, and no man who is a lawyer can deny it; and therefore it is a simple absurdity in any man, reasoning as a lawyer, to say that this bill is an abdication of the powers of the two houses.

SAMUEL JONES TILDEN

NEGRO SUFFRAGE

[Samuel Jones Tilden, an American statesman, whose contest with Rutherford B. Hayes for the Presidency of the United States caused the creation of the electoral commission, was born in New York State in 1814. From the moment he began to speak, his command of words attracted attention and caused his parents to anticipate that he would be a famous orator. His education was completed partly at Yale and partly at the University of New York. He began life by practicing law in the city of New York. Entering politics as a Democrat, he was elected to the state legislature. By the time the Civil War broke out he was a leader of his party in the state, but he first attracted wide national attention by his war upon the corrupt Tweed ring that had plundered the city of New York for years. His success in putting an end to this scandal resulted in his election as governor of New York State in 1874. His nomination as Democratic candidate for the Presidency followed two years later. The result of the election was long in doubt, but was finally decided in favor of Hayes by an electoral commission, specially created by Act of Congress. Tilden retired to private life, but remained until his death a trusted leader of the Democracy. He twice refused to become again candidate for President. At his death, in 1886, he bequeathed a large fortune to public uses; the Tilden Library, merged into the New York Public Library, being one of his benefactions. The following speech, pointing out the dangers and probable effects of Negro Suffrage, was delivered at the Democratic State Convention, Albany, 1868.]

ON the formation of the government of the United States, the question still remained to be solved, what practical character should be impressed upon it, in its actual administration. Governor Morris, who had favored a centralized system tending to aristocracy and monarchy, when asked his opinion of the Constitution, answered, "That depends on how it is construed."

During the controversies of its earlier years, men's minds

were constantly turned toward organic questions. Every measure was tested by its relations to such questions. Parties imputed to each other designs to change the character of the government. Jefferson, in the nation, and George Clinton, in this state, led the Democratic masses against a centralism which they feared would in practise assimilate our new institutions to the British system, from which the Revolution had emancipated us; and it is now historically certain that a powerful element in the Federal party of that day did in fact desire such a result. Hamilton believed Burr, even while the latter stood high in public esteem, to be capable of a Roman or French ambition, and did not deem his success in establishing a dictatorship or an empire impossible, if he could gain the presidency and wield its powers for that object. Other eminent public men entertained the same fears, in the event of a civil convulsion, which Hamilton expected. With such ideas in men's minds, the political contest of 1800 was fought and decided in the city of New York for the state and for the nation.

The result closed the first era of our governmental history. The liberal and beneficent political philosophy of Jefferson became ascendent everywhere in the public councils and in the popular opinion. The essential character of the government became fixed, and men's ideas in respect to it settled. Organic questions, debates as to the structure of the government, ceased to occupy public attention. For sixty years our controversies turned on questions of administrative policy. Eddies in the current of our progress there were. The War of 1812, even under Madison, caused a centralization in administrative measures and policies which cost us a quarter of a century of peace to remove. But, on the whole, the master-wisdom of governing little and leaving as much as possible to localities and to individuals, prevailed; and we progressively limited the sphere of governmental action, and enlarged the domain of individual conscience and judgment. These sixty years were a period of transcendent national growth and prosperity, and of universal happiness among the people.

How and why we passed from that fortunate condition into a gigantic Civil war; the moral and social causes which gradually prepared such a result; the events of that conflict,

I cannot pause to discuss. When at last we brought the contest to a successful issue, and especially when the voluntary extinction of slavery declared—what moral and material causes had already made certain—that our Northern system of society and industry are to prevail in every part of this continent which shall be occupied by us, I hoped that we might speedily restore the people of the revolted states to their true relations to the Union; and then, that we might at once begin to deal with the administrative questions which the war had cast upon us.

Questions of this sort there were, enough for a generation of the most earnest political activity. The reaction against the heresy of secession, the public necessities during the war, the lead throughout all that struggle of a party always imbued with false ideas of government and with obsolete notions of political economy, and always dominated over by class interests, had created for the time an overwhelming tendency to centralism. All our administrative systems had become buried under a fungus-growth, which was smothering all trade, and sucking out the vitality of the industries of the country.

I looked to the Democratic party as the only agency through which the government could be brought back to the liberal ideas and beneficent policies which had prevailed under Jefferson and Jackson; but before we could enter on the work of administrative and economical reform, pacification was necessary. A complete and harmonious restoration of the revolted states would have been effected if the Republican party had not proved to be totally incapable of acting in the case with any large, wise, or firm statesmanship.

This crisis was the trial of the Republican party. The question was whether it could become a permanent party in the country, continuing to govern for the present, capable of being, from time to time, called to govern; or whether it must admit itself to be but a revolutionary faction, accepted by the people during war, accepted for the venom, if not the vigor, with which it could strike, acting often "outside the Constitution," often converting the regular and lawful organs of the government into a French committee of public safety, or a Jacobin club, and now, incapable of adapting itself to the work of pacification when that has become the commanding public necessity; and, therefore, its mission being fulfilled, having nothing left to it but to die and be forever dismissed from our national history.

In this trial the Republican party completely failed. It could do nothing but strike, when to strike was no longer necessary, or wise, or humane, or Christian; and when to continue to strike was ruin to all reviving commerce and reviving industries of the victorious North, and inflicted anew, upon an exhausted people, the burdens of war, after war was ended.

The Republican party, finding no difficulty outside of itself, found a difficulty in itself which was insurmountable —it could not change its own nature. If it could have generated one leader capable of the generous ambition of pacificating the country and founding a permanent ascendency on the ultimate public opinion of the whole country, it might have lived. Even a large demagogue might have been a national benefaction. But two hundred small demagogues—not one of them able to extend his vision beyond the horizon of one congressional district, nor having much moral sway over the opinion of his constituency—found it easier and safer to stimulate the hatreds left by war, and the provincial passions which led to the war, than to act with the wise moderation of a comprehensive statesman, or even the prudent liberality of a conqueror.

The Republican party recoiled for a while on the fatal brink of the policy on which it at last embarked. It had not the courage to conciliate by magnanimity, and to found its alliances and its hopes of success upon the better qualities of human nature. It totally abandoned all relations with the white race of the ten states. It resolved to make the black the governing power in the states, and by means of them to bring into Congress twenty senators and fifty representatives—practically appointed by itself in Washington.

It is evident that the internal government of those states was not the main object of this desperate expedient. The State organizations and new electoral bodies were so managed that the twenty senators and fifty representatives could be secured to the Republican party after it refused to trust to pacification.

The effect of a gain to the Republican party of twenty senators and fifty representatives is to strengthen its hold on the Federal government against the people of the North. Nor is there the slightest doubt that the paramount object and motive of the Republican party is, by these means, to secure itself against a reaction of opinion adverse to it, in our great populous Northern commonwealths. The effect of its system and its own real purpose is to establish a domination over us of the Northern States.

When the Republican party resolved to establish negro supremacy in the ten states in order to gain to itself the representation of those states in Congress, it had to begin by governing the people of those states by the sword. The four millions and a half of whites composed the electoral bodies. If they were to be put under the supremacy of the three millions of negroes, and twenty senators and fifty representatives were to be obtained through these three millions of negroes, it was necessary to obliterate every vestige of local authority, whether it had existed before the rebellion, or been instituted since by Mr. Lincoln or by the people. A bayonet had to be set to supervise and control every local organization. The military dictatorship had to be extended to the remotest ramification of human society. That was the first necessity.

The next was the creation of new electoral bodies for those ten states, in which, by exclusions, by disfranchisements and proscriptions, by control over registration, by applying test-oaths operating retrospectively, by intimidation, and by every form of influence, three millions of negroes are made to predominate over four and a-half millions of whites.

How, my fellow-citizens, has this work been accomplished, and at what cost? The main instruments have been the Freedman's Bureau and the army of the United States.

The Freedman's Bureau is partly an eleemosynary establishment which dispenses alms to the liberated slaves, and assumes to be their friend and protector. It is to a large extent a job for its dependents and their speculative associates. But, in its principal character, it is a political machine to organize and manage the three millions of negroes. Its cost, as reported by itself to the public treasury for the last two years, is about ten millions of dollars.

The army is used to overawe the white race, and sometimes to work and sometimes to shelter the working of the political system which goes on under the military governments of the ten states.

You have seen the telegrams announcing the reduction of the army expenses. When I was in Washington, the week before last, I took some pains to ascertain the truth. I am able to inform you, from authentic data, that the monthly payments at the treasury for army expenses up to the beginning of the present month exceed twelve millions. I assert that they are now, to-day, running at the rate of one hundred and fifty millions per annum. They have not been less, but probably more, for the two years past. This does not include pensions, which are thirty-six millions more.

Remember that it is excessive taxation which crushes the industrial masses in European monarchies and despotism, and that this taxation is mainly caused by their military establishments, kept up by the ambitions of their rulers, by their mutual jealousies, and by the fears which tyrants entertain of their own peoples.

Remember that our wise ancestors warned us against standing armies, and all those false systems of government which require standing armies. They formed the Union of the states that we might be free from the jealousies of coterminous countries, which have been the usual pretext of tyrants for maintaining costly military establishments. They founded that Union on the principle of local self-government, to be everywhere carried on by the voluntary coöperation of the governed. They did not intend that one part of our country should govern another part, as European tyrants govern their subjects. Rebellion, which for a time disturbed this beneficent system, is conquered, but we do not return to government on the principles of our fathers. The Southern people are willing and anxious to do so. We refuse. See how the refusal brings upon us the calamities foretold by the prophetic statesmen and patriots of 1776 and 1787.

We have now reached a period when everything valuable in the Constitution and in the government as formed by our fathers is brought into peril. Men's minds are unsettled by the civil strifes through which we have passed. The body of traditional ideas which limited the struggles of parties within narrow and fixed boundaries is broken up. A temporary party majority, having complete sway over the legislative bodies, discards all standards—whether embodied in laws, constitutions, or in elementary and organic principles of free government—acts its own pleasure as absolutely as if it were a revolutionary convention, and deems everything legitimate which can serve its party aims.

Changes are dared and attempted by it with a success which, I trust, is but temporary—changes which revolutionize the whole nature of our government.

(1) If there be anything fundamental in government or human society, it is the question, which elements shall compose the electoral bodies from which emanate all the governing powers. The Constitution left the states with exclusive power over the suffrage, and the states have always defined and protected the suffrage from change, by their fundamental laws. Congress now usurps control over the whole subject in the ten states, and creates negro constituencies, and vests them with nearly a third of the whole representation in the Senate, and nearly a quarter of the whole representation in the House. The leaders of the Republican party also claim the power by congressional act to regulate the suffrage in the loyal states, and, without the consent of the people of these states, to alter their constitutions, and involve them in a political partnership with inferior races.

(2) Congress, by the methods and means I have traced, usurps control over the representation in the two branches of the national legislature, and packs those bodies with delegates, admitting or rejecting for party ends, and at length attempting to create a permanent majority by deputies from negro constituencies formed for that purpose.

(3) Congress has not only fettered the trade and industries of the country, for the benefit of special interests and classes, but it has absorbed many powers and functions of the state governments which are, in the words of Mr. Jefferson's celebrated Inaugural, "the most competent adminis-

trations for our domestic concerns, the surest bulwark against anti-republican tendencies;" and it is rapidly centralizing all our political institutions.

(4) Congress is systematically breaking down all the divisions of power between the coördinate departments of the Federal Government which the Constitution established, and which have always been considered as essential to the very existence of constitutional representative government.

The conviction of all our revered statesmen and patriots is, in the language of Mr. Jefferson, that "the concentration of legislative, executive, and judicial powers in the same hands is precisely the definition of despotic government." "An elective despotism," said he, "was not the government we fought for, but one that should not only be founded on free principles, but in which the powers of the government should be so divided among several bodies of magistracy as that no one could transcend their legal limits without being effectually checked and restrained by the others."

Hitherto the great right of the citizen to a voice in choosing his rulers has been safely intrenched in the constitutions of the several states. No legislative power in the land, federal or state, could touch it. No temporary political ascendency, no fluctuation of parties, could endanger it. The state constitution could be changed only through slow processes—imposing delays insuring deliberation, and generally requiring several submissions to a vote of the people. To effect a change throughout the Union would require that these processes be carried through in each state separately. But once abdicate this rightful authority of the people of the several states, acting in their organic capacity; once allow Congress to usurp jurisdiction over the suffrage of the people of the states; once admit that this fundamental right may be changed by a mere enactment of Congress, without submission to a vote of the people—and no man in any state can tell how soon his vote may be rendered worthless, or how soon it may be taken from him. Mr. Sumner avows that his object is to control the next Presidential election. Adopt his theory; establish the precedent; accustom the people to acquiesce in the usurpation; and you will have a congressional majority changing the suffrage wherever it may be a convenient means of keeping themselves in power.   An ambitious President, with a subservient majority in Congress; in possession of the machinery of the Federal Government; our political system centralized under the popular reaction against the heresy of secession, until the moral force of the states to restrain is gone—and a supreme control over the suffrage is all that is wanting to complete and consummate a practical revolution in our government.   Your future masters may indulge you a while in the forms of election, if they be allowed to make over the constituent bodies as often and as much as they please, letting in and shutting out voters to maintain their ascendency. An addition of nine hundred and thirty-one thousand negroes—most of them emancipated slaves without any of the training, or traditions, or aspirations of freemen, who would as soon vote to make their favorite an emperor as to make him a president—will be a convenient accessory.   And when their representatives get into power, who can doubt that they are capable of being made facile instruments of excluding opponents as well as of admitting allies?   How do you think Senator Brownlow and his twenty associates would vote on a bill to regulate the suffrage by admitting negroes in New York, Pennsylvania, Ohio, Indiana, or Illinois?   How would they vote on a bill to regulate the suffrage by excluding Irishmen or Germans?   Do you think they would not assert the superior rights of the negroes born in this country over foreigners?   Is it not at least prudent for all who possess the suffrage to keep the regulation of it where it now is—in the constitutions of the several states?

The Republicans have educated our people to overthrow what they called the "Slave power."   Analyze it.   What was it?   It was the influence which 350,000 heads of families, embracing 2,000,000 of the white race, owning slaves, and living intermingled with 6,000,000 of other whites not owning slaves, were capable of exercising over public opinion, thereby upon the government.   It gave us Washington, Jefferson, Madison, Monroe, Jackson, Marshall, Clay, and hosts of other statesmen and patriots; and whatever influence could be exercised by it was only through the consent of millions of civilized people of our race.   The struggle to overthrow it has cost the whole country a million of lives and four thousand millions of dollars. And now what is it proposed to the people of the great populous commonwealths of the North to accept in exchange, and as the recompense for such immense sacrifices?

The political power of the states where slavery once existed will remain, and after the next census will be enlarged by the representation of all, instead of three-fifths of the former slaves. That power in the ten States, if the system of the Republicans shall prevail and continue—at any rate for the next few years, which involve practically all the business interests of the country—is to be wielded by a few hundred adventurers through the 3,000,000 emancipated slaves; and the centralization of our governmental authorities will cause it to act vastly more upon all our interests. It will give us Hunnicut for Washington, Underwood for Jefferson, and Brownlow for Jackson. Every element of this power would be inferior in morality and intelligence to the one which has been overthrown, and its influence upon our welfare would be immensely greater. Will the people of our great Northern States accept a domination of such a "negro power," erected on the ruins of such a "slave power?"

I do not ask what will be the consequences on the white race of ten states—whether the white race will be expelled; I do not ask what will be the effects upon our industrial or commercial interests, or on the civilization of a portion of our country three and a half times as large as the French Empire.

If the authors of this policy tell you that the white people of the South deserve this infliction, I ask you whether you all deserve it? If, taking counsel of hatred, you think you are making a government for your late enemies, I remind you that you are also making a government for yourselves. Do the 25,000,000 of white people out of the ten states deserve such a government as you are imposing on them?

The masses of the Republicans do not understand the real nature of the system they are contributing to establish. They are misled by party association and party antagonism, by the animosities created by war, and the unsettled ideas which grow out of the novelty of the situation. The leaders are full of party passion and party ambition, and will not easily surrender the power of a centralized government, or the patronage and profits which are incident to an official expenditure of $500,000,000 a year. The grim Puritan of New England—whose only child, whose solitary daughter is already listening to the soft music of a Celtic wooer—stretches his hand down along the Atlantic coast to the receding and decaying African, and says: "Come, let us rule this continent together!" The twelve senators from New England, with twenty from the ten states, would require only a few from Missouri, Tennessee, West Virginia, and from new states, to make a majority.

I do not forbid the banns; I simply point to the region which stretches from the Hudson to the Missouri. It is there that the Democracy must display their standards in another, and, I trust, final battle for constitutional government and civil liberty. I invited you to that theater last year; I come now to bid you God-speed!

Every business, every industrial interest is paralyzed under excessive taxation, false systems of finance, extravagant cost of production, diminished ability to consume. You cannot obtain relief until you change your governmental policy. You cannot change that until you change the men who administer your government. The causes of the dangers in respect to our political institutions and civil liberty and the causes of your suffering in business are identical. For the safety of the one and for the relief of the other you must demand of the people a change of administration as now carried on by Congress.

ROBERT TOOMBS

REVOLUTION OR SECESSION

[Robert Toombs was born in Georgia in 1810. He was elected to
the lower House in Congress in 1845, and to the United States Senate
in 1853, and was reëlected to the latter in 1859. Being a leader of the
secession party in Georgia, he resigned his seat in the Senate when
that State left the Union, and became secretary of state for the Southern
Confederacy, in which capacity he served from February 1861 to July
of the same year. In 1862 he was elected a senator in the Confederate
Senate, and became a brigadier-general in the same year. He died at
Washington in 1885. The following was his last speech in the United
States Senate previous to his retirement therefrom shortly before the
Civil War began, and was delivered January 7, 1861.]

THE success of the Abolitionists and their allies, under
the name of the Republican party, has produced its
logical results already. They have for long years been sowing dragons' teeth, and have finally got a crop of armed
men. The Union, sir, is dissolved. That is an accomplished fact in the path of this discussion that men may as
well heed. One of your confederates has already, wisely,
bravely, boldly, confronted public danger, and she is only
ahead of many of her sisters because of her greater facility
for speedy action. The greater majority of those sister
states, under like circumstances, consider her cause as their
cause; and I charge you in their name to-day, "Touch not
Saguntum." It is not only their cause, but it is a cause
which receives the sympathy and will receive the support
of tens and hundreds of thousands of honest patriotic men
in the non-slaveholding states, who have hitherto maintained
constitutional rights, and who respect their oaths, abide by
compacts, and love justice. And while this Congress, this
Senate, and this House of Representatives, are debating
the constitutionality and the expediency of seceding from
the Union, and while the perfidious authors of this mischief

are showering down denunciations upon a large portion of the patriotic men of this country, those brave men are coolly and calmly voting what you call revolution—aye, sir, doing better than that: arming to defend it. They appealed to the Constitution, they appealed to justice, they appealed to fraternity, until the Constitution, justice, and fraternity were no longer listened to in the legislative halls of their country, and then, sir, they prepared for the arbitrament of the sword; and now you see the glittering bayonet, and you hear the tramp of armed men from your capital to the Rio Grande. It is a sight that gladdens the eyes and cheers the heart of other millions ready to second them. Inasmuch, sir, as I have labored earnestly, honestly, sincerely, with these men to avert this necessity so long as I deemed it possible, and inasmuch as I heartily approve their present conduct of resistance, I deem it my duty to state their case to the Senate, to the country, and to the civilized world.

Senators, my countrymen have demanded no new government; they have demanded no new constitution. Look to their records at home and here from the beginning of this national strife until its consummation in the disruption of the empire, and they have not demanded a single thing except that you shall abide by the Constitution of the United States; that constitutional rights shall be respected, and that justice shall be done. Sirs, they have stood by your Constitution; they have stood by all its requirements; they have performed all its duties unselfishly, uncalculatingly, disinterestedly, until a party sprang up in this country which endangered their social system—a party which they arraign, and which they charge before the American people and all mankind with having made proclamation of outlawry against four thousand millions of their property in the territories of the United States; with having put them under the ban of the empire in all the states in which their institutions exist, outside the protection of federal laws; with having aided and abetted insurrection from within and invasion from without, with the view of subverting those institutions, and desolating their homes and their firesides. For these causes they have taken up arms. I shall proceed to vindicate the justice of their demands, the patriotism of their conduct. I will show the injustice which they suffer and the rightfulness of their resistance.

I shall not spend much time on the question that seems to give my honorable friend [Mr. Crittenden] so much concern—the constitutional right of a state to secede from this Union. Perhaps he will find out after a while that it is a fact accomplished. You have got it in the South pretty much both ways. South Carolina has given it to you regularly, according to the approved plan. You are getting it just below there (in Georgia), I believe, irregularly, outside of the law, without regular action. You can take it either way. You will find armed men to defend both. I have stated that the discontented states of this Union have demanded nothing but clear, distinct, unequivocal, well-acknowledged constitutional rights; rights affirmed by the highest judicial tribunals of their country; rights older than the Constitution; rights which are planted upon the immutable principles of natural justice; rights which have been affirmed by the good and the wise of all countries, and of all centuries. We demand no power to injure any man. We demand no right to injure our confederate states. We demand no right to interfere with their institutions, either by word or deed. We have no right to disturb their peace, their tranquillity, their security. We have demanded of them simply, solely—nothing else—to give us equality, security, and tranquillity. Give us these, and peace restores itself. Refuse them, and take what you can get.

I will now read my own demands, acting under my own convictions, and the universal judgment of my countrymen. They are considered the demands of an extremist. To hold to a constitutional right now makes one considered as an extremist—I believe that is the appellation these traitors and villains, North and South, employ. I accept their reproach rather than their principles. Accepting their designation of treason and rebellion, there stands before them as good a traitor, and as good a rebel as ever descended from revolutionary loins.

What do the rebels demand? First, "that the people of the United States shall have an equal right to emigrate and settle in the present or any future acquired territories, with whatever property they may possess (including slaves), and be securely protected in its peaceable enjoyment until such territory may be admitted as a state into the Union, with or without slavery, as she may determine, on an equality with all existing states." That is our territorial demand. We have fought for this territory when blood was its price. We have paid for it when gold was its price. We have not proposed to exclude you, though you have contributed very little of blood or money. I refer especially to New England. We demand only to go into those territories upon terms of equality with you, as equals in this great confederacy, to enjoy the common property of the whole Union, and receive the protection of the common government, until the territory is capable of coming into the Union as a sovereign state, when it may fix its own institutions to suit itself.

The second proposition is, "that property in slaves shall be entitled to the same protection from the government of the United States, in all of its departments, everywhere, which the Constitution confers the power upon it to extend to any other property, provided nothing herein contained shall be construed to limit or restrain the right now belonging to every state to prohibit, abolish, or establish and protect slavery within its limits." We demand of the common government to use its granted powers to protect our property as well as yours. For this protection we pay as much as you do. This very property is subject to taxation. It has been taxed by you and sold by you for taxes. The title to thousands and tens of thousands of slaves is derived from the United States. We claim that the government, while the Constitution recognizes our property for the purposes of taxation, shall give it the same protection that it gives yours. Ought it not to be so? You say no. Every one of you upon the committee said no. Your senators say no. Your House of Representatives says no. Throughout the length and breadth of your conspiracy against the Constitution, there is but one shout of no! This recognition of this right is the price of my allegiance. Withhold it, and you do not get my obedience. This is the philosophy of the armed men who have sprung up in this country. Do you ask me to support a government that will tax my property; that will plunder me; that will demand my blood, and will not protect me? I would rather see the population of my native state laid six feet beneath her sod than they should support for one hour such a government. Protection is the price of obedience everywhere, in all countries. It is the only thing that makes government respectable. Deny it and you cannot have free subjects or citizens; you may have slaves.

We demand, in the next place, "that persons committing crimes against slave property in one state, and fleeing to another, shall be delivered up in the same manner as persons committing crimes against other property, and that the laws of the state from which such persons flee shall be the test of criminality." That is another one of the demands of an extremist and rebel. The Constitution of the United States, article four, section two, says:

"A person charged in any state with treason, felony, or other crime, who shall flee from justice and be found in another state, shall, on demand of the executive authority of the state from which he fled, be delivered up to be removed to the state having jurisdiction of the crime." But the non-slaveholding states, treacherous to their oaths and compacts, have steadily refused, if the criminal only stole a negro, and that negro was a slave, to deliver him up. It was refused twice on the requisition of my own state as long as twenty-two years ago. It was refused by Kent and by Fairfield, governors of Maine, and representing, I believe, each of the then Federal parties. We appealed then to fraternity, but we submitted; and this constitutional right has been practically a dead letter from that day to this. The next case came up between us and the State of New York, when the present senior senator [Mr. Seward] was the governor of that state; and he refused it. Why? He said it was not against the laws of New York to steal a negro, and therefore he would not comply with the demand. He made a similar refusal to Virginia. Yet these are our confederates; these are our sister states! There is the bargain; there is the compact. You have sworn to it. Both these governors swore to it. The Senator from New York swore to it. The governor of Ohio swore to it when he was inaugurated. You cannot bind them by oaths. Yet they talk to us of treason; and I suppose they expect to whip freemen into loving such brethren! They will have a good time in doing it.

It is natural we should want this provision of the Constitution carried out. The Constitution says slaves are property; the Supreme Court says so; the Constitution says so. The theft of slaves is a crime; they are a subject-matter of felonious asportation. By the text and letter of the Constitution you agreed to give them up. You have sworn to do it, and you have broken your oaths. Of course, those who have done so look out for pretexts. Nobody expected them to do otherwise. I do not think I ever saw a perjurer, however bald and naked, who could not invent some pretext to palliate his crime, or who could not, for fifteen shillings, hire an Old Bailey lawyer to invent some for him. Yet this requirement of the Constitution is another one of the extreme demands of an extremist and a rebel.

The next stipulation is that fugitive slaves shall be surrendered under the provisions of the Fugitive Slave Act of 1850, without being entitled either to a writ of habeas corpus, or trial by jury, or other similar obstructions of legislation, in the state to which he may flee. Here is the Constitution:

"No person held to service or labor in one state, under the laws thereof, escaping into another, shall, in consequence of any law or regulation therein, be discharged from such service or labor, but shall be delivered up on claim of the party to whom such service or labor may be due."

This language is plain, and everybody understood it the same way for the first forty years of your government. In 1793, in Washington's time, an Act was passed to carry out this provision. It was adopted unanimously in the Senate of the United States, and nearly so in the House of Representatives. Nobody then had invented pretexts to show that the Constitution did not mean a negro slave. It was clear; it was plain. Not only the Federal courts, but all the local courts in all the states, decide that this was a constitutional obligation. How is it now? The North sought to evade it; following the instincts of their natural character, they commenced with the fraudulent fiction that fugitives were entitled to habeas corpus, entitled to trial by jury in the state to which they fled. They pretended to believe that our fugitive slaves were entitled to more rights than their white citizens; perhaps they were right, they know one another better than I do. You may charge a white man with treason, or felony, or other crime, and you do not require any trial by jury before he is given up; there is nothing to determine but that he is legally charged with a crime and that he fled, and then he is to be delivered up upon demand. White people are delivered up every day in this way; but not slaves. Slaves, black people, you say, are entitled to trial by jury; and in this way schemes have been invented to defeat your plain constitutional obligations.

The next demand made on behalf of the South is, "that Congress shall pass effective laws for the punishment of all persons in any of the states who shall in any manner aid and abet invasion or insurrection in any other state, or commit any other act against the laws of nations, tending to disturb the tranquillity of the people or government of any other state." That is a very plain principle. The Constitution of the United States now requires, and gives Congress express power, to define and punish piracies and felonies committed on the high seas, and offenses against the laws of nations. When the honorable and distinguished Senator from Illinois [Mr. Douglas] last year introduced a bill for the purpose of punishing people thus offending under that clause of the Constitution, Mr. Lincoln, in his speech at New York, which I have before me, declared that it was a "sedition bill"; his press and party hooted at it. So far from recognizing the bill as intended to carry out the Constitution of the United States, it received their jeers and jibes. The Black Republicans of Massachusetts elected the admirer and eulogist of John Brown's courage as their governor, and we may suppose he will throw no impediments in the way of John Brown's successors. The epithet applied to the bill of the Senator from Illinois is quoted from a deliberate speech delivered by Lincoln in New York, for which, it was stated in the journals, according to some resolution passed by an association of his own party, he was paid a couple of hundred dollars. The speech should therefore have been deliberate. Lincoln denounced that

bill.   He places the stamp of his condemnation upon a
measure intended to promote the peace and security of Confederate States.   He is, therefore, the enemy of the human
race, and deserves the execration of all mankind.

We demand these five propositions. Are they not right?
Are they not just?   Take them in detail, and show that
they are not warranted by the Constitution, by the safety
of our people, by the principles of eternal justice.   We will
pause and consider them; but mark me, we will not let you
decide the question for us.

Senators, the Constitution is a compact.   It contains
all our obligations and the duties of the Federal Government.   I am content and have ever been content to sustain
it.   While I doubt its perfection, while I do not believe it
was a good compact, and while I never saw the day that
I would have voted for it as a proposition de novo, yet I
am bound to it by oath and by that common prudence
which would induce men to abide by established forms
rather than to rush into unknown dangers.   I have given to
it, and intend to give to it, unfaltering support and allegiance, but I choose to put that allegiance on the true ground,
not on the false idea that anybody's blood was shed for it.
I say that the Constitution is the whole compact.   All the
obligations, all the chains that fetter the limbs of my people, are nominated in the bond, and they wisely excluded
any conclusion against them, by declaring that "the powers
not granted by the Constitution to the United States, or
forbidden by it to the states, belonged to the states respectively or the people."   Now I will try it by that standard;
I will subject it to that test.   The law of nature, the law of
justice, would say—and it is so expounded by the publicists
—that equal rights in the common property shall be enjoyed.   Even in a monarchy the king cannot prevent the
subjects from enjoying equality in the disposition of the
public property.   Even in a despotic government this principle is recognized.   It was the blood and the money of the
whole people (says the learned Grotius, and say all the
publicists) which acquired the public property, and therefore
it is not the property of the sovereign.   This right of
equality being, then, according to justice and natural equity,
a right belonging to all states, when did we give it up?

You say Congress has a right to pass rules and regulations concerning the territory and other property of the United States. Very well. Does that exclude those whose blood and money paid for it? Does "dispose of" mean to rob the rightful owners? You must show a better title than that, or a better sword than we have.

But, you say, try the right. I agree to it. But how? By our judgment? No, not until the last resort. What then; by yours? No, not until the same time. How then try it? The South has always said, by the Supreme Court. But that is in our favor, and Lincoln says he will not stand that judgment. Then each must judge for himself of the mode and manner of redress. But you deny us that privilege, and finally reduce us to accepting your judgment. The Senator from Kentucky comes to your aid, and says he can find no constitutional right of secession. Perhaps not; but the Constitution is not the place to look for state rights. If that right belongs to independent states, and they did not cede it to the Federal Government, it is reserved to the states, or to the people. Ask your new commentator where he gets the right to judge for us. Is it in the bond?

The Northern doctrine was, many years ago, that the Supreme Court was the judge. That was their doctrine in 1800. They denounced Madison for the report of 1799, on the Virginia resolutions; they denounced Jefferson for framing the Kentucky resolutions, because they were presumed to impugn the decisions of the Supreme Court of the United States; and they declared that that court was made, by the Constitution, the ultimate and supreme arbiter. That was the universal judgment—the declaration of every free state in this Union, in answer to the Virginia resolutions of 1798, or of all who did answer, even including the State of Delaware, then under federal control.

The Supreme Court have decided that, by the Constitution, we have a right to go to the territories and be protected there with our property. You say, we cannot decide the compact for ourselves. Well, can the Supreme Court decide it for us? Mr. Lincoln says he does not care what the Supreme Court decides, he will turn us out anyhow. He says this in his debate with the honorable member from

Illinois [Mr. Douglas]. I have it before me. He said he would vote against the decision of the Supreme Court. Then you did not accept that arbiter. You will not take my construction; you will not take the Supreme Court as an arbiter; you will not take the practise of the government; you will not take the treaties under Jefferson and Madison; you will not take the opinion of Madison upon the very question of prohibition in 1820. What, then, will you take? You will take nothing but your own judgment; that is, you will not only judge for yourselves, not only discard the court, discard our construction, discard the practise of the government, but you will drive us out, simply because you will it. Come and do it! You have sapped the foundations of society; you have destroyed almost all hope of peace. In a compact where there is no common arbiter, where the parties finally decide for themselves, the sword alone at last becomes the real, if not the constitutional, arbiter. Your party says that you will not take the decision of the Supreme Court. You said so at Chicago; you said so in committee; every man of you in both houses says so. What are you going to do? You say we shall submit to your construction. We shall do it, if you can make us; but not otherwise, or in any other manner. That is settled. You may call it secession, or you may call it revolution; but there is a big fact standing before you, ready to oppose you—that fact is, freemen with arms in their hands. The cry of the Union will not disperse them; we have passed that point; they demand equal rights; you had better heed the demand.

GEORGE GRAHAM VEST

ON INDIAN SCHOOLS

[George Graham Vest was born in Kentucky in 1830. He graduated at Centre College in his native State, and after studying law
and receiving a diploma at Transylvania University he settled in Missouri. His reputation as a lawyer soon became such that in a few years
he was elected to the State legislature. When the Civil War came he
advocated Secession, and sat in the Confederate Congress—two years
in the House and one year in the Senate. When peace was restored
he was not long in gaining the ear of the people of his State, thanks to
his gift of oratory and devotion to Democratic principles. He was
elected to the United States Senate from Missouri in 1879, and has been
continuously reëlected since that year. The speech that follows was
the result of an extensive Western tour of investigation of the Indian
schools, and was delivered in the United States Senate in 1900.]

MR. PRESIDENT: I shall not take the time of the
Senate in discussing this oft-debated question as to
the contract schools. My opinions have been so emphatically and repeatedly expressed that it is hardly necessary
for me now to give information on that subject to any one
who has taken any interest in the matter.

There are people in this country, unfortunately, who
believe that an Indian child had better die an unbeliever,
an idolater even, than to be educated by the Society of
Jesus or in the Catholic Church. I am very glad to say that
I have not the slightest sympathy with that sort of bigotry
and fanaticism. I was raised a Protestant; I expect to die
one; I was never in a Catholic church in my life, and I have
not the slightest sympathy with many of its dogmas; but,
above all, I have no respect for this insane fear that the
Catholic Church is about to overturn this government. I
should be ashamed to call myself an American if I indulged
in any such ignorant belief.

I look upon this as a man of the world, practical, I hope, in all things, and especially in legislation, where my sphere of duty now is. Unfortunately I am not connected with any religious organization. I have no such prejudice as would prevent me from doing what I believed to be my duty. I would give this question of the education of Indian children the same sort of consideration that I would if I were building a house or having any other mechanical or expert business carried on. I had infinitely rather see these Indians Catholics than to see them blanket Indians on the plains, ready to go on the warpath against civilization and Christianity.

I said a few minutes ago that I was a Protestant. I was reared in the old Scotch Presbyterian church; my father was an elder in it, and my earliest impressions were that the Jesuits had horns and hoofs and tails, and that there was a faint tinge of sulphur in the circumambient air whenever one crossed your path. Some years ago I was assigned by the Senate to duty upon the committee on Indian affairs, and I was assigned by the committee, of which Mr. Dawes was then the very zealous chairman, to examine the Indian schools in Wyoming and Montana. I did so under great difficulties and with labor which I could not now physically perform. I visited every one of them. I crossed that great buffalo expanse of country where you can now see only the wallows and trails of those extinct animals, and I went to all these schools. I wish to say now what I have said before in the Senate, and it is not the popular side of this question by any means, that I did not see in all my journey, which lasted for several weeks, a single school that was doing any educational work worthy the name of educational work unless it was under the control of the Jesuits. I did not see a single government school, especially these day schools, where there was any work done at all.

Something has been said here about the difference between enrolment and attendance. I found day schools with 1,500 Indian children enrolled and not ten in attendance, except on meat days, as they called it, when beeves were killed by the agent and distributed to the tribe. Then there was a full attendance. I found schools where there were old, broken-down preachers and politicians receiving

$1,200 a year and a house to live in for the purpose of conducting these Indian day schools, and when I cross-examined them, as I did in every instance, I found that their actual attendance was about three to five in the hundred of the enrolment.   I do not care what reports are made, for they usually come from interested parties.   You cannot educate the children with the day schools.

In 1850 Father De Smet, a self-sacrificing Christian Jesuit, went, at the solicitation of the Flatheads, to their reservation in Montana.   The Flatheads sent two runners, young men, to bring the black robes to educate them and teach them the religion of Christ.   Both of these runners were killed by the Blackfeet and never reached St. Louis. They then sent two more.   One of them was killed, and the other made his way down the Missouri River after incredible hardships and reached St. Louis.   Father De Smet and two young associates went out to the Flathead reservation and established the mission of St. Mary in the Bitter Root and St. Ignatius on the Jocko reservation.   The Blackfeet burned the St. Mary mission, killed two of the Jesuits and thought they had killed the other—Father Ravaille.   I saw him when on this committee, lying in his cell at the St. Mary's mission, paralyzed from the waist down, but performing surgical operations, for he was an accomplished surgeon, and doing all that he possibly could do for humanity and religion.   He had been fifty-two years in that tribe of Indians.   Think of it!   Fifty-two years.   Not owning the robe on his back, not even having a name, for he was a number in the semi-military organization called the Company of Jesus; and if he received orders at midnight to go to Africa or Asia he went without question, because it was his duty to the cause of Christ, and for no other consideration or reason.

Father De Smet established these two missions and undertook to teach the Indian children as we teach our children in the common schools by day's attendance.   It was a miserable failure.   The Jesuits tried it for years, supported by contributions from France, not a dollar from the government, and they had to abandon the whole system.   They found that when the girls and boys went back to the tepee at night all the work of the day by the Jesuits was obliterated. They found that ridicule, the great weapon of the Indian in the tepee, was used to drive these children away from the educational institutions established by the Jesuits. When the girl went back to the tepee with a dress on like an American woman and attempted to speak the English language, and whom the nuns were attempting to teach how to sew and spin, and wash and cook, she was ridiculed as having white blood in her veins, and the result was that she became the worst and most abandoned of the tribe, because it was neccessary in order to reinstate herself with her own people that she should prove the most complete apostate from the teachings of the Jesuits.

After nearly twenty years of this work by the Jesuits they abandoned it, and they established a different system, separating the boys and the girls, teaching them how to work, for that is the problem, not how to read or spell, nor the laws of arithmetic, but how to work and to get rid of this insane prejudice taught by the Indians from the beginning that nobody but a squaw should work, and that it degrades a man to do any sort of labor, or in fact to do anything except to hunt and go to war.

The hardest problem that can be proposed to the human race is how to make men self-dependent. There can be no self-respect without self-dependence. There can be no good government until a people are elevated up to the high plane of earning their bread in the sweat of their faces. When you come to educate negroes and Indians there is but one thing that will ever lift them out of the degradation in which long years of servitude and nomadic habits have placed them, and that is to teach them that the highest and greatest and most elevating thing in the human race is to learn how to work and to make themselves independent.

I take off my hat, metaphorically, whenever I think of this negro in Alabama—Booker Washington. He has solved that problem for his race, and he is the only man who has ever done it. Fred Douglass was a great politician, but he never discovered what was necessary for the negro race in this country. I have just returned from the South after a sojourn of five weeks upon the Gulf of Mexico.

The negro problem is the most terrible that ever confronted a civilized race upon the face of the earth. You cannot exterminate them; you cannot extradite them; you must make them citizens as they are and as they will continue to be. You must assimilate them. Exportation is a dream of the philanthropist, demonstrated to be such by the experiment in Liberia. Mr. Lincoln tried it, and took his contingent fund immediately after the war, shipped negroes to a colony in the West Indies, and those who were left from the fever after two years came back to the United States, and every dollar expended was thrown away. Washington, this negro in Alabama, has struck the keynote. It will take years to carry it out, and he has the prejudices of his own race and the prejudices of the ignorant whites against him; but he deserves the commendation of all the people, not only of the United States, but those of the civilized world.

Mr. President, the Jesuits have elevated the Indian wherever they have been allowed to do so without interference of bigotry and fanaticism and the cowardice of insectivorous politicians who are afraid of the A. P. A. and the votes that can be cast against them in their district and states. They have made him a Christian, and above even that have made him a workman able to support himself and those dependent upon him. Go to the Flathead reservation, in Montana, and look from the cars of the Northern Pacific Railroad, and you will see the result of what Father De Smet and his associates began and what was carried on successfully until the A. P. A. and the cowards who are afraid of it struck down the appropriation. There are now four hundred Indian children upon that reservation without one dollar to give them an hour's instruction of any kind. That is the teaching of many professors of the religion of Christ in the Protestant churches. I repudiate it. I would be ashamed of myself if I did not do it, and if it were the last accent I ever uttered in public life it would be to denounce that narrow-minded and unworthy policy based upon religious bigotry.

This A. P. A. did me the greatest honor in my life during their last session in this city, two years ago. They passed a resolution unanimously demanding that I should be impeached because I said what I am saying now. Mr. President, the knowledge of the Constitution of this country

2018 GEORGE GRAHAM VEST

developed by that organization in demanding the impeachment of a United States senator for uttering his honest opinion in this chamber puts them beyond criticism. It would be cowardly and inhuman to say one word about ignorance so dense as that.

Mr. President, as I said, go through this reservation and look at the work of the Jesuits, and what is seen? You find comfortable dwellings, herds of cattle and horses, intelligent, self-respecting Indians. I have been to their houses and found that under the system adopted by the Jesuits, the new system, as I may call it, after the failure of that which was attempted for twenty years, to which I have alluded, after they had educated these boys and girls and they had intermarried, the Jesuits would go out and break up a piece of land and build them a house, and that couple became the nucleus of civilization in the neighborhood. They had been educated under the system which prevented them from going back to the tepee after a day's tuition. The Jesuits found that in order to accomplish their purpose of teaching them how to work and to depend upon themselves it was necessary to keep them in school, a boarding-school, by day and night, and to allow even the parents to see them only in the presence of the brothers or the nuns.

I undertake to say now—and every Senator here who has passed through that reservation will corroborate my statement—that there is not in this whole country an object lesson more striking than that to be seen from the cars of the Northern Pacific Railroad, the fact that these Jesuits alone have solved the problem of rescuing the Indians from the degradation in which they were found.

Mr. President, these Jesuits are not there, as one of them told me, for the love of the Indian. Old Father Ravaille told me, lying upon his back in that narrow cell, with the crucifix above him, "I am here not for the love of the Indian, but for the love of Christ," without pay except the approval of his own conscience. If you send one of our people, a clergyman, a politician even, to perform this work among the Indians, he looks back to the fleshpots of Egypt. He has a family, perchance, that he cannot take with him on the salary he receives. He is divided between the habits and customs and luxuries of civilized life and the self-sacrificing duties that devolve upon him in this work of teaching the Indians.

The Jesuit has no family. He has no ambition. He has no idea except to do his duty as God has given him to see it; and I am not afraid to say this, because I speak from personal observation, and no man ever went among these Indians with more intense prejudice against the Jesuits than I had when I left the city of Washington to perform that duty. I made my report to the secretary of the interior, Senator Teller, now on this floor, and I said in that report what I say here and what I would say anywhere and be glad of the opportunity to say it.

Mr. President, every dollar you give these day schools might as well be thrown into the Potomac River under a ton of lead. You will make no more impression upon the Indian children than if you should take that money and burn it and expect its smoke by some mystic process to bring them from idolatry and degradation to Christianity and civilization. If you can have the same system of boarding schools supported by the government that the Jesuits have adopted after long years of trial and deprivation, I grant that there might be something done in the way of elevating this race.

The old Indians are gone, hopelessly gone, so far as civilization and Christianity are concerned. They look upon all work as a degradation and that a squaw should bear the burden of life. The young Indian can be saved. There are 3,000 of them to-day in the Dakotas—in South Dakota, I believe—who are voters, exercising intelligently, as far as I know, the right of suffrage. Go to the Indian Territory, where there are the five civilized tribes, and you will see what can be done by intelligent effort, not with day schools, but with schools based upon the idea of taking the children and removing them from the injurious influence of the old Indians and teaching them the arts of civilization and of peace.

If I have ever done anything in my whole career in this chamber of which I am sincerely proud it is that upon one occasion I obtained an appropriation of $10,000 for an industrial school at St. Ignatius, in Montana. A few years afterward, in passing through to the Pacific coast, I stopped over to see that school. They heard I was coming and met me at the depot with a brass band, the instruments in the hands of Indian boys, and they played without discrimination Hail Columbia and Dixie. They had been taught by a young French nobleman whom I had met two years before at the mission, who had squandered the principal portion of his fortune in reckless dissipation in the salons of Paris and had suddenly left that sort of life and joined the Company of Jesus and dedicated himself to the American missions.

I went up to the mission and found there these Indian boys making hats and boots and running a smithy and carrying on a mill and herding cattle. The girls and boys when they graduated, intermarrying, became heads of families as reputable and well-behaved and devoted to Christianity as any we can find in our own states. They were Catholics. That is a crime with some people in this country.

Mr. President, are we to be told that a secret political organization in this country shall dictate to us what we ought to do for this much injured race whom we have despoiled of their lands and homes and whom God has put upon us as an inheritance to be cared for? I accuse no Senator here of any other motive than a desire to do his public duty. I shall do mine, and I should gladly vote for an amendment to this bill infinitely stronger than that of the Senator from Arkansas. I would put this work, imperative upon us, in the hands of those who could best accomplish it, as I would give the building of my house to the best mechanic, who would put up a structure that suited me and met the ends I desired. If the Catholics can do it better than anybody else, let them do it. If the Presbyterian, the Methodist, the Congregationalist, or any other denomination can do it, give the work to them; but to every man who comes to me and says this is a union of church and state, I answer him, "Your statement is false upon the very face of it." Instead of teaching the Indian children that they must be Catholics in order to be good citizens, they are simply taught that work is ennobling, and with the sense of self-dependence and not of dependence upon others will come civilization and Christianity. These are my feelings, Mr. President, and I should be glad if I could put them upon the statute books.

DANIEL WOLSEY VOORHEES

ON THE TILDEN CONTROVERSY

[Daniel Wolsey Voorhees, an American statesman, and for many years one of the most distinguished leaders of the Democratic party, was born in Ohio in 1827. He received a superior academic education in Indiana, chose the law as his profession, and directed his attention to politics. Having filled local offices with credit, and established a reputation throughout Indiana as a Democrat of oratorical ability, he was elected to Congress, and in 1877 was chosen by the State legislature to the United States Senate. He retained his seat in that body for a period of twenty years, and was finally displaced by a Republican. During his senatorial career he held radical views on the money question, favoring at one time free silver coinage and a greenback currency. He died in Washington a few months after his defeat for reelection to the Senate in 1897. The following speech on the disputed Presidential election between Hayes and Tilden was delivered in the Democratic National Convention at St. Louis in 1876.]

I AM overwhelmed with gratitude to so many of my fellow-citizens of distinguished character from every part of the United States, who have done me the singular honor of calling for my presence on this occasion and under these circumstances. I cannot attribute it to anything in my humble career; I know not what to attribute it to, and I may say that at least for once in my life I am at a loss as to the manner in which I shall respond to such an overwhelming compliment as has been paid to me. I feel abashed in the presence of this mighty congregation of people who expect to hear my humble words. I am here with you, fellow-Democrats of the United States, for the exalted and patriotic purpose of endeavoring to redeem and wrench our country from the hands of despoilers and public plunderers. I am here with you for the purpose of trying to better unite the scattered, shattered, broken bands of our Union by gathering together in one mighty brotherhood, looking in one another's faces, renewing ancient friend-ship, steadying the column, turning its head toward victory and glory in the future as we have done in the past.

We are entering upon a new century. Portions of the last century were full of glory. The closing years of our last century, however, have had tears and blood com-mingled, sorrow and gloom. The cypress of mourning has been in thousands of households, but with the coming of this new century there comes a new dispensation, the dawn of a revelation of glory such as shall eclipse the past years of the century that has gone by. Standing, as I do, one of the humble representatives of the great valley of the Mis-sissippi, we stand in a central point to invoke union, to invoke harmony, to invoke a compromise of conflicting opinions in the Democratic ranks. There is nothing, my friends, in the differences and divergences of opinion in the Democratic party that cannot be honorably, easily, smoothly, and harmoniously adjusted, so that when the lines of battle are formed, there shall be no heartburnings, no divisions, no collisions of thought. There is no reason why we should not thus adjust our differences, if differences we have; and standing, as I do, one of the representatives of the great Mississippi Valley, we appeal to the people of the far East. We say to them: "What is for your pros-perity is likewise for ours." You all rest upon the pros-perity of the agricultural interests of the mighty Mississippi Valley. The foundation of commercial glory and greatness is the farmer's plow and the sickle and the rich harvest. We freight your ships, we make your cities prosper. You, in turn, benefit us in a thousand ways. We interlace and interchange and bind our interests together, when we prop-erly consider it. We appeal to you now. Give us a living chance in this convention and in this contest, and we will make a glorious return in October for your final charge upon the enemy.

I stand in your presence neither arrogant nor suppliant. I stand for absolute justice, willing to concede everything that is just to everybody else, only asking the same mete to ourselves. Let us not be extreme to each other; let us not seek to be distasteful. Man's talent to be disagreeable to his fellow-man is quite sufficient without cultivating it at

all. We should cultivate amiability and friendship rather.
I make these remarks to our brethren of the East. We
have fought a thousand battles with you for the Democracy, and never one against you. Our scores of political
conflict are upon our breasts and none upon our backs.

To our old-time brethren of the South a word or two
also! I am one of the men surely that needs no apology
to look my Southern brother in the eye and expect him to
believe that I speak to him with no forked tongue. No
political battle was ever so hot, the clouds of obloquy and
storm and danger never ran so low or black over the heads
of the Democracy with whom I have worked and toiled for
years, as to deter us from standing by all the constitutional
rights and guaranties of our oppressed Southern brothers.
I say to my Southern brethren who know me, and whom
I know, do not in this hour of national counsel, this hour
of national preparation for the great conflict against the
Radical foe arrayed against you and led, as was well said
by the distinguished gentleman from New York, by the
pirate's flag of the bloody shirt,—do not in this hour leave
us in the Northwest, wounded, helpless, to be scalped and
murdered upon the field of battle. We have no personal
animosities to gratify, we have no personal aims to subserve. If there is one man who can get more votes than
another, were my own brother a candidate, I should be for
that other man. The times are too serious, the issues too
mighty, for a personal thought to intervene.

Three times in the last twelve years we in the Northwest have charged the enemy's lines under the head of the
gallant Democracy of New York. If it has to be so again
we will dress in parade, and even if it be a forlorn hope, we
will fight it like men. I say there are no heartburnings,
there are no animosities to gratify. Men of this convention, it was no purpose of mine to speak here. I feel like
apologizing for it, but your voice sent me here. I did not
desire to speak, but I belong to that class of men who cannot speak and say nothing. I must say something. And
what I say is the utterance of a sincere heart. In the counsel of old, tried, cherished, and beloved friends, let us purify
our hearts for this great work that is before us. Let us
look narrowly to our motives. Let us look narrowly to our

duties, and when the sun goes down upon the finished work of this convention, I pray Almighty God that it may be as ordered, that in November your country will stand redeemed, disenthralled, and reënfranchised in all the rights of a free people, from the tyrannical bond that has crushed and oppressed us so long.   That is my prayer.

SIR ROBERT WALPOLE

ON A MOTION FOR HIS REMOVAL

[Sir Robert Walpole, Earl of Orford, was born in Norfolk about 1676. He was educated at Eton and at King's College, Cambridge. He entered Parliament as a Whig, and speedily became a power there. He was appointed secretary of war, but this he resigned in 1710. In 1712 he was imprisoned for a time in the Tower on an ill-founded charge of corruption. On the accession of George I. (1714), Walpole acquired great influence at court, becoming paymaster-general of the forces, and later first lord of the treasury, and twice chancellor of the exchequer. This office he resigned in 1717, against the wishes of the king. He opposed the South Sea act, and when the crash came all eyes were turned to him. He was appointed first lord of the treasury in 1721, and by his exertions the national credit was restored. He died in March, 1745. In 1741 his enemies in Parliament petitioned the king to remove him from office, and the following speech regarding this movement was delivered in the House of Commons, 1741.]

IT has been observed by several gentlemen, in vindication of this motion, that if it should be carried, neither my life, liberty, nor estate will be affected. But do the honorable gentlemen consider my character and reputation as of no moment? Is it no imputation to be arraigned before this House, in which I have sat forty years, and to have my name transmitted to posterity with disgrace and infamy? I will not conceal my sentiments, that to be named in Parliament as a subject of inquiry, is to me a matter of great concern. But I have the satisfaction, at the same time, to reflect, that the impression to be made depends upon the consistency of the charge and the motives of the prosecutors.

I shall now consider the articles of accusation which they have brought against me, and which they have not thought fit to reduce to specific charges; and I shall consider these in the same order as that in which they were placed by the honorable member who made the motion. First, in regard to foreign affairs; secondly, to domestic affairs; and, thirdly, to the conduct of the war.

(1) As to foreign affairs, I must take notice of the uncandid manner in which the gentlemen on the other side have managed the question, by blending numerous treaties and complicated negotiations into one general mass.

To form a fair and candid judgment of the subject, it becomes necessary not to consider the treaties merely insulated, but to advert to the time in which they were made, to the circumstances and situation of Europe when they were made, to the peculiar situation in which I stand, and to the power which I possessed. I am called repeatedly and insidiously prime and sole minister. Admitting, however, for the sake of argument, that I am prime and sole minister in this country, am I, therefore, prime and sole minister of all Europe? Am I answerable for the conduct of other countries as well as for that of my own? Many words are not wanting to show that the particular view of each court occasioned the dangers which affected the public tranquillity; yet the whole is charged to my account. Nor is this sufficient. Whatever was the conduct of England, I am equally arraigned. If we maintained ourselves in peace, and took no share in foreign transactions, we are reproached for tameness and pusillanimity. If, on the contrary, we interfered in these disputes, we are called Don Quixotes, and dupes to all the world. If we contracted guaranties it was asked, Why is the nation wantonly burdened? If guaranties were declined, we were reproached with having no allies.

I have, however, sir, this advantage, that all the objections now alleged against the conduct of the administration to which I have the honor to belong, have already been answered to the satisfaction of a majority of both Houses of Parliament, and I believe to the satisfaction of a majority of the better sort of people in the nation. I need, therefore, only repeat a few of these answers that have been made already, which I shall do in the order of time in which the several transactions happened; and consequently must begin with our refusing to accept the sole mediation offered us by Spain, on the breach between that court and the court of France, occasioned by the dismission of the Infanta of Spain.

I hope it will not be said we had any reason to quarrel with France upon that account; and therefore, if our accepting of that mediation might have produced a rupture with France, it was not our duty to interfere unless we had something very beneficial to expect from the acceptance. A reconciliation between the courts of Vienna and Madrid, it is true, was desirable to all Europe as well as to us, provided it had been brought about without any design to disturb our tranquillity or the tranquillity of Europe. But both parties were then so high in their demands that we could hope for no success; and if the negotiation had ended without effect, we might have expected the common fate of arbitrators, the disobliging of both. Therefore, as it was our interest to keep well with both, I must still think it was the most prudent part we could act to refuse the offered mediation.

The next step of our foreign conduct, exposed to reprehension, is the Treaty of Hanover. Sir, if I were to give the true history of that treaty, which no gentleman can desire I should, I am sure I could fully justify my own conduct. But as I do not desire to justify my own without justifying his late Majesty's conduct, I must observe that his late Majesty had such information as convinced not only him, but those of his council, both at home and abroad, that some dangerous designs had been formed between the emperor and Spain at the time of their concluding the treaty at Vienna, in May, 1725; designs, sir, which were dangerous not only to the liberties of this nation, but to the liberties of Europe.

I do not pretend, sir, to be a great master of foreign affairs. In that post in which I have the honor to serve his Majesty, it is not my business to interfere; and as one of his Majesty's council, I have but one voice. But if I had been the sole adviser of the Treaty of Hanover, and of all the measures which were taken in pursuance of it, from what I have said I hope it will appear that I do not deserve to be censured either as a weak or a wicked minister on that account.

The next measures which incurred censure were the guaranty of the Pragmatic Sanction by the second Treaty of Vienna, and the refusal of the Cabinet to assist the House of Austria, in conformity with the articles of that guaranty.

As to the guaranty of the Pragmatic Sanction, I am really surprised to find that measure objected to. It was so universally approved of, both within doors and without, that till this very day I think no fault was ever found with it, unless it was that of being too long delayed. If it was so neccessary for supporting the balance of power in Europe, as has been insisted on in this debate, to preserve entire the dominions of the House of Austria, surely it was not our business to insist upon a partition of them in favor of any of the princes of the empire. But if we had, could we have expected that the House of Austria would have agreed to any such partition even for the acquisition of our guaranty? The king of Prussia had, it is true, a claim upon some lordships in Silesia; but that claim was absolutely denied by the court of Vienna, and was not at that time so much insisted on by the late king of Prussia. Nay, if he had lived till this time, I believe it would not now have been insisted on; for he acceded to that guaranty without any reservation of that claim; therefore I must look upon this as an objection which has since arisen from an accident that could not then be foreseen or provided against.

(2) I now come, sir, to the second head, the conduct of domestic affairs. And here a most heinous charge is made, that the nation has been burdened with unnecessary expenses, for the sole purpose of preventing the discharge of our debts and the abolition of taxes. But this attack is more to the dishonor of the whole Cabinet council than to me. If there is any ground for this imputation, it is a charge upon king, lords, and commons, as corrupted or imposed upon. And they have no proof of these allegations, but affect to substantiate them by common fame and public notoriety!

No expense has been incurred but what has been approved of, and provided for, by Parliament. The public treasure has been duly applied to the uses to which it was appropriated by Parliament, and regular accounts have been annually laid before Parliament of every article of expense. If by foreign accidents, by the disputes of foreign states among themselves, or by their designs against us, the nation has often been put to an extraordinary expense, that expense cannot be said to have been unnecessary; because if by saving it we had exposed the balance of power to danger, or ourselves to an attack, it would have cost, perhaps, a hundred times that sum before we could recover from that danger, or repel that attack.

(3) I shall now advert to the third topic of accusation—the conduct of the war. I have already stated in what manner, and under what circumstances, hostilities commenced; and as I am neither general nor admiral—as I have nothing to do either with our navy or army—I am sure I am not answerable for the prosecution of it. But were I to answer for everything, no fault could, I think, be found with my conduct in the prosecution of the war. It has from the beginning been carried on with as much vigor, and as great care of our trade, as was consistent with our safety at home, and with the circumstances we were in at the beginning of the war. If our attacks upon the enemy were too long delayed, or if they have not been so vigorous or so frequent as they ought to have been, those only are to blame who have for many years been haranguing against standing armies; for, without a sufficient number of regular troops in proportion to the numbers kept up by our neighbors, I am sure we can neither defend ourselves nor offend our enemies. On the supposed miscarriages of the war, so unfairly stated, and so unjustly imputed to me, I could, with great ease, frame an incontrovertible defense. But as I have trespassed so long on the time of the House, I shall not weaken the effect of that forcible exculpation so generously and disinterestedly advanced by the right honorable gentleman who so meritoriously presides at the admiralty.

If my whole administration is to be scrutinized and arraigned, why are the most favorable parts to be omitted? If facts are to be accumulated on one side, why not on the other? And why may not I be permitted to speak in my own favor? Was I not called by the voice of the king and of the nation to remedy the fatal effects of the South Sea project, and to support declining credit? Was I not placed at the head of the treasury when the revenues were in the greatest confusion? Is credit revived, and does it now flourish? Is it not at an incredible height? and if so, to whom must that circumstance be attributed? Has not tranquillity been preserved both at home and abroad, notwithstanding a most unreasonable and violent opposition? Has the true interest of the nation been pursued, or has trade flourished? Have gentlemen produced one instance of this exorbitant power; of the influence which I extend to all parts of the nation; of the tyranny with which I oppress those who oppose, and the liberality with which I reward those who support me? But having first invested me with a kind of mock dignity, and styled me a prime minister, they impute to me an unpardonable abuse of that chimerical authority which they only have created and conferred. If they are really persuaded that the army is annually established by me, that I have the sole disposal of posts and honors, that I employ this power in the destruction of liberty and the diminution of commerce, let me awaken them from their delusion. Let me expose to their view the real condition of the public weal. Let me show them that the Crown has made no encroachments, that all supplies have been granted by Parliament, that all questions have been debated with the same freedom, as before the fatal period in which my counsels are said to have gained the ascendency—an ascendency from which they deduce the loss of trade, the approach of slavery, the preponderance of prerogative, and the extension of influence. But I am far from believing that they feel those apprehensions which they so earnestly labor to communicate to others; and I have too high an opinion of their sagacity not to conclude that, even in their own judgment, they are complaining of grievances that they do not suffer, and promoting rather their private interest than that of the public.

What is this unbounded sole power which is imputed to me? How has it discovered itself, or how has it been proved?

What have been the effects of the corruption, ambition, and avarice with which I am so abundantly charged?

Have I ever been suspected of being corrupted? A strange phenomenon, a corrupter himself not corrupt! Is ambition imputed to me? Why then do I still continue a commoner? I, who refused a white staff and a peerage? I had, indeed, like to have forgotten the little ornament about my shoulders [the garter], which gentlemen have so repeatedly mentioned in terms of sarcastic obloquy. But surely, though this may be regarded with envy or indignation in another place, it cannot be supposed to raise any resentment in this House, where many may be pleased to see those honors which their ancestors have worn, restored again to the Commons.

Have I given any symptoms of an avaricious disposition? Have I obtained any grants from the Crown since I have been placed at the head of the treasury? Has my conduct been different from that which others in the same station would have followed? Have I acted wrong in giving the place of auditor to my son, and in providing for my own family? I trust that their advancement will not be imputed to me as a crime, unless it shall be proved that I placed them in offices of trust and responsibility for which they were unfit.

But while I unequivocally deny that I am sole and prime minister, and that to my influence and direction all the measures of the government must be attributed, yet I will not shrink from the responsibility which attaches to the post I have the honor to hold; and should, during the long period in which I have sat upon this bench, any one step taken by government be proved to be either disgraceful or disadvantageous to the nation, I am ready to hold myself accountable.

To conclude, sir, though I shall always be proud of the honor of any trust or confidence from his Majesty, yet I shall always be ready to remove from his councils and presence when he thinks fit; and therefore I should think myself very little concerned in the event of the present question, if it were not for the encroachment that will thereby be made upon the prerogatives of the Crown. But I must think that an address to his Majesty to remove one of his servants without so much as alleging any particular crime against him, is one of the greatest encroachments that was ever made upon the prerogatives of the Crown. And therefore, for the sake of my master, without any regard for my own, I hope all those that have a due regard for our Constitution, and for the rights and prerogatives of the Crown, without which our Constitution cannot be preserved, will be against this motion.

GEORGE WASHINGTON

FIRST INAUGURAL ADDRESS

[George Washington was born at Pope's Creek, Westmoreland County, Va., 1732. His first public service was in acting as messenger from Governor Dinwiddie of Virginia to the commandant of the French forces near Lake Erie to protest against their eastern encroachments. He was then nineteen, and held the appointment of one of the adjutants-general of Virginia with the rank of major. He went as a delegate to the first Continental Congress in 1775. In the following year he was nominated commander-in-chief of the colonial forces then assembled before Boston and accepted the post, at the same time declining all remuneration for services, relying upon Congress to reimburse him for actual expenses. He compelled the British evacuation of Boston, March 17, 1776, and finally brought about the surrender of Cornwallis at Yorktown, October 19, 1781. He surrendered his commission at Annapolis on December 23d, and retired to Mt. Vernon to spend a few years in quiet, before emerging again to preside over the Convention of 1787, met to form the Articles of Confederation for the government of the States. He was chosen the first president under the Constitution and served two terms. He died at Mt. Vernon, December 14, 1799. His first inaugural address was delivered in New York City April 30, 1789 ; the farewell address was issued September 19, 1796.]

AMONG the vicissitudes incident to life, no event could have filled me with greater anxieties than that of which the notification was transmitted by your order, and received on the fourth day of the present month. On the one hand, I was summoned by my country, whose voice I can never hear but with veneration and love, from a retreat which I had chosen with the fondest predilection, and, in my flattering hopes, with an immutable decision, as the asylum of my declining years; a retreat which was rendered every day more necessary as well as more dear to me, by the addition of habit to inclination, and of frequent interruptions in my health to the gradual waste committed on it by time; on the other hand, the magnitude and difficulty of the trust to which the voice of my country called me, being sufficient to awaken, in the wisest and most experienced of her citizens, a distrustful scrutiny into his qualifications, could not but overwhelm with despondence one who, inheriting inferior endowments from nature, and unpracticed in the duties of civil administration, ought to be peculiarly conscious of his own deficiencies. In this conflict of emotions, all I dare aver is that it has been my faithful study to collect my duty from a just appreciation of every circumstance by which it might be affected. All I dare hope is, that if, in executing this task, I have been too much swayed by a grateful remembrance of former instances, or by an affectionate sensibility to this transcendent proof of the confidence of my fellow-citizens, and have thence too little consulted my incapacity as well as disinclination for the weighty and untried cares before me, my error will be palliated by the motives which misled me, and its consequences be judged by my country, with some share of the partiality in which they originated.

Such being the impression under which I have, in obedience to the public summons, repaired to the present station, it would be peculiarly improper to omit, in this first official act, my fervent supplications to that Almighty Being who rules over the universe, who presides in the councils of nations, and whose providential aids can supply every human defect, that his benediction may consecrate to the liberties and happiness of the people of the United States a government instituted by themselves for these essential purposes, and may enable every instrument employed in its administration to execute, with success, the functions allotted to his charge. In tendering this homage to the great Author of every public and private good, I assure myself that it expresses your sentiments not less than my own; nor those of my fellow-citizens at large less than either. No people can be bound to acknowledge and adore the invisible hand which conducts the affairs of men, more than the people of the United States. Every step by which they have advanced to the character of an independent nation seems to have been distinguished by some token of providential agency. And, in the important revolution just accomplished, in the system of their united government, the tranquil deliberations and voluntary consent of so many distinct communities, from which the event has resulted, cannot be compared with the means by which most governments have been established, without some return of pious gratitude, along with a humble anticipation of the future blessings which the past seems to presage. These reflections, arising out of the present crisis, have forced themselves too strongly on my mind to be suppressed. You will join with me, I trust, in thinking that there are none under the influence of which the proceedings of a new and free government can more auspiciously commence.

By the article establishing the Executive Department, it is made the duty of the President " to recommend to your consideration such measures as he shall judge necessary and expedient." The circumstances under which I now meet you will acquit me from entering into that subject further than to refer you to the great constitutional charter under which we are assembled; and which, in defining your powers, designates the objects to which your attention is to be given. It will be more consistent with those circumstances and far more congenial with the feelings which actuate me, to substitute, in place of a recommendation of particular measures, the tribute that is due to the talents, the rectitude, and the patriotism which adorn the characters selected to devise and adopt them. In these honorable qualifications, I behold the surest pledges, that as, on one side, no local prejudices or attachments, no separate views nor party animosities, will misdirect the comprehensive and equal eye which ought to watch over this great assemblage of communities and interests—so, on another, that the foundations of our national policy will be laid in the pure and immutable principles of private morality; and the preeminence of a free government be exemplified by all the attributes which can win the affections of its citizens and command the respect of the world.

I dwell on this prospect with every satisfaction which an ardent love for my country can inspire; since there is no truth more thoroughly established than that there exists, in the economy and course of nature, an indissoluble union between virtue and happiness—between duty and advantage

—between the genuine maxims of an honest and magnanimous policy and the solid rewards of public prosperity and felicity—since we ought to be no less persuaded that the propitious smiles of heaven can never be expected on a nation that disregards the eternal rules of order and right which heaven itself has ordained—and since the preservation of the sacred fire of liberty, and the destiny of the republican model of government, are justly considered as deeply, perhaps as finally, staked on the experiment intrusted to the hands of the American people.

Besides the ordinary objects submitted to your care, it will remain with your judgment to decide how far an exercise of the occasional power delegated by the fifth article of the Constitution is rendered expedient, at the present juncture, by the nature of objections which have been urged against the system, or by the degree of inquietude which has given birth to them. Instead of undertaking particular recommendations on this subject, in which I could be guided by no lights derived from official opportunities, I shall again give way to my entire confidence in your discernment and pursuit of the public good. For I assure myself that, while you carefully avoided every alteration which might endanger the benefits of a united and effective government, or which ought to await the future lessons of experience, a reverence for the characteristic rights of freemen and a regard for the public harmony will sufficiently influence your deliberations on the question how far the former can be more impregnably fortified, or the latter be safely and more advantageously promoted.

To the preceding observations I have one to add, which will be most properly addressed to the House of Representatives. It concerns myself, and will therefore be as brief as possible.

When I was first honored with a call into the service of my country, then on the eve of an arduous struggle for its liberties, the light in which I contemplated my duty required that I should renounce every pecuniary compensation. From this resolution I have in no instance departed. And being still under the impressions which produced it, I must decline, as inapplicable to myself, any share in the personal emoluments which may be indispensably included in a permanent provision for the Executive Department; and must accordingly pray that the pecuniary estimates for the station in which I am placed may, during my continuation in it, be limited to such actual expenditures as the public good may be thought to require.

Having thus imparted to you my sentiments, as they have been awakened by the occasion which brings us together, I shall take my present leave, but not without resorting once more to the benign Parent of the human race, in humble supplication, that, since he has been pleased to favor the American people with opportunities for deliberating in perfect tranquillity, and dispositions for deciding with unparalleled unanimity, on a form of government for the security of their union and the advancement of their happiness, so his divine blessing may be equally conspicuous in the enlarged views, the temperate consultations, and the wise measures on which the success of this government must depend.

FAREWELL ADDRESS

THE period for a new election of a citizen to administer the executive government of the United States being not far distant, and the time actually arrived when your thoughts must be employed in designating the person who is to be clothed with that important trust, it appears to me proper, especially as it may conduce to a more distinct expression of the public voice, that I should now apprise you of the resolution I have formed, to decline being considered among the number of those out of whom a choice is to be made.

I beg you, at the same time, to do me the justice to be assured that this resolution has not been taken without a strict regard to all the considerations appertaining to the relation which binds a dutiful citizen to his country; and that in withdrawing the tender of services, which silence in my situation might imply, I am influenced by no diminution of zeal for your future interest, no deficiency of grateful respect for your past kindness, but am supported by a full conviction that the step is compatible with both.

The acceptance of, and continuance hitherto in, the office to which your suffrage has twice called me have been a uniform sacrifice of inclination to the opinion of duty and to a deference for what appeared to be your desire. I constantly hoped that it would have been much earlier in my power, consistently with motives which I was not at liberty to disregard, to return to that retirement from which I had been reluctantly drawn. The strength of my inclination to do this, previous to the last election, had even led to the preparation of an address to declare it to you; but mature reflection on the then perplexed and critical posture of our affairs with foreign nations, and the unanimous advice of persons entitled to my confidence, impelled me to abandon the idea.

I rejoice that the state of your concerns, external as well as internal, no longer renders the pursuit of inclination incompatible with the sentiment of duty or propriety, and am persuaded, whatever partiality may be retained for my services, that, in the present circumstances of our country, you will not disapprove my determination to retire.

The impressions with which I first undertook the arduous trust were explained on the proper occasion. In the discharge of this trust, I will only say that I have, with good intentions, contributed toward the organization and administration of the government the best exertions of which a very fallible judgment was capable. Not unconscious in the outset of the inferiority of my qualifications, experience in my own eyes, perhaps still more in the eyes of others, has strengthened the motives to diffidence of myself; and every day, the increasing weight of years admonishes me more and more that the shade of retirement is as necessary to me as it will be welcome. Satisfied that if any circumstances have given peculiar value to my services, they were temporary, I have the consolation to believe that, while choice and prudence invite me to quit the political scene, patriotism does not forbid it.

In looking forward to the moment which is intended to terminate the career of my public life, my feelings do not permit me to suspend the deep acknowledgment of that debt of gratitude which I owe to my beloved country for the many honors it has conferred upon me; still more for the steadfast confidence with which it has supported me; and for the opportunities I have thence enjoyed of manifesting my inviolable attachment, by services faithful and persevering, though in usefulness unequal to my zeal. If benefits have resulted to our country from these services, let it always be remembered to your praise, and as an instructive example in our annals, that under circumstances in which the passions, agitated in every direction, were liable to mislead, amid appearances sometimes dubious, vicissitudes of fortune often discouraging, in situations in which not infrequently want of success has countenanced the spirit of criticism, the constancy of your support was the essential prop of the efforts, and a guaranty of the plans by which they were effected. Profoundly penetrated with this idea, I shall carry it with me to my grave, as a strong incitement to unceasing vows that heaven may continue to you the choicest tokens of its beneficence; that your union and brotherly affection may be perpetual; that the free Constitution, which is the work of your hands, may be sacredly maintained; that its administration in every department may be stamped with wisdom and virtue; that, in fine, the happiness of the people of these states, under the auspices of liberty, may be made complete by so careful a preservation and so prudent a use of this blessing as will acquire to them the glory of recommending it to the applause, the affection, and adoption of every nation which is yet a stranger to it.

Here, perhaps, I ought to stop. But solicitude for your welfare, which cannot end but with my life and the apprehension of danger, natural to that solicitude, urge me, on an occasion like the present, to offer to your solemn contemplation, and to recommend to your frequent review, some sentiments which are the result of much reflection, of no inconsiderable observation, and which appear to me all-important to the permanency of your felicity as a people. These will be offered to you with the more freedom, as you can only see in them the disinterested warnings of a parting friend, who can possibly have no personal motive to bias his counsel. Nor can I forget, as an encouragement to it, your indulgent reception of my sentiments on a former and not dissimilar occasion.

Interwoven as is the love of liberty with every ligament of your hearts, no recommendation of mine is necessary to fortify or confirm the attachment.

The unity of government which constitutes you one people is also now dear to you. It is justly so, for it is a main pillar in the edifice of your real independence, the support of your tranquillity at home, your peace abroad; of your safety, of your prosperity; of that very liberty which you so highly prize. But as it is easy to foresee that, from different causes and from different quarters, much pains will be taken, many artifices employed, to weaken in your minds the conviction of this truth; as this is the point in your political fortress against which the batteries of internal and external enemies will be most constantly and actively (though often covertly and insidiously) directed, it is of infinite moment that you should properly estimate the immense value of your national union to your collective and individual happiness: that you should cherish a cordial, habitual, and immovable attachment to it; accustoming yourselves to think and speak of it as of the palladium of your political safety and prosperity; watching for its preservation with jealous anxiety; discountenancing whatever may suggest even a suspicion that it can in any event be abandoned; and indignantly frowning upon the first dawning of every attempt to alienate any portion of our country from the rest, or to enfeeble the sacred ties which now link together the various parts.

For this you have every inducement of sympathy and interest. Citizens, by birth or choice, of a common country, that country has a right to concentrate your affections. The name of American, which belongs to you in your national capacity, must always exalt the just pride of patriotism more than any appellation derived from local discriminations. With slight shades of differences, you have the same religion, manners, habits, and political principles. You have in a common cause fought and triumphed together; the independence and liberty you possess are the work of joint counsels, and joint efforts of common dangers, sufferings, and successes.

But these considerations, however powerfully they address themselves to your sensibility, are greatly outweighed by those which apply more immediately to your interest. Here every portion of our country finds the most commanding motives for carefully guarding and preserving the union of the whole.

The North, in an unrestrained intercourse with the South, protected by equal laws of a common government, finds in the productions of the latter great additional resources of maritime and commercial enterprise and precious materials of manufacturing industry. The South, in the same intercourse, benefiting by the agency of the North, sees its agriculture grow and its commerce expand. Turning partly into its own channels the seamen of the North, it finds its particular navigation invigorated; and, while it contributes, in different ways, to nourish and increase the general mass of the national navigation, it looks forward to the protection of a maritime strength, to which itself is unequally adapted. The East, in a like intercourse with the West, already finds, and, in the progressive improvement of interior communications by land and water, will more and more find, a valuable vent for the commodities which it brings from abroad, or manufactures at home. The West derives from the East supplies requisite to its growth and comfort, and, what is perhaps of still greater consequence, it must of necessity owe the secure enjoyment of indispensable outlets for its own productions to the weight, influence, and the future maritime strength of the Atlantic side of the Union, directed by an indissoluble community of interest as one nation. Any other tenure by which the West can hold this essential advantage, whether derived from its own separate strength, or from an apostate and unnatural connection with any foreign power, must be intrinsically precarious.

While, then, every part of our country thus feels an immediate and particular interest in union, all the parts combined cannot fail to find in the united mass of means and efforts greater strength, greater resource, proportionably greater security from external danger, a less frequent interruption of their peace by foreign nations; and, what is of inestimable value, they must derive from union an exemption from those broils and wars between themselves, which so frequently afflict neighboring countries not tied together by the same governments, which their own rival ships alone would be sufficient to produce, but which opposite foreign alliances, attachments, and intrigues would stimulate and embitter. Hence, likewise, they will avoid the necessity of those overgrown military establishments which, under any form of government, are inauspicious to liberty, and which are to be regarded as particularly hostile to republican liberty. In this sense it is that your union ought to be considered as a main prop of your liberty, and that the love of the one ought to endear to you the preservation of the other.

These considerations speak a persuasive language to every reflecting and virtuous mind, and exhibit the continuance of the Union as a primary object of patriotic desire. Is there a doubt whether a common government can embrace so large a sphere? Let experience solve it! To listen to mere speculation in such a case were criminal. We are authorized to hope that a proper organization of the whole with the auxiliary agency of governments for the respective subdivisions will afford a happy issue to the experiment. It is well worth a fair and full experiment. With such powerful and obvious motives to union, affecting all parts of our country, while experience shall not have demonstrated its impractibility, there will always be reason to distrust the patriotism of those who in any quarter may endeavor to weaken its bands.

In contemplating the causes which may disturb our Union, it occurs as matter of serious concern that any ground should have been furnished for characterizing parties by geographical discriminations, Northern and Southern, Atlantic and Western; whence designing men may endeavor to excite a belief that there is a real difference of local interests and views. One of the expedients of party to acquire influence within particular districts is to misrepresent the opinions and aims of other districts. You cannot shield yourselves too much against the jealousies and heart-burnings which spring from these misrepresentations; they tend to render alien to each other those who ought to be bound together by fraternal affection. The inhabitants of our Western country have lately had a useful lesson on this head; they have seen, in the negotiation by the Executive, and in the unanimous ratification of the Senate, of the treaty with Spain, and in the universal satisfaction at that event, throughout the United States, a decisive proof how unfounded were the suspicions propagated among them of a policy in the general government and in the Atlantic States unfriendly to their interests in regard to the Mississippi; they have been witnesses to the formation of two treaties, that with Great Britain and that with Spain, which secure to them everything they could desire, in respect to our foreign relations, toward confirming their prosperity. Will it not be their wisdom to rely for the preservation of these advantages on the Union by which they were procured? Will they not henceforth be deaf to those advisers, if such there are, who would sever them from their brethren and connect them with aliens?

To the efficacy and permanency of your Union, a government for the whole is indispensable. No alliance, however strict, between the parts can be an adequate substitute; they must inevitably experience the infractions and interruptions which all alliances in all times have experienced. Sensible of this momentous truth, you have improved upon your first essay, by the adoption of a constitution of government better calculated than your former for an intimate union, and for the efficacious management of your common concerns. This government, the offspring of our own choice, uninfluenced and unawed, adopted upon full investigation and mature deliberation, completely free in its principles, in the distribution of its powers, uniting security with energy, and containing within itself a provision for its own amendment, has a just claim to your confidence and your support. Respect for its authority, compliance with its laws, acquiescence in its measures, are duties enjoined by the fundamental maxims of true liberty. The basis of our political systems is the right of the people to make and to alter their constitutions of government. But the Constitution which at any time exists, till changed by an explicit and authentic act of the whole people, is sacredly obligatory upon all. The very idea of the power and the right of the people to establish government presupposes the duty of every individual to obey the established government.

All obstructions to the execution of the laws, all combinations and associations, under whatever plausible character, with the real design to direct, control, counteract, or awe the regular deliberation and action of the constituted authorities, are destructive of this fundamental principle, and of fatal tendency. They serve to organize faction, to give it an artificial and extraordinary force; to put in the place of the delegated will of the nation the will of a party, often a small but artful and enterprising minority of the community; and, according to the alternate triumphs of different parties, to make the public administration the mirror of the ill-concerted and incongruous projects of faction, rather than the organ of consistent and wholesome plans digested by common counsels and modified by mutual interests.

However combinations or associations of the above description may now and then answer popular ends, they are likely, in the course of time and things, to become potent engines by which cunning, ambitious, and unprincipled men will be enabled to subvert the power of the people and to usurp for themselves the reins of government, destroying afterward the very engines which have lifted them to unjust dominion.

Toward the preservation of your government, and the permanency of your present happy state, it is requisite, not only that you steadily discountenance irregular oppositions to its acknowledged authority, but also that you resist with care the spirit of innovation upon its principles, however specious the pretexts. One method of assault may be to effect, in the forms of the Constitution, alterations which will impair the energy of the system, and thus to undermine what cannot be directly overthrown. In all the changes to which you may be invited, remember that time and habit are at least as necessary to fix the true character of governments as of other human institutions; that experience is the surest standard by which to test the real tendency of the existing constitution of a country; that facility in changes, upon the credit of mere hypothesis and opinion, exposes to perpetual change, from the endless variety of hypothesis and opinion; and remember, especially, that for the efficient management of your common interests, in a country so extensive as ours, a government of as much vigor as is consistent with the perfect security of liberty is indispensable. Liberty itself will find in such a government, with powers properly distributed and adjusted, its surest guardian. It is, indeed, little else than a name, where the government is too feeble to withstand the enterprises of faction, to confine each member of the society within the limits prescribed by the laws, and to maintain all in the secure and tranquil enjoyment of the rights of person and property.

I have already intimated to you the danger of parties in the state, with particular reference to the founding of them on geographical discriminations. Let me now take a more comprehensive view, and warn you in the most solemn manner against the baneful effects of the spirit of party generally.

This spirit, unfortunately, is inseparable from our nature, having its root in the strongest passions of the human mind. It exists under different shapes in all governments, more or less stifled, controlled, or repressed; but, in those of the popular form, it is seen in its greatest rankness, and is truly their worst enemy.

The alternate domination of one faction over another, sharpened by the spirit of revenge, natural to party dissension, which in different ages and countries has perpetrated the most horrid enormities, is itself a frightful despotism. But this leads at length to a more formal and permanent despotism. The disorders and miseries which result gradually incline the minds of men to seek security and repose in the absolute power of an individual; and sooner or later the chief of some prevailing faction, more able or more fortunate than his competitors, turns this disposition to the purpose of his own elevation, on the ruins of public liberty.

Without looking forward to an extremity of this kind (which, nevertheless, ought not to be entirely out of sight), the common and continual mischiefs of the spirit of party are sufficient to make it the interest and duty of a wise people to discourage and restrain it.

It serves always to distract the public councils and enfeeble the public administration. It agitates the community with ill-founded jealousies and false alarms, kindles the animosity of one part against another, foments occasionally riot and insurrection. It opens the door to foreign influence and corruption, which finds a facilitated access to the government itself through the channels of party passions. Thus the policy and the will of one country are subjected to the policy and will of another.

. There is an opinion that parties in free countries are useful checks upon the administration of the government and serve to keep alive the spirit of liberty. This within certain limits is probably true; and in governments of a monarchical cast, patriotism may look with indulgence, if not with favor, upon the spirit of party. But in those of the popular character, in governments purely elective, it is a spirit not to be encouraged. From their natural tendency, it is certain there will always be enough of that spirit for every salutary purpose. And there being constant danger of excess, the effort ought to be, by force of public opinion, to mitigate and assuage it. A fire not to be quenched, it demands a uniform vigilance to prevent its bursting into a flame, lest, instead of warming, it should consume.

It is important, likewise, that the habits of thinking in a free country should inspire caution in those intrusted with its administration, to confine themselves within their respective constitutional spheres, avoiding in the exercise of the powers of one department to encroach upon another. The spirit of encroachment tends to consolidate the powers of all the departments into one, and thus to create, whatever the form of government, a real despotism. A just estimate of that love of power, and proneness to abuse it, which predominates in the human heart, is sufficient to satisfy us of the truth of this position. The necessity of reciprocal checks in the exercise of political power, by dividing and distributing it into different depositaries, and constituting each the guardian of the public weal against invasions by the others, has been evinced by experiments ancient and modern, some of them in our country and under our own eyes. To preserve them must be as necessary as to institute them. If, in the opinion of the people, the distribution or modification of the constitutional powers be in any particular wrong, let it be corrected by an amendment in the way which the Constitution designates. But let there be no change by usurpation; for though this, in

one instance, may be the instrument of good, it is the cus-
tomary weapon by which free governments are destroyed.
The precedent must always greatly overbalance in permanent evil any partial or transient benefit which the use can
at any time yield.

Of all the dispositions and habits which lead to political prosperity, religion and morality are indispensable supports. In vain would that man claim the tribute of patriotism, who should labor to subvert these great pillars of
human happiness, these firmest props of the duties of men
and citizens. The mere politician, equally with the pious
man, ought to respect and to cherish them. A volume
could not trace all their connections with private and public
felicity. Let it simply be asked: Where is the security for
property, for reputation, for life, if the sense of religious
obligation desert the oaths which are the instruments of
investigation in courts of justice? And let us with caution
indulge the supposition that morality can be maintained
without religion. Whatever may be conceded to the influence of refined education on minds of peculiar structure,
reason and experience both forbid us to expect that national
morality can prevail in exclusion of religious principle.

It is substantially true that virtue or morality is a necessary spring of popular government. The rule, indeed,
extends with more or less force to every species of free
government. Who that is a sincere friend to it can look
with indifference upon attempts to shake the foundation of
the fabric?

Promote, then, as an object of primary importance,
institutions for the general diffusion of knowledge. In proportion as the structure of a government gives force to
public opinion, it is essential that public opinion should be
enlightened.

As a very important source of strength and security,
cherish public credit. One method of preserving it is to
use it as sparingly as possible, avoiding occasions of expense
by cultivating peace, but remembering also that timely disbursements to prepare for danger frequently prevent much
greater disbursements to repel it, avoiding likewise the
accumulation of debt, not only by shunning occasions of
expense, but by vigorous exertion in time of peace to dis-

charge the debts which unavoidable wars may have occasioned, not ungenerously throwing upon posterity the burden which we ourselves ought to bear. The execution of these maxims belongs to your representatives, but it is necessary that public opinion should coöperate. To facilitate to them the performance of their duty, it is essential that you should practically bear in mind that toward the payment of debts there must be revenue; that to have revenue there must be taxes; that no taxes can be devised which are not more or less inconvenient and unpleasant; that the intrinsic embarrassment, inseparable from the selection of the proper objects (which is always a choice of difficulties), ought to be a decisive motive for a candid construction of the conduct of the government in making it, and for a spirit of acquiescence in the measures for obtaining revenue, which the public exigencies may at any time dictate.

Observe good-faith and justice toward all nations; cultivate peace and harmony with all. Religion and morality enjoin this conduct; and can it be that good policy does not equally enjoin it? It will be worthy of a free, enlightened, and, at no distant period, a great nation, to give to mankind the magnanimous and too novel example of a people always guided by an exalted justice and benevolence. Who can doubt that, in the course of time and things, the fruit of such a plan would richly repay any temporary advantages which might be lost by a steady adherence to it? Can it be that Providence has not connected the permanent felicity of a nation with its virtue? The experiment, at least, is recommended by every sentiment which ennobles human nature. Alas! is it rendered impossible by its vices?

In the execution of such a plan, nothing is more essential than that permanent, inveterate antipathies against particular nations, and passionate attachments for others, should be excluded; and that, in place of them, just and amicable feelings toward all should be cultivated. The nation which indulges toward another a habitual hatred or a habitual fondness is in some degree a slave. It is a slave to its animosity or to its affection, either of which is sufficient to lead it astray from its duty and its interest.

Antipathy in one nation against another disposes each more readily to offer insult and injury, to lay hold of slight causes of umbrage, and to be haughty and intractable, when accidental or trifling occasions of dispute occur. Hence, frequent collisions, obstinate, envenomed, and bloody contests. The nation, prompted by ill-will and resentment, sometimes impels to war the government, contrary to the best calculations of policy. The government sometimes participates in the national propensity, and adopts through passion what reason would reject; at other times it makes the animosity of the nation subservient to projects of hostility instigated by pride, ambition, and other sinister and pernicious motives. The peace often, sometimes perhaps the liberty, of nations, has been the victim.

So, likewise, a passionate attachment of one nation for another produces a variety of evils. Sympathy for the favorite nation, facilitating the illusion of an imaginary common interest in cases where no real common interest exists, and infusing into one the enmities of the other, betrays the former into a participation in the quarrels and wars of the latter without adequate inducement or justification. It leads also to concessions to the favorite nation of privileges denied to others which is apt doubly to injure the nation making the concessions; by unnecessarily parting with what ought to have been retained, and by exciting jealousy, ill-will, and a disposition to retaliate, in the parties from whom equal privileges are withheld. And it gives to ambitious, corrupted, or deluded citizens (who devote themselves to the favorite nation) facility to betray or sacrifice the interests of their own country, without odium, sometimes even with popularity; gilding, with the appearance of a virtuous sense of obligation, a commendable deference for public opinion, or a laudable zeal for public good, the base or foolish compliances of ambition, corruption, or infatuation.

As avenues to foreign influence in innumerable ways, such attachments are particularly alarming to the truly enlightened and independent patriot. How many opportunities do they afford to tamper with domestic factions, to practice the art of seduction, to mislead public opinion, to influence or awe the public councils? Such an attachment of a small or weak toward a great and powerful nation dooms the former to be the satellite of the latter.

Against the insidious wiles of foreign influence (I conjure you to believe me, fellow-citizens) the jealousy of a free people ought to be constantly awake, since history and experience prove that foreign influence is one of the most baneful foes of republican government. But that jealousy to be useful must be impartial; else it becomes the instrument of the very influence to be avoided, instead of a defense against it. Excessive partiality for one foreign nation and excessive dislike of another cause those whom they actuate to see danger only on one side, and serve to veil and even second the arts of influence on the other. Real patriots who may resist the intrigues of the favorite are liable to become suspected and odious, while its tools and dupes usurp the applause and confidence of the people, to surrender their interests.

The great rule of conduct for us in regard to foreign nations is, in extending our commercial relations, to have with them as little political connection as possible. So far as we have already formed engagements, let them be fulfilled with perfect good faith. Here let us stop.

Europe has a set of primary interests which to us have none, or a very remote, relation. Hence she must be engaged in frequent controversies, the causes of which are essentially foreign to our concerns. Hence, therefore, it must be unwise in us to implicate ourselves by artificial ties in the ordinary vicissitudes of her politics, or the ordinary combinations and collisions of her friendships or enmities.

Our detached and distant situation invites and enables us to pursue a different course. If we remain one people under an efficient government, the period is not far off when we may defy material injury from external annoyance; when we may take such an attitude as will cause the neutrality we may at any time resolve upon to be scrupulously respected; when belligerent nations, under the impossibility of making acquisitions upon us, will not lightly hazard the giving us provocation; when we may choose peace or war, as our interest, guided by justice, shall counsel.

Why forego the advantages of so peculiar a situation?

129

Why quit our own to stand upon foreign ground? Why,
by interweaving our destiny with that of any part of Europe,
entangle our peace and prosperity in the toils of European
ambition, rivalship, interest, humor, or caprice?

It is our true policy to steer clear of permanent alliances
with any portion of the foreign world; so far, I mean, as
we are now at liberty to do it; for let me not be understood
as capable of patronizing infidelity to existing engagements.
I hold the maxim no less applicable to public than to private
affairs, that honesty is always the best policy. I repeat it,
therefore, let those engagements be observed in their genuine
sense. But, in my opinion, it is unnecessary, and would
be unwise, to extend them.

Taking care always to keep ourselves by suitable establishments on a respectable defensive posture, we may safely
trust to temporary alliances for extraordinary emergencies.

Harmony, liberal intercourse with all nations, are recommended by policy, humanity, and interest. But even our
commercial policy should hold an equal and impartial hand;
neither seeking nor granting exclusive favors or preferences;
consulting the natural course of things; diffusing and diver-
sifying by gentle means the streams of commerce, but forcing nothing; establishing (with powers so disposed, in order
to give trade a stable course, to define the rights of our
merchants, and to enable the government to support them)
conventional rules of intercourse, the best that present circumstances and mutual opinion will permit, but temporary,
and liable to be from time to time abandoned or varied, as
experience and circumstances shall dictate; constantly keeping in view that it is folly in one nation to look for disinterested favors from another; that it must pay with a portion
of its independence for whatever it may accept under that
character; that, by such acceptance, it may place itself in
the condition of having given equivalents for nominal favors,
and yet of being reproached with ingratitude for not giving
more. There can be no greater error than to expect or cal-
culate upon real favors from nation to nation. It is an
illusion, which experience must cure, which a just pride
ought to discard.

In offering to you, my countrymen, these counsels of
an old and affectionate friend, I dare not hope they will

make the strong and lasting impression I could wish; that they will control the usual current of the passions, or prevent our nation from running the course which has hitherto marked the destiny of nations. But, if I may even flatter myself that they may be productive of some partial benefit, some occasional good; that they may now and then recur to moderate the fury of party spirit, to warn against the mischiefs of foreign intrigue, to guard against the impostures of pretended patriotism; this hope will be a full recompense for the solicitude for your welfare, by which they have been dictated.

How far in the discharge of my official duties I have been guided by the principles which have been delineated, the public records and other evidences of my conduct must witness to you and to the world. To myself, the assurance of my own conscience is, that I have at least believed myself to be guided by them.

In relation to the still subsisting war in Europe, my proclamation of the twenty-second of April, 1793, is the index of my plan. Sanctioned by your approving voice, and by that of your representatives in both Houses of Congress, the spirit of that measure has continually governed me, uninfluenced by any attempts to deter or divert me from it.

After deliberate examination, with the aid of the best lights I could obtain, I was well satisfied that our country, under all the circumstances of the case, had a right to take, and was bound in duty and interest to take, a neutral position. Having taken it, I determined, as far as should depend upon me, to maintain it, with moderation, perseverance, and firmness.

The considerations which respect the right to hold this conduct, it is not necessary on this occasion to detail. I will only observe that, according to my understanding of the matter, that right, so far from being denied by any of the belligerent powers, has been virtually admitted by all.

The duty of holding a neutral conduct may be inferred, without anything more, from the obligation which justice and humanity impose on every nation, in cases in which it is free to act, to maintain inviolate the relations of peace and amity toward other nations.

The inducements of interest for observing that conduct will best be referred to your own reflections and experience. With me a predominant motive has been to endeavor to gain time to our country to settle and mature its yet recent institutions, and to progress without interruption to that degree of strength and consistency which is necessary to give it, humanly speaking, the command of its own fortunes.

Though, in reviewing the incidents of my administration, I am unconscious of intentional error, I am nevertheless too sensible of my defects not to think it probable that I may have committed many errors. Whatever they may be, I fervently beseech the Almighty to avert or mitigate the evils to which they may tend. I shall also carry with me the hope that my country will never cease to view them with indulgence; and that, after forty-five years of my life dedicated to its service with an upright zeal, the faults of incompetent abilities will be consigned to oblivion, as myself must soon be to the mansions of rest.

Relying on its kindness in this as in other things, and actuated by that fervent love toward it, which is so natural to a man who views in it the native soil of himself and his progenitors for several generations, I anticipate with pleasing expectation that retreat in which I promise myself to realize, without alloy, the sweet enjoyment of partaking, in the midst of my fellow-citizens, the benign influence of good laws under a free government, the ever favorite object of my heart, and the happy reward, as I trust, of our mutual cares, labors, and dangers.

DANIEL WEBSTER

REPLY TO HAYNE

[Daniel Webster, eminent American statesman, orator, and jurist, was born in New Hampshire, 18th January 1782. He spent his early days in the town of Salisbury. At Exeter and then at Darmouth College he showed unusual talent for speaking, and was chosen the orator for the Fourth of July. He completed his law studies in Boston, and was admitted to the bar in March 1805. His defense of the Dartmouth College case before the Supreme Court of the United States in 1818 was a masterly exposition of constitutional law. He went to the House of Representatives from Massachusetts in 1823, and in 1827 was transferred to the Senate. Here he delivered his great "Reply to Hayne," a statement of the constitutional sanctions of union as against Nullification and the doctrine of State rights. When California applied for admission in 1850 he made his famous "seventh of March" speech in the Senate, in which he seemed to contradict his earlier expressions on the subject of slavery, to endeavor to conciliate the slaveholding element, and to brand the abolition element for mischievous disorderliness. He favored the Fugitive Slave law—most repugnant to the North. Nothing could ever undo the effect of this speech; and along with his chances for the presidential office went some of his personal popularity. He lived but two years longer, dying at his country home at Marshfield, Mass., October 24, 1852. The reply to Hayne, on the Foote Resolution, was made in the Senate, in 1830; the eulogy on Adams and Jefferson, at Faneuil Hall, Boston, 1826; the oration, at Bunker Hill, in 1825.]

M R. PRESIDENT: When the mariner has been tossed for many days in thick weather, and on an unknown sea, he naturally avails himself of the first pause in the storm, the earliest glance of the sun, to take his latitude, and ascertain how far the elements have driven him from his true course. Let us imitate this prudence, and, before we float further on the waves of this debate, refer to the point from which we departed, that we may at least be able to conjecture where we now are. I ask for the reading of the resolution before the Senate.

The secretary read the resolution, as follows:—

Resolved, That the Committee on Public Lands be instructed to in-quire and report the quantity of public land remaining unsold within each State and Territory, and whether it be expedient to limit for a cer-tain period the sales of the public lands to such lands only as have heretofore been offered for sale, and are now subject to entry at the minimum price.   And, also, whether the office of Surveyor-general, and some of the land offices, may not be abolished without detriment to the public interest ; or whether it be expedient to adopt measures to hasten the sales and extend more rapidly the surveys of the public lands.

We have thus heard, sir, what the resolution is which is actually before us for consideration; and it will readily occur to every one that it is almost the only subject about which something has not been said in the speech, running through two days, by which the Senate has been entertained by the gentleman from South Carolina.   Every topic in the wide range of our public affairs, whether past or present— everything, whether general or local, whether belonging to national politics or party politics—seems to have attracted more or less of the honorable member's attention, save only the resolution before the Senate.   He has spoken of every-thing but the public lands; they have escaped his notice. To that subject, in all his excursions, he has not paid even the cold respect of a passing glance.

When this debate, sir, was to be resumed, on Thursday morning, it so happened that it would have been convenient for me to be elsewhere.   The honorable member, however, did not incline to put off the discussion to another day.   He had a shot, he said, to return, and he wished to discharge it. That shot, sir, which he thus kindly informed us was com-ing, that we might stand out of the way, or prepare our-selves to fall before it and die with decency, has now been received.   Under all advantages, and with expectation awakened by the tone which preceded it, it has been dis-charged, and has spent its force.   It may become me to say no more of its effect, than that, if nobody is found, after all, either killed or wounded, it is not the first time in the history of human affairs that the vigor and success of the war have not quite come up to the lofty and sounding phrase of the manifesto.

The gentleman, sir, in declining to postpone the debate, told the Senate, with the emphasis of his hand upon his heart, that there was something rankling *here*, which he wished to relieve. [Mr. Hayne rose and disclaimed having used the word "rankling."] It would not, Mr. President, be safe for the honorable member to appeal to those around him, upon the question whether he did in fact make use of that word. But he may have been unconscious of it. At any rate, it is enough that he disclaims it. But still, with or without the use of that particular word, he had yet something here, he said, of which he wished to rid himself by an immediate reply. In this respect, sir, I have a great advantage over the honorable gentleman. There is nothing here, sir, which gives me the slightest uneasiness; neither fear, nor anger, nor that which is sometimes more troublesome than either—the consciousness of having been in the wrong. There is nothing, either originating here, or now received by the gentleman's shot. Nothing original here, for I had not the slightest feeling of disrespect or unkindness toward the honorable member. Some passages, it is true, had occurred since our acquaintance in this body, which I could have wished might have been otherwise; but I had used philosophy and forgotten them. I paid the honorable member the attention of listening with respect to his first speech; and when he sat down, though surprised, and I must say even astonished, at some of his opinions, nothing was farther from my intention than to commence any personal warfare. Through the whole of the few remarks I made in answer, I avoided, studiously and carefully, everything which I thought possible to be construed into disrespect. And, sir, while there is thus nothing originating here which I have wished at any time, or now wish, to discharge, I must repeat, also, that nothing has been received here which rankles, or in any way gives me annoyance. I will not accuse the honorable member of violating the rules of civilized war; I will not say that he poisoned his arrows. But whether his shafts were or were not dipped in that which would have caused rankling if they had reached their destination, there was not, as it happened, quite strength enough in the bow to bring them to their mark. If he wishes now to gather up those shafts, he must look for them elsewhere; they will not be found fixed and quivering in the object at which they were aimed.

The honorable member complained that I had slept on his speech. I must have slept on it, or not slept at all. The moment the honorable member sat down, his friend from Missouri rose, and, with much honeyed commendation of the speech, suggested that the impressions which it had produced were too charming and delightful to be disturbed by other sentiments or other sounds, and proposed that the Senate should adjourn. Would it have been quite amiable in me, sir, to interrupt this excellent good feeling? Must I not have been absolutely malicious, if I could have thrust myself forward, to destroy sensations thus pleasing? Was it not much better and kinder, both to sleep upon them myself, and to allow others also the pleasure of sleeping upon them? But if it be meant, by sleeping upon his speech, that I took time to prepare a reply to it, it is quite a mistake. Owing to other engagements, I could not employ even the interval between the adjournment of the Senate and its meeting the next morning, in attention to the subject of this debate. Nevertheless, sir, the mere matter of fact is undoubtedly true. I did sleep on the gentleman's speech, and slept soundly. And I slept equally well on his speech of yesterday, to which I am now replying. It is quite possible that in this respect, also, I possess some advantage over the honorable member, attributable, doubtless, to a cooler temperament on my part; for, in truth, I slept upon his speeches remarkably well.

But the gentleman inquires why he was made the object of such a reply. Why was he singled out? If an attack has been made on the East, he, he assures us, did not begin it; it was made by the gentleman from Missouri. Sir, I answered the gentleman's speech because I happened to hear it; and because, also, I choose to give an answer to that speech, which, if unanswered, I thought most likely to produce injurious impressions. I did not stop to inquire who was the original drawer of the bill. I found a responsible endorser before me, and it was my purpose to hold him liable, and to bring him to his just responsibility without delay. But, sir, this interrogatory of the honorable member was only introductory to another. He proceeded to ask me whether I had turned upon him in this debate, from the consciousness that I should find an overmatch, if I ventured on a contest with his friend from Missouri. If, sir, the honorable member, *modestiæ gratia*, had chosen thus to defer to his friend, and to pay him compliments, without intentional disparagement to others, it would have been quite according to the friendly courtesies of debate, and not at all ungrateful to my own feelings. I am not one of those, sir, who esteem any tribute of regard, whether light and occasional, or more serious and deliberate, which may be bestowed on others, as so much unjustly withholden from themselves. But the tone and the manner of the gentleman's question forbid me that I thus interpret it. I am not at liberty to consider it as nothing more than a civility to his friend. It had an air of taunt and disparagement, something of the loftiness of asserted superiority, which does not allow me to pass over it without notice. It was put as a question for me to answer, and so put as if it were difficult for me to answer whether I deemed the member from Missouri an overmatch for myself in debate here. It seems to me, sir, that this is extraordinary language, and an extraordinary tone, for the discussions of this body.

Matches and overmatches! Those terms are more applicable elsewhere than here, and fitter for other assemblies than this. Sir, the gentleman seems to forget where and what we are. This is a senate, a senate of equals, of men of individual honor and personal character, and of absolute independence. We know no masters, we acknowledge no dictators. This is a hall for mutual consultation and discussion; not an arena for the exhibition of champions. I offer myself, sir, as a match for no man; I throw the challenge of debate at no man's feet. But then, sir, since the honorable member has put the question in a manner that calls for an answer, I will give him an answer; and I tell him, that, holding myself to be the humblest of the members here, I yet know nothing in the arm of his friend from Missouri, either alone or when aided by the arm of his friend from South Carolina, that need deter even me from espousing whatever opinions I may choose to espouse, from debating whatever I may choose to debate, or from speaking whatever I may see fit to say, on the floor of the Senate.

Sir, when uttered as matter of commendation or compliment, I should dissent from nothing which the honorable member might say of his friend. Still less do I put forth any pretensions of my own. But when put to me as a matter of taunt, I throw it back, and say to the gentleman that he could possibly say nothing less likely than such a comparison to wound my pride of personal character. The anger of its tone rescued the remark from intentional irony, which otherwise, probably, would have been its general acceptation. But, sir, if it be imagined that by this mutual quotation and commendation; if it be supposed that, by casting the characters of the drama, assigning to each his part, to one the attack, to another the cry of onset; or if it be thought that, by a loud and empty vaunt of anticipated victory, any laurels are to be won here; if it be imagined, especially, that any or all these things will shake any purpose of mine, I can tell the honorable member, once for all, that he is greatly mistaken, and that he is dealing with one of whose temper and character he has yet much to learn. Sir, I shall not allow myself, on this occasion—I hope on no occasion,—to be betrayed into any loss of temper; but if provoked, as I trust I never shall be, into crimination and recrimination, the honorable member may, perhaps, find that in that contest there will be blows to take as well as blows to give; that others can state comparisons as significant, at least, as his own, and that his impunity may possibly demand of him whatever powers of taunt and sarcasm he may possess. I commend him to a prudent husbandry of his resources. . . .

On yet another point, I was still more unaccountably misunderstood. The gentleman had harangued against "consolidation." I told him, in reply, that there was one kind of consolidation to which I was attached, and that was the consolidation of our Union; and that this was precisely that consolidation to which I feared others were not attached; that such consolidation was the very end of the Constitution—the leading object, as they had informed us themselves, which its framers had kept in view. I turned to their communication, and read their very words—"the consolidation of the Union"—and expressed my devotion to this sort of consolidation. I said, in terms, that I wished not in the slightest degree to augment the powers of this government; that my object was to preserve, not to enlarge; and that by consolidating the Union I understood no more than the strengthening of the Union, and perpetuating it. Having been thus explicit, having thus read from the printed book the precise words which I adopted, as expressing my own sentiments, it passes comprehension how any man could understand me as contending for an extension of the powers of the government, or for consolidation in that odious sense in which it means an accumulation, in the Federal Government, of the powers properly belonging to the States.

I repeat, sir, that, in adopting the sentiments of the framers of the Constitution, I read their language audibly, and word for word; and I pointed out the distinction, just as fully as I have now done, between the consolidation of the Union and that other obnoxious consolidation which I disclaim. And yet the honorable member misunderstood me. The gentleman had said that he wished for no fixed revenue—not a shilling. If by a word he could convert the Capitol into gold, he would not do it. Why all this fear of revenue? Why, sir, because, as the gentleman told us, it tends to consolidation. Now, this can mean neither more nor less than that a common revenue is a common interest, and that all common interests tend to preserve the union of the states. I confess I like that tendency; if the gentleman dislikes it, he is right in deprecating a shilling of fixed revenue. So much, sir, for consolidation. . . .

Professing to be provoked by what he chose to consider a charge made by me against South Carolina, the honorable member, Mr. President, has taken up a crusade against New England. Leaving altogether the subject of the public lands, in which his success, perhaps, had been neither distinguished nor satisfactory, and letting go, also, of the topic of the tariff, he sallied forth in a general assault on the opinions, politics, and parties of New England, as they have been exhibited in the last thirty years. . . .

New England has, at times—so argues the gentleman—held opinions as dangerous as those which he now holds. Suppose this were so; how should he therefore abuse New England? If he finds himself countenanced by acts of hers, how is it that, while he relies on these acts, he covers, or seeks to cover, their authors with reproach? But, sir, if in the course of forty years there have been undue effervescences of party in New England, has the same thing happened nowhere else? Party animosity and party outrage, not in New England, but elsewhere, denounced President Washington, not only as a Federalist, but as a Tory, a British agent, a man who in his high office sanctioned corruption. But does the honorable member suppose, that if I had a tender here who should put such an effusion of wickedness and folly into my hand, that I would stand up and read it against the South? Parties ran into great heats again in 1799 and 1800. What was said, sir, or rather what was not said, in those years, against John Adams, one of the committee that drafted the Declaration of Independence, and its admitted ablest defender on the floor of Congress? If the gentleman wishes to increase his stores of party abuse and frothy violence, if he has a determined proclivity to such pursuits, there are treasures of that sort south of the Potomac, much to his taste, yet untouched. I shall not touch them. . . . The gentleman's purveyors have only catered for him among the productions of one side. I certainly shall not supply the deficiency by furnishing him samples of the other. I leave to him, and to them, the whole concern. It is enough for me to say that if, in any part of this their grateful occupation, if in all their researches they find anything in the history of Massachusetts, or of New England, or in the proceedings of any legislative or other public body, disloyal to the Union, speaking slightingly of its value, proposing to break it up, or recommending non-intercourse with neighboring states, on account of difference in political opinion, then, sir, I give them all up to the honorable gentleman's unrestrained rebuke; expecting, however, that he will extend his buffetings in like manner, to all similar proceedings, wherever else found. . . .

Mr. President, in carrying his warfare, such as it was, into New England, the honorable gentleman all along professes to be acting on the defensive. He chooses to consider me as having assailed South Carolina, and insists that he comes forth only as her champion, and in her defense. Sir, I do not admit that I made any attack whatever on South Caro-

lina.   Nothing like it.   The honorable member, in his first
speech, expressed opinions, in regard to revenue and some
other topics, which I heard with both pain and with surprise.
I told the gentleman I was aware that such sentiments were
entertained out of the government, but had not expected
to find them advanced in it; that I knew there were persons
in the South who speak of our Union with indifference or
doubt, taking pains to magnify its evils, and to say nothing
of its benefits; that the honorable member himself, I was
sure, could never be one of these; and I regretted the
expression of such opinions as he had avowed, because I
thought their obvious tendency was to encourage feelings
of disrespect to the Union, and to impair its strength.
This, sir, is the sum and substance of all I said on the subject.   And this constitutes the attack which called on the
chivalry of the gentleman, in his own opinion, to harry us
with such a foray among the party pamphlets and party
proceedings in Massachusetts!   If he means that I spoke
with dissatisfaction or disrespect of the ebullitions of individuals in South Carolina, it is true.   But if he means that
I assailed the character of the State, her honor, or patriotism,
that I reflected on her history or her conduct, he had not
the slightest ground for any such assumption. . . . I shall
not acknowledge that the honorable member goes before
me in regard for whatever of distinguished talent or distinguished character South Carolina has produced.   I claim
part of the honor, I partake in the pride of her great names.
I claim them for my countrymen, one and all, the Lau-
renses, the Rutledges, the Pinckneys, the Sumters, the
Marions—Americans all—whose fame is no more to be
hemmed in by State lines than their talents and patriotism
were capable of being circumscribed within the same narrow limits.   In their generation they served and honored
the country, and the whole country; and their renown is
of the treasures of the whole country.   Him whose honored name the gentleman himself bears—does he esteem
me less capable of gratitude for his patriotism, or sympathy
for his sufferings, than if his eyes had first opened upon the
light of Massachusetts, instead of South Carolina?   Sir,
does he suppose it in his power to exhibit a Carolina name
so bright as to produce envy in my bosom?   No, sir; in-

creased gratification and delight, rather. I thank God that, if I am gifted with little of the spirit which is able to raise mortals to the skies, I have yet none, as I trust, of that other spirit which would drag angels down. When I shall be found, sir, in my place here in the Senate, or elsewhere, to sneer at public merit, because it happens to spring up beyond the little limits of my own state or neighborhood; when I refuse, for any such cause, or for any cause, the homage due to American talent, to elevated patriotism, to sincere devotion to liberty and the country; or, if I see an uncommon endowment of Heaven, if I see extraordinary capacity and virtue, in any son of the South; and if, moved by local prejudices or gangrened by state jealousy, I get up here to abate the tithe of a hair from his just character and just fame, may my tongue cleave to the roof of my mouth!

Sir, let me recur to pleasing recollections; let me indulge in refreshing remembrances of the past; let me remind you that, in early times, no states cherished greater harmony, both of principle and feeling, than Massachusetts and South Carolina. Would to God that harmony might again return! Shoulder to shoulder they went through the Revolution, hand in hand they stood round the administration of Washington, and felt his own great arm lean on them for support. Unkind feeling, if it exist, alienation, and distrust, are the growth, unnatural to such soils, of false principles since sown. They are weeds, the seeds of which that same great arm never scattered.

Mr. President, I shall enter upon no encomium of Massachusetts; she needs none. There she is. Behold her, and judge for yourselves. There is her history; the world knows it by heart. The past, at least, is secure. There is Boston, and Concord, and Lexington, and Bunker Hill; and there they will remain forever. The bones of her sons, falling in the great struggle for independence, now lie mingled with the soil of every state from New England to Georgia, and there they will lie forever. And, sir, where American liberty raised its first voice, and where its youth was nurtured and sustained, there it still lives, in the strength of its manhood, and full of its original spirit. If discord and disunion shall wound it, if party strife and blind ambition shall hawk and tear it, if folly and madness, if uneasiness under salutary and necessary restraint shall succeed in separating it from that Union, by which alone its existence is made sure, it will stand, in the end, by the side of that cradle in which its infancy was rocked; it will stretch forth its arm with whatever of vigor it may still retain, over the friends who gather round it; and it will fall at last, if fall it must, amidst the profoundest monuments of its own glory, and on the very spot of its origin.

There yet remains to be performed, Mr. President, by far the most grave and important duty which I feel to be devolved upon me by this occasion. It is to state, and to defend, what I conceive to be the true principles of the Constitution under which we are here assembled. I might well have desired that so weighty a task should have fallen into other and abler hands. I could have wished that it should have been executed by those whose character and experience give weight and influence to their opinions, such as cannot possibly belong to mine. But, sir, I have met the occasion, not sought it; and I shall proceed to state my own sentiments, without challenging for them any particular regard, with studied plainness, and as much precision as possible.

I understand the honorable gentleman from South Carolina to maintain that it is a right of the state legislatures to interfere whenever, in their judgment, this government transcends its constitutional limits, and to arrest the operation of its laws.

I understand him to maintain this right, as a right existing under the Constitution, not as a right to overthrow it on the ground of extreme necessity, such as would justify violent revolution.

I understand him to maintain an authority on the part of the states, thus to interfere, for the purpose of correcting the exercise of power by the general government, of checking it, and of compelling it to conform to their opinion of the extent of its powers.

I understand him to maintain that the ultimate power of judging of the constitutional extent of its own authority is not lodged exclusively in the general government, or any branch of it; but that, on the contrary, the states may lawfully decide for themselves, and each state for itself, whether, in a given case, the act of the general government transcends its power.

I understand him to insist that if the exigencies of the case, in the opinion of any state government, require it, such state government may, by its own sovereign authority, annul an act of the general government which it deems plainly and palpably unconstitutional.

This is the sum of what I understand from him to be the South Carolina doctrine, and the doctrine which he maintains. I propose to consider it, and compare it with the Constitution. Allow me to say, as a preliminary remark, that I call this the South Carolina doctrine only because the gentleman himself has so denominated it. I do not feel at liberty to say that South Carolina, as a state, has ever advanced these sentiments. I hope she has not, and never may. That a great majority of her people are opposed to the tariff laws is doubtless true. That a majority, somewhat less than that just mentioned, conscientiously believe these laws unconstitutional, may probably also be true. But that any majority holds to the right of direct state interference at state discretion, the right of nullifying acts of Congress by acts of state legislation, is more than I know, and what I shall be slow to believe.

That there are individuals besides the honorable gentleman who do maintain these opinions, is quite certain. I recollect the recent expression of a sentiment, which circumstances attending its utterance and publication justify us in supposing was not unpremeditated. "The sovereignty of the state—never to be controlled, construed, or decided on, but by her own feelings of honorable justice."

[Mr. Hayne here rose and said that, for the purpose of being clearly understood, he would state that his proposition was in the words of the Virginia Resolution, as follows: "That this assembly doth explicitly and peremptorily declare that it views the powers of the Federal Government as resulting from the compact to which the states are parties, as limited by the plain sense and intention of the instrument constituting that compact, as no farther valid than they are authorized by the grants enumerated in that compact; and that, in case of a deliberate, palpable, and dangerous exercise of other powers not granted by the said compact, the states that are parties thereto have the right, and are in duty bound to interpose for arresting the progress of the evil, and for maintaining within their respective limits the authorities, rights, and liberties appertaining to them."]

Mr. Webster resumed:—

I am quite aware, Mr. President, of the existence of the resolution which the gentleman read, and has now repeated, and that he relies on it as his authority. I know the source, too, from which it is understood to have proceeded. I need not say that I have much respect for the constitutional opinions of Mr. Madison; they would weigh greatly with me always. But before the authority of his opinion be vouched for the gentleman's proposition, it will be proper to consider what is the fair interpretation of that resolution, to which Mr. Madison is understood to have given his sanction. As the gentleman construes it, it is an authority for him. Possibly, he may not have adopted the right construction. That resolution declares that, in the case of the dangerous exercise of powers not granted by the general government, the states may interpose to arrest the progress of the evil. But how interpose, and what does this declaration purport? Does it mean no more than that there may be extreme cases, in which the people, in any mode of assembling, may resist usurpation, and relieve themselves from a tyrannical government? No one will deny this. Such resistance is not only acknowledged to be just in America, but in England also. Blackstone admits as much, in the theory, and practice, too, of the English Constitution. We, sir, who oppose the Carolina doctrine, do not deny that the people may, if they choose, throw off any government when it becomes oppressive and intolerable, and erect a better in its stead. We all know that civil institutions are established for the public benefit, and that when they cease to answer the ends of their existence they may be changed. But I do not understand the doctrine now contended for to be that which, for the sake of distinction, we may call the right of revolution. I understand the gentleman to maintain that, without revolution, without civil commotion, without rebellion, a remedy for supposed abuse and transgression of the

130

powers of the general government lies in a direct appeal to the interference of the state governments.

[Mr. Hayne here arose and said: He did not contend for the mere right of revolution, but for the right of constitutional resistance. What he maintained was, that in a case of plain, palpable violation of the Constitution by the general government, a state may interpose, and that this interposition is constitutional.]

Mr. Webster resumed: So, sir, I understood the gentleman, and am happy to find that I did not misunderstand him. What he contends for is that it is constitutional to interrupt the administration of the Constitution itself, in the hands of those who are chosen and sworn to administer it, by the direct interference, in form of law, of the states, in virtue of their sovereign capacity. The inherent right in the people to reform their government I do not deny; and they have another right, and that is, to resist unconstitutional laws, without overturning the government. It is no doctrine of mine that unconstitutional laws bind the people. The great question is, Whose prerogative is it to decide on the constitutionality or unconstitutionality of the laws? On that the main debate hinges. The proposition that in case of a supposed violation of the Constitution by Congress the states have a constitutional right to interfere and annul the law of Congress is the proposition of the gentleman. I do not admit it. If the gentleman had intended no more than to assert the right of revolution for justifiable cause, he would have said only what all agree to. But I cannot conceive that there can be a middle course between submission to the laws, when regularly pronounced constitutional, on the one hand, and open resistance, which is revolution or rebellion, on the other. I say the right of a state to annul a law of Congress cannot be maintained but on the ground of the inalienable right of man to resist oppression; that is to say, upon the ground of revolution. I admit that there is an ultimate violent remedy, above the Constitution and in defiance of the Constitution, which may be resorted to when a revolution is to be justified. But I do not admit that under the Constitution, and in conformity with it, there is any mode in which a state government, as a member of the Union, can interfere and stop the progress of the general government by force of her own laws, under any circumstances whatever.

This leads us to inquire into the origin of this government and the source of its power. Whose agent is it? Is it the creature of the state legislatures or the creature of the people? If the government of the United States be the agent of the state governments, then they may control it, provided they can agree in the manner of controlling it; if it be the agent of the people, then the people alone can control it, restrain it, modify or reform it. It is observable enough that the doctrine for which the honorable gentleman contends leads him to the necessity of maintaining, not only that this general government is the creature of the states, but that it is the creature of each of the states, severally, so that each may assert the power for itself of determining whether it acts within the limits of its authority. It is the servant of four-and-twenty masters, of different wills and different purposes, and yet bound to obey all. This absurdity (for it seems no less) arises from a misconception as to the origin of this government and its true character. It is, sir, the people's Constitution, the people's government, made for the people, made by the people, and answerable to the people. The people of the United States have declared that this Constitution shall be supreme law. We must either admit the proposition or deny their authority. The states are, unquestionably, sovereign, so far as their sovereignty is not affected by this supreme law. But the state legislatures, as political bodies, however sovereign, are yet not sovereign over the people. So far as the people have given power to the general government, so far the grant is unquestionably good, and the government holds of the people, and not of the state governments. We are all agents of the same supreme power, the people. The general government and the state governments derive their authority from the same source. Neither can, in relation to the other, be called primary, though one is definite and restricted, and the other general and residuary. The national government possesses those powers which it can be shown the people have conferred on it, and no more. All the rest belongs to the state governments, or to the people themselves. So far as the people have restrained

DANIEL WEBSTER

state sovereignty by the expression of their will, in the Constitution of the United States, so far, it must be admitted, state sovereignty is effectually controlled. I do not contend that it is, or ought to be, controlled farther. The sentiment to which I have referred propounds that state sovereignty is only to be controlled by its own "feeling of justice"—that is to say, it is not to be controlled at all, for one who is to follow his own feelings is under no legal control. Now, however men may think this ought to be, the fact is that the people of the United States have chosen to impose control on state sovereignties. There are those, doubtless, who wish they had been left without restraint; but the Constitution has ordered the matter differently. To make war, for instance, is an exercise of sovereignty; but the Constitution declares that no state shall make war. To coin money is another exercise of sovereign power; but no state is at liberty to coin money. Again, the Constitution says that no sovereign state shall be so sovereign as to make a treaty. These prohibitions, it must be confessed, are a control on the state sovereignty of South Carolina, as well as of the other states, which does not arise "from her own feelings of honorable justice." The opinion referred to, therefore, is in defiance of the plainest provisions of the Constitution.

There are other proceedings of public bodies which have already been alluded to, and to which I refer again, for the purpose of ascertaining more fully what is the length and breadth of that doctrine denominated the Carolina doctrine, which the honorable member has now stood up on this floor to maintain. In one of them I find it resolved that "the tariff of 1828, and every other tariff designed to promote one branch of industry at the expense of others, is contrary to the meaning and intention of the federal compact, and such a dangerous, palpable, and deliberate usurpation of power, by a determined majority, wielding the general government beyond the limits of its delegated powers, as calls upon the states which compose the suffering minority, in their sovereign capacity, to exercise the powers which, as sovereigns, necessarily devolve upon them when their contract is violated."

Observe, sir, that this resolution holds the tariff of 1828, and every other tariff designed to promote one branch of industry at the expense of another, to be such a dangerous, palpable, and deliberate usurpation of power as calls upon the states in their sovereign capacity to interfere by their own authority. This denunciation, Mr. President, you will please to observe, includes our old tariff of 1816, as well as all others; because that was established to promote the interest of the manufacturers of cotton, to the manifest and admitted injury of the Calcutta cotton trade. Observe, again, that all the qualifications are here rehearsed and charged upon the tariff which are necessary to bring the case within the gentleman's proposition. The tariff is a usurpation; it is a dangerous usurpation; it is a palpable usurpation; it is a deliberate usurpation. It is such a usurpation, therefore, as calls upon the states to exercise their right of interference. Here is a case, then, within the gentleman's principles, and all his qualifications of his principles. It is a case for action. The Constitution is plainly, dangerously, palpably, and deliberately violated; and the states must interpose their own authority to arrest the law. Let us suppose the state of South Carolina to express the same opinion, by the voice of her legislature. That would be very imposing; but what then? It so happens that, at the very moment when South Carolina resolves that the tariff laws are unconstitutional, Pennsylvania and Kentucky resolve exactly the reverse. They hold those laws to be both highly proper and strictly constitutional. And now, sir, how does the honorable member propose to deal with this case? How does he relieve us from this difficulty upon any principle of his? His construction gets us into it; how does he propose to get us out?

In Carolina the tariff is a palpable, deliberate usurpation; Carolina, therefore, may nullify it, and refuse to pay the duties. In Pennsylvania it is both clearly constitutional and highly expedient; and there the duties are to be paid. And yet we live under a government of uniform laws, and under a Constitution, too, which contains an express provision, as it happens, that all duties shall be equal in all states. Does not this approach absurdity?

If there be no power to settle such questions, independent of either of the states, is not the whole Union a rope of sand? Are we not thrown back again precisely upon the old Confederation?

It is too plain to be argued. Four-and-twenty inter-preters of constitutional law, each with a power to decide for itself, and none with authority to bind anybody else, and this constitutional law the only bond of their union! What is such a state of things but a mere connection during pleasure, or, to use the phraseology of the times, during feeling? And that feeling, too, not the feeling of the peo-ple, who established the Constitution, but the feeling of the state governments.

In another of the South Carolina addresses, having pre-mised that the crisis requires "all the concentrated energy of passion," an attitude of open resistance to the laws of the Union is advised. Open resistance to the laws, then, is the constitutional remedy, the conservative power of the state, which the South Carolina doctrines teach for the redress of political evils, real or imaginary. And its authors further say that, appealing with confidence to the Constitution itself to justify their opinions, they cannot consent to try their accuracy by the courts of justice. In one sense, indeed, sir, this is assuming an attitude of open resistance in favor of liberty. But what sort of liberty? The liberty of establishing their own opinions in defiance of the opinions of all others; the liberty of judging and deciding exclusively themselves in a matter in which others have as much right to judge and decide as they; the liberty of placing their own opinion above the judgment of all others, above the laws, and above the Constitution. This is their liberty, and this is the fair result of the proposition contended for by the honorable gentleman. Or, it may be more properly said, it is identical with it, rather than a result from it. . . .

Sir, the human mind is so constituted that the merits of both sides of a controversy appear very clear, and very pal-pable, to those who respectively espouse them; and both sides usually grow clearer as the controversy advances. South Carolina sees unconstitutionality in the tariff; she sees oppression there also, and she sees danger. Pennsyl-vania, with a vision not less sharp, looks at the same tariff, and sees no such thing in it; she sees it all constitutional, all useful, all safe. The faith of South Carolina is strengthened by opposition, and she now not only sees, but resolves, that the tariff is palpably unconstitutional, oppressive, and dangerous; but Pennsylvania, not to be behind her neighbors, and equally willing to strengthen her own faith by a confident asseveration, resolves also, and gives to every warm affirmative of South Carolina a plain, downright, Pennsylvania negative. South Carolina, to show the strength and unity of her opinion, brings her assembly to a unanimity, within seven voices; Pennsylvania, not to be outdone in this respect any more than in others, reduces her dissentient fraction to a single vote. Now, sir, again I ask the gentleman, What is to be done? Are these states both right? Is he bound to consider them both right? If not, which is in the wrong? Or, rather, which has the best right to decide? And if he, and if I, are not to know what the Constitution means, and what it is, till those two state legislatures, and the twenty-two others, shall agree in its construction, what have we sworn to when we have sworn to maintain it? I was forcibly struck, sir, with one reflection, as the gentleman went on in his speech. He quoted Mr. Madison's resolutions to prove that a state may interfere in a case of deliberate, palpable, and dangerous exercise of a power not granted. The honorable member supposes the tariff law to be such an exercise of power; and that consequently a case has arisen in which the state may, if it see fit, interfere by its own law. Now it so happens, nevertheless, that Mr. Madison deems this same tariff law quite constitutional. Instead of a clear and palpable violation, it is, in his judgment, no violation at all. So that, while they use his authority in a hypothetical case, they reject it in the very case before them. All this, sir, shows the inherent futility—I had almost used a stronger word—of conceding this power of interference to the state, and then attempting to secure it from abuse by imposing qualifications of which the states themselves are to judge. One of two things is true—either the laws of the Union are beyond the discretion and beyond the control of the states, or else we have no constitution of general government, and are thrust back again to the days of the Confederation. . . .

I must now beg to ask, sir, whence is this supposed right of the states derived? Where do they find the power to interfere with the laws of the Union? Sir, the opinion which the honorable gentleman maintains is a notion founded in a total misapprehension, in my judgment, of the origin of this government, and of the foundation on which it stands. I hold it to be a popular government, erected by the people; those who administer it responsible to the people; and itself capable of being amended and modified, just as the people may choose it should be. It is as popular, just as truly emanating from the people, as the state governments. It is created for one purpose; the state governments for another. It has its own powers; they have theirs. There is no more authority with them to arrest the operation of a law of Congress, than with Congress to arrest the operation of their laws. We are here to administer a constitution emanating immediately from the people, and trusted by them to our administration. It is not the creature of the state governments. . . .

This government, sir, is the independent offspring of the popular will. It is not the creature of state legislatures; nay, more, if the whole truth must be told, the people brought it into existence, established it, and have hitherto supported it, for the very purpose, amongst others, of imposing certain salutary restraints on state sovereignties. The states cannot now make war; they cannot contract alliances; they cannot make, each for itself, separate regulations of commerce; they cannot lay imposts; they cannot coin money. If this Constitution, sir, be the creature of state legislatures, it must be admitted that it has obtained a strange control over the volitions of its creators.

The people, then, sir, erected this government. They gave it a Constitution, and in that Constitution they have enumerated the powers which they bestow on it. They have made it a limited government. They have defined its authority. They have restrained it to the exercise of such powers as are granted; and all others, they declare, are reserved to the states, or the people. But, sir, they have not stopped here. If they had, they would have accomplished but half their work. No definition can be so clear as to avoid the possibility of doubt; no limitation so precise as to exclude all uncertainty. Who, then, shall construe this grant of the people? Who shall interpret their will, where it may be supposed they have left it doubtful? With whom do they repose this ultimate right of deciding on the powers of the government? Sir, they have settled all this in the fullest manner. They have left it with the government itself, in its appropriate branches. Sir, the very chief end, the main design, for which the whole Constitution was framed and adopted, was to establish a government that should not be obliged to act through state agency, or depend on state opinion or state discretion. The people had had quite enough of that kind of government under the Confederation. Under that system, the legal action, the application of law to individuals, belonged exclusively to the states. Congress could only recommend; their acts were not of binding force till the states had adopted and sanctioned them. Are we in that condition still? Are we yet at the mercy of state discretion and state construction? Sir, if we are, then vain will be our attempt to maintain the Constitution under which we sit.

But, sir, the people have wisely provided, in the Constitution itself, a proper, suitable mode and tribunal for settling questions of constitutional law. There are in the Constitution grants of powers to Congress, and restrictions on these powers. There are also prohibitions on the states. Some authority must, therefore, necessarily exist, having the ultimate jurisdiction to fix and ascertain the interpretation of these grants, restrictions, and prohibitions. The Constitution has itself pointed out, ordained, and established that authority. How has it accomplished this great and essential end? By declaring, sir, that "the Constitution and the laws of the United States, made in pursuance thereof, shall be the supreme law of the land, anything in the constitution or laws of any state to the contrary notwithstanding."

This, sir, was the first great step. By this the supremacy of the Constitution and the laws of the United States are declared. The people so will it. No state law is to be valid which comes in conflict with the Constitution, or any law of the United States passed in pursuance of it. But who shall decide this question of interference? To whom lies the last appeal? This, sir, the Constitution itself decides also, by declaring, "that the judicial power shall extend to all cases arising under the Constitution and laws of the United States." These two provisions cover the whole ground. They are, in truth, the keystone of the arch! With these it is a government; without them, a confederation. In pursuance of these clear and express provisions, Congress established, at its very first session, in the judicial act, a mode for carrying them into full effect, and for bringing all questions of constitutional power to the final decision of the Supreme Court. It then, sir, became a government. It then had the means of self-protection; and but for this it would, in all probability, have been now among things which are past. Having constituted the government, and declared its powers, the people have further said that since somebody must decide on the extent of these powers, the government shall itself decide, subject always, like other popular governments, to its responsibility to the people. And now, sir, I repeat, how is it that a state legislature acquires any power to interfere? Who or what gives them the right to say to the people: "We, who are your agents and servants for one purpose, will undertake to decide that your other agents and servants, appointed by you for another purpose, have transcended the authority you gave them!" The reply would be, I think, not impertinent: "Who made you a judge over another's servants? To their own masters they stand or fall."

Sir, I deny this power of state legislatures altogether. It cannot stand the test of examination. Gentlemen may say that in an extreme case a state government may protect the people from intolerable oppression. Sir, in such a case the people might protect themselves without the aid of the state governments. Such a case warrants revolution. It must make, when it comes, a law for itself. A nullifying act of a state legislature cannot alter the case, nor make resistance any more lawful. In maintaining these sentiments, sir, I am but asserting the rights of the people. I state what they have declared, and insist on their right to declare it. They have chosen to repose this power in the general government, and I think it my duty to support it like other constitutional powers.

For myself, sir, I do not admit the competency of South

Carolina or any other state to prescribe my constitutional duty, or to settle, between me and the people, the validity of laws of Congress for which I have voted. I decline her umpirage. I have not sworn to support the Constitution according to her construction of the clauses. I have not stipulated by my oath of office or otherwise to come under any responsibility, except to the people, and those whom they have appointed to pass upon the question, whether laws, supported by my votes, conform to the Constitution of the country. And, sir, if we look to the general nature of the case, could anything have been more preposterous than to make a government for the whole Union, and yet leave its powers subject, not to one interpretation, but to thirteen or twenty-four interpretations? Instead of one tribunal, established by all, responsible to all, with power to decide for all, shall constitutional questions be left to four-and-twenty popular bodies, each at liberty to decide for itself, and none bound to respect the decisions of others; and each at liberty, too, to give a new constitution on every new election of its own members? Would anything, with such a principle in it, or rather with such a destitution of all principle, be fit to be called a government? No, sir. It should not be denominated a constitution. It should be called, rather, a collection of topics for everlasting controversy; heads of debate for a disputatious people. It would not be a government. It would not be adequate to any practical good, or fit for any country to live under.

To avoid all possibility of being misunderstood, allow me to repeat again in the fullest manner that I claim no powers for the government by forced or unfair construction. I admit that it is a government of strictly limited powers; of enumerated, specified, and particularized powers; and that whatsoever is not granted is withheld. But notwithstanding all this, and however the grant of powers may be expressed, its limit and extent may yet, in some cases, admit of doubt; and the general government would be good for nothing, it would be incapable of long existing, if some mode had not been provided in which those doubts as they should arise might be peaceably but authoritatively solved.

And now, Mr. President, let me run the honorable

gentleman's doctrine a little into its practical application. Let us look at his probable modus operandi. If a thing can be done, an ingenious man can tell how it is to be done, and I wish to be informed how this state interference is to be put in practice without violence, bloodshed, and rebellion. We will take the existing case of the tariff law. South Carolina is said to have made up her opinion upon it. If we do not repeal it (as we probably shall not), she will then apply to the case the remedy of her doctrine. She will, we must suppose, pass a law of her legislature declaring the several Acts of Congress, usually called the tariff laws, null and void, so far as they respect South Carolina, or the citizens thereof. So far, all is a paper transaction, and easy enough. But the collector at Charleston is collecting the duties imposed by these tariff laws. He, therefore, must be stopped. The collector will seize the goods if the tariff duties are not paid. The state authorities will undertake their rescue, the marshal, with his posse, will come to the collector's aid, and here the contest begins. The militia of the state will be called out to sustain the nullifying act. They will march, sir, under a very gallant leader; for I believe the honorable member himself commands the militia of that part of the state. He will raise the nullifying act on his standard, and spread it out as his banner! It will have a preamble, setting forth that the tariff laws are palpable, deliberate, and dangerous violations of the Constitution! He will proceed, with this banner flying, to the custom-house in Charleston,

"All the while
Sonorous metal blowing martial sounds."

Arrived at the custom-house, he will tell the collector that he must collect no more duties under any of the tariff laws. This he will be somewhat puzzled to say, by the way, with a grave countenance, considering what hand South Carolina herself had in that of 1816. But, sir, the collector would not, probably, desist at his bidding. He would show him the law of Congress, the Treasury instruction, and his own oath of office. He would say, he should perform his duty, come what might.

Here would ensue a pause; for they say that a certain

stillness precedes the tempest. The trumpeter would hold his breath awhile, and before all this military array should fall on the custom-house, collector, clerks, and all, it is very probable some of those composing it would request of their gallant commander-in-chief to be informed upon a little point of law; for they have, doubtless, a just respect for his opinions as a lawyer, as well as for his bravery as a soldier. They know he has read Blackstone and the Constitution, as well as Turenne and Vauban. They would ask him, therefore, somewhat concerning their rights in this matter. They would inquire whether it was not somewhat dangerous to resist a law of the United States. What would be the nature of their offense, they would wish to learn, if they, by military force and array, resisted the execution in Carolina of a law of the United States, and it should turn out, after all, that the law *was constitutional?* He would answer, of course, treason. No lawyer could give any other answer. John Fries, he would tell them, had learned that some years ago. How, then, they would ask, do you propose to defend us? We are not afraid of bullets, but treason has a way of taking people off that we do not much relish. How do you propose to defend us? "Look at my floating banner," he would reply; "see there the nullifying law!"

Is it your opinion, gallant commander, they would then say, that if we should be indicted for treason, that same floating banner of yours would make a good plea in bar? "South Carolina is a sovereign state," he would reply. That is true; but would the judge admit our plea? "These tariff laws," he would repeat, "are unconstitutional, palpably, deliberately, dangerously." That may all be so; but if the tribunal should not happen to be of that opinion, shall we swing for it? We are ready to die for our country, but it is rather an awkward business, this dying without touching the ground! After all, that is a sort of hemp tax worse than any part of the tariff.

Mr. President, the honorable gentleman would be in a dilemma like that of another great general. He would have a knot before him which he could not untie. He must cut it with his sword. He must say to his followers, "Defend yourselves with your bayonets"; and this is war —civil war.

Direct collision, therefore, between force and force, is the unavoidable result of that remedy for the revision of unconstitutional laws which the gentleman contends for. It must happen in the very first case to which it is applied. Is not this the plain result? To resist by force the execution of a law, generally, is treason. Can the courts of the United States take notice of the indulgence of a state to commit treason? The common saying that a state cannot commit treason herself is nothing to the purpose. Can she authorize others to do it? If John Fries had produced an Act of Pennsylvania, annulling the law of Congress, would it have helped his case? Talk about it as we will, these doctrines go the length of revolution. They are incompatible with any peaceable administration of the government. They lead directly to disunion and civil commotion; and therefore it is that at their commencement, when they are first found to be maintained by respectable men, and in a tangible form, I enter my public protest against them all.

The honorable gentleman argues that if this government be the sole judge of the extent of its own powers, whether that right of judging be in Congress or the Supreme Court, it equally subverts state sovereignty. This the gentleman sees, or thinks he sees, although he cannot perceive how the right of judging in this matter, if left to the exercise of state legislatures, has any tendency to subvert the government of the Union. The gentleman's opinion may be that the right ought not to have been lodged with the general government; he may like better such a Constitution as we should have had under the right of state interference; but I ask him to meet me on the plain matter of fact. I ask him to meet me on the Constitution itself. I ask him if the power is not found there, clearly and visibly found there?

But, sir, what is this danger, and what are the grounds of it? Let it be remembered that the Constitution of the United States is not unalterable. It is to continue in its present form no longer than the people who established it shall choose to continue it. If they shall become convinced that they have made an injudicious or inexpedient partition and distribution of power between the state governments and the general government, they can alter that distribution at will.

If anything be found in the national Constitution, either by original provision or subsequent interpretation, which ought not to be in it, the people know how to get rid of it. If any construction, unacceptable to them, be established so as to become practically a part of the Constitution, they will amend it at their own sovereign pleasure. But while the people choose to maintain it as it is, while they are satisfied with it, and refuse to change it, who has given, or who can give, to the legislatures a right to alter it, either by interference, construction, or otherwise? Gentlemen do not seem to recollect that the people have any power to do anything for themselves. They imagine there is no safety for them any longer than they are under the close guardianship of the state legislatures. Sir, the people have not trusted their safety, in regard to the general Constitution, to these hands. They have required other security, and taken other bonds. They have chosen to trust themselves, first, to the plain words of the instrument, and to such construction as the government themselves, in doubtful cases, should put on their powers, under their oaths of office, and subject to their responsibility to them, just as the people of a state trust to their own governments with a similar power. Second, they have reposed their trust in the efficacy of frequent elections, and in their own power to remove their own servants and agents whenever they see cause. Third, they have reposed trust in the judicial power, which, in order that it might be trustworthy, they have made as respectable, as disinterested, and as independent as was practicable. Fourth, they have seen fit to rely, in case of necessity, or high expediency, on their known and admitted power to alter or amend the Constitution, peaceably and quietly, whenever experience shall point out defects or imperfections. And, finally, the people of the United States have at no time, in no way, directly or indirectly, authorized any state legislature to construe or interpret their high instrument of government, much less to interfere, by their own power, to arrest its course and operation.

If, sir, the people in these respects had done otherwise than they have done, their Constitution could neither have been preserved, nor would it have been worth preserving.

And if its plain provisions shall now be disregarded, and these new doctrines interpolated in it, it will become as feeble and helpless a being as its enemies, whether early or more recent, could possibly desire. It will exist in every state but as a poor dependent on state permission. It must borrow leave to be; and will be, no longer than state pleasure, or state indiscretion, sees fit to grant the indulgence, and to prolong its poor existence.

But, sir, although there are fears, there are hopes also. The people have preserved this, their own chosen Constitution, for forty years, and have seen their happiness, prosperity, and renown grow with its growth, and strengthen with its strength. They are now, generally, strongly attached to it. Overthrown by direct assault, it cannot be; evaded, undermined, NULLIFIED, it will not be, if we, and those who shall succeed us here, as agents and representatives of the people, shall conscientiously and vigilantly discharge the two great branches of our public trust, faithfully to preserve and wisely to administer it.

Mr. President, I have thus stated the reasons of my dissent to the doctrines which have been advanced and maintained. I am conscious of having detained you and the Senate much too long. I was drawn into the debate with no previous deliberation, such as is suited to the discussion of so grave and important a subject. But it is a subject of which my heart is full, and I have not been willing to suppress the utterance of its spontaneous sentiments. I cannot, even now, persuade myself to relinquish it without expressing once more my deep conviction that since it respects nothing less than the union of the states, it is of most vital and essential importance to the public happiness. I profess, sir, in my career hitherto to have kept steadily in view the prosperity and honor of the whole country, and the preservation of our Federal Union. It is to that Union we owe our safety at home, and our consideration and dignity abroad. It is to that Union that we are chiefly indebted for whatever makes us most proud of our country. That Union we reached only by the discipline of our virtues in the severe school of adversity. It has its origin in the necessities of disordered finance, prostrate commerce, and ruined credit. Under its benign influences these great interests immediately awoke, as from the dead, and sprang forth with newness of life. Every year of its duration has teemed with fresh proofs of its utility and its blessings; and although our territory has stretched out wider and wider, and our population spread farther and farther, they have not outrun its protection or its benefits. It has been to us all a copious fountain of national, social, and personal happiness.

I have not allowed myself, sir, to look beyond the Union, to see what might lie hidden in the dark recess behind. I have not coolly weighed the chances of preserving liberty when the bonds that unite us together shall be broken asunder. I have not accustomed myself to hang over the precipice of disunion, to see whether, with my short sight, I can fathom the depth of the abyss below; nor could I regard him as a safe counsellor in the affairs of this government, whose thoughts should be mainly bent on considering, not how the Union may be best preserved, but how tolerable might be the condition of the people when it should be broken up and destroyed. While the Union lasts we have high, exciting, gratifying prospects spread out before us, for us and our children. Beyond that I seek not to penetrate the veil. God grant that in my day at least that curtain may not rise! God grant that on my vision never may be opened what lies behind! When my eyes shall be turned to behold for the last time the sun in heaven, may I not see him shining on the broken and dishonored fragments of a once glorious Union—on states dissevered, discordant, belligerent; on a land rent with civil feuds, or drenched, it may be, in fraternal blood! Let their last feeble and lingering glance rather behold the gorgeous ensign of the Republic, now known and honored throughout the earth, still full high advanced, its arms and trophies streaming in their original lustre, not a stripe erased or polluted, not a single star obscured, bearing for its motto no such miserable interrogatory as "What is all this worth?" nor those other words of delusion and folly, "Liberty first and Union afterward"; but everywhere, spread all over in characters of living light, blazing on all its ample folds, as they float over the sea and over the land, and in every wind under the whole heavens, that other sentiment, dear to every true American heart—Liberty *and* Union, now and forever, one and inseparable!

ADAMS AND JEFFERSON

This is an unaccustomed spectacle. For the first time, fellow-citizens, badges of mourning shroud the columns and overhang the arches of this hall. These walls, which were consecrated so long ago to the cause of American liberty, which witnessed her infant struggles, and rung with the shouts of her earliest victories, proclaim now that distinguished friends and champions of the great cause have fallen. It is right that it should be thus. The tears which flow, and the honors that are paid when the founders of the Republic die, give hope that the Republic itself may be immortal. . . .

Adams and Jefferson are no more; and we are assembled, fellow-citizens—the aged, the middle-aged, and the young—by the spontaneous impulse of all, under the authority of the municipal government, with the presence of the Chief Magistrate of the Commonwealth, and others, its official representatives, the university, and the learned societies, to bear our part in those manifestations of respect and gratitude which universally pervade the land. Adams and Jefferson are no more. On our fiftieth anniversary, the great day of national jubilee, in the very hour of public rejoicing, in the midst of echoing and reëchoing voices of thanksgiving, while their own names were on all tongues, they took their flight together to the world of spirits.

If it be true that no one can safely be pronounced happy while he lives; if that event which terminates life can alone crown its honors and its glory, what felicity is here! The great epic of their lives, how happily concluded! Poetry itself has hardly closed illustrious lives and finished the career of earthly renown by such a consummation. If we had the power we could not wish to reverse this dispensation of the Divine Providence. The great objects of life were accomplished; the drama was ready to be closed; it has closed; our patriots have fallen; but so fallen at such age,

with such coincidence on such a day, that we cannot rationally lament that that end has come which we knew could not be long deferred. Neither of these great men, fellow-citizens, could have died at any time without leaving an immense void in our American society. They have been so intimately and for so long a time blended with the history of the country, and especially so united in our thoughts and recollections with the events of the Revolution, that the death of either would have touched the strings of public sympathy. We should have felt that one great link connecting us with former times was broken; that we had lost something more, as it were, of the presence of the Revolution itself and of the Act of Independence, and were driven on by another great remove from the days of our country's early distinction to meet posterity and to mix with the future. Like the mariner whom the ocean and the winds carry along till he sees the stars which have directed his course, and lighted his pathless way, descend one by one beneath the rising horizon, we should have felt that the stream of time had borne us onward till another great luminary whose light had cheered us, and whose guidance we had followed, had sunk away from our sight.

But the concurrence of their death on the anniversary of Independence has naturally awakened stronger emotions. Both had been Presidents; both had lived to great age; both were early patriots; and both were distinguished and even honored by their immediate agency in the Act of Independence. It cannot but seem striking and extraordinary that these two should live to see the fiftieth year from the date of that Act; that they should complete that year; and that then, on the day which had fast linked forever their own fame with their country's glory, the heavens should open to receive them both at once. As their lives themselves were the gifts of Providence, who is not willing to recognize in their happy termination, as well as in their long continuance, proofs that our country and its benefactors are objects of his care? . . .

We are not assembled, therefore, fellow-citizens, as men overwhelmed with calamity by the sudden disruption of the ties of friendship or affection, or as in despair for the Republic, by the untimely blighting of its hopes. Death has not surprised us by an unseasonable blow. We have, indeed, seen the tomb close; but it has closed only over mature years, over long-protracted public service, over the weakness of age, and over life itself only when the ends of living had been fulfilled. These suns, as they rose slowly, and steadily, amidst clouds and storms, in their ascendant, so they have not rushed from their meridian to sink suddenly in the west. Like the mildness, the serenity, the continuing benignity of a summer's day, they have gone down with slow-descending, grateful, long-lingering light, and now that they are beyond the visible margin of the world, good omens cheer us from "the bright track of their fiery car."

There were many points of similarity in the lives and fortunes of these great men. They belonged to the same profession, and had pursued its studies and its practice, for unequal lengths of time indeed, but with diligence and effect. Both were learned and able lawyers. They were natives and inhabitants, respectively, of those two of the Colonies which, at the Revolution, were the largest and most powerful, and which naturally had a lead in the political affairs of the times. When the Colonies became, in some degree, united, by the assembling of a general congress, they were brought to act together, in its deliberations, not indeed at the same time, but both at early periods. Each had already manifested his attachment to the cause of the country, as well as his ability to maintain it, by printed addresses, public speeches, extensive correspondence, and whatever other mode could be adopted, for the purpose of exposing the encroachments of the British Parliament and animating the people to a manly resistance. Both were not only decided, but early friends of Independence. While others yet doubted, they were resolved; while others hesitated, they pressed forward. They were both members of the committee for preparing the Declaration of Independence, and they constituted the sub-committee appointed by the other members to make the draft. They left their seats in Congress, being called to other public employments, at periods not remote from each other, although one of them returned to it, afterwards, for a short time. Neither of them was of the assembly of great men which formed the present Constitution, and neither was at any time member of Congress under its provisions. Both have been public ministers abroad, both Vice-Presidents, and both Presidents. These coincidences are now singularly crowned and completed. They have died together; and they died on the anniversary of liberty.

When many of us were last in this place, fellow-citizens, it was on the day of that anniversary. We were met to enjoy the festivities belonging to the occasion, and to manifest our grateful homage to our political fathers.

We did not, we could not here, forget our venerable neighbor of Quincy. We knew that we were standing, at a time of high and palmy prosperity, where he had stood in the hour of utmost peril; that we saw nothing but liberty and security, where he had met the frown of power; that we were enjoying everything, where he had hazarded everything; and just and sincere plaudits rose to his name from the crowds which filled this area and hung over these galleries. He whose grateful duty it was to speak to us, on that day, of the virtues of our fathers, had, indeed, admonished us that time and years were about to level his venerable frame with the dust. But he bade us hope that the "sound of a nation's joy, rushing from our cities, ringing from our valleys, echoing from our hills, might yet break the silence of his aged ear; that the rising blessings of grateful millions might yet visit, with glad light, his decaying vision." Alas! that vision was then closing forever! Alas! the silence which was then settling on that aged ear was an everlasting silence! For, lo! in the very moment of our festivities, his freed spirit ascended to God who gave it! Human aid and human solace terminate at the grave, or we would gladly have borne him upward on a nation's outspread hands; we would have accompanied him, and with the blessings of millions, and the prayers of millions, commended him to the Divine favor. . . .

The eloquence of Mr. Adams resembled his general character, and formed, indeed, a part of it. It was bold, manly, and energetic; and such the crisis required. When public bodies are to be addressed on momentous occasions, when great interests are at stake and strong passions excited, nothing is valuable in speech further than it is connected with high intellectual and moral endowments. Clearness, force, and earnestness are the qualities which produce conviction. True eloquence, indeed, does not consist in speech. It cannot be brought from far. Labor and learning may toil for it; but they will toil in vain. Words and phrases may be marshaled in every way; but they cannot compass it. It must exist in the man, in the subject, and in the occasion. Affected passion, intense expression, the pomp of declamation, all may aspire after it; they cannot reach it. It comes, if it come at all, like the outbreaking of a fountain from the earth, or the bursting forth of volcanic fires, with spontaneous, original, native force. The graces taught in the schools, the costly ornaments, and studied contrivances of speech, shock and disgust men, when their own lives, and the fate of their wives, their children, and their country hang on the decision of the hour. Then words have lost their power, rhetoric is vain, and all elaborate oratory contemptible. Even genius itself then feels rebuked and subdued, as in the presence of higher qualities. Then patriotism is eloquent; then self-devotion is eloquent. The clear conception, outrunning the deductions of logic—the high purpose—the firm resolve—the dauntless spirit, speaking on the tongue, beaming from the eye, informing every feature, and urging the whole man onward, right onward, to his object—this, this is eloquence; or, rather, it is something greater and higher than all eloquence—it is action, noble, sublime, godlike action.

In July, 1776, the controversy had passed the stage of argument. An appeal had been made to force, and opposing armies were in the field. Congress then was to decide whether the tie which had so long bound us to the parent state was to be severed at once and severed forever. All the Colonies had signified their resolution to abide by this decision, and the people looked for it with the most intense anxiety. And surely, fellow-citizens, never, never were men called to a more important political deliberation. If we contemplate it from the point where they then stood, no question could be more full of interest; if we look at it now, and judge of its importance by its effects, it appears in still greater magnitude.

Let us, then, bring before us the assembly, which was

about to decide a question thus big with the fate of empire. Let us open their doors, and look in upon their deliberations. Let us survey the anxious and careworn countenances—let us hear the firm-toned voices of this band of patriots.

Hancock presides over this solemn sitting, and one of those not yet prepared to pronounce for absolute independence is on the floor, and is urging his reasons for dissenting from the Declaration:—

"Let us pause! This step, once taken, cannot be retraced. This resolution, once passed, will cut off all hope of reconciliation. If success attend the arms of England, we shall then be no longer colonies, with charters and with privileges. These will all be forfeited by this act; and we shall be in the condition of other conquered people—at the mercy of the conquerors. For ourselves, we may be ready to run the hazard; but are we ready to carry the country to that length? Is success so probable as to justify it? Where is the military, where the naval, power, by which we are to resist the whole strength of the arm of England? for she will exert that strength to the utmost. Can we rely on the constancy and perseverance of the people?—or will they not act as the people of other countries have acted, and, wearied with a long war, submit, in the end, to a worse oppression? While we stand on our old ground, and insist on redress of grievances, we know we are right, and are not answerable for consequences. Nothing, then, can be imputable to us. But if we now change our object, carry our pretensions further, and set up for absolute independence, we shall lose the sympathy of mankind. We shall no longer be defending what we possess, but struggling for something which we never did possess, and which we have solemnly and uniformly disclaimed all intention of pursuing, from the very outset of the troubles. Abandoning thus our old ground, of resistance only to arbitrary acts of oppression, the nations will believe the whole to have been mere pretense, and they will look on us, not as injured, but as ambitious, subjects. I shudder before this responsibility. It will be on us, if, relinquishing the ground we have stood on so long, and stood on so safely, we now proclaim Independence, and carry on the war for that object, while these cities burn, these pleasant fields whiten and bleach with the bones of their owners, and these streams run blood. It will be upon us, it will be upon us, if, failing to maintain this unseasonable and ill-judged Declaration, a sterner despotism, maintained by military power, shall be established over our posterity, when we ourselves, given up by an exhausted, a harassed, a misled people, shall have expiated our rashness and atoned for our presumption on the scaffold."

It was for Mr. Adams to reply to arguments like these. We know his opinions, and we know his character. He would commence with his accustomed directness and earnestness :—

" Sink or swim, live or die, survive or perish, I give my hand and my heart to this vote. It is true, indeed, that in the beginning we aimed not at Independence. But there's a divinity which shapes our ends. The injustice of England has driven us to arms ; and blinded to her own interest, for our good, she has obstinately persisted, till Independence is now within our grasp. We have but to reach forth to it, and it is ours. Why, then, should we defer the Declaration ? Is any man so weak as now to hope for a reconciliation with England, which shall leave either safety to the country and its liberties, or safety to his own life and his own honor ? Are not you, sir, who sit in that chair—is not he, our venerable colleague near you—are you not both already the proscribed and predestined objects of punishment and of vengeance? Cut off from all hope of royal clemency, what are you, what can you be, while the power of England remains, but outlaws? If we postpone independence, do we mean to carry on, or to give up the war? Do we mean to submit to the measures of Parliament, Boston Port Bill and all? Do we mean to submit, and consent that we ourselves shall be ground to powder, and our country and its rights trodden down in the dust? I know we do not mean to submit. We never shall submit. Do we intend to violate that most solemn obligation ever entered into by men— that plighting, before God, of our sacred honor to Washington, when, putting him forth to incur the dangers of war, as well as the political hazards of the times, we promised to adhere to him, in every extremity, with our fortunes and our lives ? I know there is not a man here who would not rather see a general conflagration sweep over the land, or an earthquake sink it, than one jot or tittle of that plighted faith fall to the ground. For myself, having twelve months ago in this place moved you that George Washington be appointed commander of the forces, raised or to be raised, for defense of American liberty, may my right hand forget her cunning and my tongue cleave to the roof of my mouth, if I hesitate or waver in the support I give him. The war, then, must go on. We must fight it through. And, if the war must go on, why put off longer the Declaration of Independence? That measure will strengthen us. It will give us character abroad. The nations will then treat with us, which they never can do while we acknowledge ourselves subjects in arms against our sovereign. Nay, I maintain that England herself will sooner treat for peace with us on the footing of Independence, than consent, by repealing her acts, to acknowledge that her whole conduct towards us has been a course of injustice and oppression. Her pride will be less wounded by submitting to that course of things which now predestinates our independence, than by yielding the points in controversy to her rebellious subjects. The former she would regard as the result of fortune; the latter she would feel as her own deep disgrace. Why, then—why, then, sir, do we not, as soon as possible, change this from a civil to a national war? And since we must fight it through, why not put ourselves in a state to enjoy all the benefits of victory, if we gain the victory?

"If we fail, it can be no worse for us. But we shall not fail. The cause will raise up armies; the cause will create navies. The people —the people, if we are true to them, will carry us, and will carry themselves, gloriously through this struggle. I care not how fickle other people have been found. I know the people of these Colonies, and I know that resistance to British aggression is deep and settled in their hearts and cannot be eradicated. Every colony, indeed, has expressed its willingness to follow, if we but take the lead. Sir, the Declaration will inspire the people with increased courage. Instead of a long and bloody war for restoration of privileges, for redress of grievances, for chartered immunities, held under a British king, set before them the glorious object of entire independence, and it will breathe into them anew the breath of life. Read this Declaration at the head of the army; every sword will be drawn from its scabbard, and the solemn vow uttered to maintain it, or to perish on the bed of honor. Publish it from the pulpit; religion will approve it, and the love of religious liberty will cling round it, resolved to stand with it, or fall with it. Send it to the public halls; proclaim it there; let them hear it, who heard the first roar of the enemy's cannon; let them see it, who saw their brothers and their sons fall on the field of Bunker Hill, and in the streets of Lexington and Concord, and the very walls will cry out in its support.

"Sir, I know the uncertainty of human affairs, but I see, I see clearly, through this day's business. You and I, indeed, may rue it. We may not live to the time when this Declaration shall be made good. We may die; die, colonists; die, slaves; die, it may be, ignominiously and on the scaffold. Be it so. Be it so. If it be the pleasure of heaven that my country shall require the poor offering of my life, the victim shall be ready at the appointed hour of sacrifice, come when that hour may. But while I do live, let me have a country, or at least the hope of a country, and that a free country!

"But, whatever may be our fate, be assured, be assured, that this Declaration will stand. It may cost treasure, and it may cost blood; but it will stand, and it will richly compensate for both. Through the thick gloom of the present I see the brightness of the future as the sun in heaven. We shall make this a glorious, an immortal, day. When we are in our graves, our children will honor it. They will celebrate it with thanksgiving, with festivity, with bonfires, and illuminations. On its annual return they will shed tears, copious, gushing tears, not of subjection and slavery, not of agony and distress, but of exultation, of gratitude, and of joy. Sir, before God, I believe the hour has come. My judgment approves this measure, and my whole heart is in it. All that I have, and all that I am, and all that I hope, in this life, I am now ready here to stake upon it; and I leave off as I began, that, live or die, survive or perish, I am for the Declaration. It is my living sentiment, and, by the blessing of God, it shall be my dying sentiment; independence now, and independence forever."

And so that day shall be honored, illustrious prophet and patriot!—so that day shall be honored, and, as often as it returns, thy renown shall come along with it, and the glory of thy life, like the day of thy death, shall not fail from the remembrance of men.

BUNKER HILL MONUMENT ORATION

We live in a most extraordinary age. Events so various and so important that they might crowd and distinguish centuries are in our times compressed within the compass of a single life. When has it happened that history has had so much to record in the same term of years as since the seventeenth of June, 1775? Our own Revolution, which under other circumstances might itself have been expected to occasion a war of half a century, has been achieved; twenty-four sovereign and independent states erected; and a general government established over them, so safe, so wise, so free, so practical, that we might well wonder its establishment should have been accomplished so soon were it not for the greater wonder that it should have been established at all. Two or three millions of people have been augmented to twelve; and the great forests of the West prostrated beneath the arm of successful industry; and the dwellers on the banks of the Ohio and the Mississippi become the fellow-citizens and neighbors of those who cultivate the hills of New England. We have a commerce that leaves no sea unexplored; navies which take no law from superior force; revenues adequate to all the exigencies of government, almost without taxation; and peace with all nations, founded on equal rights and mutual respect.

Europe, within the same period, has been agitated by a mighty revolution, which, while it has been felt in the individual condition and happiness of almost every man, has shaken to the center her political fabric, and dashed against one another thrones which had stood tranquil for ages. On this, our continent, our own example has been followed; and colonies have sprung up to be nations. Unaccustomed sounds of liberty and free government have reached us from beyond the track of the sun; and at this moment the dominion of European power in this continent, from the place where we stand to the South Pole, is annihilated forever.

In the meantime, both in Europe and America, such has been the general progress of knowledge; such the improvements in legislation, in commerce, in the arts, in letters, and, above all, in liberal ideas and the general spirit of the age, that the whole world seems changed.

Yet, notwithstanding that this is but a faint abstract of the things which have happened since the day of the battle of Bunker Hill, we are but fifty years removed from it; and we now stand here to enjoy all the blessings of our own condition, and to look abroad on the brightened prospects of the world, while we hold still among us some of those who were active agents in the scenes of 1775, and who are now here from every quarter of New England to visit once more, and under circumstances so affecting, I had almost said so overwhelming, this renowned theater of their courage and patriotism.

Venerable men, you have come down to us from a former generation. Heaven has bounteously lengthened out your lives that you might behold this joyous day. You are now where you stood fifty years ago this very hour, with your brothers and your neighbors, shoulder to shoulder, in the strife for your country. Behold, how altered! The same heavens are, indeed, over your heads; the same ocean rolls at your feet; but all else, how changed! You hear now no roar of hostile cannon, you see no mixed volumes of smoke and flame rising from burning Charlestown. The ground strewed with the dead and the dying; the impetuous charge; the steady and successful repulse; the loud call to repeated

assault; the summoning of all that is manly to repeated
resistance; a thousand bosoms freely and fearlessly bared in
an instant to whatever of terror there may be in war and
death; all these you have witnessed, but you witness them
no more.   All is peace.   The heights of yonder metropolis,
its towers and roofs which you then saw filled with wives
and children and countrymen in distress and terror, and
looking with unutterable emotions for the issue of the combat, have presented you to-day with the sight of its whole
happy population come out to welcome and greet you with
a universal jubilee.   Yonder proud ships, by a felicity of
position appropriately lying at the foot of this mount, and
seeming fondly to cling around it, are not means of annoyance to you, but your country's own means of distinction
and defense.   All is peace; and God has granted you this
sight of your country's happiness ere you slumber in the
grave forever.   He has allowed you to behold and to par-
také the reward of your patriotic toils; and he has allowed
us, your sons and countrymen, to meet you here, and in
the name of the present generation, in the name of your
country, in the name of liberty, to thank you!

But, alas! you are not all here!   Time and the sword
have thinned your ranks.   Prescott, Putnam, Stark, Brooks,
Read, Pomeroy, Bridge! our eyes seek for you in vain amid
this broken band.   You are gathered to your fathers, and
live only to your country in her grateful remembrance and
your own bright example.   But let us not too much grieve
that you have met the common fate of men.   You lived at
least long enough to know that your work had been nobly
and successfully accomplished.   You lived to see your
country's independence established and to sheathe your
swords from war.   On the light of liberty you saw arise the
light of peace, like

> " Another morn,
> Risen on mid-noon,"

and the sky on which you closed your eyes was cloudless.

But—ah!—Him! the first great martyr in this great
cause!   Him! the premature victim of his own self-devot-
ing heart!   Him! the head of our civil councils and the
destined leader of our military bands, whom nothing

brought hither but the unquenchable fire of his own spirit; him! cut off by Providence in the hour of overwhelming anxiety and thick gloom; falling ere he saw the star of his country rise; pouring out his generous blood like water before he knew whether it would fertilize a land of freedom or of bondage! how shall I struggle with the emotions that stifle the utterance of thy name! Our poor work may perish, but time shall endure! This monument may moulder away; the solid ground it rests upon may sink down to a level with the sea, but thy memory shall not fail! Wheresoever among men a heart shall be found that beats to the transports of patriotism and liberty, its aspirations shall be to claim kindred with thy spirit!

But the scene amid which we stand does not permit us to confine our thoughts or our sympathies to those fearless spirits who hazarded or lost their lives on this consecrated spot. We have the happiness to rejoice here in the presence of a most worthy representation of the survivors of the whole Revolutionary army.

Veterans, you are the remnant of many a well-fought field. You bring with you marks of honor from Trenton and Monmouth, from Yorktown, Camden, Bennington, and Saratoga. Veterans of half-a-century, when in your youthful days you put everything at hazard in your country's cause, good as that cause was, and sanguine as youth is, still your fondest hopes did not stretch onward to an hour like this! At a period to which you could not reasonably have expected to arrive; at a moment of national prosperity, such as you could never have foreseen, you are now met here to enjoy the fellowship of old soldiers and to receive the overflowings of a universal gratitude.

But your agitated countenances and your heaving breasts inform me that even this is not an unmixed joy. I perceive that a tumult of contending feelings rushes upon you. The images of the dead, as well as the persons of the living, throng to your embraces. The scene overwhelms you, and I turn from it. May the Father of all mercies smile upon your declining years and bless them! And when you shall here have exchanged your embraces; when you shall once more have pressed the hands which have been so often extended to give succor in adversity, or grasped in the exultation of victory; then look abroad into this lovely land, which your young valor defended, and mark the happiness with which it is filled; yea, look abroad into the whole earth and see what a name you have contributed to give to your country, and what a praise you have added to freedom, and then rejoice in the sympathy and gratitude which beam upon your last days from the improved condition of mankind.

The occasion does not require of me any particular account of the battle of the seventeenth of June, nor any detailed narrative of the events which immediately preceded it. These are familiarly known to all. In the progress of the great and interesting controversy, Massachusetts and the town of Boston had become early and marked objects of the displeasure of the British Parliament. This had been manifested in the act for altering the government of the province, and in that for shutting up the port of Boston. Nothing sheds more honor on our early history, and nothing better shows how little the feelings and sentiments of the colonies were known or regarded in England, than the impression which these measures everywhere produced in America. It had been anticipated that while the other colonies would be terrified by the severity of the punishment inflicted on Massachusetts, the other seaports would be governed by a mere spirit of gain; and that, as Boston was now cut off from all commerce, the unexpected advantage which this blow on her was calculated to confer on other towns would be greedily enjoyed. How miserably such reasoners deceived themselves! How little they knew of the depth, and the strength, and the intenseness of that feeling of resistance to illegal acts of power which possessed the whole American people! Everywhere the unworthy boon was rejected with scorn. The fortunate occasion was seized everywhere to show to the whole world that the colonies were swayed by no local interest, no partial interest, no selfish interest. The temptation to profit by the punishment of Boston was strongest to our neighbors of Salem. Yet Salem was precisely the place where this miserable proffer was spurned in a tone of the most lofty self-respect and the most indignant patriotism. "We are deeply affected," said its inhabitants, "with the sense of our public calamities; but the miseries that are now rapidly hastening on our brethren in the capital of the province greatly excite our commiseration. By shutting up the port of Boston some imagine that the course of trade might be turned hither, and to our benefit; but we must be dead to every idea of justice, lost to all feelings of humanity, could we indulge a thought to seize on wealth and raise our fortunes on the ruin of our suffering neighbors." These noble sentiments were not confined to our immediate vicinity. In that day of general affection and brotherhood, the blow given to Boston smote on every patriotic heart, from one end of the country to the other. Virginia and the Carolinas, as well as Connecticut and New Hampshire, felt and proclaimed the cause to be their own. The Continental Congress, then holding its first session in Philadelphia, expressed its sympathy for the suffering inhabitants of Boston, and addresses were received from all quarters assuring them that the cause was a common one, and should be met by common efforts and common sacrifices. The Congress of Massachusetts responded to these assurances; and in an address to the Congress at Philadelphia, bearing the official signature, perhaps among the last, of the immortal Warren, notwithstanding the severity of its suffering and the magnitude of the dangers which threatened it, it was declared that this colony "is ready, at all times, to spend and to be spent in the cause of America."

But the hour drew nigh which was to put professions to the proof and to determine whether the authors of these mutual pledges were ready to seal them in blood. The tidings of Lexington and Concord had no sooner spread than it was universally felt that the time was at last come for action. A spirit pervaded all ranks, not transient, not boisterous, but deep, solemn, determined—

> "Totamque infusa per artus
> Mens agitat molem, et magno se corpore miscet."

War, on their own soil and at their own doors, was, indeed, a strange work to the yeomanry of New England; but their consciences were convinced of its necessity, their country called them to it and they did not withhold themselves from the perilous trial. The ordinary occupations of life were abandoned; the plow was stayed in the unfinished furrow; wives gave up their husbands, and mothers gave up their sons to the battles of a civil war. Death might come, in honor, on the field; it might come, in disgrace, on the scaffold. For either and for both they were prepared. The sentiment of Quincy was full in their hearts. "Blandishments," said that distinguished son of genius and patriotism, "will not fascinate us, nor will threats of a halter intimidate; for, under God, we are determined that wheresoever, whensoever, or howsoever we shall be called to make our exit, we will die free men."

The seventeenth of June saw the four New England colonies standing here, side by side, to triumph or to fall together; and there was with them from that moment to the end of the war what I hope will remain with them forever—one cause, one country, one heart.

The battle of Bunker Hill was attended with the most important effects beyond its immediate result as a military engagement. It created at once a state of open, public war. There could now be no longer a question of proceeding against individuals as guilty of treason or rebellion. That fearful crisis was past. The appeal now lay to the sword, and the only question was whether the spirit and the resources of the people would hold out till the object should be accomplished. Nor were its general consequences confined to our own country. The previous proceedings of the colonies, their appeals, resolutions, and addresses had made their cause known to Europe. Without boasting, we may say that in no age or country has the public cause been maintained with more force of argument, more power of illustration, or more of that persuasion which excited feeling and elevated principle can alone bestow, than the Revolutionary state papers exhibit. These papers will forever deserve to be studied, not only for the spirit which they breathe, but for the ability with which they were written.

To this able vindication of their cause, the colonies had now added a practical and severe proof of their own true devotion to it, and evidence also of the power which they could bring to its support. All now saw that if America fell, she would not fall without a struggle. Men felt sympathy and regard as well as surprise when they beheld these infant states, remote, unknown, unaided, encounter the power of England, and in the first considerable battle leave more of their enemies dead on the field, in proportion to the number of combatants, than they had recently known in the wars of Europe.

Information of these events circulating through Europe at length reached the ears of one who now hears me. He has not forgotten the emotion which the fame of Bunker Hill and the name of Warren excited in his youthful breast.

Sir, we are assembled to commemorate the establishment of great public principles of liberty, and to do honor to the distinguished dead. The occasion is too severe for eulogy to the living. But, sir, your interesting relation to this country, the peculiar circumstances which surround you and surround us, call on me to express the happiness which we derive from your presence and aid in this solemn commemoration.

Fortunate, fortunate man! With what measure of devotion will you not thank God for the circumstances of your extraordinary life! You are connected with both hemispheres and with two generations. Heaven saw fit to ordain that the electric spark of liberty should be conducted, through you, from the New World to the Old; and we, who are now here to perform this duty of patriotism, have all of us long ago received it in charge from our fathers to cherish your name and your virtues. You will account it an instance of your good fortune, sir, that you crossed the seas to visit us at a time which enables you to be present at this solemnity. You now behold the field, the renown of which reached you in the heart of France, and caused a thrill in your ardent bosom. You see the lines of the little redoubt thrown up by the incredible diligence of Prescott; defended to the last extremity by his lion-hearted valor; and within which the cornerstone of our monument has now taken its position. You see where Warren fell, and where Parker, Gardner, McCleary, Moore, and other early patriots fell with him. Those who survived that day, and whose lives have been prolonged to the present hour, are now around you. Some of them you have known in the trying scenes of the war. Behold! they now stretch forth their feeble arms to embrace you. Behold! they raise their trembling voices to invoke the blessing of God on you and yours forever.

Sir, you have assisted us in laying the foundation of this edifice. You have heard us rehearse, with our feeble commendation, the names of departed patriots. Sir, monuments and eulogy belong to the dead. We give them this day to Warren and his associates. On other occasions they have been given to your more immediate companions in arms—to Washington, to Greene, to Gates, Sullivan, and Lincoln. Sir, we have become reluctant to grant these, our highest and last honors, further. We would gladly hold them yet back from the little remnant of that immortal band. "Serus in cœlum redeas." Illustrious as are your merits, yet far, oh, very far distant be the day when any inscription shall bear your name, or any tongue pronounce its eulogy!

The leading reflection to which this occasion seems to invite us respects the great changes which have happened in the fifty years since the battle of Bunker Hill was fought. And it peculiarly marks the character of the present age that, in looking at these changes and in estimating their effect on our condition, we are obliged to consider, not what has been done in our own country only, but in others also. In these interesting times, while nations are making separate and individual advances in improvement, they make, too, a common progress; like vessels on a common tide, propelled by the gales at different rates, according to their several structure and management, but all moved forward by one mighty current beneath, strong enough to bear onward whatever does not sink beneath it.

A chief distinction at the present day is a community of opinions and knowledge among men, in different nations, existing in a degree heretofore unknown. Knowledge has, in our time, triumphed, and is triumphing over distance, over difference of languages, over diversity of habits, over prejudice, and over bigotry. The civilized and Christian world is fast learning the great lesson, that difference of nation does not imply necessary hostility, and that all contact need not be war. The whole world is becoming a common field for intellect to act in. Energy of mind, genius, power, wheresoever it exists, may speak out in any tongue, and

the world will hear it.   A great chord of sentiment and
feeling runs through two continents, and vibrates over
both.   Every breeze wafts intelligence from country to
country; every wave rolls it; all give it forth, and all in
turn receive it.   There is a vast commerce of ideas; there
are marts and exchanges for intellectual discoveries, and a
wonderful fellowship of those individual intelligences which
make up the mind and opinion of the age.   Mind is the
great lever of all things; human thought is the process by
which human ends are ultimately answered; and the diffusion of knowledge, so astonishing in the last half-century,
has rendered innumerable minds, variously gifted by nature,
competent to be competitors, or fellow-workers, on the
theater of intellectual operation.

From these causes, important improvements have taken
place in the personal condition of individuals.   Generally
speaking, mankind are not only better fed and better
clothed, but they are able also to enjoy more leisure; they
possess more refinement and more self-respect.   A superior
tone of education, manners, and habits prevails.   This remark, most true in its application to our own country, is
also partly true when applied elsewhere.   It is proved by
the vastly augmented consumption of those articles of
manufacture and of commerce which contribute to the com-
forts and the decencies of life—an augmentation which has
far outrun the progress of population.   And while the unexampled and almost incredible use of machinery would
seem to supply the place of labor, labor still finds its occupation and its reward; so wisely has Providence adjusted
men's wants and desires to their condition and their
capacity.

Any adequate survey, however, of the progress made in
the last half-century, in the polite and the mechanic arts,
in machinery and manufactures, in commerce and agriculture, in letters and in science, would require volumes.   I
must abstain wholly from these subjects, and turn, for a
moment, to the contemplation of what has been done on
the great question of politics and government.   This is the
master topic of the age; and during the whole fifty years,
it has intensely occupied the thoughts of men.   The nature
of civil government, its ends and uses, have been canvassed

and investigated; ancient opinions attacked and defended; new ideas recommended and resisted by whatever power the mind of man could bring to the controversy. From the closet and the public halls the debate has been transferred to the field; and the world has been shaken by wars of unexampled magnitude, and the greatest variety of fortune. A day of peace has at length succeeded; and now that the strife has subsided, and the smoke cleared away, we may begin to see what has actually been done, permanently changing the state and condition of human society. And without dwelling on particular circumstances, it is most apparent that, from the before-mentioned causes of augmented knowledge and improved individual condition, a real, substantial, and important change has taken place, and is taking place, greatly beneficial, on the whole, to human liberty and human happiness.

The great wheel of political revolution began to move in America. Here its rotation was guarded, regular, and safe. Transferred to the other continent, from unfortunate but natural causes, it received an irregular and violent impulse; it whirled along with a fearful celerity, till at length, like the chariot wheels in the races of antiquity, it took fire from the rapidity of its own motion, and blazed onward, spreading conflagration and terror around.

We learn from the result of this experiment how fortunate was our own condition, and how admirably the character of our people was calculated for making the great example of popular governments. The possession of power did not turn the heads of the American people, for they had long been in the habit of exercising a great portion of self-control. Although the paramount authority of the parent state existed over them, yet a large field of legislation had always been open to our colonial assemblies. They were accustomed to representative bodies and the forms of free government; they understood the doctrine of the division of power among different branches and the necessity of checks on each. The character of our countrymen, moreover, was sober, moral, and religious; and there was little in the change to shock their feelings of justice and humanity, or even to disturb an honest prejudice. We had no domestic throne to overturn, no privileged orders to cast down, no violent changes of property to encounter. In the American Revolution, no man sought or wished for more than to defend and enjoy his own. None hoped for plunder or for spoil. Rapacity was unknown to it; the ax was not among the instruments of its accomplishment; and we all know that it could not have lived a single day under any well-founded imputation of possessing a tendency adverse to the Christian religion.

It need not surprise us that, under circumstances less auspicious, political revolutions elsewhere, even when well intended, have terminated differently. It is, indeed, a great achievement, it is the master-work of the world, to establish governments entirely popular, on lasting foundations; nor is it easy, indeed, to introduce the popular principle at all into governments to which it has been altogether a stranger. It cannot be doubted, however, that Europe has come out of the contest, in which she has been so long engaged, with greatly superior knowledge, and, in many respects, a highly improved condition. Whatever benefit has been acquired is likely to be retained, for it consists mainly in the acquisition of more enlightened ideas. And although kingdoms and provinces may be wrested from the hands that hold them, in the same manner they were obtained; although ordinary and vulgar power may, in human affairs, be lost as it has been won, yet it is the glorious prerogative of the empire of knowledge, that what it gains it never loses. On the contrary, it increases by the multiple of its own power; all its ends become means; all its attainments help to new conquests. Its whole abundant harvest is but so much seed-wheat, and nothing has ascertained, and nothing can ascertain, the amount of ultimate product.

Under the influence of this rapidly increasing knowledge, the people have begun, in all forms of government, to think and to reason on affairs of state. Regarding government as an institution for the public good, they demand a knowledge of its operations and a participation in its exercise. A call for the representative system, wherever it is not enjoyed, and where there is already intelligence enough to estimate its value, is perseveringly made. Where men may speak out, they demand it; where the bayonet is at their throats, they pray for it.

When Louis XIV. said " I am the State," he expressed the essence of the doctrine of unlimited power. By the rules of that system, the people are disconnected from the State; they are its subjects; it is their lord. These ideas, founded in the love of power, and long supported by the excess and the abuse of it, are yielding in our age to other opinions; and the civilized world seems at last to be proceeding to the conviction of that fundamental and manifest truth, that the powers of government are but a trust, and that they cannot be lawfully exercised but for the good of the community. As knowledge is more and more extended, this conviction becomes more and more general. Knowledge, in truth, is the great sun in the firmament. Life and power are scattered with all its beams. The prayer of the Grecian combatant, when enveloped in unnatural clouds and darkness, is the appropriate political supplication for the people of every country not yet blessed with free institutions:

> " Dispel this cloud, the light of heaven restore;
> Give me to see — and Ajax asks no more."

We may hope that the growing influence of enlightened sentiments will promote the permanent peace of the world. Wars, to maintain family alliances, to uphold or to cast down dynasties, to regulate successions to thrones, which have occupied so much room in the history of modern times, if not less likely to happen at all, will be less likely to become general and involve many nations, as the great principle shall be more and more established, that the interest of the world is peace, and its first great statute, that every nation possesses the power of establishing a government for itself. But public opinion has attained also an influence over governments which do not admit the popular principle into their organization. A necessary respect for the judgment of the world operates, in some measure, as a control over the most unlimited forms of authority. It is owing, perhaps, to this truth, that the interesting struggle of the Greeks has been suffered to go on so long, without a direct interference, either to wrest that country from its present masters, and add it to other powers, or to execute the system of pacification by force, and, with united strength, lay the neck of Christian and civilized Greece at the foot of the barbarian Turk. Let us thank God that we live in an age when something has influence besides the bayonet, and when the sternest authority does not venture to encounter the scorching power of public reproach. Any attempt of the kind I have mentioned should be met by one universal burst of indignation; the air of the civilized world ought to be made too warm to be comfortably breathed by any who would hazard it.

It is, indeed, a touching reflection, that while, in the fulness of our country's happiness, we rear this monument to her honor, we look for instruction in our undertaking to a country which is now in fearful contest, not for works of art or memorials of glory, but for her own existence. Let her be assured that she is not forgotten in the world; that her efforts are applauded, and that constant prayers ascend for her success. And let us cherish a confident hope for her final triumph. If the true spark of religious and civil liberty be kindled, it will burn. Human agency cannot extinguish it. Like the earth's central fire, it may be smothered for a time; the ocean may overwhelm it; mountains may press it down; but its inherent and unconquerable force will heave both the ocean and the land, and at some time or another, in some place or another, the volcano will break out and flame up to heaven.

Among the great events of the half-century, we must reckon, certainly, the revolution of South America; and we are not likely to overrate the importance of that revolution, either to the people of the country itself or to the rest of the world. The late Spanish colonies, now independent states, under circumstances less favorable, doubtless, than attended our own Revolution, have yet successfully commenced their national existence. They have accomplished the great object of establishing their independence; they are known and acknowledged in the world; and, although in regard to their systems of government, their sentiments on religious toleration, and their provisions for public instruction, they may have yet much to learn, it must be admitted that they have risen to the condition of settled and established states more rapidly than could have been reasonably anticipated. They already furnish an exhilarating example of the difference between free governments and despotic misrule. Their commerce at this moment creates a new activity in all the great marts of the world. They show themselves able by an exchange of commodities to bear a useful part in the intercourse of nations. A new spirit of enterprise and industry begins to prevail; all the great interests of society receive a salutary impulse; and the progress of information not only testifies to an improved condition, but constitutes itself the highest and most essential improvement.

When the battle of Bunker Hill was fought, the existence of South America was scarcely felt in the civilized world. The thirteen little colonies of North America habitually called themselves the "Continent." Borne down by colonial subjugation, monopoly, and bigotry, these vast regions of the South were hardly visible above the horizon. But in our day there hath been, as it were, a new creation. The Southern Hemisphere emerges from the sea. Its lofty mountains begin to lift themselves into the light of heaven; its broad and fertile plains stretch out in beauty to the eye of civilized man; and at the mighty being of the voice of political liberty, the waters of darkness retire.

And now let us indulge an honest exultation in the conviction of the benefit which the example of our country has produced and is likely to produce on human freedom and human happiness. And let us endeavor to comprehend in all its magnitude and to feel in all its importance the part assigned to us in the great drama of human affairs. We are placed at the head of the system of representative and popular governments. Thus far our example shows that such governments are compatible, not only with respectability and power, but with repose, with peace, with security of personal rights, with good laws and a just administration.

We are not propagandists. Wherever other systems are preferred, either as being thought better in themselves or as better suited to existing conditions, we leave the preference to be enjoyed. Our history hitherto proves, however, that the popular form is practicable, and that, with wisdom and knowledge, men may govern themselves; and the duty incumbent on us is to preserve the consistency of this cheering example and take care that nothing may weaken its

authority with the world.   If in our case the representative
system ultimately fail, popular governments must be pronounced impossible.   No combination of circumstances
more favorable to the experiment can ever be expected to
occur.   The last hopes of mankind, therefore, rest with us;
and if it should be proclaimed that our example had become
an argument against the experiment, the knell of popular
liberty would be sounded throughout the earth.

These are incitements to duty; but they are not sugges-
tions of doubt.   Our history and our condition, all that is
gone before us and all that surrounds us, authorize the
belief that popular governments, though subject to occasional variations, perhaps not always for the better in form,
may yet in their general character be as durable and permanent as other systems.   We know, indeed, that in our
country any other is impossible.   The principle of free governments adheres to the American soil.   It is bedded in it
—immovable as its mountains.

And let the sacred obligations which have devolved on
this generation and on us sink deep into our hearts.   Those
are daily dropping from among us who established our liberty and our government.   The great trust now descends
to new hands.   Let us apply ourselves to that which is presented to us as our appropriate object.   We can win no
laurels in a war for independence.   Earlier and worthier
hands have gathered them all.   Nor are there places for us
by the side of Solon, and Alfred, and other founders of
states.   Our fathers have filled them.   But there remains
to us a great duty of defense and preservation; and there
is opened to us also a noble pursuit to which the spirit of
the times strongly invites us.   Our proper business is improvement.   Let our age be the age of improvement.   In
a day of peace let us advance the arts of peace and the
works of peace.   Let us develop the resources of our land,
call forth its powers, build up its institutions, promote all
its great interests, and see whether we also, in our day and
generation, may not perform something worthy to be remembered.   Let us cultivate a true spirit of union and harmony.   In pursuing the great objects which our condition
points out to us, let us act under a settled conviction, and
a habitual feeling that these twenty-four states are one

country. Let our conceptions be enlarged to the circle of our duties. Let us extend our ideas over the whole of the vast field in which we are called to act. Let our object be our country, our whole country, and nothing but our country. And by the blessing of God may that country itself become a vast and splendid monument, not of oppression and terror, but of wisdom, of peace, and of liberty, upon which the world may gaze with admiration, forever.

THE DUKE OF WELLINGTON

ON CATHOLIC EMANCIPATION

[Arthur Wellesley, afterward Duke of Wellington, British soldier and statesman, was born in Ireland in 1769. He was educated at Eton and at the military college of Angers, France. In 1787 he entered the army as ensign, and in 1793 became lieutenant-colonel of the Thirty-third Regiment. He was sent to India with this regiment in 1796, and there, at Seringapatam, in Mysore, and at Assaye, displayed great military ability. In 1807, after is return to Great Britain, he was appointed Irish Secretary; and in 1808 he took command of troops sent to operate against the French in the Spanish Peninsula, where he won high distinction. After a brilliant military career, during which he defeated the army of Napoleon Bonaparte at the memorable battle of Waterloo, in 1815, he was appointed prime minister of England in 1828, and held that office until 1830. Catholic Emancipation, in advocating which he delivered the following speech in the House of Lords, in 1829, was the most notable event of his ministry. In his later years he was called the "Iron Duke." The Duke was foreign secretary in Peel's Cabinet (1834–35) and a member of his administration (1841–46). He died at Walmer Castle, Kent, September 14, 1852, and was buried in St. Paul's Cathedral, London, next to the tomb of Lord Nelson.]

IT is now my duty to move that your lordships read this bill a second time, and to explain to your lordships the grounds on which I recommend this measure to your consideration. I may be under the necessity of requesting a larger portion of your time and attention, upon this occasion, than I have hitherto been in the habit of occupying; but I assure you, my lords, that it is not my intention to take up an instant of your time with respect to myself, or my own conduct in this transaction, any further than to express my regret that I should differ in opinion on this subject from so many of those for whom I entertain the highest respect and regard. However, my lords, I must say that I have considered the part which I have taken upon this subject as the performance of a public duty absolutely incumbent upon me; and that no private regard, no respect for the opinion of any noble lord, would have induced me to depart from the course which I have considered it my duty to adopt. I must say, likewise, this, that comparing my own opinion with that of others upon this subject, I have, during the period I have been in office, had opportunities of forming a judgment upon this subject which others have not had; and they will admit that I should not have given the opinion I have given, if I was not intimately and firmly persuaded that that opinion was a just one.

My lords, the point which I shall first bring under your lordships' consideration is the state of Ireland. I know that by some it has been considered that the state of Ireland has nothing to do with this question—that it is a subject which ought to be left entirely out of our consideration. My lords, they tell us that Ireland has been disturbed for the last thirty years, that to such disturbance we have been accustomed, and that it does not at all alter the circumstances of the case, as they have hitherto appeared. My lords, it is perfectly true that Ireland has been disturbed during the long period I have stated; but within the last year or two there have been circumstances of particular aggravation. Political circumstances have in a considerable degree occasioned that aggravation; but besides this, my lords, I must say, although I have no positive legal proof of the fact, that I have every reason to believe that there has been a considerable organization of the people for the purposes of mischief. My lords, this organization is, it appears to me, to be proved not only by the declarations of those who formed and who arranged it, but likewise by the effects which it has produced in the election of church-wardens throughout the country; in the circumstances attending the election for the county of Clare; in the circumstances that preceded and followed that election; in the proceedings of a gentleman who went at the head of a body of men to the north of Ireland; in the simultaneous proceedings of various bodies of men in the south of Ireland, in Thurles, Templemore, Killenaule, Cahir, Clonmel, and other places; in the proceedings of another gentleman in the King's County; and in the recall of the former gentleman from the north of Ireland by the Roman Catholic Association. In all these circumstances it is quite obvious to me that there was an organization and direction of some superior authority. This organization has certainly produced a state of society in Ireland which we have not heretofore witnessed, and an aggravation of all the evils which before afflicted that unfortunate country.

My lords, late in the year a considerable town was attacked in the middle of the night by a body of people who came from the neighboring mountains, the town of Augher. They attacked it with arms, and were driven from it with arms by the inhabitants of the town. This is a state of things which I feel your lordships will admit ought not to exist in a civilized country. Later in the year still, a similar event occurred in Charleville; and in the course of last autumn the Roman Catholic Association deliberated upon the propriety of adopting, and the means of adopting, the measure of ceasing all dealings between Roman Catholics and Protestants. Is it possible to believe that supposing these dealings had ceased, that supposing this measure had been carried into execution, as I firmly believe it was in the power of those who deliberated upon it to carry it into execution; is it possible to believe that those who could cease these dealings would not likewise have ceased to carry into execution the contracts into which they had entered? Will any man say that people in this situation are not verging toward that state in which it would be impossible to expect from them that they would be able to perform the duties of jurymen, or to administer justice between man and man for the protection of the lives and properties of his Majesty's subjects? My lords, this is the state of society to which I wished to draw your attention, and for which it is necessary that Parliament should provide a remedy. But before I proceed to consider what those remedies ought to be, I wish just to show you what the effect of this state of society has been upon the King's prerogative.

My lords, his Majesty could not create a peer, and the reason he could not create a peer was this. His Majesty's servants could not venture to recommend to him to incur the risks of an election, and those which might have attended any accident at the election which might have occasioned the shedding of blood. Such a disaster must have been productive of an immediate civil war in the country; and not only was that the case, my lords, but I confess that I had the strongest objection to give another triumph to the Roman Catholic Association. Then we are asked, "Why do you not carry the law into execution?" My lords, I have upon former occasions stated to your lordships how the law stood in respect to the association; and your lordships will observe that in all I have stated hitherto there was no resistance to the law. The magistrates were not called upon to act. There was no resistance to the King's troops; indeed, except in the case of the procession to the north of Ireland, they were never called into duty. There was no instance, therefore, in which the law could be carried into execution. When we hear, therefore, noble lords reproaching the government for not carrying into execution the law in Ireland, as it was carried into execution in England, the observation shows that they do not understand the state of things in Ireland. The truth of the matter is that in England, when the law was carried into execution in the year 1819, a large body of persons assembled for an illegal purpose; they resisted the order of the magistrates to disperse, and, having resisted that order, the magistrates directed the troops to disperse them. But in the case in Ireland there were no circumstances of the same kind; no order was given to disperse, no order could be given to disperse, because no magistrates were present; and, if they had been present, there were no troops to disperse them. The truth is, the state of society was such as rendered these events probable at every hour; and it was impossible that the magistrates could be at every spot, and at all times, to put an end to these outrages, which really are a disgrace to the country in which they take place. My lords, neither the law, nor the means in the possession of government, enabled government to put an end to these things. It was necessary, therefore, to come to Parliament. Now, let us see what chance there was of providing a remedy to this state of things by coming to Parliament.

My lords, we all know perfectly well that the opinion of the majority in another place is, that the remedy for this state of things in Ireland is a repeal of the disabilities affecting his Majesty's Roman Catholic subjects. We might have gone and asked Parliament to put down the Roman Catholic Association; but what chance had we of prevailing upon Parliament to pass such a bill without being prepared to come forward and state that we were ready to consider the whole condition of Ireland, with a view to apply a remedy to that which Parliament had stated to be the cause of the disease? Suppose that Parliament had given us a bill to put down the Roman Catholic Association, would such a law as that which passed lately be a remedy for the state of things I have already described to your lordships as existing in Ireland? Would it do any one thing toward putting an end to the organization which, I have stated to your lordships, exists; toward putting an end to the mischiefs which are the consequences of that organization, toward giving you the means of getting the better of the state of things existing in Ireland, without some further measure to be adopted? But, my lords, it is said, "If that will not do, let us proceed to blows!" What is meant by "proceeding to blows" is civil war! Now, I believe that every government must be prepared to carry into execution the laws of the country by the force placed at its disposal; not by the military force, unless it should be absolutely necessary, but by the military force in case that should be necessary; and, above all things, to endeavor to overcome resistance to the law, in case the disaffected or the ill-disposed are inclined to resist the authority or sentence of the law; but in this case, as I have already stated to your lordships, there was no resistance of the law; nay, I will go further, and will say that I am positively certain that this state of things existing in Ireland for the last year and a-half, bordering upon civil war, being attended by nearly all the evils of civil war, might have continued a considerable time longer, to the great injury and disgrace of the country, and nevertheless those who managed this state of things, those who were at its head, would have taken care to prevent any resistance to the law, which must have ended, they knew as well as I do, in the only way in which a struggle against the King's government could end. They knew perfectly well they would have been the first victims of that resistance; but knowing that, and knowing as I do that they are sensible, able men, and perfectly aware of the materials upon which they have to work, I have not the smallest doubt that the state of things which I have stated to your lordships would have continued, and that you would never have had an opportunity of putting it down in the manner some noble lords imagine. But, my lords, even if I had been certain of such means of putting it down, I should have considered it my duty to avoid those means. I am one of those who have probably passed a longer period of my life engaged in war than most men, and principally in civil war; and I must say this, that if I could avoid, by any sacrifice whatever, even one month of civil war in the country to which I was attached, I would sacrifice my life in order to do it. I say that there is nothing which destroys property, cuts up prosperity by the roots, and demoralizes character, to the degree that civil war does. In such a crisis the hand of every man is raised against his neighbor, against his brother, and against his father; servant betrays master, and the whole scene ends in confusion and devastation. Yet, my lords, this is the resource to which we must have looked; these are the means which we must have applied, in order to have put an end to this state of things, if we had not made the option of bringing forward the measures for which I say I am responsible. But let us look a little farther. If civil war is so bad when it is occasioned by resistance to the government, if it is so bad in the case I have stated, and so much to be avoided, how much more is it to be avoided when we are to arm the people in order that we may conquer one part of them by exciting the other part against them.

My lords, I am sure there is not a man who hears me whose blood would not shudder at such a proposition if it were made to him; and yet that is the resource to which we should be pushed at last by continuing the course we have been adopting for the last few years. I entreat your lordships not to look at it in this point of view only, but let us revert a little to what passed on a former similar occasion. My lords, I am old enough to remember the rebellion in 1798. I was not employed in Ireland at the time. I was employed in another part of his Majesty's dominion; but, my lords, if I am not mistaken, the Parliament of Ireland at that time walked up to my lord-lieutenant with an unanimous address, beseeching his excellency to take every means to put down that unnatural rebellion, and promising their full support in order to carry those measures into execution. The lord-lieutenant did take measures, and did succeed in putting down that rebellion. Well, my lords, what happened in the very next session? The government proposed to put an end to the parliament, and to form a legislative union between the two kingdoms, for the purpose, principally, of proposing this very measure; and, in point of fact, the very first measure that was proposed after this legislative union, after those successful endeavors to put down this rebellion, was the very measure with which I am now about to trouble your lordships. Is it possible noble lords can believe that supposing there was such a contest as that which I have anticipated—is it possible noble lords can believe that such a contest could be carried on without the consent of the other House of Parliament? I am certain, my lords, that when you look at the division of opinion which prevails in both Houses of Parliament; when you look at the division of opinion which prevails in every family of this kingdom and of Ireland—in every family, I say, from the most eminent in station down to the lowest in this country; when you look at the division of opinion that prevails among the Protestants of Ireland on this subject, I am convinced that you will see that there would be a vast difference in a contest carried on now and that which was carried on on former occasions.

Having now gone through the general principles which induced me to consider it desirable to bring forward this measure, I will now explain generally the provisions of the bill. The bill is, in itself, very simple. It concedes the Roman Catholics the power of holding every office in the state, except a few connected with the administration of the church; and it also concedes to them the power of becoming members of Parliament.

I have already stated to your lordships my opinion respecting the expediency of granting seats in Parliament to Roman Catholics; and I do not conceive that the concession of seats in Parliament can in any manner affect any question relative to the Church of England. In the first place, I beg your lordships to recollect that at the time those laws to which I have before alluded—the one passed in the thirtieth of Charles II., and the other at the period of the Revolution—were enacted, it was not the church that was in danger; it was the state. It was the state that was in danger, and from what? Not because the safety of the church was threatened. No! but because the sovereign on the throne was suspected of Popery, and because the successor to the throne was actually a Papist. Those laws were adopted because of the existence of a danger which threatened the state, and not of one which threatened the church. On the contrary, at that period danger to the church was apprehended, not from Roman Catholics, but from Dissenters from the Church of England. I would ask of your lordships, all of whom have read the history of those times, whether any danger to the church was apprehended from the Roman Catholics? No! Danger to the church was apprehended from the Dissenters, who had become powerful by the privileges granted to them under the Act of Parliament passed at the period of the Revolution. I think, therefore, that it is not necessary for me to enter into any justification of myself for having adopted this measure, on account of any danger which might be apprehended from it to the church. Roman Catholics will come into Parliament under this bill, as they went into Parliament previous to the Act of the thirtieth of Charles II. They sat in Parliament up to that period, and were not obliged to take the oath of supremacy. By this bill they will be required to take the oath of allegiance, in which a great part of the oath of supremacy is included, namely, that part which refers to the jurisdiction of foreign potentates; and I must say that the church, if in danger, is better secured by this bill than it was previous to the thirtieth of Charles II., though the object for which that Act was recognized at the period of the Revolution, namely, to keep out the house of Stuart from the throne, has long since ceased to exist, by the extinction of that family. It is the opinion of nearly every considerable man in the country—of nearly all those who are competent to form a judgment on the question—that the time is now arrived for repealing these laws. Circumstances have been gradually tending toward their repeal since the extinction of the House of Stuart, and at last the period has come when it is quite clear that the repeal can be no longer delayed with safety to the state.

But, my lords, I know that there are many in this house, and many in this country, who think, and I am free to admit that I was formerly of the same opinion myself, that the state ought to have some security for the church against the proceedings of the Roman Catholic clergy, besides the oaths imposed by the Act of Parliament, to which I have already alluded. Now I confess that on examining into the question, and upon looking more minutely than I had before leisure to do, at the various Acts of Parliament by which the Church of England is constituted, and which form the foundation on which it rests, I can think of no sort of arrangement capable of being carried into execution in this country which can add to the security of the Established Church.

I beg your lordships to attend for a moment whilst I explain the situation of the kingdom of Prussia with respect to the Roman Catholic religion. The King of Prussia exercises the power which he does over the Roman Catholic Church in his various dominions, under different concordats made with the Pope—in Silesia, under a concordat made by the sovereigns of the House of Austria with the Pope; in the territories on the left bank of the Rhine, under a concordat made by Bonaparte with the Pope; and in the territories on the right bank of the Rhine, under a concordat made by the former sovereigns of those countries with the Pope. Each of those concordats supposes that the Pope possesses some power in the country, which he is enabled to concede to the sovereign with whom the concordat is made. That is a point which we can never yield to any sovereign whatever. There is no sovereign, be he whom he may, who has any power in this country to confer upon his Majesty. We must keep our sovereign clear from such transactions. We can, therefore, have no security of that description, not even a veto on the appointment of a Roman Catholic bishop, without detracting in some degree from the authority and dignity of the sovereign, and without admitting that the Pope has something to concede to his Majesty.

Now let us suppose another security. Suppose it were arranged that his Majesty should have the nomination of the Catholic bishops. If he nominated them, he must also give them jurisdiction, he must give them dioceses. I should like to know in what part of Ireland, or England, the King could fix upon a spot where he could, consistently with the oath he has taken, nominate a Catholic bishop, or give him a diocese? The King is sworn to maintain the rights and privileges of the bishops and the clergy of this realm, and of the churches committed to their charge. Now, consistently with that oath, how could the King appoint a bishop of the Roman Catholic religion, and would not the Established Church lose more than it gained by the assumption of such a power on the part of his Majesty?

Then, my lords, there is another security, which some noble lords think it desirable to have, namely, the obtaining, by government, of copies of all correspondence between the Catholic clergy and the court of Rome; and the supervising of that correspondence, in order to prevent any danger resulting to the Established Church. Upon that point I must say that I feel the greatest objection to involve the government of this country in such matters. That correspondence, we are told, turns on spiritual affairs. But I will suppose, for the sake of argument, that it turns on questions of excommunication. Is it, then, to be suffered that the Pope and his Majesty, or his Majesty's Secretary of State, acting for him, should make law for this country? For that would be the result of communications between the Catholic clergy of this realm and the Pope being submitted to his Majesty's inspection, or to the inspection of his Majesty's Secretary of State. Such a security amounts to a breach of the Constitution, and it is quite impossible that it could be made available. It would do more injury to the Constitution and to the church than anything that could be done by the Roman Catholics themselves, when placed by this bill in the same situation as Dissenters.

With respect to communications with the court of Rome, that has already been provided against and prevented by laws still in existence. Your lordships are aware that those laws, like many others regarding the Roman Catholic religion, are not strictly enforced; but still, if indulgence should be abused, if the conduct of those persons whose actions those laws are intended to regulate, should be such as to render necessary the interference of the government, the very measure which is now before your lordships will enable government to interfere in such a manner as not only to answer the object of its interference, but also to give satisfaction to this House and to the country.

Another part of the bill has for its object the putting an end to the order of the Jesuits and other monastic orders in this country. If your lordships will look at the Act passed in the year 1791, you will probably see that at that time, as well as in this, it was possible for one person to make laws through which another might drive a coach and four. My noble and learned friend [Eldon] will excuse me, I hope, for saying that, notwithstanding all the pains which he took to draw up the Act of 1791, yet the fact is, of which there cannot be the slightest doubt, that large religious establishments have been regularly formed, not only in Ireland, but also in this country. The measure which I now propose for your lordships' adoption will prevent the increase of such establishments, and, without oppression to any individuals, without injury to any body of men, will gradually put an end to those which have been already formed. There is no man more convinced than I am of the absolute necessity of carrying into execution that part of the present measure which has for its object the extinction of monastic orders in this country. I entertain no doubt whatever that if that part of the measure be not carried into execution we shall very soon see this country and Ireland inundated by Jesuits and regular monastic clergy, sent out from other parts of Europe, with means to establish themselves within his Majesty's kingdom. When I recommend this measure to your lordships' attention, you have, undoubtedly, a right to ask what are the reasons I have for believing that it will effect the purpose for which it is intended. My lords, I believe that it will answer its object, not only from the example of all Europe, but from the example of what occurred in a part of this kingdom on a former occasion. If I am not mistaken, at the time that the

Episcopalians labored under civil disabilities in Scotland, the state of society there was as bad as the state of Ireland is at the present moment. Your lordships know that abroad, in other parts of Europe, in consequence of the diffusion of civil privileges to all classes, the difference between Protestant and Catholic is never heard of. I am certain that I can prove to your lordships what I state, when I say that the state of society in Scotland previous to the concession of civil privileges to the Episcopalians was as bad as the present state of society in Ireland.

I hope your lordships will give me leave to read a petition which has been sent to me this day, and which was presented to the Scottish Parliament at the period when those concessions were about to be made, and your lordships will perceive that the petition is almost a model of many petitions which have been read in this House respecting the question under discussion. I am therefore in expectation that, should the present bill pass this House, there will be no longer occasion for those complaints which have been expressed to your lordships, and that the same happy and peaceful state of things which has in the last century prevailed in Scotland will also prevail in Ireland. I will, with your lordship's permission, read the petition I have alluded to, and I think that, after you have heard it, you will be of the same opinion as I am with respect to the similarity it bears to many petitions which have been presented to your lordships on the Catholic question. The petition states that " to grant toleration to that party (the Episcopalians), in the present circumstances of the church, must unavoidably shake the foundation of our present happy Constitution; overthrow those laws on which it is settled; grievously disturb that peace and tranquillity which the nation has enjoyed since the late Revolution; disquiet the minds of his Majesty's best subjects; increase animosity; confirm discord and tumult; weaken and enervate the discipline of the church; open the door to unheard-of vices, and to Popery as well as to other errors; propagate and cherish disaffection to the government; and bring the nation under the danger of falling back into those mischiefs and calamities from which it had lately escaped by the Divine blessing. We therefore humbly hope that no concession will be granted to that party, which would be to establish iniquity by law, and bring upon the country manifold calamities and disasters, from which we pray that government may preserve the members of the High Court of Parliament.''

I sincerely hope that, as the prophecy contained in this petition has not been fulfilled, a similar prophecy respecting the passing of the present bill, contained in many petitions presented to your lordships, will also not be fulfilled.

But, my lords, I have other grounds besides those which I have already stated for supposing that the proposed measure will answer the object in view. There is no doubt that, after this measure shall have been adopted, the Roman Catholics can have no separate interest, as a separate sect, for I am sure that neither this House nor the other House of Parliament will be disposed to look upon the Roman Catholics, nor upon anything that respects Ireland, with any other eye than that with which they regard whatever affects the interest of Scotland or of this country. For my own part, I will state that if I am disappointed in the hopes which I entertain that tranquillity will result from this measure, I shall have no scruple in coming down and laying before Parliament the state of the case, and calling on Parliament to enable government to meet whatever danger might have arisen. I shall act with the same confidence that Parliament will support me then, as I have acted in the present case.

Having now explained to your lordships the grounds on which this measure has been brought forward; the state of Ireland; the state of public opinion on the question; the divisions of the government and of the Parliament; the pretenses (for so I must call them) which have been urged against the claims of the Catholics, founded on Acts passed previous to the Revolution; having, my lords, likewise stated to you the provisions of the measure which I propose as a remedy for these inconveniences, I will trouble your lordships no further, except by beseeching you to consider the subject with the coolness, moderation, and temper recommended in his Majesty's speech from the throne.

WILLIAM WILBERFORCE

HORRORS OF THE BRITISH SLAVE-TRADE

[William Wilberforce, the great English statesman, orator, philanthropist and abolitionist-colleague of Thomas Clarkson, was born in Hull in 1759. He completed a course at Cambridge, inherited a large fortune, and was made a member of Parliament. At thirty he began a systematic agitation against slavery, but the cause was not popular, and he had to face the most disheartening indifference. He was not, however, to be daunted. He set about acquiring a knowledge of the workings of the institution of slavery, and in the course of a few years had equipped himself with an array of figures and facts that furnished him material in debate. For nineteen years his energies were obsorbed by the cause of Emancipation, and the fame of his crusade filled the world. At last, in 1807, his efforts were crowned with success. The traffic in slaves ended in the British dominions, and Wilberforce could "lay his head upon his pillow and remember that the slave-trade was no more." He died in 1833 at London, and was buried in Westminster Abbey. His indignation at the horrors of the slave-trade in the British West Indies is shown in the ensuing speech, made in the House of Commons, in 1789.]

IN opening, concerning the nature of the slave-trade, I need only observe that it is found by experience to be just such as every man who uses his reason would infallibly conclude it to be. For my own part, so clearly am I convinced of the mischiefs inseparable from it, that I should hardly want any further evidence than my own mind would furnish, by the most simple deductions. Facts, however, are now laid before the House. A report has been made by his Majesty's Privy Council, which, I trust, every gentleman has read, and which ascertains the slave-trade to be just such in practice as we know, from theory, it must be. What should we suppose must naturally be the consequence of our carrying on a slave-trade with Africa? With a country vast in its extent, not utterly barbarous, but civilized in a very small degree? Does any one suppose a slave-trade would help their civilization? Is it not plain that she must suffer from it? That civilization must be checked; that her barbarous manners must be made more barbarous; and that the happiness of her millions of inhabitants must be prejudiced with her intercourse with Britain? Does not every one see that a slave-trade carried on around her coasts must carry violence and desolation to her very center? That in a continent just emerging from barbarism, if a trade in men is established, if her men are all converted into goods, and become commodities that can be bartered, it follows they must be subject to ravage just as goods are; and this, too, at a period of civilization when there is no protecting legislature to defend this their only sort of property, in the same manner as the rights of property are maintained by the legislature of every civilized country. We see, then, in the nature of things, how easily the practices of Africa are to be accounted for. Her kings are never compelled to war, that we can hear of, by public principles, by national glory, still less by the love of their people. In Europe it is the extension of commerce, the maintenance of national honor, or some great public object, that is ever the motive to war with every monarch; but in Africa it is the personal avarice and sensuality of their kings; these two vices of avarice and sensuality, the most powerful and predominant in natures thus corrupt, we tempt, we stimulate in all these African princes, and we depend upon these vices for the very maintenance of the slave-trade. Does the king of Barbessin want brandy? He has only to send his troops, in the night-time, to burn and desolate a village; the captives will serve as commodities, that may be bartered with the British trader. What a striking view of the wretched state of Africa does the tragedy of Calabar furnish! Two towns, formerly hostile, had settled their differences, and by an intermarriage among their chiefs, had each pledged themselves to peace; but the trade in slaves was prejudiced by such pacifications, and it became, therefore, the policy of our traders to renew the hostilities. This, their policy, was soon put in practice, and the scene of carnage which followed was such that it is better, perhaps, to refer gentlemen to the Privy Council's report than to agitate their minds by dwelling on it.

The slave-trade, in its very nature, is the source of such kind of tragedies; nor has there been a single person, almost, before the Privy Council, who does not add something by his testimony to the mass of evidence upon this point. Some, indeed, of these gentlemen, and particularly the delegates from Liverpool, have endeavored to reason down this plain principle: some have palliated it; but there is not one, I believe, who does not more or less admit it. Some, nay most, I believe, have admitted the slave-trade to be the chief cause of wars in Africa.

Having now disposed of the first part of this subject, I must speak of the transit of the slaves in the West Indies. This, I confess, in my own opinion, is the most wretched part of the whole subject. So much misery condensed in so little room is more than the human imagination had ever before conceived. I will not accuse the Liverpool merchants; I will allow them, nay, I will believe them to be men of humanity; and I will therefore believe, if it were not for the multitude of these wretched objects, if it were not for the enormous magnitude and extent of the evil which distracts their attention from individual cases, and makes them think generally, and therefore less feelingly, on the subject, they never would have persisted in the trade. I verily believe, therefore, if the wretchedness of any one of the many hundred negroes stowed in each ship could be brought before their view, and remain within the sight of the African merchant, that there is no one among them whose heart would bear it. Let any one imagine to himself six or seven hundred of these wretches chained two and two, surrounded with every object that is nauseous and disgusting, diseased, and struggling under every kind of wretchedness! How can we bear to think of such a scene as this? One would think it had been determined to heap on them all the varieties of bodily pain, for the purpose of blunting the feelings of the mind; and yet, in this very point (to show the power of human prejudice), the situation of the slaves has been described by Mr. Norris, one of the Liverpool delegates, in a manner which I am sure will convince the House how interest can draw a film over the eyes so thick that total blindness could do no more; and how it is our duty, therefore, to trust not to the reasonings of interested men, or to their way of coloring a transaction. "Their apartments," says Mr. Norris, "are fitted up as much for their advantage as circumstances will admit. The right ankle of one, indeed, is connected with the left ankle of another by a small iron fetter, and if they are turbulent, by another on their wrists. They have several meals a day; some of their own country provisions, with the best sauces of African cookery; and, by the way of variety, another meal of pulse, etc., according to European taste. After breakfast they have water to wash themselves, while their apartments are perfumed with frankincense and lime-juice. Before dinner they are amused after the manner of their country. The song and the dance are promoted," and, as if the whole were really a scene of pleasure and dissipation, it is added that games of chance are furnished. "The men play and sing, while the women and girls make fanciful ornaments with beads, which they are plentifully supplied with." Such is the sort of strain in which the Liverpool delegates, and particularly Mr. Norris, gave evidence before the Privy Council. What will the House think when, by the concurring testimony of other witnesses, the true history is laid open. The slaves, who are sometimes described as rejoicing at their captivity, are so wrung with misery at leaving their country, that it is the constant practice to set sail in the night, lest they should be sensible of their departure. The pulse which Mr. Norris talks of are horse beans; and the scantiness of both water and provision was suggested by the very legislature of Jamaica, in the report of their committee, to be a subject that called for the interference of Parliament.

Mr. Norris talks of frankincense and lime-juice, when the surgeons tell you the slaves are stowed so close that there is not room to tread among them, and when you have it in evidence from Sir George Younge, that even in a ship which wanted two hundred of her complement the stench was intolerable. The song and the dance are promoted, says Mr. Norris. It had been more fair, perhaps, if he had explained that word "promoted." The truth is, that for the sake of exercise these miserable wretches, loaded with chains, oppressed with disease and wretchedness, are forced to dance by the terror of the lash, and sometimes by the actual use of it. "I," says one of the other evidences, "was employed to dance the men, while another person danced the women." Such, then, is the meaning of the word "promoted"; and it may be observed, too, with respect to food, that an instrument is sometimes carried out, in order to force them to eat, which is the same sort of proof how much they enjoy themselves in that instance also. As to their singing, what shall we say when we are told that their songs are songs of lamentation upon their departure, which, while they sing, are always in tears, insomuch that one captain (more humane, as I should conceive him, therefore, than the rest) threatened one of the women with a flogging, because the mournfulness of her song was too painful for his feelings? In order, however, not to trust too much to any sort of description, I will call the attention of the House to one species of evidence, which is absolutely infallible. Death, at least, is a sure ground of evidence, and the proportion of deaths will not only confirm, but, if possible, will even aggravate our suspicion of their misery in the transit. It will be found, upon an average of all ships of which evidence has been given at the Privy Council, that, exclusive of those who perish before they sail, not less than twelve and one-half per cent. perish in the passage. Besides these, the Jamaica report tells you that not less than four and one-half per cent. die on shore before the day of sale, which is only a week or two from the time of landing. One-third more die in the seasoning, and this in a country exactly like their own, where they are healthy and happy, as some of the evidences would pretend. The diseases, however, which they contract on shipboard, the astringent washes used to hide their wounds, and the mischievous tricks employed to make them up for sale, are, as the Jamaica report says—a most precious and valuable report, which I shall often have to advert to—one principal cause of this mortality. Upon the whole, however, here is a mortality of about fifty per cent., and this among negroes who are not bought unless quite healthy at first, and unless (as the phrase is with cattle) they are sound in wind and limb. How, then, can the House refuse its belief to the multiplied testimonies, before the Privy Council, of the savage treatment of the negroes in the middle passage? Nay, indeed, what need is there of any evidence? The number of deaths speaks for itself, and makes all such inquiry superfluous.   As soon as ever I had arrived thus far in my investigation of the slave-trade, I confess to you, sir, so enormous, so dreadful, so irremediable did its wickedness appear, that my own mind was completely made up for the abolition.   A trade founded in iniquity, and carried on as this was, must be abolished, let the policy be what it might.   Let the consequences be what they would, I from this time determined that I would never rest till I had effected its abolition.

When we consider the vastness of the continent of Africa; when we reflect how all other countries have for some centuries past been advancing in happiness and civilization; when we think how in this same period all improvement in Africa has been defeated by her intercourse with Britain; when we reflect that it is we ourselves that have degraded them to that wretched brutishness and barbarity which we now plead as the justification of our guilt; how the slave-trade has enslaved their minds, blackened their character, and sunk them so low in the scale of animal beings that some think the apes are of a higher class, and fancy the orang-outang has given them the go-by.   What a mortification must we feel at having so long neglected to think of our guilt, or attempt any reparation! It seems, indeed, as if we had determined to forbear from all interference until the measure of our folly and wickedness was so full and complete, until the impolicy which eventually belongs to vice was become so plain and glaring that not an individual in the country should refuse to join in the abolition; it seems as if we had waited until the persons most interested should be tired out with the folly and nefariousness of the trade, and should unite in petitioning against it.

Let us then make such amends as we can for the mischiefs we have done to the unhappy continent: let us recollect what Europe itself was no longer ago than three or four centuries.   What if I should be able to show this House that in a civilized part of Europe, in the time of our

Henry VII., there were people who actually sold their own children? What if I should tell them that England itself was that country? What if I should point out to them that the very place where this inhuman traffic was carried on was the city of Bristol? Ireland at that time used to drive a considerable trade in slaves with these neighboring barbarians; but a great plague having infested the country, the Irish were struck with a panic, suspected (I am sure very properly) that the plague was a punishment sent from heaven for the sin of the slave-trade, and therefore abolished it. All I ask, therefore, of the people of Bristol is, that they would become as civilized now as Irishmen were four hundred years ago. Let us put an end at once to this inhuman traffic—let us stop this effusion of human blood. The true way to virtue is by withdrawing from temptation; let us then withdraw from these wretched Africans those temptations to fraud, violence, cruelty, and injustice which the slave-trade furnishes. Wherever the sun shines, let us go round the world with him, diffusing our beneficence; but let us not traffic, only that we may set kings against their subjects, subjects against their kings, sowing discord in every village, fear and terror in every family, setting millions of our fellow-creatures a-hunting each other for slaves, creating fairs and markets for human flesh through one whole continent of the world, and, under the name of policy, concealing from ourselves all the baseness and iniquity of such a traffic. Why may we not hope, erelong, to see Hans-towns established on the coast of Africa, as they were on the Baltic? It is said the Africans are idle, but they are not too idle, at least, to catch one another; seven hundred to one thousand tons of rice are annually bought of them; by the same rule, why should we not buy more? At Gambia one thousand of them are seen continually at work; why should not some more thousands be set to work in the same manner? It is the slave-trade that causes their idleness and every other mischief. We are told by one witness, "They sell one another as they can;" and while they can get brandy by catching one another, no wonder they are too idle for any regular work.

I have one word more to add upon a most material point; but it is a point so self-evident that I shall be ex-

tremely short.   It will appear from everything which I
have said that it is not regulation, it is not mere palliatives,
that can cure this enormous evil.   Total abolition is the only
possible cure for it.   The Jamaica report, indeed, admits
much of the evil, but recommends it to us so to regulate
the trade that no persons should be kidnapped or made
slaves contrary to the custom of Africa.   But may they not
be made slaves unjustly, and yet by no means contrary to
the custom of Africa?   I have shown they may; for all the
customs of Africa are rendered savage and unjust through
the influence of this trade; besides, how can we discriminate between the slaves justly and unjustly made?   Or,
if we could, does any man believe that the British captains
can, by any regulation in this country, be prevailed upon
to refuse all such slaves as have not been fairly, honestly,
and uprightly enslaved?   But granting even that they should
do this, yet how would the rejected slaves be recompensed?
They are brought, as we are told, from three or four thousand miles off, and exchanged like cattle from one hand to
another, until they reach the coast.   We see, then, that it
is the existence of the slave-trade that is the spring of all
this internal traffic, and that the remedy cannot be applied
without abolition.   Again, as to the middle passage, the
evil is radical there also; the merchant's profit depends
upon the number that can be crowded together, and upon
the shortness of their allowance.   Astringents, escharotics,
and all the other arts of making them up for sale, are of the
very essence of the trade; these arts will be concealed both
from the purchaser and the legislature; they are necessary
to the owner's profit, and they will be practiced.   Again,
chains and arbitrary treatment must be used in transporting
them; our seamen must be taught to play the tyrant, and
that deprivation of manners among them (which some very
judicious persons have treated of as the very worst part of
the business) cannot be hindered, while the trade itself continues.   As to the slave merchants, they have already told
you that if two slaves to a ton are not permitted, the trade
cannot continue; so that the objections are done away by
themselves on this quarter; and in the West Indies, I have
shown that the abolition is the only possible stimulus
whereby a regard to population, and consequently to the

happiness of the negroes, can be effectually excited in those islands.

I trust, therefore, I have shown that upon every ground the total abolition ought to take place. I have urged many things which are not my own leading motives for proposing it, since I have wished to show every description of gentleman, and particularly the West India planters, who deserve every attention, that the abolition is politic upon their own principles also. Policy, however, sir, is not my principle, and I am not ashamed to say it. There is a principle above everything that is political; and when I reflect upon the command which says: "Thou shalt do no murder," believing the authority to be Divine, how can I dare to set up any reasonings of my own against it? And, sir, when we think of eternity, and of the future consequences of all human conduct, what is there in this life that should make any man contradict the dictates of his conscience, the principles of justice, the laws of religion, and of God? Sir, the nature of all the circumstances of this trade are now laid open to us; we can no longer plead ignorance, we cannot evade it, it is now an object placed before us, we cannot pass it; we may spurn it, we may kick it out of our way, but we cannot turn aside so as to avoid seeing it; for it is brought now so directly before our eyes that this House must decide, and must justify to all the world, and to their own consciences, the rectitude of the grounds and principles of their decision. A society has been established for the abolition of this trade, in which Dissenters, Quakers, Churchmen—in which the most conscientious of all persuasions have all united, and made a common cause in this great question. Let not Parliament be the only body that is insensible to the principles of national justice. Let us make reparation to Africa, so far as we can, by establishing a trade upon true commercial principles, and we shall soon find the rectitude of our conduct rewarded by the benefits of a regular and a growing commerce.

THE EMPEROR WILLIAM II. OF GERMANY

MOSES AND AMALEK

[William II., German Emperor and King of Prussia, was born in 1859. He was brought into the world by a village doctor, who accidentally maimed the arm of the new-born babe. The young Prince was educated for a military career. The religious influences under which he grew up profoundly influenced his character, as is evidenced by his speeches. He entered the army, and was steadily promoted until he reached the rank of colonel. In 1888 he ascended the throne. Once Emperor, William II. resolved to establish an energetic personal sway. In the execution of this policy he has concerned himself with almost every department of national endeavor. Politically he has sought to found a colonial empire. Since the retirement of Bismarck, early in his reign, William has had three able chancellors, but they were all mere agents of the imperial will. Considered in the light of his oratory, William is a remarkable man. The tone of every one of his speeches is that of assurance. "My policy is good, and I am in the hands of God as His great instrument." Such is the message he seems eager to convey to the world in the more than nine hundred set speeches he has delivered since his reign began. The following sermon, showing the Emperor's figurative style of oratory, was addressed to his men on board the royal yacht, in August, 1900.]

IT is a most impressive picture that our text to-day brings before our souls. Israel wanders through the desert from the Red Sea to Mount Sinai. But suddenly the heathen Amalekites stop them and want to prevent their advance, and a battle ensues. Joshua leads the young men of Israel to the fight, the swords clash together, and a hot and bloody struggle begins in the valley of Rephidim. But, see! whilst the fight is going on, the pious men of God, Moses, Aaron, and Hur, go to the top of the hill. They lift up their hands to heaven; they pray. Down in the valley the fighting hosts; at the top of the mountain the praying men. This is the holy battle-picture of our text. Who does not understand to-day what it tells us? Again, a heathenish Amalekite has stirred in distant Asia with great power and much cunning. By burning and murder it is sought to prevent the entrance of European trade and European genius, the triumphal march of Christian morals and Christian faith. Again the command of God has been issued: "Choose us out men, and go out, fight with Amalek." A hot and bloody struggle has begun. Many of our brothers stand already under fire, many are on their way to the enemy's coasts, and you have seen them, the thousands who at the call, "Volunteers to the fore! Who will be the guardian of the empire?" now assembled, to enter the fight with flying colors. But you, who remain behind at home, who are bound by other sacred duties, say, do you not hear God's call, which He makes to you, and which says to you, "Go up on the mountain; raise up thy hands to the heavens"? The prayer of the just can do much if it be earnest.

Thus let it be. Yonder, far away, the hosts of fighters; here at home, the hosts of praying men. May this be the holy battle-picture of our days. May this peaceful morning hour remind us—may it remind us of the sacred duty of intercession, of the sacred power of intercession. The sacred duty of intercession! Certainly it is an enthusiastic moment when a ship with young men on board weighs anchor. Did you not see the warriors' eyes flash? Did you not hear their many-voiced hurrahs! But when the native shores vanish, when one enters the glowing heat of the Red Sea or the heavy waters of the ocean, how easily brightness and enthusiasm grow weary! Certainly it is a sublime moment when, after a long voyage, in the distance the straight lines of the German forts can be seen, and the black, red, and white flags of the German colony become visible, and comrades in arms stand on the shore waiting to give a hearty reception. But the long marches in the burning sun, the long nights of bivouac in the rain! How easily gayety and strength vanish! Certainly it is a longed-for moment when at last the drums beat to the charge and the bugles are blown to advance when a command is given:

"Forward! At the enemy!" But then, when amid the roar of the guns and the flashing of the shells, comrades fall to the right and left, and hostile batteries still refuse to yield—how easily at such a moment the bravest hearts begin to tremble!

Christian, in order that our brothers over yonder may remain gay even in the greatest distress, faithful in the most painful duty, courageous in the greatest danger, they want something more than ammunition and sharp weapons —more even than youthful courage and fiery enthusiasm. They want a blessing from above, vital power from above; otherwise, they cannot win and remain victorious. And the heavenly world opens only to prayer. Prayer is the golden key to the treasury of our God. But he who has it has also the promise that to him who asks shall be given. Or shall we remain idle? Woe to us if we are idle whilst they are carrying on a hard and bloody piece of work; woe to us if we only look on curiously at the great struggle! This would be Cain's spirit with the cruel words "Am I my brother's keeper?" This would be unfaithfulness toward our brave brothers who are staking their lives. Never! We will mobilize not only battalions of warriors, but also a holy force of praying men. Yes. How much there is to ask for our brothers going into the field! They are to be the strong arm which punishes assassins. They are to be the mailed fist which strikes in among them. They are to stand up with the sword in their hands for our most sacred possessions. So we shall accompany them with our prayers, out on to the heaving waves, on their marches, into the roar of the battle, and into the peacefulness of the hospitals; shall pray to God that they may stand at their posts like men, that they may fight their battles courageously and heroically, that they may bear their wounds bravely and calmly, that God may give those who die under fire a blessed end and the reward of faithfulness—in short, that He may make the warriors heroes, and the heroes victors, and then bring them home to the land of their fathers with the laurels round their puggarees and the medals on their breasts.

Or do we, perhaps, not believe in the sacred power of intercession? Well, then, what does our text say? "And it came to pass, when Moses held up his hand, that Israel prevailed." The earnest prayers of a Moses made the swords of the enemy blunt. They pushed themselves like a wedge between the enemy's lines, made them waver, and brought victory to the flying banners of Israel. Should not our prayers be able to do what the prayers of Moses did? God has not taken back one syllable of His promise; heart-felt prayer can still to-day cast down the dragon banner into the dust and plant the banner of the cross on the walls. And Moses does not stand alone with his intercession. Look yonder. There on the heights of Sodom stands Abraham, interceding before his God, and with his prayers he prays Lot out of the burning city. And should not our prayers succeed in praying our fighting comrades out of the fire of the battles? Look yonder. There in Jerusalem lies the young Christian community on its knees. Their leader, their father, lies imprisoned in a dungeon, and, see, with their prayers they summon the angel of God into the prison, and he leads forth Peter unharmed. And our prayers— should not they have the power even to-day to burst the doors of the oppressed prisoners and the persecuted, and to place an angel at their side? Yes, the God of old lives still, the great Ally rules still the Holy God, who cannot let sin and acts of violence triumph, but will carry on His holy cause against an unholy people; the Almighty God, who can shatter the strongest walls as if they were spider's webs, and who can disperse the greatest crowds like heaps of sand; the merciful, faithful God, whose fatherly heart looks after the well-being of His children, who hears every sigh, and who sympathizes with every distress. Pious prayers open His fatherly hands, and they are filled with blessing. Earnest prayer opens His fatherly heart, and it is full of love. Yes, true, continuous prayer fetches the living God down from heaven and places Him among us. And if God is for us, who shall be against us?

Up in the Tavern there hang strange bells on the heights. No man's hand rings them. Still and dumb they hang in the sunshine. But when the storm winds blow, they be-gin to swing, and commence to ring, and deep down in the valley their song is heard. God the Lord has hung the prayer bell in every man's heart. In sunshine and happiness how often it hangs still and dumb. But when

KAISER WILHELM II.

Photogravure after a painting

the stormy winds of distress break forth, then it begins to
ring. How many a comrade who has forgotten how to
pray will, out yonder, in the fight for life or death, fold his
hands again! Distress teaches us to pray, and so shall it
also be at home. Let the serious days which have come
upon us, let the war-storm which has come on, set the
bells ringing again. Let us pray for our fighting brothers.
Not only now and then, in a solemn hour. No, no; let us
be true in prayer. As our fathers once in war-times rang
the bells every evening and bared their heads at the sound
and prayed, so also let us not forget intercession for a day.
Moses held up his hands until the going down of the sun,
and Joshua discomfited Amalek and his people with the
edge of the sword. Our fight is not brought to an end in
a day. But do not let the hands become tired or idle until
the victory has been gained. Let our prayers be a fiery
wall around the camp of our brothers. How the thought
will strengthen them, make them enthusiastic, and excite
them, that thousands, nay, millions, at home bear them in
their praying hearts! The King of all kings calls volunteers
to the fore. Who will be the praying one for the empire?
Oh, if one could only say here, "The King called, and all
—all came!" Not one of us must be wanting. History
will one day describe the fights of these days. But man
sees only what he has before him; he can say only what the
wisdom of the leaders, the courage of the troops, the sharp-
ness of the weapons, have done. But eternity will some
time reveal still more—it will show how the secret prayers
of the believers were a great power in these fights, how the
old promise is again fulfilled. "Then they cry unto the
Lord in their trouble, and He saveth them out of their distress." And thus, keep to prayer. Amen.

Almighty God, dear Heavenly Father, Thou Lord of
Hosts and Ruler of Battles, we raise, praying, our hands to
Thee. On Thy heart we lay the thousands of brothers-in-
arms, whom Thou thyself hast called to battle. Protect
with Thy almighty protection the breasts of our sons.
Lead our men to victory. On Thy heart we lay the
wounded and sick. Be Thou their comfort and their
strength, and heal their wounds which they receive for
king and fatherland. On Thy heart we lay all those whom

Thou hast ordained to die on the field of battle.   Stand by
them in the last struggle, and give them everlasting peace.
On Thy heart we lay our people.   Preserve, sanctify, increase the enthusiasm with which we are now all imbued.
Lord our God, we trust in Thee.   Lead Thou us in battle.
We boast, Lord, that Thou wilt help us, and in Thy name
we unroll the banner.   Lord, we will not leave Thee; then
wilt Thou bless us.   Amen.

WILLIAM WIRT

AGAINST AARON BURR

[William Wirt, LL.D., an American statesman, author, and jurist, was born of Swiss-German descent in Maryland in 1772. He received an academic education, and after studying law, he practiced in Virginia, and became very prominent at the bar. In public life his rise was a rapid one, although the offices he held were mainly such as an eminent lawyer would capably fill. Thus he was a chancellor in Virginia, United States district attorney for Virginia, and, finally, attorney-general of the United States for three successive terms, or twelve years in all. Nor must it be overlooked that he played a prominent part in the prosecution of Aaron Burr for treason.

The notable writings of William Wirt include "Letters of a British Spy," which ran through a dozen editions ; a series of essays called "The Old Bachelor," and "Sketches of the Life and Character of Patrick Henry." The last named work was a masterpiece of its kind, and edition after edition was exhausted. Wirt delivered at Washington the memorial oration on the death of Adams and Jefferson, who, as every American knows, died within a few hours of each other on the fiftieth anniversary of American independence. Wirt died at Washington in 1834. The speech that follows, a scorching denunciation of the character of Aaron Burr, on trial for treason in attempting to seize Texas and other adjacent territory and establish a rival republic at the south and southwest, was delivered in the U. S. Circuit Court at Richmond, Va., in 1807.]

LET us put the case between Burr and Blennerhassett. Let us compare the two men and settle this question of precedence between them. It may save a good deal of troublesome ceremony hereafter.

Who Aaron Burr is, we have seen in part already. I will add, that beginning his operations in New York, he associates with him men whose wealth is to supply the necessary funds. Possessed of the mainspring, his personal labor contrives all the machinery. Pervading the Continent from New York to New Orleans, he draws into his plan, by every allurement which he can contrive, men of all ranks and descriptions. To youthful ardor he presents danger and glory; to ambition, rank and titles and honors; to avarice, the mines of Mexico. To each person whom he addresses he presents the object adapted to his taste. His recruiting officers are appointed. Men are engaged throughout the continent. Civil life is indeed quiet upon its surface, but in its bosom this man has contrived to deposit the materials which, with the slightest touch of his match, produce an explosion to shake the continent. All this his restless ambition has contrived; and in the autumn of 1806 he goes forth for thē last time to apply this match. On this occasion he meets with Blennerhassett.

Who is Blennerhassett? A native of Ireland, a man of letters, who fled from the storms of his own country to find quiet in ours. His history shows that war is not the natural element of his mind. If it had been, he never would have exchanged Ireland for America. So far is an army from furnishing the society natural and proper to Mr. Blennerhassett's character, that on his arrival in America he retired even from the population of the Atlantic States, and sought quiet and solitude in the bosom of our Western forests. But he carried with him taste and science and wealth; and lo, the desert smiled! Possessing himself of a beautiful island in the Ohio, he rears upon it a palace and decorates it with every romantic embellishment of fancy. A shrubbery that Shenstone might have envied blooms around him. Music that might have charmed Calypso and her nymphs is his. An extensive library spreads its treasures before him. A philosophical apparatus offers to him all the secrets and mysteries of nature. Peace, tranquillity, and innocence shed their mingled delights around him. And to crown the enchantment of the scene, a wife, who is said to be lovely even beyond her sex, and graced with every accomplishment that can render it irresistible, had blessed him with her love, and made him the father of several children. The evidence would convince you that this is but a faint picture of the real life. In the midst of all this peace, this innocent simplicity, and this tranquillity, this feast of the mind, this pure banquet of the heart, the destroyer comes; he comes to change this paradise into a hell. Yet the flowers do not wither at his approach. No monitory shuddering through the bosom of their unfortunate possessor warns him of the ruin that is coming upon him. A stranger presents himself. Introduced to their civilities by the high rank which he had lately held in his country, he soon finds his way to their hearts by the dignity and elegance of his demeanor, the light and beauty of his conversation, and the seductive and fascinating power of his address. The conquest was not difficult. Innocence is ever simple and credulous. Conscious of no design itself, it suspects none in others. It wears no guard before its breast. Every door and portal and avenue of the heart is thrown open, and all who choose it enter. Such was the state of Eden when the serpent entered its bowers. The prisoner, in a more engaging form, winding himself into the open and unpracticed heart of the unfortunate Blennerhassett, found but little difficulty in changing the native character of that heart and the objects of its affection. By degrees he infuses into it the poison of his own ambition. He breathes into it the fire of his own courage; a daring and desperate thirst for glory; an ardor panting for great enterprises, for all the storm and bustle and hurricane of life. In a short time the whole man is changed, and every object of his former delight is relinquished. No more he enjoys the tranquil scene; it has become flat and insipid to his taste. His books are abandoned. His retort and crucible are thrown aside. His shrubbery blooms and breathes its fragrance upon the air in vain; he likes it not. His ear no longer drinks the rich melody of music; it longs for the trumpet's clangor and the cannon's roar. Even the prattle of his babes, once so sweet, no longer affects him; and the angel smile of his wife, which hitherto touched his bosom with ecstasy so unspeakable, is now unseen and unfelt. Greater objects have taken possession of his soul. His imagination has been dazzled by visions of diadems, of stars, and garters, and titles of nobility. He has been taught to burn with restless emulation at the names of great heroes and conquerors. His enchanted island is destined soon to relapse into a wilderness; and in a few months we find the beautiful and tender partner of his bosom, whom he lately "permitted not the winds of" summer "to visit too roughly," we find her shivering at midnight, on the wintry banks of the Ohio, and mingling her tears with the torrents that froze as they fell. Yet this unfortunate man, thus deluded from his interest and his happiness, thus seduced from the paths of innocence and peace, thus confounded in the toils that were deliberately spread for him, and overwhelmed by the mastering spirit and genius of another—this man, thus ruined and undone, and made to play a subordinate part in this grand drama of guilt and treason, this man is to be called the principal offender, while he by whom he was thus plunged in misery is comparatively innocent, a mere accessory! Is this reason? Is it law? Is it humanity? Sir, neither the human heart nor the human understanding will bear a perversion so monstrous and absurd! so shocking to the soul! so revolting to reason! Let Aaron Burr, then, not shrink from the high destination which he has courted, and having already ruined Blennerhassett in fortune, character, and happiness, forever, let him not attempt to finish the tragedy by thrusting that ill-fated man between himself and punishment.

Upon the whole, sir, reason declares Aaron Burr the principal in this crime, and confirms herein the sentence of the law; and the gentleman, in saying that his offense is of a derivative and accessorial nature, begs the question, and draws his conclusions from what, instead of being conceded, is denied. It is clear from what has been said that Burr did not derive his guilt from the men on the island, but imparted his own guilt to them; that he is not an accessory, but a principal; and, therefore, that there is nothing in the objection which demands a record of their conviction before we shall go on with our proof against him.

But suppose you should think otherwise, suppose you were of opinion that on principles of law and reason (notwithstanding the seeming injustice and inhumanity of considering him as inferior in guilt to them) Aaron Burr was not a principal, but an accessorial offender in the treason; would you, for that reason, stop the evidence from going to the jury? Now, to inquire whether the conduct of Aaron Burr makes him liable as a principal or accessory, is only arguing in a different shape the whole question, whether he have committed an overt act of war or not. The jury are to consult and decide whether he be a principal offender or not. Whether he be a principal or accessory is a question of fact, which they are sworn to decide. The court must judge of the weight of evidence, before it can say that the accused is either a principal or accessory. Suppose one part of the evidence contradicts another. Is it not judging of the weight of evidence to decide whether he be a principal or accessory? If it be not, I know not what judging of the weight of evidence is. Nothing is more peculiarly within the exclusive province of the jury than the sufficiency or insufficiency of the evidence.

But the court never says that the evidence is or is not sufficient to prove what it is intended to establish. No court has such right. The course in such cases is to give instructions in a general charge to the jury, after all the evidence shall have been heard. Will you, because of your impressions on this subject, from a merely partial view of the evidence, compel the jury also to decide on that necessarily partial view? If you do, do you not thereby divest the jury of their peculiar functions? Their province should not be invaded. The invasion is big with danger and terror. I trust that you will see this subject in the awful light in which it really stands, and that you will suffer the trial to take its natural course.

Mr. Martin has referred you to a number of cases from Cooper and other authors, but they do not prove the position intended. The court, in all these cases, leaves the jury to decide on the overt act. You will find those cases to amount simply to this—a dialogue between the court and the counsel of the prisoner as to the overt act. The court was required to say whether the overt act was proved or not. There was no judicial determination. The judge merely told his opinion; but he told the jury at the same time that the decision belonged to them and not to him.

There is a wide difference between criminal and civil cases; and as it is of much more importance to preserve the trial by jury in the former, to protect the lives of the people against unjust persecutions, than, in mere civil suits, to preserve the rights of property, the Constitution has secured that trial in all criminal prosecutions.

Should the court interfere for the purpose of stopping the evidence, and to wrest the cause from the jury, in favor

of the accused, would there not be a reciprocal right? If
it can interfere to save the prisoner, can they not interfere
equally against him? A thing unprecedented in the annals
of jurisprudence. Have the counsel, on either side, a right
to call on the other side, to state all their evidence, before
it be introduced, and then to address the court without
hearing it, if they think they have a better chance before
the court than the jury? Has either party a right to substitute the court for the jury, or the jury for the court, at
pleasure; to address the court on facts, or the jury on points
of law? Such an attempt would not be a greater encroachment on the right of the proper tribunal than the present
motion is on the rights of the jury.

HENRY ALEXANDER WISE

KNOW–NOTHINGISM

[Henry Alexander Wise, American statesman and soldier, was born in Drummondtown, Va., December 3, 1806. He graduated at Washington College, Pa., in 1825, studied law, and established a practice in his native county. He was elected to Congress in 1833, and in 1840 secured the nomination of John Tyler as Vice-President, who, after becoming President, appointed him United States Minister to Brazil. After this diplomatic service, Wise was nominated for governor of Virginia, in 1854, and took an active part in the presidential campaign, during which he made numerous speeches against the "Know-Nothings," a political organization, the motto of which was "America for Americans," one of their principles being hostility to Roman Catholicism and their chief object being the diverting of the rapidly increasing anti-slavery excitement into another channel. Wise was elected governor, and during his term of office he signed, in 1859, the death-warrant of John Brown, who was hanged for treason in attempting to incite a negro insurrection. The same year he published a treatise on territorial government, maintaining the right of Congress over the institution of slavery. At the outbreak of the Civil War, Wise was appointed a brigadier-general in the Confederate army. He died in Richmond, Va., in 1876. The following speech was delivered in Alexandria, Va., in 1854.]

THERE is a Know-Nothing member elected from Masssachusetts to the Congress of the United States. There is a United States senator-elect of the Know-Nothings, who confesses the accusation which I make, that the new party of the Know-Nothings was formed especially for the sake of abolitionism. [Cheers and hisses.] And there is a Know-Nothing governor—one of the nine who are all ready to take the same ground. [Stamping of feet and some hisses.] Then, gentlemen, I have here an Act of the Know-Nothing Legislature of Pennsylvania, which proposes to give citizenship to the fugitive slaves of the

South.   I have here also an article, which is too long for
me to read, exhausted as I am, from the Worcester " Evening Journal," an organ of Governor Gardner and Senator
Wilson, which says to you boldly that the American organ
at Washington is a pro-slavery organ, that it is not a true
Know-Nothing organ, and that they speak for the North
when they claim that they have already one hundred and
sixty votes of the non-slaveholding States organized, eleven
more than sufficient to elect a President of the United
States, without a single electoral vote from the slaveholding States.

Now, gentlemen, having swept the northern and the
northwestern non-slaveholding States of the Union, the next
onset is on the soil of Virginia.   This Worcester Journal
boasts that Maryland and Virginia are already almost
Northern States; and, pray, how do they propose to operate the South?   Having swept the North—Massachusetts,
New York, Pennsylvania, and all those other States—the
question was: How can this "ism" be wedged in in the
South?   And the devil was at the elbow of these preachers
of "Christian politics," to tell them precisely how.   [Cat-
calls, derisive cheers, and other manifestations of the Know-
Nothing element of the meeting.]   There were three elements in the South, and in Virginia particularly, to which
they might apply themselves.   There is the religious element—the Protestant bigotry and fanaticism—for Protestants, gentlemen, have their religious zeal without knowledge, as well as the Catholics.   [A voice: "True enough,
sir."]   It is an appeal to the one hundred and three thousand Presbyterians, to the three hundred thousand Baptists,
to the three hundred thousand Methodists of Virginia.
Well, how were they to reach them?   Why, just by raising
a fuss about the Pope.   [Laughter.]   The Pope!—the
Pope, now so poor "that none can do him reverence," so
poor that Louis Napoleon, who requires every soldier in
his kingdom to be at Sebastopol, has to leave a guard of
muskets at Rome!   Once on a time crowned heads could
bow down and salute him; but now, who cares for a Pope
in Italy?   Gentlemen, the Pope is here.   Priestcraft at
home is what you have to dread, more than all the Popes
in the world.   I believe, intellectually, and in my heart as

well as in my head, in evangelical Christianity. I believe there is no other certain foundation for this Republic but the pure and undefiled religion of Jesus Christ of Nazareth. And the man of God who believes in the Father, in the divinity of the Son, and in the Holy Ghost—the preacher in the pulpit, at the baptismal font, by the sick bed, at the grave pointing

. . . "men to Heaven and leading the way,"

I honor. No man honors him more than I. But the priest who deserts the spiritual kingdom for the carnal kingdom, is "of the earth, *earthy,*" whoever he be—Episcopalian, Baptist, or Methodist; whoever leaves the pulpit to form a dark-lantern, secret political society, in order that he may become a Protestant pope by seizing on political power—he is a hypocrite, whoever he be. [Some applause, and cries of "Good!"] Jesus Christ of Nazareth settled that question. When the Jews expected Him to put on a prince's crown and seat Himself on the actual throne of David, He asked for a penny to be shown Him. A penny was brought to Him, a metal coin, assayed, clipped, stamped with the image of the state, representative of the civil power, stamped with Cæsar's image. "Whose image and superscription is this?" "It is Cæsar's." "Then render unto Cæsar the things that be Cæsar's, and unto God the things that be God's." [Applause.] "My kingdom is not of this world." My kingdom is a spiritual kingdom. Cæsar's kingdom is a carnal kingdom, and I tell you, that if I stood alone in the State of Virginia, and if priestcraft—if the priests of my own mother church—dared to lay their hands on the political power of our people, or to use their churches to wield political influence, I would stand, even if I stood alone, as Patrick Henry stood in the Revolution, between the parsons and the people. [Applause, and a cry: "I'm with you."] I want no Pope, either Catholic or Protestant. I will pay Peter's pence to no pontiff—Episcopalian, Presbyterian, Baptist, Methodist, or any other. [Applause, and cries of "Good!"] They not only appeal to the religious element, but they raise a cry about the Pope. These men, many of whom are neither Episcopalian nor Presbyterian, Baptist, Methodist, Congregationalist, Lutheran, or what not—who

are men of no religion, who have no church, who do not
say their prayers, who do not read their Bible, who live
God-defying lives every day of their existence, are now
seen with faces as long as their dark-lanterns, with the
whites of their eyes turned up in holy fear lest the Bible
be shut by the Pope! [Laughter, applause, and derisive
cheers.] Men who were never known before on the face of
God's earth to show any interest in religion, to take any
part with Christ or His kingdom, are all of a sudden very
deeply interested for the word of God and against the Pope!
It would be well for them that they joined a church which
does believe in the Father, and in the Son, and in the Holy
Ghost. Let us see, my friends, what Know-Nothingism
believes in. Do you know that, gentlemen? [Holding up
a small pamphlet, amid great laughter and excitement.]
That is your formulary of the Grand Council of the United
States of North America, from the press of Damerill and
Moore, Number 10 Devonshire Street, Boston, 1854.

And now, let us see how the book reads. The first
page of the cover of the blue book—and it is not only blue,
real Boston blue, but it is a Mazarin blue—[laughter]—
contains the following, in tabular form. Now, listen to the
Know-Nothing reading. Gentlemen, I want to show you
their religion. I read from the blue book:

"The organization shall be known by the name of the Grand Council of the United States of North America. Its jurisdiction and power
shall extend to all states, districts, and territories of the United States
of North America. A person, to become a member of any subordinate Council, must be twenty-one years of age, he must believe in the
existence of a Supreme Being, as the Creator and Preserver of the
Universe."

No Christ acknowledged! No Saviour of Mankind!
No Holy God! No Heavenly Dove of Grace! Go, go,
you Know-Nothings, to the city of Baltimore, and in a certain street there you will see two churches. One is inscribed "To Monos Theos,"—To the One God; on the
other is the inscription, "As for us, we preach Christ crucified,"—to the Jews a stumbling-block, and to the Greeks,
foolishness. The one inscribed, "To Monos Theos," is
the Unitarian church; the other, inscribed "We preach
Christ crucified," is the Catholic! [Cries of "Good, good!"

and cheers.] Is it, I ask, for any orthodox Trinitarian
Christian church to join an association that is inscribed,
like the Unitarian church of Baltimore, "To Monos Theos"
—To the One God? Is it for them to join or to countenance an association that so lays out its religion as to catch
men like this? I put it to all the religious societies—to the
Presbyterians, Episcopalians, the Methodists, and the Baptists—whether they mean to renounce the divinity of Christ
and the operation of the Holy Spirit, when they give countenance to the secret society which is inscribed To the One
God.

But, gentlemen, the Know-Nothings appeal not only to
the religious element, but to the political element, and to
the agrarian element. Not only do they ask the Protestants to out-Herod Herod, to out-Catholic Catholics, to
out-Jesuit Jesuits, by adopting their Machiavellian creed,
but they appeal to a forlorn party in the State of Virginia
—a minority party, broken down at home and disorganized;
they appeal to them as affording them a house of refuge.
[Cheers and laughter.] There is a paper published in this
town by one of the most respectable gentlemen of the
state, who some time ago published an article which, I
must confess, I did not expect to see in print from his pen.
The Alexandria "Gazette," one of the most respectable of
the Whig papers of the United States, edited by one
of the most conservative and respectable gentlemen that
I know of among my acquaintances, one who has been
advocating the doctrine and practice of conversationism
ever since I knew him, is now proposing a fusion between
the Know-Nothing and the Whig parties, simply for the
reason that "the Whigs are tired of standing at the rack
without fodder." [Voice in the crowd: "Oh, go along,"
and laughter.] One who used, as I well remember, to denounce corruption and the spoils system very sweepingly,
is now actually maintaining that the Whigs will not, and
cannot, upon principle, any longer adhere to conversationism, because they are tired of waiting for office. [Laughter
and cheers.] Not only that, but my friend the editor has
lately published this short article:

"We are pleased to see that with regard to Mr. Wise, the Democratic candidate for governor, the opposition is generally conducted

with entire respect to his character as a citizen and a man and with a full acknowledgment on all hands of his many excellent personal qualities. The opposition do not think he is the best qualified man for the office of governor, but they admit his talents. In seeking his defeat, they mainly desire to defeat the political organization which he upholds."

Remember, you Democrats who have joined with Mr. Snowden in upholding the Know-Nothing cause, that the very object of the Whigs in forming the Know-Nothing society is to break up the organization to which you belong! [Cheers.] You Democrats have these gentlemen in a minority out of doors, but the moment they get you into a Know-Nothing lodge, they have you in a minority indoors. [Renewed cheers.] But the article goes on:

"They contend themselves, that as a former violent opponent of the party at whose head he is now placed, there is too much political inconsistency in him to entitle him to the position he seeks."

How, then, can Mr. Snowden, how can the conservative Whigs of Alexandria, to punish my inconsistency, join hands with Democrats and go over to them in Know-Nothing lodges? [Cheers.] They tell us they cannot give the grip in public to the Whigs of the North, because the Northern Whigs have become abolitionized. Here are two gentlemen who cannot shake hands with each other in our presence—one is a Whig of the North and the other a Whig of Alexandria. They cannot any longer keep up their Whig organization; but let the Whig of the North, abolitionized as he is, become a Know-Nothing, and let the Whig of the South, pro-slavery as he is, become a Know-Nothing, then, behind the curtain, these gentlemen can shake hands and "honey-fuggle" with each other. [Much laughter.] This is what is called "conversationism." This is what is called consistency. The article continues:

"They are resolved to unite in a strong and determined effort to break up the present political organization, which directs the destinies and controls the action of the state in all departments. Mr. Wise cannot expect the support of those who desire to see this change effected."

If Mr. Wise cannot expect the support of conservative Whigs, or of any Whig, how can they expect the Democrats to join them? But there is a last and worst element which they address, for which they can, as conservatives, offer me no excuse, and I come to it boldly. It is the most difficult and the hardest subject to deal with in public, in a slave-holding community. Gentlemen, the last convention of Virginia betrayed the important fact to the North, as well as to ourselves, that out of the one hundred and twenty-five thousand voters in the State of Virginia but twenty-five thousand to thirty thousand are slave-holding voters. About one out of five is a slave-holder. I say it boldly,—and no man will dispute it who has been in Norfolk and Portsmouth,—that the last and worst element that is appealed to is the agrarian element—appealing to the white laborers of the state against the black laborers of the state! [Cheers.] Go all over the state, and tell me where Know-Nothingism is rankest and most violent! [Voice in the crowd: "Down on the wharves," and great laughter.] I tell you that you'll not only find it on the wharves in Alexandria, as has been said, and well said, in the crowd, but you will find it worse than anywhere else around the wharves of Portsmouth navy-yard. The very men who have been petitioning the secretary of the navy to forbid the employment of slave-labor in Gosport navy-yards—the very men who petitioned the convention to frame a new constitution, for Virginia to make it a part of the organized system of the state that slave-holders should not allow their slaves to be taught the mechanical arts—these are the men that form the very hotbed of Know-Nothingism!

It is impossible to say what effect these three combined elements are to have upon us. I ask the Protestant Church —to recur to the religious element—how they expect in the future—if they think that Catholicism is not a pure and undefiled religion—to succeed in preaching against the Pope and the Catholics. Where a preacher has risen in the pulpit, in times past, to arraign the Pope and the Church of Rome, he has been regarded as one looking to the spiritual kingdom. But let a preacher now rise and preach against the Pope and against Catholicism, and, whether he is sincere or not, his congregation feels that he is preaching for Know-Nothingism. Why, the other day in the Isle of Wight, I saw a man from Canada, or I heard of him there, who was distributing the Bible to the State of Virginia.

Well, he may have been a man of as honest intentions as Father Hudnall, who is your distributor of the Bible, but he came all the way from Canada down to the Isle of Wight to distribute Bibles! He was asked why he distributed Bibles among us? Did he take us to be heathens? Our churches are distributing the Word. Our bishops are distributing the Word. The Bible is found in every steamboat saloon, and in every chamber of every hotel of the State. Did he take us to be heathens? No, no; he was glad to hear that we had the Bible here, but he thought perhaps he would be doing a great service to bring the Bible to us. He was called upon to take his departure, as he was known at once to be a Know-Nothing agent. He pretended merely to visit to distribute the Bible, but the fellow was all the time carrying his dark-lantern and lucifer matches in his pocket, to apply the test oath. [Laughter.] We gave him warning to go hence, and I hope he has gone. So it is with your preachers—your Protestant preachers. It is utterly impossible that they can make any inroads against the Pope and against the Catholics, so long as they are suspected of political motives, so long as they are suspected of attempting to become Protestant popes and to seize political power. Calvin and Luther, and Melancthon, and Roger Williams—all the great reformers—were men that did not go into secret places, who did not use dark-lanterns, who did not speak in whispers, but who thundered in the tones of Whitfield himself. The moment a bishop or religious leader becomes part and head of the political state, that very moment the state corrupts the church, and the church destroys the liberties of the state. As to the proscription of foreigners, let me ask the Know-Nothings themselves to return to that passage of the Bible to which I have already referred them. If they will take the fifteenth chapter of second Samuel, and read it, they will discover the whole history of Absalom, the traitor, and they will find that Absalom was not only a native born of the land, but native born of the loins of King David, the psalmist of Israel. When King David was driven toward the wilderness with his followers, he turned and saw Ittai the Gittite, and said to him, "Wherefore goest thou also with us? return to thy place, and abide with the king: for thou art a stranger, and also an exile. Whereas thou camest but yesterday, should I this day make thee go up and down with us? seeing I go whither I may, return thou, and take back thy brethren: Mercy and truth be with thee!" And Ittai, the exile and stranger, who came but yesterday, answered the king and said: "As the Lord liveth, and as my lord the king liveth, surely in what place my lord the king shall be, whither in death or life, even there also will thy servant be." And remember that the case of Absalom and of Ittai is but the prototype of an Arnold and a Lafayette. [Applause.] Who sent you alliances? You tell the people that Catholics never gave aid to civil liberty; that they never yet struck a blow for the freedom of mankind. Who gave you alliances against the Crown of England? Who but the Catholics' king, Louis XVI.? He sent you, from the court of Versailles, the joy of Washington's camp, a foreigner, who never was naturalized, but who bled at the redoubt of Yorktown! [Applause.] And not only did Lafayette bleed at the redoubt of Yorktown, when an Arnold, a native like Absalom, proved traitor, but when the German, De Kalb, fell at the field of Camden, on Southern soil, with fourteen bayonet wounds transfixing his body, and, dying, praised the Maryland militia, Gates, the Yankee native, ran seventy-five miles without looking behind him. [Applause and laughter.] And not only that. In that intense moment when the Declaration of Independence was brought into Carpenter's Hall by Rutledge, and Franklin, and Jefferson, and laid upon the table—that holy paper, which not only pledged life and honor, but fortune, too (realize that moment of intense, of deep, of profound interest, when the independence of this land hung upon the act of men!)—when, one by one, men rose from their seats and went to the table to pledge lives and fortunes and sacred honor; at length, one spare, pale-faced man rose and went and dipped the pen into the ink and signed "Charles Carroll," and when reminded that it might not be known what Charles Carroll it was, that it might not be known that it was a Charles Carroll who was pledging a principality and a fortune, he added the words "of Carrollton." [Cheers.] He was a Catholic representative from a Catholic colony.

And, sir, before George Washington was born, before

Lafayette wielded the sword, and Charles Carroll the pen, for his country—six hundred and forty years ago—on the sixteenth of June 1214, there was another scene, enacted on the face of the globe, when the general charter of all charters of freedom was gained; when one man—a man called Stephen Langton—swore the barons of England for the people, against the orders of the Pope and against the power of the king; swore the barons on the high altar of the Catholic church at St. Edmundsbury, that they would have Magna Charta or die for it. The charter which secures to every one of you to-day trial by jury, freedom of the press, freedom of the pen, the confronting of witnesses with the accused, and the opening of secret dungeons—that charter was obtained by Stephen Langton against the Pope and against the king of England, and if you Know-Nothings don't know who Stephen Langton was, you know nothing, sure enough. [Laughter and cheers.] He was a Catholic archbishop of Canterbury. [Renewed cheers.] I come here not to praise the Catholics, but I come here to acknowledge historical truths, and to ask of Protestants what has heretofore been the pride and boast of Protestants—tolerance of opinions in religious faith. [Applause.] All we ask is tolerance. All we ask is, that if you hate the Catholics because they have proscribed heretics, you won't out-proscribe proscription. If you hate Catholics because they have nunneries and monasteries and Jesuit secret orders, don't out-Jesuit the Jesuit, by going into dark-lantern secret chambers to apply test oaths. If you hate the Catholics because you say they encourage the Machiavellian expediency of telling lies sometimes, don't swear yourselves not to tell the truth. [Cheers.] Here are the oaths—the oaths that bind you, under no circumstances, to disclose who you are or what you are, and that bind you not only to political, but to social, proscription. Here is your book—your Bible—which requires you to stick up your notices between midnight and daybreak. [Laughter.] I don't object to secrecy. I am a member of a secret order, and I am proud to be a brother Mason. [Loud cheers.] And I am left at liberty by my order to say, that as to its ends, its purposes, its designs, Masonry has no secrets. [Renewed cheering.] Its ends, its purposes, its aims, are

to make a brotherhood of charity amongst men. Its end
is the end of a Christian law of religion. I know not how
any Mason can be a Know-Nothing. Masonry binds its
members to respect and obey the laws of the land in which
we live; and when the Constitution of the United States
declares that no religious test shall be made a qualification
for office, Masonry dares not interpose by conspiring, in a
secret association, to attempt to make a religious test a
qualification for office. When Virginia has an act of religious freedom—an act that is no longer a mere statute law,
but that is now part of the organic law, and which says that
no man shall be burdened for religious opinion's sake—
Masonry dares not conspire to burden any man for opinion's
sake. Masonry has no secret but the simple test by which
it recognizes its brotherhood. It is bound to respect the
law and tolerate difference of opinion in religion and politics. I do not complain of secrecy, but I complain of
secrecy for political objects. What is your object? Is it
to assail the Constitution of the United States? To conspire to contradict the Constitution of the United States
and the law of the land? Is it to conspire against the Constitution and laws, and swear men by test oaths—the most
odious instruments of tyranny that intolerance has ever
devised? It is not only to proscribe all Protestants, and
natives too, who will not unite with you in proscribing
Catholics and foreigners; it goes further than that. It destroys all individuality in the man. You bring in your
novice. You swear him, to do—what? To give us his
conscience, his judgment, his will, to the judgment and the
conscience and the will of an association of men who are
not willing that others should enslave them, but by their
test-oaths enslave themselves. And to what are they
sworn? They are sworn to passive obedience, to non-
resistance, and to take the sign and grip. Here is your
organization. [Holding up a document.] I will not take
time to read it, but I will state that your Grand National
Council of the United States claims power over individual
judgment. All power is concentrated in that National
Council. And has it come to this? Has Virginia been so
provincialized in the Union that her sons will consent, not
to be guided by their own individual wills, by their own

individual conscience, by their own individual judgments, but to be sworn by the test oath to take a sign which comes from an outside State?

When that is submitted to by the people of Virginia, they can no longer call themselves a free, sovereign, and independent state. You are subdued—you are conquered—you are provincialized—you have lost your individuality. And not only are these appliances brought to bear upon us, but, gentlemen, emissaries are everywhere at work. The "New York Herald" has taken up this election, and has proclaimed to the world that it is arranged in New York already.

At this moment I have to endure that the Whig presses of the state have forgotten what they owe to the State—not to me—so far as to publish the Herald's reports, which insult the state, as well as me. That is tolerated. I care nothing about the "Herald." I am looking at higher game. I am looking at the Absaloms, at the Arnolds, at the traitors of the North, who, wielding the power of the "Herald," have thought to put the South and slavery down, by putting me down, and I suppose the Know-Nothings are very confident that they will succeed. Let me tell them that I would as soon die a martyr in this cause as in any other cause. Let me say to them, When you have fastened together the Whigs and Know-Nothings and Democrats; when you get those who are blindly leaving their party, to place themselves in the toils of your machinery, those who are either seeking office or are disappointed in not getting office; when you have put me down; when you have crushed the slave-holding power in my election—why, then follows a revolution, a social and political revolution, not only in the State of Virginia, but in the whole South! Gentlemen, what is to follow from this? Where is it to end? What is to follow? They have swept the North. They claim they have got a majority in the Senate of the United States; but, if I am elected governor of the State of Virginia, what will be your state of things? The next Congress will assemble on the first Monday in December next. If I be elected governor of the State of Virginia, I shall be sworn in on the first of January next. And now I tell you what will be the consequence. When I take the oath to support the Constitution of the

State of Virginia, I will remember that I shall be invested with the militia power of the State of Virginia, to repel invasion and to suppress insurrection. No man loves and adores the Union of this land more than I. I have been taught to venerate and to cherish the Union of these states. It is the holiest of all earthly things. I would gladly give my life, my blood, as a sacrifice to save it, if required. But I know the main pillars of the Union, the main props and supporters of this palladium, are the two pillars of State-rights and State sovereignty! [Applause.] If you place me, with your sword in my hand, by that great pillar of Virginia sovereignty, I promise you to bear and forbear to the last extremity. I will suffer much, suffer long, suffer almost anything but dishonor. But it is, in my estimation, with the union of the states as it is with the union of matrimony. You may suffer almost anything but dishonor; but when honor is touched the union must be dissolved. [Loud and prolonged cheering.] I will not say that. I take back the words. I will not allow myself to contemplate a dissolution of the Union. [Renewed cheers.] No, we will try to save it. But when the worst comes to the worst, if compelled to draw the sword of Virginia, I will draw it. And, by the gods of the state and her holy altars! if I am compelled to draw it, I shall flesh it, or it shall pierce my body. [Enthusiastic cheering.] And I tell you more. We have abolitionists in this state. If I should have to move, some of the first, I fear, against whom I should have to act, would be some of those within our own limits. But I will not confine myself to the State of Virginia. My motto will be

"Woe to the coward, that was ever born,
Who did not draw the sword before he blew his horn."

[Loud cheers.]

Gentlemen, I was in a very poor plight to speak to you to-night. Perhaps I have spoken already too long, although I have not said one-half of what I would say to you, or produced half the evidence which I have with me. All I have to say to the Democracy is, that all you want is active, earnest organization. [Cheers.] Remember that if these Know-Nothings hold together, they are a sworn committee of vigilance. Go to work, then; organize actively everywhere.

Appoint your vigilance committees, but take special care that no Know-Nothings are, secretly and unknown to you, upon them. [Cheers.] Be prepared. I have gone through most of Eastern Virginia, and in spite of their vaunting, I defy them to defeat me. [Great cheering.] There are "Indians in the bushes," but I'll whack in the bayonet, and lunge to every shrub in the state, till I drive them out. [Enthusiastic cheering.] I tell them distinctly there shall be no compromise, no parley. I will come to no terms. They shall either crush me or I shall crush them in this state. [Great applause.] Of the conscientious and considerate and conservative members of the Whig party I would ask where can they find anything in form, shape, tendency, or result that promises so much destructiveness as Know-Nothingism? I challenge them to compare Know-Nothingism with Democracy, and to tell me what it is in Democracy that they cannot show in comparison with Know-Nothingism. I will say that I do expect that the Democratic nomination in this election will gain the support of some of the brightest jewels of the Whig party in this state. [Cheers and laughter.] I hail them, and extend to them the right hand of fellowship; and I believe that if Know-Nothingism can claim no other good deed, it will at least effect a reorganization of the Democratic party of the state of Virginia upon higher ground, more affiliated, stronger, and abler to serve itself and the country, than it has been for the last twenty-five years. Let them, then, boast of their thirty thousand, and forty thousand, and fifty thousand majorities. We will take our old and usual majority—I shall be satisfied with that. [Cheers and laughter.] And to obtain it I would not flatter you, the people, "if you were Neptune for his trident, or Jove for his power to hinder." I will deceive no man. I will "honey-fuggle" no voter. [Laughter.] I will condescend to nothing unbecoming a gentleman. I will conduct this canvass throughout in such a manner as will command your respect and preserve my own self-respect. God grant that I may live through the campaign! If I continue to speak as I have been doing, I doubt very much whether I can survive it. But "sink or swim, live or die," I will do my duty; and "if Rome falls, I am innocent."

GENERAL INDEX

THIS Index has been constructed with special regard to its practical usefulness, rather than for elaborate exhibition of entries. The aim is to take
the point of view of the reader searching for a subject, an illustration, a
quotable passage, or the like, and enable him directly to find it. To this
end concreteness and plainness of expression have been constantly sought.

A

	VOL.	PAGE
Abbott, Dr. Lyman, quoted by Pres-		
ident Roosevelt	15	1759
Abdication of Ferdinand, its effects		
in Spanish America	12	682
Abnegation of General Gordon	15	1814
Abolition in District of Columbia,		
not favored by Van Buren	15	1858
Abolition Movement, beginning of the	12	499
Of the National Bank by Andrew		
Jackson	11	216
Of Slavery, the, Emilio Castelar		
on	12	523
Of slave-trade a pressing duty	14	1645
Abolitionists and Kossuth	13	1276
Abraham, Heights of, Washington on		
the	13	1306
Absolutism, in the Middle Ages	13	895
Napoleonic, saved France	12	513
Occasional, its efficacy in the Ro-		
man republic	12	513
Abuses, civil service, Presidents not		
chief sinners in	12	792
Abzate, Spanish-American	12	684
Accomplices of Warren Hastings in		
spoliation	15	1879
Accumulation of armaments in the		
Transvaal	11	101
Achievement, English, Ireland's part		
in, Richard Lalor Sheil on	15	1865
Acland, Sir T	14	1540
Acquisition of wealth, evil methods		
in	13	1232
Acropolis, its ruins in the moonlight	15	1927
Act, Coercion, the	14	1498
Act, George the First, its purport	13	1100

	VOL.	PAGE
Act, McKinley, produced large sur-		
pluses	15	1906
Navigation, in American colonies	14	1427
Ninth William, its purport	13	1100
Of Union between Ireland and		
England, its tardy fruits	15	1869
Redemption, of 1875	13	1224
Action, President's power of, limited	15	1783
Acts, x. 38, quoted by Leo XIII	14	1331
xx. 28, quoted by Leo XIII	14	1328
Adams, John, biography of	11	1
John, complains of the predomi-		
nating materialism	13	1278
John, his summary of Otis on		
Writs of Assistance	14	1529
John, Inaugural Address of	11	1
John, James Otis on eloquence of	11	viii
John, on dangers to American		
liberties	11	4
John, on the retirement of Wash-		
ington	11	5
John, on the safeguards of the		
Constitution	11	6
Adams, John Quincy	11	x
John Quincy, biography of	11	8
John Quincy, condemned and de-		
posed by Democratic party	15	1861
John Quincy, his election op-		
posed by Democrats	15	1858
John Quincy, in civil service ap-		
pointments	12	789
John Quincy, speech of, on the		
Constitutional War Power over		
Slavery	11	17
Adams and Jefferson, Daniel Web-		
ster on	15	2082
Adams, Samuel, biography of	11	21

	VOL.	PAGE
Adams, Samuel, speech on American Independence.............	11	21
Addison, his lack of strength and vigor......................	11	xxiii
Address, "Corner-Stone," The, by Alexander Hamilton Stephens	15	1936
Farewell, of George Washington	15	2036
First Inaugural, of George Washington....................	15	2032
Inaugural, of Benjamin Harrison	13	1137
Inaugural, of John Adams......	11	1
By Napoleon Bonaparte, to his army at the beginning of the Italian campaign...........	11	290
To troops after War of Third Coalition, by Napoleon Bonaparte......................	11	293
To troops, on beginning of the Russian campaign, by Napoleon Bonaparte.............	11	294
To troops on conclusion of first Italian campaign, by Napoleon Bonaparte.............	11	292
Addresses to his army, Napoleon's..	11	289
Administration, how far to be upheld	15	1843
Admission of new territories in 1889.	13	1146
Adoption of the Constitution, centennial of..................	13	1138
Adrian, Emperor, unique example of self-denial.................	12	621
Advantages, geographical, of the United States..................	13	1257
Adversity worse than death........	14	1569
Advice, Jefferson's, to the Mandan Indians..................	13	1261
Æschines, abuse of Demosthenes by.	12	823
A calumniator.................	12	825
Against crowning Demosthenes.	11	38
A third-rate actor..............	12	869
Biography of..................	11	38
Bribed by Philip..............	12	832
Hireling of Philip and Alexander	12	832
His advantages over Demosthenes......................	12	822
His career contrasted with that of Demosthenes.............	12	880
His early life stigmatized by Demosthenes.................	12	879
Æschines of Cothocidæ, ambassador to Philip..................	12	828
Affectation destroys eloquence......	12	xiii
Afghanistan, Russia's abstention from, to the credit of Clarendon and Granville..........	13	1091
Africa, deplorable state of..........	14	1640
Difficulty of eradicating slave-trade in....................	14	1635
Africa, human sacrifices among negroes in....................	14	1641
Its diamonds and mineral products........................	14	1740
North, to be secured by the British....................	14	1739
Poor prospect of civilizing......	14	1638
African barbarity, instances of......	14	1635
Africans, importation of, for agricultural labor, granted to the South......................	15	1933
Sale of wives, children and themselves by, in gambling........	14	1633
African slave-trade.................	14	1630
"Age of Reason," Paine's, blasphemous......................	13	958
Aggrandizement, territorial, on American soil, by foreigners, to be prohibited.............	15	1766
Aggression, criminal, disclaimed by President McKinley.........	15	1835
Agincourt........................	15	1953
Agitation against slavery begun in the North in 1835...........	12	467
Agoncillo and Santico, great leaders in Aguinaldo's party........	15	1920
Agriculturist, American, the, buys at prices fixed in Washington...	13	1078
American, the, sells at prices fixed in Liverpool..........	13	1079
Aguesseau, d', the great chancellor of France.....................	13	1217
Aguinaldo, activity of, on the sea...	15	1838
And Dewey at Cavité.........	15	1838
And Dewey confer.............	15	1837
An obstacle to military occupation of the Philippines.......	15	1919
His name coupled with Washington's.....................	15	1920
How treated by the United States	13	1197
On the withdrawal of American troops from Manila..........	15	1917
Called a catspaw..............	15	1836
Ajax, his prayer for light..........	14	1589
Alaska discussed in the Canadian Parliament.................	13	1301
Alaskan frontier a stumbling-block to Canadians and Americans.	13	1300
Albuera, Irish soldiers at........	15	1871
Alexander, his claims, and Cæsar's, on man's homage............	14	1720
Of Macedon, a robber chief.....	12	728
The Great...................	12	673
Alexandria, English fleet in the harbor of......................	15	1809
Its fortifications demolished by Admiral Seymour...........	15	1810

	VOL.	PAGE
Alexandria, The Christians at, demolish the Serapeum.	13	1054
Algiers, Virginia likened to	14	1590
Aliens, Irish unjustly stigmatized as.	15	1870
Property-owners by treaty	14	1410
"All men are created equal," interpreted by Stephen A. Douglas	14	1362
Alleghanies, the	14	1596
Alleghany river, the	14	1701
Alliance, the Holy, due to Charles James Fox	14	1720
The Holy, wrecked in the Crimean War	11	249
Alsace, delegates from, Gambetta's address to	13	1037
Alsatian textile industries and annexation.	11	162
Amalgamation of black and white race abhorrent	14	1361
Ambassadors to Philip, dilatoriness of	12	828
Amendment, Chase's, why he offered it.	13	937
Fifth, the, deductions from	14	1343
Fourteenth, the	11	ix
Proposed, to preclude secession, unnecessary.	13	1061
Tenth, the, deductions from	14	1343
Thirteenth, the	11	ix
To the Constitution, against slavery, opposed by slavery party	15	1855
Amendments, Fifth and Tenth, passed by anti-slavery Congress.	14	1343
America, war between, and England, criminal.	13	1302
Central and South, in need of steamship lines.	14	1402
Discovery of, the salvation of the world.	13	899
Irishman's gratitude to	14	1584
Its only debt to great nations.	13	968
Like Russia, cannot be great in commerce or manufactures.	14	1714
Shuts out English goods.	14	1733
South, the emancipation of	12	676
To be what Athens was.	14	1586
What the Age Owes to, William Maxwell Evarts on	13	962
American and Filipino civilization compared.	11	80
American citizenship, like Roman, an inviolable passport from the days of Andrew Jackson.	11	214
Not valued by the Chinese	14	1572
American colonies fired by oratory.	13	vii
American interests abroad to be safeguarded.	13	1144
American liberty, column erected to	13	1217
American republic, causes of progress of the, since Civil War	11	x
American revolutionists, Filipinos compared with.	15	1836
Americans, called by John Randolph "a nation of sharks".	14	1722
Endowments and advantages of.	13	1257
American Stamp Act, why repealed.	13	1101
Ames, Fisher, biography of	11	43
On the British Treaty	11	43
Amiens, peace of, its futility	12	507
Amphipolis.	12	836
Analogies, Roman, unsuitable to English policy.	13	1097
Analysis, secret of eloquence eludes.	11	xiv
Anarchism, extreme development of capitalist liberalism.	11	164
Its intellectual fathers.	11	163
Anarchist assassinations, manufacture of	11	172
Anarchy, remedial legislation for.	13	1151
And chaos, feudal system in Europe result of.	13	894
Ancient colonies no parallel to modern.	14	1424
Ancient republics of Sparta, Rome and Athens.	14	1604
Anderson, Gen. T. M., assures Aguinaldo of American support.	15	1838
Andersonville, horrors of.	13	1208
Andersonville and Libby prisons.	13	1254
Angels and Little Breeches.	15	1928
Anglo-Saxon, the, his political nature	13	1229
Anglo-Turkish convention eclipses fiction.	13	1095
Animals, domestic, raising of, among the Indians, advised by President Jefferson.	13	1266
Annals, tiresome, their blessedness.	12	729
Annexation bitterly opposed by Hawaiians.	12	627
By force, is "criminal aggression".	15	1835
Of foreign slave states, contemplated by American slaveholders.	15	1855
Of Hawaii, contradicts Declaration of Independence	12	625
Of Hawaii, favored by Republicans inconsistently.	12	623
Of Hawaii, tantamount to admission of a slave state.	12	624
To be decided by Hawaiian votes	12	626
Anti-slave trade act of 1808, repeal of, contemplated by American slave-holders.	15	1855

	VOL.	PAGE
Aphidna.	12	830
Appomattox, Candidate from	12	719
Appropriations, not mandatory, but permissive, Secretary Carlisle and	15	1905
Of Congress to Philippine War	15	1921
Arabian Nights quoted by John Randolph.	14	1724
Arabia's rebellion in Egypt	15	1809
Arabs, slaughter of six thousand	15	1812
Arbitration, treaty of, with the United States, advocated in English Parliament	13	1032
Arcadians, abettors of Philip	12	835
Archipelago, Philippine	14	1491
Areopagus, at Athens, punishes a child for cruelty	13	915
The, a court of manners and behavior.	13	915
Argives abettors of Philip	12	835
Argos.	14	1746
Argument, best, in a case, statement of the case.	12	41
Aristides.	11	42
Aristocracy, an, the Democratic party raise, in a republic.	15	1863
Exclusive of liberty	13	1270
Of idleness, in Ingersoll's "Vision of War".	13	1240
Aristonicus.	12	829
Aristophon.	12	836
Aristotle on good taste.	14	vii
Aristratus.	12	832
Armies, standing, subversive of liberty.	13	976
Arms of the British army in South Africa, not obsolete.	11	103
Army, German, education in the	11	253
And navy in higher offices of the South in vast majority till 1861	15	1935
Of the United States, the, born of the martial spirit of brave people.	11	135
Of the United States, the, represents military spirit of whole nation.	11	134
United States, the, Thomas F. Bayard on.	11	134
Arnold, Dr., on the Jews.	14	1546
Arrogance, American, in British press	13	1301
Art, great, its power to move the will.	13	v
Spanish, under the monarchy and under the republic, contrasted.	12	521
Success in, an international asset	14	1399
Articles of Confederation, the, statements in, regarding slavery.	14	1606
Arts, oratory the most personal of.	13	vii
Asia, Central, Russia's position in, forced upon her.	13	1090
Filipinos the only Christian people in.	11	79
Asp, for the breast of the poor, the needle the.	13	1241
Assassination, eminent victims of.	13	1151
Justin McCarthy accused of conniving at.	14	1366
Of rulers, its futility.	13	1150
Assassination, political, reactionary outcome of.	11	167
Assassinations, attempted, of European rulers.	11	169
Assaye, Irish soldiers at.	15	1870
Assigny, d', on excellence of oratory.	14	vi
Assistance, Writs of, James Otis on.	14	1526
Writs of, the worst instruments of tyranny.	14	1526
Associations, philanthropic, must be religious.	14	1329
Aston, in the Gladstone redistribution scheme.	15	1824
Athenian greatness, causes of, Pericles on.	14	1563
Athenians, on receiving bad news.	14	1746
Remained in their fatherland.	14	1564
Their excellence in war.	14	1568
Athens, all-sufficiency of, in war and peace.	14	1564
A minister to Greece merely a minister to.	15	1926
Its government a model to other states.	14	1565
Manner of living at.	14	1566
Population of Kansas greater than that of.	15	1953
Subject to the mindless Ottoman	14	1586
Atlanta, heroes of.	11	228
Attachment, Government by, John Philpot Curran on.	12	774
Power of, its limitations.	12	775
Attica, a fortress against.	12	836
Attainder, bills of, and ex post facto laws.	14	1609
Audience, an, enthusiasm of, how to be measured.	13	xii
"Augmenter of the State," McKinley so styled by Stedman.	13	1161
Austerlitz of American politics, the.	12	719
Australia, High tariff on British goods.	14	1734
Austria, aggressor, with Prussia, in last Napoleonic wars.	13	997
Empress of, assassinated by Luccheni.	13	1151

	VOL.	PAGE
Austria, her absurd defense in occupying Venetian territory.....	13	1012
Income tax in................	11	354
Received Venice from the French in 1797....................	13	1011
Authority, local and federal........	14	1344
Authors, distinguished, proscribed in Spanish America............	12	681
Avenues, natural, of one soul's influence upon another..........	11	xvii

B

	VOL.	PAGE
Bacon, Augustus Octavius, biography of....................	11	77
Resolution of, declaring Filipinos ought to be free..	13	1197
Speech of, on the Character and Capacity of Filipinos.........	11	77
Bacon, Lord, on the *post nati* of Scotland.....................	14	1547
On vain speaking.............	15	ix
Badajos, the Irish at.............	15	1871
Bailey, Joseph Walden, biography of	11	84
On Porto Rico................	11	xi
On the Porto Rico tariff........	11	84
Bajazet, a robber chief............	12	728
Baker, General, why defeated by the Mahdi.....................	15	1811
"Balancers" in the French National Convention................	13	917
Baldwin, Abraham, at the Congress of 1789....................	14	1339
Balfour, Arthur James, biography of.	11	99
Speech of, on Boer War........	11	99
Ball at the palace of Athens, American minister's report of a.....	15	1927
Ballot, freedom of the, a condition of American national life.......	13	1147
Gift of the, to twelve peoples, saved Rome................	13	1061
Ballot-box not a "juggler's hat," sentiment of Benjamin Harrison.	13	1147
Baltimore favors the tariff bill......	14	1714
Riotin, quelled by General Butler	12	446
Bancroft. George, biography of......	11	110
On Andrew Jackson...........	11	110
Bandiera, the brothers............	14	1469
Bank, National, abolished by Andrew Jackson...................	11	216
Of the United States, Andrew Jackson and the..........	11	127
Of the United States, prime mover in censure of President Jackson...................	11	209
Bankers, demand of, for honest money...................	13	1223
Banks, savings, their beneficent work	15	1777

	VOL.	PAGE
Banners of America and England to be intertwined.............	13	1303
Baptist, John the, his question of Christ.....................	14	1330
Baptists divide on the slavery question........................	12	471
Barbadoes. a dancing-hall for pirate chiefs during the Civil War...	12	449
Barbarian invasion of Europe.......	14	1425
Barbarism, cannot exist in civilization........................	15	1768
Not the result of liberty........	12	802
Barrett, John, minister to Siam, his opinion of Filipino government.....................	15	1841
Bassett, Richard, at the Congress of 1789.	14	1339
Batangas, guerilla warfare in........	13	927
Batavian and Helmetic models followed in American Confederation.....................	11	2
Batoum made a merely commercial port by Berlin treaty........	13	1090
Bayard, Thomas Francis, biography of............................	11	134
On the United States Army....	11	134
Beaconsfield, Lord, biography of....	11	143
On Conservatism..............	11	143
On the gold standard, quoted by D. B. Hill..................	13	1188
Beaver, the head warrior of the Delawares.....................	13	1263
Thomas Jefferson to...........	13	1263
Bebel, August, biography of........	11	159
On Socialism and Assassination.	11	159
Bechuanaland, Krüger's grasping policy in..................	14	1738
Beckford's Vathek, cited by Wendell Phillips...................	14	1595
Beecher, Henry Ward, biography of.	11	180
His dictum on oratory.........	13	vii
In Liverpool..................	12	vi
On Raising the Flag over Fort Sumter.....................	11	180
Begums, ministers cruelly flogged...	15	1898
Deceived and robbed by Middleton, the tool of Hastings.....	15	1896
Starved into submission by Warren Hastings................	15	1888
Their destruction by Warren Hastings...................	15	1892
Their innocency..............	15	1874
Belgium, erection of the kingdom of, due to Lord Palmerston.....	13	1088
Bell, General, his order to the friendly Filipinos...................	13	927
Benares, Chief Justice Impey at.....	15	1889

	VOL.	PAGE
Beneficence, Athenian, character of.	14	1567
Benefits of Expositions	14	1398
Benevolences, illegal in England	14	1423
"Benevolent assimilation," President McKinley's order of	15	1842
Benjamin, Judah Philip, biography of	11	200
On Education the Foundation-stone of Republican Government.	11	200
Benton, Thomas Hart	11	x
Biography of	11	208
On the Political Career of Andrew Jackson	11	208
Berlin, Congress of, 1878, Lord Salisbury at the	13	1089
Berthier and Monge, Napoleon's messengers to the Directory	13	1021
Best English authors for the oratorical student	11	xxiii
Betrayers of the Constitution and freedom, the Democratic party so called	15	1864
Beveridge, Albert J., biography of	11	224
On public speaking	12	v
On the March of the Flag	11	224
Bible, good citizenship and the	15	1770
Misuse of the	15	1773
Paine's opinion of the	13	959
Pure English of the King James.	12	xi
The most democratic book	15	1773
Theodore Roosevelt on Reading the	15	1770
Bible-words misunderstood by children, example of	15	1774
Bill, Kansas-Nebraska, the, Salmon Portland Chase on	12	547
Bimetalism advocated by John Sherman	15	1911
David Bennett Hill an advocate of	11	x
David Bennett Hill favors	13	1182
Bimetalist, Great Britain as, up to 1816	13	1187
Birth, place of, unimportant in the United States	13	1248
Bishops, supremacy of	14	1328
Bismarck, Otto von, biography of	11	244
On the German police	11	172
On War and Armaments in Europe	11	244
Remedy for social democracy proposed by	11	160
Blaine, James Gillespie, biography of	11	259
Eulogized by President McKinley	14	1402
R. G. Ingersoll on the character of	13	1253
Blaine, knight-errant of political chivalry	13	1253
On a Century of Protection	11	259
The "Plumed Knight"	13	1252
Bland, Richard Parks, biography of.	11	273
On Free Silver	11	273
Blenheim, battle of	13	1028
Blennerhasset and Burr	15	2135
Blood-drinker, Danton called a.	12	802
Blunt, Mr., at the Galway jail	14	1499
In the police court	14	1500
Boats, Kentucky	14	1704
Description of	14	1704
Bœotia, property held in	12	831
Boer War, disappointments of the	11	108
Speech on the, by Arthur James Balfour	11	99
Boker, George H., his bill for diplomatic contingent expenses	15	1925
Bonaparte, Joseph, his advice to Spanish-Americans in 1808	12	682
Napoleon, address of, to his army at beginning of the Italian campaign	11	290
Address of, to his soldiers during siege of Mantua	11	293
Address of, to his soldiers on entering Milan	11	291
Address of, to his troops after War of Third Coalition	11	293
Address of, to his troops on conclusion of first Italian campaign	11	292
Addresses of, to his army	11	289
And his army could not collect excise in the United States	14	1709
Biography of	11	289
His farewell to the Old Guard	11	295
Proclamation of, to his army	11	290
The fall of, George Canning on	12	494
(See, also, under NAPOLEON.)		
Bonds, the Cleveland administration thinks its debt paid by giving	15	1908
Six per cent. Federal, absorbed by the North	14	1699
Bones of dead Chinamen, transportation of, back to China	14	1580
Book, the Red	14	1706
Books as cheap in Asia as in New York	14	1589
Bosphorus, the, military importance of, to Russia	13	1092
Bossism condemned by Governor La Follette	13	1286
Boston Massacre, John Hancock on the	13	1125
Botzaris a household word in America	15	1929

	VOL.	PAGE
Bourbon, House of, England's unjustifiable efforts to restore the..	13	1027
Its restoration favored by England.	13	1014
Political iniquities of the.	13	1001
Boyle a Christian.	13	957
Bow Begum, her vain appeal to Middleton.	15	1893
Bowie-knife, the, in Kansas.	14	1591
Boys, how to train.	15	1775
Braddock's defeat.	13	1305
Bradford, William, a refugee for conscience's sake.	13	981
Brandywine, Washington at.	13	1306
Brave, sepulcher of the.	14	1569
Breastpin worn by son of Turkish minister.	15	1925
Breckinridge, John Cabell, address of, Preceding the removal of the Senate.	11	296
Biography of.	11	296
Brewster, William, the Pilgrim Father.	13	981
Bribe, the ten-million.	15	1946
Bright, John, biography of.	11	303
On redistribution of parliamentary seats.	15	1822
On the tie that unites England and America.	11	327
On the "Trent" Affair.	11	303
Britain, Great, position of, depends on her trade.	15	173
And the United States, relations between.	13	1300
Charged by General Butler with conniving at piracies of the "Alabama".	12	451
Compared with France and America.	14	1731
Position of, depends on her trade	14	1731
Sole obstacle to universal bimetalism.	13	1184
British colonies, dangers of slave insurrections in.	14	1625
Parliamentary pledge to continue slave-trade in.	14	1628
Punishment for murdering a negro in.	14	1628
British Empire, the, an appanage implying responsibilities.	15	1786
Great task of the.	12	539
British goods, high tariff on, in Australia.	14	1734
British post garrisoned from South Carolina.	11	441
British rule in South Africa, attempted destruction of.	11	107
British subjects only intended in the Declaration of Independence.	14	1363
British system of government, the ..	14	1643
British, the, excluded by tariff from trade of foreign dependencies.	14	1732
British trade excluded from the Drifts in South Africa.	14	1738
British troops, their contaminating influence in American colonies	13	1127
Brooks, Preston S., biography of.	11	328
On the Sumner Assault.	11	328
Brougham, Lord, biography of.	11	333
On oratory in its application.	14	viii
On the orator's first step in his art.	15	vi
On the preëminence of Greek models.	14	ix
Speech of, Against Pitt and War with America.	11	333
Speech of, on Negro Emancipation.	11	338
On written speeches.	14	viii
Brown, John, a Cromwellian dug from his grave.	14	1593
An alkali in the acid of wrongdoing.	14	1594
And the Spirit of Fifty-nine, Wendell Phillips on.	14	1588
A saint.	14	1601
Conscience of Virginia moved by	14	1595
Death of, William Lloyd Garrison on the.	13	1065
His courage.	15	2009
His great qualities.	14	1592
His unjust and hasty trial.	14	1591
No insurgent.	14	1590
No Republican.	14	1349
Peculiarity of his attempt.	14	1351
Sympathy of all parties for.	14	1600
Brownlow, Governor, his plea for Tennessee's readmission to the Union.	13	1058
Brutality, British, in American press	13	1301
Bryan, William Jennings, Answer to, by W. Bourke Cockran.	12	710
Biography of.	11	352
On the Income Tax.	11	352
Bryce, James, on South Africa.	14	1745
Bubble republic, bursting of the.	11	313
Buckner at Fort Donelson, his wise submissiveness.	13	1057
Buenos Ayres, periodicals of, in 1818.	12	685
Buffalo, address of William McKinley at.	14	1397
Pan-American Exposition.	14	1398
Buluwayo reached by the railway.	14	1736
Bullets, age of, yields to age of brains	14	1588

	VOL.	PAGE
Bulwer, Sir Henry, on the ground-		
work of the orator's art	14	vi
Bunker Hill, battle of	13	1306
Bunker Hill Monument Oration, by		
Daniel Webster	15	2090
Bureau, the Freedmen's, its object	15	1996
Bureaus of the people in Italy	14	1325
Burgess, one, summoned from Calais		
to Parliament	14	1424
Burgesses, House of, in Virginia	13	983
Burke, Edmund	11	ix
Biography of	11	368
His opinion of the Declaration of		
Independence	13	965
His style now out of date	12	xi
On Conciliation with America	11	368
On the freedom of dependencies,		
quoted by Senator Hoar	13	1213
Sheridan's eulogy on	15	1877
Burlingame, Anson, biography of	11	429
On Massachusetts and Sumner	11	429
Burr, Aaron, character of	15	2135
William Wirt against	15	2135
Bursting of the "bubble republic,"		
said of the Civil War	11	313
Business depression under the Glad-		
stone administration	15	1831
Business men of Chicago, their cour-		
age	13	1298
Butler, Benjamin Franklin, answers		
his calumniators	12	447
Biography of	12	445
On the Character and Results of		
the War	12	445
Butler, Charles, annotator of Coke	14	1719
Never read Adam Smith	14	1719
Butler, Pierce	14	1339
At the Congress of 1789	14	1339
Byzantine Septennat, in France, a		
disguised monarchy	13	1046
Byzantium, Siege of	12	836
Saved from Philip by Demos-		
thenes	11	41

C

	VOL.	PAGE
Cabinet ministers, seats given to, in		
Congress by the new Southern		
constitution	15	1938
Cable, a Pacific, to be laid	14	1402
Cæsar, a warning to Napoleon	12	513
An epoch-maker	13	896
Cited by Sheridan as an example		
of successful guilt	15	1877
His canon of honesty for kings	13	915
His image and superscription	13	1236
His mercifulness equalled by		
Washington's	14	1587

	VOL.	PAGE
Cæsarians, French republican party		
charged with being	13	1044
Cæsarism in France, a hideous leprosy	13	1047
Caird, John, observation of, that a		
speech cannot be repeated	14	x
On oratory in modern life	14	x
Calcutta, Warren Hasting's action in		
the Council at	15	1874
Caldwell, victim of British cruelty	13	1130
Calhoun, John Caldwell, biography of	12	457
His Last Speech, on Slavery	12	457
On dangers of patronage	12	785
On free trade and slavery as cor-		
ner-stones of party policy	11	266
On Nullification and the Force		
Bill	12	485
On the spoils system	12	797
California, Acquisition of, by the		
United States	13	939
Chinese labor in, more injurious		
than beneficial	14	1576
Discovery of gold in, its effects		
on prosperity of the country	11	268
People of, generous to a fault	14	1579
Self-government in	12	476
California, trip to, in 1849, liberalizing	13	1242
Caligula, his cruelty	14	1747
Callisthenes, decree of	12	829
Campaign, the presidential, of 1896,		
and William McKinley	13	1159
Campo Formio, treaty of	13	1021
Canaan, the curse of	14	1528
Canada, development of grain pro-		
duction in	13	1071
High tariff on British goods	14	1734
Unwilling to separate from Great		
Britain	14	1395
Canada, British colonies and, com-		
missioners of	14	1398
England, and the United States,		
Sir Wilfrid Laurier on	13	1297
Canal, Isthmian, to be built	14	1402
Canal bill, the Hepburn	14	1490
Canandaigua, treaty of, between the		
United States and the Six		
Nations	14	1728
Candles, wax, two thousand, lighted		
the palace at Athens	15	1928
Caney, El, heroes of	11	228
Cannibalism at British deliverance		
of Naples	13	1026
Canning, George, biography of	12	494
On the Fall of Bonaparte	12	494
Why his name is to be honored	13	1088
Cape Colony, its attitude towards re-		
form	14	1741
Paid for British intervention	14	1738

	VOL.	PAGE
Capital, corporate, not to be indiscriminately assailed...........	15	1778
Invested in Eastern [New England] lands, dwindles in value.	13	1070
Capitalist magnates to German Emperor on assassination of Empress of Austria.............	11	161
Capital punishment, not the most powerful of deterrents.......	14	1746
Robespierre against...........	14	1746
Capo d'Istria, a household word in America....................	15	1929
Caprivi, fall of, how hastened.......	11	160
Carlyle, Thomas, his definition of poetry.....................	11	xvi
On public speaking............	12	vi
Carnot, Lazare Nicolas Marguerite, biography of..............	12	510
Against Imperialism in France.	12	510
Carr, victim of British cruelty.......	13	1130
Carroll, Daniel, at the Congress of 1789.....................	14	1339
Carthage, the modern, England as...	12	507
Carthagena, British expedition against, aided by American colonists..................	11	25
Cart-whip, abstract love of the, Canning's phrase of the Jamaica slave system...............	13	910
Caserio, the assailant of Carnot.....	11	160
Castelar, Emilio, biography of......	12	517
On the Abolition of Slavery.....	12	523
Speech of, a Plea for Republican Institutions................	12	517
Castel de Nuovo, Naples, British treachery at................	13	1026
Castes and classes in England.......	14	1705
Castile and Aragon, sovereigns of the patrons of Columbus........	13	979
Catherall on perspicuity...........	15	vii
Catherine of Russia................	14	1607
Cato, the elder, his denunciation of Carthage...................	13	1275
Cato, the younger, cause of his suicide	12	523
Caucasians and Europeans once slaves	15	1850
Caucus, a Tory, Bright's description of House of Lords as........	15	1829
Caucus system, the, its advantages to the Democratic party.......	15	1857
Cavalier party in the Commonwealth	12	747
Cavité, heroes of..................	11	228
Cavour, Count Camillo Benso di, biography of..............	12	530
On Rome and Italy...........	12	530
Cawn, Hyder Beg, his villainy......	15	1892
Cayuga Indians..................	14	1728
	VOL.	PAGE
Censure of the Senate unjust to President Jackson...............	11	208
Census of laboring population.......	12	690
Centennial, the, of the battle of Yorktown......................	13	1138
Of the Declaration of Independence.....................	13	1138
Of the United States Supreme Court....................	13	1138
Cephisophon of Rhamnus, ambassador to Philip...............	12	828
Cervera, his fleet at Santiago.......	14	1400
Cession of the Philippines to the United States a necessity of the situation...............	15	1915
Chaffee, General, popular misapprehension of his official report...	13	928
Chamberlain, Joseph, biography of..	12	536
On Splendid Isolation.........	12	541
On the True Conception of Empire.....................	12	536
Chambers, upper parliamentary, originated in England...........	13	1050
Channing, W. E., on rhetoric.......	15	viii
Chaplin, Mr., his speech on protection	13	1079
Charity, law of, carried out by the Apostles.................	14	1331
Two-fold, spiritual and corporal.	14	1330
Charlemagne, a controller of historic crises.....................	13	896
Charles Stuart plots against the Commonwealth..................	12	748
Charles I., of England, execution of..	11	168
Charleston, S. C., rebellion in, considered as a riot...............	12	446
Charlestown, Mass., destruction of...	14	1316
The heights of, refuge of defeated British....................	13	985
Va., people of, terrified by John Brown....................	14	1596
Charter, The People's, Macaulay on..	14	1377
Six points of the people's.......	14	1379
Charters and laws give to Ireland equal rights with England....	13	1113
Chartists, Macaulay's fairness to....	14	1383
Petition of, quoted from.......	14	1381
Their proposed remedy delusive.	14	1384
Chase, Salmon Portland, biography of.........................	12	547
On the Kansas-Nebraska Bill...	12	547
Chase's amendment, object of its author.......................	13	937
Chateaubriand on a representative republic...................	13	984
Châtelet, Court of the.............	14	1479
Chatham, Earl of.................	11	ix
Biography of.................	12	563

VOL. PAGE

Chatham, Earl of, his leaving the Commons fatal to British policy in America.............. 15 1787
On the Right of Taxing America 12 563
Cheating favored by change in currency standard............. 12 716
"Cheers for the living, tears for the dead," sentiment in Ingersoll's "Vision of War"............. 13 1240
Chesterfield, on the human face..... 15 viii
On necessity of style............ 14 v
Chicago, its characteristic festival... 13 1298
Robbed in tax payments by fraud and forgery.......... 13 1285
Chicago fire, horrors of the......... 13 1298
Chief-Justice of India an accomplice of Hastings, so declared by Sheridan.................... 15 1879
Child, Lydia Maria, sympathy of, with abolition, roused by John Brown.................... 14 1601
Childe Harold, Byron's, quoted by William M. Springer......... 15 1929
Children, against pampering........ 15 1775
Of dead soldiers, educated by the state at Athens......... 14 1571
Should be taught the meaning of Scriptural words......... 15 1774
Chinamen owned body and soul by the Chinese Six Companies... 14 1580
Chinese, the, as lawbreakers........ 14 1574
Exclusion of the, George Clement Perkins on............ 14 1572
Immigration of, no partisan question.................... 14 1572
Number of, in the United States. 14 1573
Secret societies among........ 14 1575
Their unsanitary way of living.. 14 1580
Choate, Rufus, biography of........ 12 575
On the Preservation of the Union 12 575
Christ Church, Boston, beacon light on, in April, 1775.......... 13 985
Christian, John Locke a............ 13 957
Sir Isaac Newton a........... 13 956
Christianity, right to attack the sanctions of, denied.............. 13 954
Testimony of great intellects to the truth of................ 13 957
The basis of British law........ 13 954
The foundation of the British judicial fabric............... 13 956
Truths of, celebrated by all the best and wisest............. 13 959
Why attacks upon, by lovers of liberty, are deplorable....... 13 961
Why Deists cannot hurt....... 13 960
Chunar, Chief-Justice Impey at..... 15 1889

VOL. PAGE

Chunar, Treaty of................ 15 1884
Church, a, without a bishop, in New England.................. 13 1230
Of England, the, and free trade. 12 704
The Spanish, an enemy to the human conscience........... 12 519
Churchill, Lord Randolph, biography of............................ 12 592
On the Desertion of Gordon.... 12 592
Cicero, Marcus Tullius, biography of. 12 598
Calls eloquence republican..... 14 ix
Fourth Philippic of........... 12 598
On different kinds of orators.... 14 vi
On dignity of oratory.......... 14 vi
On excellence of oratory........ 14 vii
On the Agrarian Law.......... 12 604
On the perfect orator.......... 14 xii
Quoted on the secret of eloquence.................... 11 xiv
Says writing is the best training for speaking................ 11 xxii
Cinderella of the Cape, Rhodesia is the..................... 14 1735
Citizen, French, what makes a...... 14 1752
An honorable, described by Demosthenes. .*................ 12 888
A well-disposed, two things characterize.................... 12 891
Citizenship, American, conditions of obtaining................... 13 1143
American, sacrificed to Chinese labor...................... 14 1576
French, after the Revolution... 14 1537
National.................... 11 ix
State....................... 11 ix
Civil authority, supremacy of the, over the military, essential in a republic.................. 13 1258
Civil government, its end.......... 13 1126
Modifications of the Gospel superior to.................... 14 1326
Civil servants, requisites in........ 12 787
Civil service, appointments in, dictated by public considerations.. 12 788
Qualifications for the.......... 13 1145
Examinations, for the, objections to, answered........... 12 796
Civil War, benefits of the, to the South. 11 195
Results of the................ 11 187
Civilization, American standard of, despised by Chinese immigrants..................... 14 1572
Based on mutual confidence.... 12 716
Law the first essential of....... 15 1767
Of the Filipinos and that of Americans compared........ 11 80

	VOL.	PAGE
Clark, Champ, biography of	12	615
On the Annexation of Hawaii	12	615
Classes and caste in England	14	1705
Clay, Henry, biography of	12	632
On Dictators in American Politics	12	632
On The American System	12	642
On the Compromise of 1850	12	663
On the dangers of patronage	12	785
On the Emancipation of South America	12	676
On the Seminole War	12	672
Tariff views of	13	1141
Clement XIV a victim of assassination	11	168
Cleon of Cottiocidæ, ambassador to Philip	12	828
Clergy, the, how taxed	14	1424
Cleveland, Grover, biography of	12	687
His approval of large, low-priced importations	15	1907
Declared the McKinley Act inefficient for revenue	15	1906
His plan for meeting the deficiency	15	1910
On Tariff Revision	12	687
Cleveland, the city of, John Brown's courage in	14	1592
Climate, the English, favorable to labor	14	1703
Clitarchus	12	836
Clymer, George, in Congress of 1789	14	1339
Coal-beds, English, cities favored by	14	1705
Coal consumers robbed of two hundred millions by coal operators	13	1284
Coal-fields, anthracite, controlled by railway company	13	1283
Coal in England	14	1705
Coaling stations, need of, by the United States navy	13	1144
Coal problem, Governor La Follette on the	13	1283
Cobden, Richard, biography of	12	698
On Free Trade with All Nations	12	698
Cochrane, Lord, terrorized the French with one vessel	12	449
Cockran, William Bourke, biography of	12	710
His Answer to William J. Bryan	12	710
William J. Bryan's financial ideas opposed by	11	x-xi
Coercion in Ireland	14	1508
Coin, sense of the term	13	1225
Coinage, free bimetallic, its advantages	13	1183
Free bimetallic, what it has effected	13	1185
Collier, Jeremy, on the countenance of the orator	15	viii
Collusion, friendly and fraudulent, familiarity of Hastings and Middleton	15	1887
Colonial government, Spanish and English, contrasted	13	983
Colonies, American, constitutions of, varied	14	1427
American, early government of	14	1426
American, how founded	14	1425
American, how harassed by Great Britain	14	1315
American, of various kinds	14	1425
Charter	14	1425
Disputes between, referred to England	14	1426
French, commissioners of	14	1398
Greek, in Asia	14	1424
In the reign of Charles I	14	1425
Not dependencies	12	537
Not for profit of mother country	12	537
The twelve united	14	1313
Tyrian, in Africa	14	1424
Were represented in British Parliament	14	1428
Colonists, early American, their character and aims	13	1229
Colony, a great and unterrified, Virginia	14	1717
Color question, the, in South Africa	14	1742
Northern zeal without knowledge on the	15	1940
Colored races take the British side in South African difficulties	14	1731
Colton, remark of, on antithesis	15	viii
Criticism of oratory by	14	vi
Columbian Exposition, the, its spirit and object	13	905
Columbian Oration, the, by Chauncey Mitchell Depew	13	893
Columbus, Christopher, as one of the world's benefactors	13	898
Controller of a great historic crisis	13	896
His offer to John of Portugal	13	897
His place in the history of liberty	13	979
His promises	13	978
His time of sailing epochal	13	895
Intellectual improvement since day of	13	903
Interest roused by the theories of	13	898
The apostle of human equality	13	894
Comet, nebulous tail of a, Democrats in free states compared to	15	1857
Commandment, Christ's new	14	1330

VOL. PAGE

Commerce, agriculture and encouragement of, essential in a republic. 13 1258
Dangers to American. 14 1454
Of America, its object. 13 1278
Of Great Britain, unrivaled. . . . 14 1643
Of Spanish America, restricted by Spain. 12 681
Of the United States, early, due to Southern capital. 14 1699
Of the United States, power of Congress to regulate. 15 1937
Of Venice and Genoa, its object. 13 1277
We have, not freedom, Ireland's complaint. 13 1101
Common ground, the orator must meet his audience on. . . . . . . 13 xii
Commons, House of, its authority. . . 15 1829
Commonwealth, a great, never established by natural religion. . . . 13 961
Spirit of ancient Athenian. 12 868
Compact between Schouvaloff and Salisbury in 1878 denounced by W. E. Gladstone. 13 1094
Company, the Virginia. 14 1425
Compensation, requirement of, for British depredations. 14 1407
For disturbance bill. 14 1375
Competition, agricultural, between Eastern and Western states. . 13 1069
Excellence of. 12 654
Reduces price of manufactures. 12 654
Strangled by trusts. 12 693
United States agriculture in, with British. 13 1069
Without hostility. 14 1398
Competitive examination the only remedy for spoils system. . . . 12 796
Compromise, the Missouri, abrogated by the Democratic party. . . . 15 1861
The Missouri, its effect. 12 667
The Missouri, its provisions. . . . 12 551
Of 1850, Henry Clay on the. . . . 12 663
Acts, a mutual concession. 12 665
Conciliation with America, Edmund Burke on. 11 368
Condemnation of Louis XVI, Camille Desmoulins advocates the. . . . 13 913
Condition, a, and not a theory. 12 695
Miserable, of the masses. 14 1333
Of savings-banks, published. . . . 15 1777
Of commerce, the new, under the trust system. 15 1776
Confederation, African, attitude of the Dutch towards. 14 1741
American, based on Batavian and Helvetic models. 11 2

VOL. PAGE

Confederation, American, articles of, too weak for union. 13 896
Canadian, a compromise. 14 1389
Canadian, and American precedent. 14 1392
Canadian, Sir John A. Macdonald on. 14 1387
German, the, formed dikes and palisades for German protection. 11 249
In South Africa, advantages of. . 14 1740
In South Africa, prospects of. . . . 14 1745
United States styled a, by John Randolph. 14 1713
Confidence, mutual, the basis of civilization. 12 716
Confiscated, exportable products of America. 14 1412
Conflict, irrepressible, between slavery and free labor, the Civil War an. 15 1853
Irrepressible, The, William Henry Seward on. 15 1849
Congress, duty of, to meet deficiencies. 15 1909
Fifty-sixth, its eminence. 14 1492
Pan-American. 14 1403
Power of, to interfere with slavery. 11 19
Relation of, to taxation. 14 1447
Slavery in territories not to be prohibited by, according to the Dred Scott decision. 14 1356
State legislatures and, agents of the people. 14 1452
Taxation as governed by. 13 1123
Congresses and Reunions, Catholic, in Italy. 14 1334
Conkling, Roscoe, biography of. 12 719
Speech of, Nominating General Grant for a Third Term. . . . 12 719
Connecticut votes for the tariff bill. . 14 1715
Connections of England, how treated by her. 12 768
Conquest, Athenian empire of Periclean age extended by. 14 1564
And annexation, spirit of, repudiated by a republic. 13 1043
Conscience, freedom of, its result. . . 13 969
Consciences, American, troubled by Philippine war. 15 1842
Consequences of East India Company's importation of tea. 13 1133
Conservatism, Lord Beaconsfield on. 11 143
Considerations, public, alone should dictate civil service appointment. 12 788

VOL. PAGE

Conspiracy, foul and unmanly, of Warren Hastings........... 15 1886

Constantinople, 1453, fall of, its results....................... 13 976

Constitution, Athenian, original at Athens.................... 14 1565

British, changeable by Parliament...................... 14 1462

British, its fundamental principle......................... 14 1319

British, in a moving state 14 1423

British, one of its wisest provisions...................... 15 1938

British, peculiar excellency of the 12 764

British, Robespierre's opinion of the...................... 14 1753

British, subverted by the taxation of Americans........... 13 965

Freest, in Europe, enjoyed by France..................... 13 989

French, revision of the......... 15 1828

Of the Confederate States...... 15 1936

Of the Confederate States, secured all ancient rights, franchises and liberties.......... 15 1936

Of the United States, and amendments, the frame of the government................... 14 1338

Of the United States, being republican, by the Democratic party made aristocratic...... 15 1863

Of the United States, defects in the...................... 14 1392

Of the United States, evolved from Articles of Confederation and completed in May, 1787. 11 14

Of the United States, framers of the, and slavery............ 14 1338

Of the United States, Jubilee of the, John Quincy Adams on the...................... 11 8

Of the United States, modeled on the British.............. 14 1392

Of the United States, Marshall on the 14 1440

Of the United States, objects of its formation............... 14 1709

Of the United States, quoted by Garfield 13 1059

Of the United States, under what conditions to be amended.... 13 1056

Of the United States, Jackson charged with violating the... 12 640

Constitutional history of the United States in oratory............ 11 ix

Constitutional Laws, Leon Gambetta on the................... 13 1043

VOL. PAGE

Contention, political and religious, caused by Chinese immigration...................... 14 1574

Contract labor of Chinese worse than African slave-labor.......... 14 1576

Contra-dance, American minister leads a, with the Queen of Greece.................... 15 1927

Control of slavery by Federal authority.................... 14 1339

Controversialist, rights of a......... 13 954

Controversy, the Tilden, Daniel Wolsey Voorhees on............. 15 2021

Contumacy of the Begums alleged by Middleton................. 15 1888

Convention of Tennesseans........ 11 113

With Nicaragua and Costa Rica. 14 1490

Conviction, aggressive, characteristic of free eloquence............. 12 v

Cook, Joseph, and Ingersoll, contrasted.................... 12 x

Coolies in the United States........ 14 1575

Cooper Union Speech, Abraham Lincoln's.................... 14 1337

Coöperation, Aguinaldo's, with Dewey against the Spaniards....... 15 1837

Copenhagen, battle of, its consequences................... 12 672

Corcoran, Patrick, of the Cork "Examiner".................... 14 1502

Corn laws, arguments for their repeal 14 1542

Repeal of, proposed by Peel.... 14 1539

Corner-stone Address, the, by Alexander Hamilton Stephens.... 15 1936

Cornwall in the Gladstone re-distribution scheme.............. 15 1825

Cornwallis, Lord, quoted on Virginia. 14 1717

Corporations, great, their legal limitations.................... 13 1142

How to safeguard the people's rights from................. 15 1778

Large, would not feel free trade. 15 1780

Not to be punished because they are big..................... 15 1778

Public-service, their control of city, state, and national legislatures.................... 13 1285

Corrupt government of the Transvaal 11 100

Corruption of Greek states by Philip. 12 831

Corwin, Thomas, speech of, Against War with Mexico........... 12 724

Biography of................. 12 724

Cosenza, enslaved................. 14 1467

The memory of its martyrs..... 14 1468

Country, our, when right to be kept right; when wrong to be put right...................... 15 1848

	VOL.	PAGE
Courage, as well as honesty, must go to make character	15	1772
Athenian, its character	14	1566
Court of last resort, war is the	13	1061
Court, Supreme, influenced in Dred Scott decision	15	1861
Cousins, Robert G., biography of	12	738
On the "Maine" Disaster	12	738
Covenant, the presidential, with the people	13	1138
Cowardice, Demosthenes charged with	11	41
Cradle of Liberty, Faneuil Hall the	13	1270
Crassus, the punisher of Spartacus	12	526
Crawford's law of 1820, degrading effect of	12	794
Sinister object of	12	793
Credit, individual, at an end in the United States	14	1711
Creditor nation, America a	13	1163
Crime, inexpiable, of the Jews	14	1545
Criminals suffer worse things than death	14	1748
Crises of history, men who have controlled	13	896
Crisis in South Africa, Cecil Rhodes on the	14	1730
Croats, whiskered	14	1512
Croly, Archbishop, and free trade	12	703
Cromwell, Oliver, biography of	12	741
Cited by Sheridan as an example of successful guilt	15	1877
Controller of a great historic crisis	13	896
Napoleon and, resemblances between	13	1016
On the Dissolution of Parliament	12	741
Sincerity of, questionable	13	1016
Crowley, P., San Francisco Chief of Police on the Chinese	14	1575
Crown, Oration of Demosthenes on the	12	821
Crown Point, Americans possess themselves of	14	1318
Cruelties, English, towards men of other races	13	1206
Of Warren Hastings	15	1885
Cruelty and oppression of British troops	13	1127
Ctesiphon, opinion of, concerning Demosthenes	12	834
Party to the proceedings against Demosthenes	12	822
Prosecuted on account of Demosthenes	12	824
Cuba, American treatment of, a cause for pride	15	1766

	VOL.	PAGE
Cuba and the Philippines, their relations to the United States different	15	1919
Commissioners of	14	1398
Described by Castelar	12	524
Forests of, 15,000,000 acres in extent	11	235
Horrors of slavery in	12	525
How treated by the United States	13	1196
Soap-and-water, common-school civilization for	11	235
Spanish cruelties in	15	1916
Cubans, the, superiority of the Filipinos to	11	78
Cultivation, the small, advantages of, on British farms	13	1077
The small, on peasant properties	13	1077
Culture involved in oratory	13	vii
Cunning of Chinese law-breakers	14	1575
Curran, John Philpot, biography of	12	764
His Farewell to the Irish Parliament	12	769
His method of practicing declamation	11	xix
On Government by Attachment	12	774
Overcomes natural disabilities in oratorical studies	11	xix
Speech of, In Behalf of Rowan	12	764
Currency, national, question of, a question of honesty	12	711
President Cleveland suggested national bank notes as the sole	15	1910
Single standard of, in Sweden, Denmark, Italy, and Belgium	13	1222
Curtis, George William, biography of	12	780
Speech of, His Sovereignty Under His Hat	12	780
On the Spoils System	12	782
Curtis, Judge, his opinion on negroes and the Constitution	14	1358
On the scope of the Constitution	14	1358
Custom-house of New York, civil service reform in the	12	791
Cyprus, cession of, to England, a bribe	13	1096
The possession and administration of, worthless to England	13	1096
Cyrsilus, punishment of, for unpatriotic counsel	12	868
Czar Nicholas, attitude of, towards Austria	11	250
Czar of Russia, the, Cecil Rhodes on	14	1737

D

| Dagger, the theory of the, by Mazzini, quoted | 14 | 1368 |

	VOL.	PAGE
Dakota half a century ago	15	1769
Population of, compared with that of five original states	13	1139
Dallas, Secretary of Treasury, 1815, advocated protection	12	649
Damascus, road to, taken by Governor Taft	13	930
Danton, Georges Jacques, biography of	12	799
Characterized by Castelar	12	524
Defamed	14	1433
His speech, Let France be Free	12	800
His speech, Squeezing the Sponge	12	802
His speech, To Dare Again, Ever to Dare	12	799
Quoted by Charles Sumner	15	1959
Dardanelles, military importance of the	13	1093
"Dare Again, Ever to Dare," maxim of Georges Jacques Danton	12	799
Darien, Isthmus of	14	1491
Canal across	14	1481
Davis, Cushman Kellogg, biography of	12	804
One of the makers of the American treaty with Spain	13	923
On the United States in Hawaii	12	804
Davis, Jefferson, biography of	12	815
Speech of, on Withdrawal from the Union	12	815
Day, William R., one of the makers of the American treaty with Spain	13	923
Dawes, Charles G., dictum of, on a great man	12	x
Dawes, Senator Henry L., on the spoils system	12	783
Dead in battle, the, how honored at Athens	14	1563
Dead men not assailed by envy, sentiment of Pericles	14	1570
Death as a legal penalty, essentially unjust	14	1746
Debate and action, Athenian eminence in both	14	1566
Debating society, advantage of frequenting the	11	xviii
Debt, national, the, interest of, must be paid	14	1385
Public, of the United States, engrossed by Northern people	14	1699
United States, bought by North to its enrichment	14	1699
Debts, English laws exact payment of	14	1705
Decalogue, qualities expressed by the, are paramount	15	1771
Decatur, a, for Virginia	14	1590
Decay of the Roman republic, Sallust on the	14	1724
Decision, Dred Scott, based on assumed history	14	1357
Decisions, judicial, of varying authority as precedents	14	1357
Judicial, two uses of	14	1357
Declamatory act of Parliament enslaves Ireland	13	1104
Declaration of Independence, Burke's opinion of the	13	965
Centennial of the	13	1138
Its inclusiveness, according to Lincoln	14	1361
The, did not apply to negroes	14	1358
Declaration of Right required by Ireland	13	1104
Decree proposed by Robespierre in the National Assembly	14	1756
Defalcations, alarming, about 1838	14	1647
Lessons taught by	14	1658
Of the Government, Sargeant Smith Prentiss on the	14	1646
Defense, Jean Paul Marat's	14	1433
Defenses, public, systematically commenced by President Jackson	11	214
Deficiency in the treasury discreditable to the United States	15	1908
Deists cannot hurt Christianity	13	960
Delaware, Washington crossing the	13	1306
Delawares, the, help of, refused by Jefferson in a war with the European powers	13	1264
Warned by Jefferson not to disturb traffic on the Mississippi	13	1264
Deliberate courage of the Athenians	14	1566
Delicacies at Athens, native, added to by importation	14	1565
Delphic utterances of hope, in reconstruction times, deluding	13	1057
Deming, Mr., his propositions to prevent secession	13	1061
Democracy, Christian, in Italy	14	1325
Christian, Pope Leo XIII, on	14	1323
Christian, the term objectionable to some	14	1325
Christian, what it ought to be	14	1326
Its favorite maxims	14	1441
Its financial results appalling	13	1232
Originated at Athens	14	1565
Preferred to monarchy	14	1440
Social, would abrogate the right of ownership	14	1326
Democrats of Phlya, ambassador to Philip	12	828

	VOL.	PAGE
Democratic hatred of centralism, conspicuous in Andrew Jackson	11	124
Democratic Party, disclaiming by the, of the policy of slavery extension	15	1860
In free states, a mere appendage.	15	1857
Its record	15	1860
Sectional and local	15	1587
Democrats, non-slavery, as unreasonable to look for as Protestants in the Roman Propaganda	15	1857
Demosthenes, according to Æschines, an oratorical roarer	12	viii
Æschines against the crowning of	11	38
Æschines on the delivery of the Oration on the Crown by	12	vii
Biography of	12	821
Crimes imputed to	12	824
Describes his early training	12	878
Describes the fortune of his life	12	879
Hesiod quoted against	11	39
How he fortified Athens	12	887
Imitated by Brougham, in defense of Queen Caroline	11	viii
Oration of, On the Crown	12	821
Private life and public measures of	12	823
Proved incorruptible by Philip	12	887
Spoke for the liberties of Greece.	11	viii
Undefeated by ambassadors of Philip	12	875
Denmark, agreement between England and	14	1412
Departments, heads of, given seats in Congress by the Southern constitution	15	1938
Dependencies, British, support British trade	14	1732
Depew, Chauncey Mitchell, biography of	13	893
His Columbian Oration	13	893
Depons, his testimony to Spanish oppression	12	681
On character of Spanish Americans	12	684
Depression, agricultural, in England, reciprocity a quack remedy for	13	1078
Business, under the Gladstone administration	15	1830
Derby, Earl of, biography of	13	908
On the Emancipation of British Negroes	13	908
Desmoulins, Camille, Speech of, Advocating the Condemnation of Louis XVI	13	913
His charges against Louis XVI.	13	915
Biography of	13	913
Despatches, bilingual, of the minister to Greece	15	1926
Despot, President, in office	14	1393
President, Jackson traduced, as a	11	213
Despotism, free labor and, incompatible	15	1852
Spanish colonial, described	12	680
The slave oligarchy an awful	13	1065
The spoils system perverts a republic into a	12	787
Destiny, manifest, a freebooter's plea	12	629
A pernicious phrase	12	628
Of mankind, a community in	13	1273
Destruction, Italy governed to	11	178
Of barbarism, cost of	12	539
De Tocqueville on public opinion in France	14	1589
Developments, economical, during the McKinley administration.	13	1162
Dewey, George, Admiral, Aguinaldo's forces armed by	15	1837
And McKinley, on the Philippine question	13	921
His brilliant feat of arms	15	1835
His victory desecrated by "criminal aggression "	15	1846
On the character of the Filipinos.	15	1836
On the intelligence and capacity of the Filipinos	11	78
On the superior intelligence of the Filipinos	15	1836
Why he called for troops to Manila	15	1915
Dexter, Samuel, Red Jacket's Reply to	14	1726
Diabolical traffic in life of the last Napoleonic wars	13	1011
Diaz, Porfirio, his dictatorship	15	1844
Dictators in American Politics	12	632
Difficulty, the Egyptian, and Arabi.	15	1809
The South-African (Boer) War.	11	99
Dinas Island Speech, The, by Charles Phillips	14	1583
Dingley bill, effect of the	13	1163
Favors sugar kings and annexation	12	622
Dionysius of Corinth	14	1719
Dionysius of Halicarnassus, opinion of, that oratory requires laborious study	14	ix
Diplomatist, McKinley as a	13	1161

VOL. PAGE

Directory, Napoleon's message to the, on the British government 13 1021

Disability, civil, of Roman Catholics not inflicted for religious error. 14 1546

Discovery of the system of a representative republic styled by Chateaubriand a great event.. 13 984

Disgrace to British government, Gordon's fate a................. 15 1817

Disinterestedness professed by Cromwell...................... 12 756

Disraeli, his assumed confidence in Sir Robert Peel............. 14 1540

Disraeli, his venomous attacks on Peel........................ 14 1540

Dissension, in discussing social problems, danger of............. 14 1334

Distress, agricultural, in England.... 13 1068

Dockyards and arsenals, national, slavery abolished in........ 15 1858

Dole, Sanford B., and the annexation of Hawaii.................. 12 626

Dolliver, Jonathan Prentiss, on the American Occupation of the Philippines................. 13 919

Biography of................. 13 919

On the Philippines........... 11 xi

Domain, the unsettled national, dedicated by the Ordinance of 1787 to free labor.......... 15 1854

Domestic and Foreign affairs, William Ewart Gladstone on..... 13 1068

Donelson, Fort, Buckner at........ 13 1057

Donoughmore, Lord................ 14 1522

Don Quixote and Sancho Panza, Charles Sumner compares two Senators with............. 15 1957

Doughfaceism, Northern, on the slavery question............... 11 266

Douglas, Stephen Arnold, biography of........................ 13 933

His Nebraska bill............. 14 1360

His pro-slavery speech at Columbus, Ohio.................. 14 1337

In the Dred Scott decision...... 14 1357

On the authority of the Supreme Court..................... 14 1358

Quoted by Abraham Lincoln... 14 1337

Reply of, to Lincoln.......... 13 933

Douglass, Frederick, did not discover the needs of the negro race.. 15 2016

Placed on social equality with whites..................... 13 940

Dramatic power of Ingersoll........ 12 viii

Dreams, the, of poetic youth, become next day the charter of nations................... 14 1600

VOL. PAGE

Dred Scott case, The.............. 15 1855

Dred Scott Decision, Abraham Lincoln on the................. 14 1361

According to Lincoln, erroneous. 14 1357

Contains two propositions...... 14 1356

Court divided in the.......... 14 1356

Not unanimous............... 14 1358

Passed by a judiciary fixed in Democratic interests........ 15 1860

Tended to spread slavery through the territories.... 15 1855

"Dregs and rinsings of human intellect," said of modern economists...................... 14 1718

Dreyfus iniquity, the............. 15 1846

Drifts question in South Africa...... 14 1738

Dryden's Virgil, quoted by Gladstone 13 1097

Dulcinea del Toboso, allusion to, by Sumner.................... 15 1957

Dutch, the, attitude of, on the question of African confederation. 14 1741

Dynamite explosion, the Salford.... 14 1371

E

Earnestness, not loud............. 12 viii

Easthope, Sir J., and the Chartists.. 14 1386

East India Company, the, allowed to import tea to colonies....... 13 1133

East Indies, the, treaty provisions concerning................. 14 1418

Ebal and Gerizim, cited by Garfield as an example to the republic. 13 1063

Eblis, Hall of, in Beckford's "Vathek," scene in the................ 14 1595

Ecclesiastes, quoted by Cromwell... 12 756

Economists, modern, a feeble herd.. 14 1718

Economy in public expenditures.... 13 1220

Education, in oratory, what it involves...................... 13 vii

In republics, Montesquieu on.. 11 203

Of the young in American history, inculcating Patriotism.. 11 205

Popular, not sufficient without spiritual teaching........... 15 1771

Public, in England, due to American example............... 13 969

The Foundation-Stone of Republican Government, Judah Philip Benjamin on......... 11 200

Edward the First and the Marches of Wales.................... 14 1424

Egypt, interests of England in...... 15 1819

Election, popular right of, an essential principle of the United States government.......... 13 1258

Primary, a, how it should be conducted................... 13 1286

	VOL.	PAGE
Election, The Tilden-Hayes, Allen Granbery Thurman on	15	1986
Polish, a	14	1724
Election laws, reform of	13	1147
Elections, primary, importance of, discussed by Governor La Follette	13	1286
Electors, American, must be educated	13	1147
Elegance and frugality combined at Athens	14	1566
Eleusis	12	830
Elizabeth, Queen	14	1607
Elk river	14	1701
Elliot, Sir Henry, on English support of Turkey	13	1091
Eloquence, a good style essential to	11	xiv
Introduction by George F. Hoar.	11	xiv
Eloquence of St. Paul on Mars' Hill	12	v
Of the Sermon on the Mount	12	v
Strained, irrational	12	xii
The secret of, eludes analysis	11	xiv
What it is, according to Castelar	12	518
Emancipation, Catholic	14	1510
Catholic, Rowan's plea for	12	766
Catholic, the Duke of Wellington on	15	2107
Negro, Lord Brougham on	11	338
Of Caucasians, recent	15	1850
Of slaves, Jefferson on	14	1350
Of Spanish America, moral causes of	13	990
Proclaimed in the French Convention	12	523
Emancipation Proclamation, the, expanded national industries	13	1140
Emancipator, Lincoln the great	12	780
Embargo, the, recommended by Jefferson	11	263
Embassies, the principal occupied, up to 1861, by Southerners	15	1935
Emerson, C. W., on the Power of Oratory	13	v
Emerson, Ralph Waldo, quoted	13	ix
Essays of, as speeches	12	xi
Emigration, early Athenians averse to	14	1564
Emmet, Robert, biography of	13	941
Denies being an emissary of France	13	945
Deprecates the dishonoring of his memory	13	947
His Protest against Sentence as a Traitor	13	941
Emmons on the rules of rhetoric	15	vii
Emperor, history of the word	13	975
Emperors, Roman, half of them murdered	13	1024
Empire, British, the, defined	12	538
British, Shakespeare s description of the	15	1806
British, strength of the	12	543
Lust of, not found among Americans	15	1916
Questions of, Earl of Rosebery on	15	1785
Responsibility of	15	1807
The North contending for, remark of Lord John Russell	11	314
The word, in what sense used of Britain	15	1786
True conception of	12	536
"Empire and Liberty," not applicable to England	13	1097
Emuckfaw and Tohopeka, battles of, won by Andrew Jackson	11	118
Encyclical letters, effect of, told by Pope Leo XIII	14	1324
England, advantages of the institutions of	14	1705
Called "a nation of shopkeepers"	11	25
Crushed the aspirants to universal dominion	13	1098
Described as the seat of progressive liberty	13	980
During the American Civil War	12	451
Her advantages as a manufacturing country	14	1689
Her superiority in manufacture	14	1703
Is greatest strategist of history	11	239
Surrender of legislative authority offered by, to America, in 1778	13	1109
To share the fate of vanished empires	14	1586
Treatment of Napoleonic countenancers by, arbitrary	13	1010
Sufficiency of, for her own requirements	12	503
Englanders, Little, have not ceased to exist	12	545
Rhodesia's constitution the best reply to	14	1734
English Bible, the, the purest fountain of English speech	12	xi
English colonies, slave trade in, destructive to England	14	1629
English Lecompton bill, its basis	15	1861
Englishmen apostrophized by Whittier	13	1299
Entangling engagements, avoidance of, the fourth principle of Gladstone's foreign policy	13	1086
Entertainment, Arabian Nights cited	14	1724
Envy spares the dead	14	1570

	VOL.	PAGE
Epochs, one of the greatest in American history, the secession	15	1936
Three epochal men, in United States history, marked by the history of the Senate	11	300
Equality, before God and men, the one idea of republicans	15	1864
For America, demanded by Jackson	11	128
Of rights, in South Africa, Dutch views concerning	14	1743
Of trade, in Madagascar	14	1732
What it meant at Athens	14	1565
Error, religious, not punishable by law	14	1545
Errors of the legislator who inflicts death	14	1748
Equilibrium between legislative representation of North and South	12	461
Eras, three, in the history of slavery in the United States	12	559
Erskine, Lord Thomas, advocate of freedom of the press	13	1217
Biography of	13	949
Quoted by Senator Hoar	13	1215
Speech of, Against Thomas Paine	13	949
Eubulus of Anaphlestus, ambassador to Philip	12	828
Eulogy of Washington by Charles James Fox	13	1025
Europe, concert of its maintenance the third principle of Gladstone's foreign policy	13	1086
Enriched by experience of America	13	904
European affairs, American policy regarding	13	1143
Authority overridden by the agreement of Salisbury and Schouvaloff	13	1096
Statesmen, their selfish policy towards America	13	1140
Eutaw Springs, battle of	13	1307
Evarts, William Maxwell, biography of	13	962
On what the Age owes to America	13	962
Evasion of the legal obligations, protected in John Randolph's day	14	1705
Everett, Edward, biography of	13	972
On the History of Liberty	13	972
Example, American, old world enlightenment due to the	13	900
Excise, commissioners of, inquisitorial	14	1707
Hardships of	14	1707
In the United States, declared impracticable	14	1708

	VOL.	PAGE
Excise, System of, in the United States, impossibility of, predicted	14	1709
Exclusion of foreigners, the best policy of France	13	1043
Exclusiveness, trade, is obsolete	14	1402
Execution, public, called cowardly assassination	14	1747
Executive, the, why unable to reform civil service	12	790
Exotics, foreigners who remain	12	652
Expansion, imperialism and, distinguished	15	1847
In Africa, British	14	1731
In South Africa, Sir William Harcourt an opponent of	14	1735
In trade a pressing problem	14	1402
Of American territories, from 1789 to the present day	11	233
Expedient, how a word of tyrannical import	13	1101
Expenses, diplomatic, of the minister to Turkey	15	1925
Exports, British, increased by free trade	13	1084
American, in foreigner's hands	14	1689
Exposition, the Pan-American	14	1398
Expositions are the timekeepers of progress	14	1398
Expunging resolution, the, of Colonel Thomas Hart Benton	11	208
Extermination dreaded by Filipinos under the Americans	11	82

F

	VOL.	PAGE
Fairfax, Lord, representatives of	14	1463
Falsehood of Warren Hastings, Sheridan on the	15	1876
Fame, the, of founders of states	13	963
Of the signers of the Declaration of Independence	13	963
Fanaticism, its origin	15	1940
Fanatics, in the cause of false liberty	15	1944
Faneuil Hall, speech in, by Louis Kossuth	13	1269
Farewell Address, Washington's, warnings contained in	14	1347
Farini, his "Roman States," quoted	14	1368
Farms, hill, in Scotland, high rents of	13	1073
Farragut, Admiral, between Port Hudson and Vicksburg	12	448
Fashoda Settlement	14	1737
Fathers, the, their opinion on slavery supports Republicans	14	1346
Favoritism, personal, the root of the spoils system	12	793

	VOL.	PAGE
Federal Constitution, the, Alexander Hamilton on	13	1117
Federal control of slavery, acknowledged by Georgia	14	1339
Tacitly acknowledged by North Carolina	14	1339
Federal Government, the, and State legislatures	13	1176
Objections to the	14	1443
Federalist, The, cited by Garfield	13	1059
On the Presidential veto	11	217
Federalists, Spanish, do not threaten property	12	518
The, and Anti-Federalists	13	1172
Federal Republicans, Spanish, their platform	12	518
Fénelon, on the use of oratory	15	v
Ferdinand and Isabella, relations of, with Columbus	13	978
Ferdinand VII of Spain, his rule intolerable in South America	13	990
Feudal system, failure of the	13	894
Feudal system, the, made men masters and slaves	14	1511
Feudatories of the British Empire knit together by the Boer war	11	108
Few, William, at the Congress of 1789	14	1339
Filipinos, a people fighting for their rights	13	1195
Character and capacity of the, by Augustus Octavius Bacon	11	77
Compared with Cubans and Mexicans	15	1836
Congress has not declared war with the	13	1195
Did not expect subjugation by the United States	15	1839
How slandered	15	1836
Nearest in civilization to Americans	11	80
Only Christian nation of Asia	13	1209
Only Christian people in Asia	11	79
Ordered to leave Manila	15	1840
Ought to be granted freedom and independence	15	1844
Practically allies of the United States	15	1838
Refused audience during peace negotiations with Spain	15	1840
Superior to the Cubans	11	78
Their dread of extermination through American occupation	11	82
Financial conditions under Cleveland, caused by deficiency of revenue	15	1908
Fingal, Lord	14	1517
Fist-fight, a, and coming to the point	12	ix
Fitzsimmons, Thomas, at the Congress of 1789	14	1339
Flag, March of the, by Albert J. Beveridge	11	224
Question of the, in Africa Confederation	14	1740
Raising the, over Fort Sumter, Henry Ward Beecher on	11	180
Flathead reservation, the	15	2017
Fleet, Athenian, successes of the	14	1567
British, depredations of the, among American shipping	14	1316
Cervera's	14	1400
Florida held by colored Union troops	12	448
Force, as a factor of government, before Christ	13	894
Forces, Athenian, how distributed and employed	14	1566
Forehead of Democratic party, laws of slavery written on the	15	1862
Form and function, the married harmony of	13	1241
Fort Franklin, an Indian murdered at	14	1727
Fort Pitt, an Indian murdered near	14	1727
Fort Sumter, Raising the Flag over, Henry Ward Beecher on	11	180
Fortunes, making of, benefits the community	15	1762
Of war, destruction of Spanish fleet at Manila, one of the	15	1921
Foundation, the original American government built on a sandy	15	1939
Founders of American Constitution, Alexander Hamilton one of the	11	ix
The, of American liberty and prosperity	13	1217
The, of states, their fame	13	963
Four million bodies in chains	13	1240
Four million souls in fetters	13	1240
Fox, Charles James, biography of	13	994
Charles James, his eulogy of Washington	13	1025
Charles James, his ignorance of Adam Smith	14	1719
Charles James, his political erudition	14	1719
Charles James, On the Rejection of Napoleon's Overtures	13	994
Charles James, lauded as a public debater by John Randolph	14	1719
Foxe, John, his "Book of Martyrs"	15	1868
Frame of the government, the, is the Constitution and amendments	14	1338
Framers of the government, the, the 39 who signed the original instrument	14	1338

	VOL.	PAGE
France, connection of, with Emmet's rebellion	13	945
Covetous of Egypt	13	991
Republican after American model	13	969
Shuts out English manufactures.	14	1733
Small land properties in, not favorable to the production of wheat	13	1074
Francis, G. H., observation of, that eloquence is power	14	vii
Franco-Prussian campaign, completeness of German successes in the	11	136
Franklin, Benjamin	14	1585
On liberty and country	15	1856
Noted anti-slavery man	14	1343
Frederick the Great, his stubborn perseverance	12	621
Free coinage of silver, advocated by W. S. Holman	13	1221
Freedom, how destroyed by institution of standing armies	13	976
Human	14	1737
Idea of, in Declaration of Independence	13	902
Love of, in Charles Sumner	13	1291
Love of, should inspire British foreign policy	13	1087
Lovers of, opposed to advocates of power	13	1172
Of conscience, as a promoter of religion	13	969
Of the press, and the people's sovereignty	13	970
To the slave who touches British soil	12	767
Free labor, contrasted with slavery	15	1851
German in origin	15	1851
Or slavery, antagonistic systems of, in the United States	15	1853
Free press, advantages of a	13	950
Free ships make free goods	14	1411
Free Silver, Richard Parks Bland on.	11	273
Free Soilers, the, and Kossuth	13	1276
Free States, Democratic party not a party of all the	15	1857
Free trade, at time of Calhoun, one of the corner-stones of Democratic policy	11	266
Gladstone's belief in	14	1732
Good results of, in Great Britain.	13	1083
Lowered property values, 1817–1824	12	643
Merely the British colonial system	12	651
Ruined commerce and navigation, 1817–'24	12	643
Freight rates in coal transportation, their exorbitancy	13	1284
French and Dutch plans against British India in 1784	13	1023
French National Convention, Thomas Paine to the	14	1532
French Republic, the President of the, not a monarch in expectation	13	1049
French Revolution, the wars of, enriched the United States	12	647
Consequences of the, in European political opinion	12	501
French trade policy in Madagascar	14	1732
Friendly rivalry in industrial competition, advantages of	14	1398
Friendly sentiments of Jefferson towards the Mandan Indians	13	1262
Frontier, Alaskan, the, a stumbling-block	13	1300
Froude, James Anthony, his dictum that free nations cannot govern subject provinces	11	86
Influence of his writings	12	537
Frye, William Pierce, biography of	13	1030
One of the makers of the American treaty with Spain	13	923
On the Republican Party	13	1030
Fugitive Slave Act of 1850	15	2008
Fugitive Slave Bill	12	558
Fugitive Slave Law, the, a Democratic measure	15	1859
Of 1850, a concession to the South	15	1933
Unconstitutional	11	432
Webster's opinion of the	11	437
Fundamental fact of American life, acceptance of the law of work is the	15	1761
Funeral oration, after Leuctra, Demosthenes chosen to speak the	12	884
At Athens, difficulties of delivering the	14	1564
Fyzabad, the palace of, scene of violence in	15	1892

G

	VOL.	PAGE
Gage, General, hostile attempts of	14	1318
Galena, price of lead at, under the tariff	12	655
Galgacus, his advice to ancient Britons	12	631
Gama, Spanish American	12	684
Gambetta, Leon, biography of	13	1037
On the Constitutional Laws	13	1043
To the Delegates from Alsace	13	1037
Ganges, the river, a scene of suffering under Warren Hastings	15	1873

	VOL.	PAGE
Ganilh, Charles, alluded to by John Randolph.	14	1717
And other economists, on tariff problems.	14	1719
Gates, General Horatio, Washington's praise of.	13	1307
Garfield, James Abram, biography of	13	1054
At the Republican convention of 1880.	12	781
On the Restoration of the South.	13	1054
Garrison, William Lloyd, biography of.	13	1065
On the Death of John Brown.	13	1065
Geese, Capitoline, the.	14	1709
Gem, the Indian's, costs more than it comes to.	15	1926
General government, preservation of the, essential to good government in the United States.	13	1258
Genet, M., reason of his recall from Washington.	12	454
Genoa, English oppression of, in Napoleonic wars.	13	1010
George II., a glorious monarch.	13	1127
His mistresses.	14	1723
Act of, on slave trade.	14	1628
"George Griswold," the, sent to feed the starving poor of Lancashire	12	450
Georgia, internal improvements in, under the Confederate Constitution.	15	1937
German origin of free labor.	15	1851
German police and anarchists, Bismarck on.	11	172
German soldiers, why superior to Russians or French.	11	252
Germantown, Washington at.	13	1306
German unity, due to American example.	13	969
Germany, English manufactures shut out by.	14	1733
Position of, as a war power, between France and Russia.	11	248
Seizure of Samoa by.	13	1031
Gestures, rules for use of.	11	xviii
Gettysburg, Lincoln's speech at.	12	v
Ghent, treaty of, disturbs native American commerce.	12	648
Gibbon, Edward, describes no such depravity as that of Warren Hastings.	15	1891
His account of the fall of the Alexandrian Serapeum.	13	1054
On foreign dependencies, quoted by Senator Hoar.	13	1214
Gibson, Mr., on Gladstone's Egyptian policy.	15	1817
Giddings, Joshua R., in Chicago convention.	12	781
Gideon, cited by Cromwell.	12	749
Gilman, Nicholas, at the Congress of 1789.	14	1339
"Give me liberty, or give me death," sentiment of Patrick Henry.	13	1181
Gladstone administration, business depression under the.	15	1831
Gladstone government, the bloody and cowardly.	12	595
Gladstone, William Ewart, an autocrat.	15	1832
Apostle of Midlothian campaign.	15	1814
Biography of.	13	1068
His acquiescence in Russia's extensions in Asia.	13	1090
His delay in the Khartum crisis.	15	1815
His selfish employment of political victory.	15	1824
His unconstitutional innovations	15	1832
On Domestic and Foreign affairs.	13	1068
On expansion in South Africa.	14	1731
Quoted by D. B. Hill.	13	1183
Right in logic, wrong in practice.	14	1732
Glasgow, ships built at, ostensibly for China, during the Civil War.	12	450
Glorious period of life.	14	1569
God and the people, their relations.	14	1469
God's dealings with the Jews, cited by Garfield.	13	1062
Gold, as coin, its prestige gone.	13	1235
Demand for, instead of notes, caused by deficiency.	15	1907
"Golden Eagle," piracy of the.	12	448
Golden Rule, importance of the.	15	1771
Goldsmith, Oliver, quoted by Henry Alexander Wise.	15	2143
Good, the doing and preventing of.	14	1376
Goods, British, excluded by Canada.	14	1734
Gordon, General, Lord Salisbury on the Abandonment of.	15	1808
At Khartum, did not ask for troops.	15	1814
His fate predicted by Lord Salisbury.	15	1812
Letter of, from Khartum.	15	1817
Mission of, to Khartum, absurd.	15	1811
The Desertion of, Lord Randolph Churchill on.	12	592
The sending of, to Khartum, an act of folly.	15	1816
Gospel, laws of the, superior to human contingencies.	14	1326
Of Matthew, xxv. 35, quoted by Leo XIII.	14	1330

	VOL.	PAGE
Governed, consent of the, doctrine of	13	1216
Governing elements, public opinion and education as	14	1589
Government, an independent, for the Filipinos	15	1844
A system of, based upon popular judgment, superior to one of pomp and precedent	11	4
At home, a good, the first principle of Gladstone's foreign policy	13	1086
By the unseen, in South Africa	14	1744
Confederate, the, first in history built on foundation of slavery	15	1939
Consolidation of, the worst of evils	13	1173
Corrupted for party uses	14	1656
Essential principles of the, expounded by Jefferson	13	1258
Executive department of the, two-thirds of officers in the, Southerners, up to 1861	15	1935
Filipino, should be in harmony with their own notions	15	1844
First principles of, dissertation on	14	1533
Framers of the, their view of slavery	14	1338
Frequent changes in the national, undesirable	14	1380
Good, the sum of, what it is	13	1258
Independent Filipino, at Malolos	15	1841
Judicial decisions of the, to be obeyed	14	1358
Military, extended over the Philippines by President McKinley	15	1842
National, objects of the	14	1445
The Federal, and the control of slavery	14	1338
The Federal, controlled by the South up to 1861	15	1934
Powers of the, overrated	14	1384
Without consent of the governed, a contradiction	14	1590
Without consent of the governed, unrighteous	13	1216
Governments, how they oppose their true end and object	14	1702
In the Philippines, Spanish, American, and Filipino, compared	15	1841
Gradual abolition of slavery, consideration of	14	1639
Graham, Sir James, on the Crimean War	11	325
Grain, price of, how depressed in the United States	13	1071
Grain, price of, under free trade and under protection, compared	13	1084
Produced upon large properties of France	13	1075
Production of, in Canada, development of the	13	1071
Unprecedented production of, in the United States	13	1070
Granada, capture of, an epoch in European history	13	897
Grant, Ulysses S., and the Alabama claims	13	1031
Unhindered by inadequate salaries of his cabinet	15	1925
His common sense	13	1155
His part in the spoils system	12	792
In civil service reform	12	790
Nominating, for a Third Term, speech of Roscoe Conkling	12	719
Surrender of civil service reform by	12	791
Granville on suitableness in style	14	v
Grattan, Henry, speech of, against English Imperialism	13	1100
Biography of	13	1100
Gray, George, one of the makers of the American treaty with Spain	13	923
Gray, Thomas, on Milton, quoted by Lord Erskine	13	958
Great Britain, Address to the People of, by Richard Henry Lee	14	1313
Censure and imitation of, by the United States	14	1706
Greatheart, Bunyan's hero, alluded to by Theodore Roosevelt	15	1770
Cited by Theodore Roosevelt	15	1775
Greatness, British, built on an amalgamation of races	14	1733
Greece, republics of, flourished under mild laws	14	1749
Republics of, short-lived	13	973
Greek colonies in Asia	14	1424
Greene, General Nathanael	13	1307
Greenville, the treaty of	13	1263
Treaty of, closed the Indian wars	13	1265
Grenville, George, and Lord North, preferred to tariff proposers	14	1712
Grievances, American, enumerated by Burke	11	410
Charged by the North to England during the Civil War	12	453
Of Uitlanders to be redressed	14	1737
Grote, George, on oratory	15	v
Grotius quoted	15	2010
Guttenberg, Johann, forged the hammer of liberty	13	895

H

	VOL.	PAGE
Habeas Corpus Bill, the	13	1111
Hale, Lord, Chief-Justice, referred to.	14	1431
Hall, J., on sophistry	15	viii
Hamilton, Alexander, biography of..	13	1117
Noted anti-slavery man	14	1343
On the Expediency of Adopting the Federal Constitution.	13	1117
On the presidential veto, in The "Federalist".	11	217
Hamlet, Shakespeare's, quoted by R. B. Sheridan.	15	1889
Hancock, John, biography of	13	1125
On the Boston massacre	13	1125
Hannibal, his patience equaled by Washington's.	14	1587
Hanover, the treaty of	15	2027
Harbors, subjects for retrenchment.	14	1660
Harcourt, Sir William, and the South African railway.	14	1736
Defeated at Derby by the imperialists.	14	1736
On an African transcontinental railway.	14	1736
An opponent of Cecil Rhodes	14	1735
Hardinge, Sir Henry.	15	1871
Harper's Ferry, another Lexington	14	1591
John Brown at	14	1590
John Brown's enterprise at	14	1349
Not a Republican.	14	1349
Harrison, Benjamin, biography of..	13	1137
Calls dogmatic free-traders "students of maxims, not of markets "	11	260
Inaugural Address of	13	1137
Harrison, William Henry, swept away by the spoils system	12	792
Hartington, Lord, on Gladstone's delay in the Gordon matter	15	1815
On local government in Ireland.	14	1505
On redistribution.	15	1823
Hartz River, Boer commando on	14	1738
Harvard, Cuban teachers visit	13	1202
Harvey, Lord, and the Grand Duke of Tuscany.	13	1009
Recalled on complaint of Grand Duke of Tuscany.	13	1010
Hastings, Warren, accountable for the crimes of his agents	15	1900
And his tool, Middleton, at odds.	15	1887
Erskine's defense of, based on the necessity of injustice in subjugating dependencies	13	1215
His duplicity.	15	1874
His tribute to Burke's eloquence	11	xvi
Pocketed a bribe.	15	1884
	VOL.	PAGE
Hastings, Warren, treachery of, suspected by Nabob of Oude	15	1892
Hat, His Sovereignty Under His, speech of George William Curtis.	12	780
Hawaii, Annexation of, Champ Clark on the	11	xi
Annexation of, pushed by sugar kings.	12	622
As a strategic base	12	617
Climate of, unfit for Anglo-Americans.	12	622
Of no use to the United States..	12	617
Porto Rico and, fields for American immigration	11	235
The Annexation of, Champ Clark on	12	615
The United States in, Cushman Kellogg Davis on	12	804
Three reasons for annexing	12	619
Unprofitable to the United States.	12	616
Hay, John, biography of	13	1149
His poem, "Little Breeches," quoted.	15	1928
On William McKinley	13	1149
Hayes, Rutherford B., his part in civil service reform	12	792
Hayne, Robert Young, and Daniel Webster.	11	x
Biography of.	13	1170
His predictions concerning the effect of the protective tariff in 1824.	12	644
On Foote's Resolution	13	1170
Reply to, speech of Daniel Webster.	15	2053
Hayti, slave insurrection in	14	1350
Hazewell, Governor, his fame	13	1272
Hazlitt, William, on the requisites in an orator.	14	vii
Heart and conscience, as well as mind, need education	15	1771
Hebrews, Epistle to the, quoted by Cromwell.	12	761
Helots, British, in the Transvaal	14	1742
Henry IV, of France, a victim of assassination	11	168
Henry VIII, first to issue parliamentary writs in Wales	14	1424
Henry, Patrick, and the cry of treason	15	1962
Biography of.	13	1178
On the Federal Constitution	14	1441
To the Convention of Delegates.	13	1178
Hepburn Canal Bill, the	14	1492
Herbert, Lord, and affectation in oratory.	15	v

	VOL.	PAGE
Hereditary nobles, all Eastern countries, save Turkey, possess	14	1707
Hermitage, Jackson retires to the	11	130
Heroes in the palace at Athens	15	1929
Hesiod, quoted against Demosthenes	11	39
Hicks, in the Sudan, wretchedly equipped	15	1810
Highlanders, after Culloden, emigrate to America	13	981
Hildebrand an epoch-maker	13	896
Hildreth, E., on the rarity of oratory	15	v
Hill, David Bennett, biography of	13	1182
Speech of, For Bimetalism	13	1182
Hillsborough, the unprovoked murders planned by	13	1128
History, American, best learned from study of political speeches	11	viii
Not all the chapters of alike important	13	972
True, is the history of liberty	13	973
Hoar, George Frisbie, biography of	13	1194
On the Philippine occupation	11	xi
Quotes the "Ars Poetica" of Horace	11	xiv
Repeats Brougham's advice to oratorical students	11	viii
Speech of, on Subjugation of the Philippines	13	1194
Hödel and Nobiling not social democrats	11	163
Hofmeyr, Jan, unpopular in the Transvaal	14	1739
Holland a model for America	14	1443
Relations of, with Spain	14	1424
Holman, William Steele, biography of	13	1220
On Economy in Public Expenditures	13	1220
Home Rule, John Morley on Irish	14	1497
Homer, Athenians need no	14	1567
Quoted by Daniel Webster	15	2102
Honesty, first, courage next, brains last, in character	15	1772
Horace, "Ars Poetica" of, quoted by George Frisbie Hoar	11	xiv
Quoted by John Randolph	14	1704
Quoted by Lord Chatham	12	567
Quoted by S. P. Chase	12	549
Horan, Alderman, his bold defiance of English custom laws	13	1107
Horse-power of steam engines in the United States, in 1860 and in 1890	13	1243
Hospitality of Virginians, the	14	1716
Hostilities, cessation of, upon what based in the Philippines	15	1922
Hottentots, the Irish people styled	14	1506
House, a man's, his castle	14	1528
House of Commons, Irish, the, bought by British gold	15	1869
Houston, Sam, on the government of the territories	12	476
Hugo, Victor, and "the road to Damascus"	13	930
Huguenots, Christian liberty brought by the	13	1217
Driven by Louis XIV to America	13	981
Humboldt, Alexander von, on the character of South Americans	12	684
Hume, David, on Jewish prosecutions	14	1557
On the methods of Louis XIV	13	1003
Humphreys, B. G., his proclamation in reconstruction times	13	1057
Hungary, restored liberties of, due to America	13	969
Hunnicut, in exchange	15	2001
Huxley, on the value of the Bible	15	1772
Hypocrites, French republican party accused of being	13	1044

I

	VOL.	PAGE
Idea, Republican party owes strength to its one	15	1864
Ideal civil service, unattainable	13	1145
Ideas, starting of, results in violence	14	1593
Strangle statutes	14	1601
Idealism in statesmanship	13	1198
Ideals in statesmanship, what they have effected	13	1199
Sentimentalities and, political, practical uses of	13	1199
Ideas, comparison of, educational	14	1983
Of Jefferson, on slavery, fundamentally wrong	15	1939
Ignorance of Chinese immigrants	14	1573
Illinois, Lincoln the glory of	13	1298
Illustrious men, the world the sepulcher of	14	1569
Iloilo, why the Spaniards evacuated	15	1921
Immigration, American, prospective, in Hawaii and Porto Rico	11	235
Chinese, a severe law needed to check	14	1573
Chinese, no partisan question	14	1572
To America, nations represented by	13	905
To the United States should not be indiscriminate	13	904
Immorality the cause of misery among workingmen	14	1329
Immortality of Pitt, character of the	11	337
Imperialism, American, meaning of	15	1834
English, Henry Grattan against	13	1100

	VOL.	PAGE
Imperialism in France, Carnot against	12	510
Policy of, Carl Schurz on the...	15	1834
Imperialists, why British workmen are	14	1733
Imperial sentiment, solidarity of....	12	541
Impey, Sir Elijah, Chief-Justice of Bengal, a perjurer..........	15	1880
Importation increased the delicacies of Athens..................	14	1565
Imprisonment for debt, abolition of, in the United States........	13	1248
Improvements, internal, provided for in the Confederate constitution	15	1937
In the harbor of Charleston, to be provided for by local tax..	15	1938
Inaugural Address, First, of Thomas Jefferson..................	13	1255
Incarnation, Milton on the.........	13	958
Incas of Peru, Spanish despotism erected on ruined stones of the	12	680
Income tax, Ward McAllister on the.	11	365
In Defense of His Colleagues, address of Justin McCarthy....	14	1365
Indemnities, France, Naples, and Denmark, compelled by Andrew Jackson to pay........	11	213
Independence, American, Samuel Adams on.................	11	21
And Union of America inseparable.....................	13	967
Declaration of, the, compared with Magna Charta and the Petition of Rights..........	13	901
Declaration of, importance of the, in history..............	13	962
Declaration of, its meaning....	14	1362
Declaration of, world-wide importance of the.............	13	901
Filipinos deceived as to American recognition of...........	15	1839
Filipino struggle for..........	15	1836
Of Spanish America, important to the United States in 1818..	12	683
Should be guaranteed to Filipinos.....................	15	1844
The Child, born in speeches of James Otis..............	11	viii
India, British, plans of French and Dutch against..............	13	1023
British, Egypt the road to.....	15	1819
Indian populations, ten states relieved from incumbrance of, by Andrew Jackson........	11	215
Indians, the, elevated by the Jesuits.	15	2017
Jefferson promises justice and protection to..............	13	1267
Warned by Jefferson against joining English forces......	13	1267
Indictment of Ctesiphon, text of the.	12	833
Indignity to Knights of Malta by Paul of Russia............	13	1013
Individual, and his Property, Stirner's book on the..........	11	165
Industrial development can be controlled by law..............	15	1777
Industrial importance of the Chinese.	14	1573
Industrial success an international asset.....................	14	1399
Industries, American, blighted by Chinese immigration........	14	1572
And labor of Americans not considered in Cleveland policy...	15	1907
Expanded in every direction by the Emancipation Proclamation.......................	13	1140
Infant, falsity of the term......	12	689
Inferiority of the negro, a truth of slow development...........	15	1939
Ingalls, John James, biography of..	13	1229
On the Political Situation...	13	1229
Ingersoll, Robert G., biography of..	13	1238
His oratorical bearing........	12	viii
His redundant rhetoric tedious.	12	xi
Never spoke loud as an orator..	12	vi
On "Blaine—the Plumed Knight ".................	13	1252
On "The Vision of War "......	13	1238
Reunion Address by..........	13	1241
What orations of, will live.....	12	vii
Ingraham, Captain, dictating terms to the fleet of the Cæsars....	14	1591
Inquisition, the Holy.............	14	1599
The Spanish, treatment of the Jews by.................	14	1561
Insanity and fanaticism, compared..	15	1940
Insincerity fatal to eloquence......	12	xv
Instability of popular government without a senate............	13	1119
Institutions, American, not studied by the Chinese immigrant....	14	1573
English, and English policy inseparable..............	14	1706
Insubordination, military dangers of.	12	676
Insurrection among slaves, Republicans charged with stirring up	14	1348
Intellectual and literary power of the Bible......................	15	1774
Intervention of Great Britain in South Africa................	14	1738
Invasion, foreign, fatal to democracy	15	1847
Invention, modern, results of.......	14	1399
Success in, an international asset	14	1399
Inventions, mechanical, embitter labor difficulties..............	14	1323
Ireland, condition of..............	14	1507

	VOL.	PAGE
Ireland, famine in	14	1540
Governed by laws of English Parliament	13	1104
Grattan's description of the condition of	13	1106
Of America, Kentucky the	12	652
The case of, contrasted with that of the colonies	14	1431
Irish, the, driven by oppression to America	13	981
Submission of the, causes English oppression	13	1108
Iron, imported by the Confederate government, and tariff of millions paid on it	15	1938
Isaiah, book of, quoted by Cromwell.	12	747
Quoted in Christ's answer to John the Baptist	14	1330
Isolation, Splendid; Joseph Chamberlain on	12	541
Istamboul	15	1930
Italians made bloodthirsty by oppression	11	177
Italian unity, revival of, due to America	13	969
Italy, cry of, "Out with the foreigners"	13	1043
Governed to destruction	11	178
Her tradition of glory	14	1471
Income tax in	11	354
Joseph Mazzini, To the Young Men of	14	1467

J

	VOL.	PAGE
Jackson, Andrew, and the spoils system	12	792
Arbitrary rule of	14	1654
Bancroft on	11	110
Benton on the Political Career of	11	208
Clay's estimate of	12	636
Conscientiously refuses to sign address to Washington	11	115
Defied United States Bank and Congress in 1832	11	217
Dictum of, "the Union: it must be preserved "	11	126
First taught the country the meaning of the veto	11	217
His action towards the Senate condemned	12	637
His arbitrary military conduct	12	674
His piety	11	130
Last hours of	11	131
Opened up the West	11	123
Pioneer aspect of	11	112
Popularity of, in Tennessee	11	116

	VOL.	PAGE
Jackson, Andrew, practically impeached	12	636
Quoted by W. S. Holman	13	1228
Retires to the Hermitage	11	130
Secret of the greatness of	11	132
Shamelessly and lawlessly condemned by the Senate	11	212
Traduced as a despot	11	213
Veto, tribunitial, revived by	11	124
War trophies of	11	220
"Jacob Bell," capture of the	12	448
Jael and the Canaanite captain	13	1156
Jaghires, the seizure of, by Warren Hastings	15	1879
Jamaica, cruelty of slave law in	13	909
Rebellion of Coromantine negroes in	14	1624
Twenty-seven thousand negroes imported to, in two years and a half	14	1624
Jamestown	14	1597
Janissaries, political, turned out from military academy	14	1721
Janus, temple of, never closed in British empire	12	539
Japan, a country where tortures and death have increased crime	14	1748
Jefferson, Thomas, allusion to	11	x
Biography of	13	1255
First imperialist of the republic.	11	233
His feelings on taking the presidency	13	1259
His ideas on the tariff and the surplus	11	262
His letter on British seizures	14	1413
Ideas of slavery held by	15	1939
Inaugural Address of, 1801	13	1255
On civil service appointments	12	788
Speech of, to the Chiefs of Various Indian Tribes	13	1265
To Beaver, the head warrior of the Delawares	13	1263
Trading houses among the Mandan Indians to be established by	13	1261
To the Wolf and People of the Mandan nation	13	1260
Jeffreys, Judge George	14	1599
Jesuits, the	15	2016
Jews, not debased	14	1559
Reparation due to	14	1556
Sir Robert Peel on the Disabilities of the	14	1544
Johnson, William S., at the Congress of 1789	14	1339
Joint-stock companies, as essentially democratic	12	653

	VOL.	PAGE
Jokes not found in Webster's speeches	12	vii
Jones, Paul, on the coast of England	12	448
Jonson, Ben, on the use of words	15	viii
Journal, Dublin, the, its contents	14	1519
Juan, San	11	228
Judas Iscariot and the race of Benedict Arnolds, descendants of, among Democrats	12	455
Judges, in the American colonies, made agents of oppression by England	13	1133
In the American colonies, refused British pay	13	1133
Judges' Bill, the	13	1111
Judgment on crime by a free people needs no legal procedure	13	917
Judicial fabric, British, based on Christianity	13	956
Judiciary, Federal, defended	14	1455
Federal, objections to the	14	1458
Judson, L. C., on clearness and conciseness	15	vi
Junius, and falsehood in wit	15	viii
Junta, Filipino, its proclamation of welcome to Americans	15	1837
Jupiter, Dodonæan, declared fortune of Athens good	12	878
Jurisdiction of Great Britain owned by the colonies	14	1426
Jurisprudence, a monument to	13	1217
Jury, trial by, how established in the United States	14	1465
Jus commercii	14	1547
Jus honorum	14	1547
Jus suffragii	14	1547
Justice, charity and, linked together by Christ's law	14	1331
Asked for by the South in 1850	12	483
For Ireland, Daniel O'Connell on	14	1522
Sacred to Christian Democracy	14	1326
To all men, equal and exact, essential to good government	13	1258

K

	VOL.	PAGE
Kansas, agitation in, upon slavery	15	1859
Charles Sumner on The Crime Against	15	1952
Democratic party forced a slave code upon	15	1859
Its central position	15	1953
Kent, Chancellor, on the establishment of distant territorial governments	11	85
Kentucky, operations of the Union armies in	12	447

	VOL.	PAGE
Kenyon, Lord, on church reformers	13	953
Khartum, fate of garrison at	15	1811
Khedive's throne shaken	15	1810
Kidnapping of slaves in Africa	14	1631
King, horror felt by Romans for the title of	13	975
King, Rufus	14	1339
At the Congress of 1789	14	1339
Stood for prohibition of slavery	14	1341
Voted for slavery prohibition in Congress, 1819–'20	14	1341
Kings, divine right of	13	977
Divine right of, challenged by American independence	13	904
Mediæval, more tyrannous than the Cæsars	13	977
Kingston, a coal depot for Confederate boats during the Civil War	12	449
Kipling, Rudyard, quoted by Robert G. Cousins	12	740
Knowledge, of men, required in the orator	13	xiii
Power and, need in dealing with trusts	15	1781
Know-nothingism, Henry Alexander Wise on	15	2141
Kolokotronis, a household word in America	15	1929
Kossuth, Louis, biography of	13	1269
His speech in Faneuil Hall	13	1269
On American prosperity and intelligence	13	1271
Krüger, Stephanus Johannes Paulus, and conventions	14	1476
And the British Empire	14	1737
His importance overestimated	14	1737

L

	VOL.	PAGE
Labor, among people of the Pacific Coast	14	1575
And legislation	15	1762
Charitable, how to be conducted	14	1330
Chinese, debasing	14	1576
Chinese, not independent	14	1577
Colored, in California	14	1743
Free, its results in America	15	1851
Free, prevailed in Europe, excepting in Russia and Turkey	15	1852
Honorableness of	14	1577
Of the Chinese immigrant, servile	14	1573
Organized, against the annexation of Hawaii	12	624
Servile contract, of China, to be wiped out in the United States	14	1576
Labor and capital, relations between	14	1324
Their proper relations	13	1233

	VOL.	PAGE
Lacedæmon, Tyrtæus, the poetic orator of	11	v
Lacedæmonians, reliance of, upon confederates in war	14	1566
Lafayette, Washington's letter to, on slavery	14	1347
La Follette, Robert Marion, biography of	13	1281
His address on Which shall Rule, Manhood or Money?	13	1281
La Fontaine, quoted by Thiers	15	1975
Laguna, Province of, guerilla warfare in	13	927
Lamar, Lucius Quintus Cincinnatus, biography of	13	1289
His Eulogy of Charles Sumner	13	1289
La Marck, meeting of, with Mirabeau	14	1481
Lamia, Keats's, cited by Wendell Phillips	14	1589
Land-holding system of Scotland, not to be safely changed	13	1073
Land in Great Britain and New England, prices of, compared	13	1070
Land league, the Irish, object of its foundation	14	1374
Land, monopoly of, complained of, by the Chartists	14	1382
America has one-seventh of the world's good land	13	1247
Small properties in, not advantageous	13	1074
Landor on bad oratory	14	ix
Lands, public, Senate resolution on	15	2054
Langdon, John, at the Congress of 1789	14	1339
Lasthenes, his treachery	12	832
Latitudinarianism of President Jackson	12	635
Laurier, Sir Wilfrid, biography of	13	1297
On Canada, England and the United States	13	1297
Law, a cruel, concerning slaves	15	1945
As a factor in prosperity	15	1762
British, based on Christianity	13	955
Contempt for, in Spain	12	519
Marcus Tullius Cicero, on the Agrarian	12	604
Natural and Christian, imposes obedience	14	1328
Predominance of, needed in the commercial world	15	1777
Scientific proof of	15	1812
The first essential of civilization	15	1767
The McKinley, better than that of Wilson	15	1907
The odious, of 1793, its repeal urged by Thaddeus Stevens	15	1948
Lawlessness of educated and influential classes, its result	13	1142
Laws, American, not respected by Chinese	14	1574
Inflicting the death penalty, the work of tyrants	14	1747
Roman code of, tyrannical	14	1314
Lee, Henry, biography of	13	1304
His Eulogy of Washington	13	1304
Lee, Richard Henry, biography of	14	1313
His Address to the People of Great Britain	14	1313
Lee, Robert E., his common sense	13	1155
In Virginia	13	1057
Left, the, in French legislature, Gambetta belonged to	13	1052
Legislation, American right of, infringed by the British government	14	1314
Canadian, between 1841 and 1867	14	1388
Remedial, required against the influx of Chinese	14	1579
Legitimate monarchy, attempt to restore, in France, shameless	13	1045
Leicester, Joseph, his speech in Trafalgar Square	14	1372
Leo XIII, Pope, biography of	14	1323
On Christian Democracy	14	1323
Quotes Mark vii. 2	14	1330
Leonidas, his land trod by slaves	14	1585
Lèse-majesté, a crime invented by tyrants	14	1747
Letters, proportionate number of, annually posted to each inhabitant in the countries of Europe	13	1246
Revived by arrival of Greeks in Italy	13	976
Leuctra, allusion to	12	825
Defeat of, Demosthenes disclaims responsibility for the	12	875
Epitaph on those who fell at	12	885
Measures of Demosthenes after battle of	12	876
Not decided by want of Athenian preparation	12	887
Not regretted by Æschines	12	886
Thebans victorious at battle of	12	843
Levelers, the, their treachery	12	750
Levre, Antoine de, his advice to Charles V	13	915
Lewis, Captain, sent by President Jefferson to visit the trans-Mississippi Indians	13	1260
Lex Porcia, effects of, at Rome	14	1749
Lexington, battle of	14	1591

	VOL.	PAGE
Liberal government, the, its blindness in the matter of Gordon.	15	1815
Liberality, mutual, of the Athenians.	14	1567
Liberal ministry, members of the, called eccentric comets.	15	1813
Liberals, the, aimlessness of, in Egyptian campaign.	15	1812
Guilty of bloodshed in Egypt.	15	1812
Refused warning about Gen. Gordon.	15	1813
Their blunders in Egypt.	15	1811
Warned by Gordon of Khartum's condition.	15	1814
Liberators, Cuban, glory of.	13	1200
Liberties, the, of colonial America, British orators advocate.	11	ix
Of Greece, list of those who sold them to Philip.	12	886
Outraged, French Revolution caused by.	11	ix
Liberty, ancient Athenians scorned to live without freedom.	12	868
Barbarism not induced by.	12	802
Contrasted with violence.	14	1593
Exclusiveness the doom of.	13	1270
Faneuil Hall, the cradle of.	13	1270
Franklin talked of, to courtiers of Louis XVI.	13	903
Growth of, in Germany.	14	1512
History of, by Edward Everett.	13	972
History of, the only real history.	13	973
Meaning of, to a Roman.	13	1097
Name of, the, made odious by the French Revolution.	13	989
Never established in states of Greece and Rome.	13	975
Not secured by books or education.	14	1589
Of the press, theme of British oratory.	11	ix
Of the slave, theme of British oratory.	11	ix
Personal, and personal rights, in keeping of the nation, not of each state.	13	1056
Religious, the theme of British oratory.	11	ix
Spirit of, illustrated the Pass of Thermopylæ.	14	1604
The birthright of all humanity.	13	1291
The schoolhouse the fortress of.	13	1246
Universality of.	14	1604
Life, arguments against taking human.	14	1747
Business, a sharp struggle.	14	1398
Civic and social, inconceivable without the Bible.	15	1770
Life, decencies and modesties of, among the Filipinos.	11	80
Unsafe outside limits of Athens.	15	1926
Life-work of men of achievement, based on the teachings of the Bible.	15	1770
Lighthouses, economy in.	14	1661
Limit, an upper, placed in the Rhodesia tariff on British goods.	14	1735
Lincoln, Abraham, abolition, proclamation of.	11	ix
As great as Washington.	13	1298
Biography of.	14	1337
Cardinal doctrine of the political creed of.	13	1216
Controller of a great historic crisis.	13	896
Demolished the idol god slavery in 1863.	13	1055
Great Emancipator, the.	12	780
Had mastered the Bible.	15	1771
His appeal to the Southern people.	14	1346
His Cooper Union speech.	14	1337
His Douglas campaign speech.	12	vii
His famous letter to Greeley.	12	623
His ideals.	13	1199
Master of style.	11	x
On Senator Douglas's "Popular Sovereignty".	15	1841
On the Dred Scott Decision.	14	1356
Speeches of, which will live.	12	vii
Lion, the, in the way of Spain, not the Filipinos, but the United States.	15	1921
Literature, direct power of, on the will.	13	v
And Dogma, Arnold's, worth of.	12	xiii
Litigation, interstate.	14	1459
Living, cost of, how increased by high tariff.	12	691
Lobbyists, Richard Parks Bland on.	11	273
Locke, John, a Christian believer.	13	957
Had expounded the theory on which the American Constitution is based.	11	16
Locomotion, modern, its universality	14	1399
Logansport speech, President Roosevelt's, quoted and endorsed by Governor La Follette.	13	1283
Long, historian of Jamaica, recommends stopping slave importations.	14	1622
Lords, House of, abolition of the.	15	1831
Description of the, by Bright.	15	1829
Power of the, in dissolving Parliament.	15	1827

	VOL.	PAGE
Losses of Americans in the Spanish war, compared with losses in other wars	11	229
Loudness of voice, inconsistent with earnestness	12	viii
Loud voice, not needed in oratory	12	vi
Louis XIV, aim of, at universal dominion	13	1098
Drove Germans to America	13	981
His designs on Egypt	13	991
His nefarious political methods	13	1002
Hume on	13	1003
Quoted by Daniel Webster	15	2102
Louis XVI, a tyrant in revolt against a nation	13	914
Camille Desmoulins on	13	915
Condemned by Desmoulins, not as a man but as a king	13	915
Friendly with Leopold of Austria	13	997
Louisiana, acquisition of, at first objected to	13	939
Florida, Texas and, made slave states, as concession to the South	15	1934
Its purchase by Jefferson, the constitutionality of	11	92
On the Admission of, by Josiah Quincy	14	1663
Purchased in 1803	14	1340
To be tilled by free labor, or Massachusetts and New York by slaves	15	1853
Lounsberry, Professor, on the mind's capacity for ignorance	15	1772
Louw, Mr., his independence of spirit among the Boers	14	1730
In South Africa, character of	14	1731
Love, the flight of the soul towards God	14	1471
Lowell, James Russell, quoted by Charles Sumner	15	1962
Luccheni, antecedents of	11	174
Crime of	11	175
Luke xi. 41, quoted by Leo XIII	14	1331
Luther as an example to presidents	12	790
Controller of a great historic crisis	13	896
Lycurgus, the laws of, and slavery	14	1604
Lyons, Lord, his correspondence with Northern politicians	12	454

M

	VOL.	PAGE
McAllister, Ward, on the income tax	11	365
MacArthur, General	13	1197
McCarthy, Justin, accused of conniving at assassination	14	1366

	VOL.	PAGE
McCarthy, Justin, biography of	14	1365
In Defense of His Colleagues	14	1365
Macaulay, Lord, biography of	14	1377
On persuasion	15	vii
On the People's Charter	14	1377
Macdonald, Sir John A., biography of	14	1387
On Canadian Confederation	14	1387
"Macedonian," frigate, sent with bread to starving Ireland	12	450
McEnery resolution, the	13	1197
Machiavelli, French republican party styled followers of	13	1044
Subtlety of, alluded to by Sumner	15	1956
Machine, political, evolution of the	13	1286
Machinery, monopoly of, charged by the Chartists	14	1382
McKinley, William, administration of, and industrial development	13	1162
A Memnon voice	13	1164
And Canada	13	1300
And the Spanish war	13	1161
A party man	13	1165
A protectionist	13	1157
As a law student	13	1155
As governor of Ohio	13	1158
A soldier in the Civil War	13	1154
As President	13	1160
Buffalo speech of	14	1397
Continues the expansion policy of Jefferson	11	234
Continues the policy of Jefferson, Monroe and Madison	11	231
Enrolled among founders of states	13	921
Grossly insulted in the Senate	15	1922
His absorption in industrial and commercial questions	13	920
His feelings on victory over Spain	13	924
His forbearance under contradiction	15	1922
His foreign policy, a dangerous precedent	15	1843
His journeys South	13	1164
His last days	13	1167
His personality	13	1159
His presence at Buffalo in 1901	13	1165
His reëlection	13	1164
His speech at Buffalo, quoted	13	1166
In Congress	13	1157
In political life	13	1156
John Hay on	13	1149
On the Civil War	13	1302
War policy of	13	1160
McKinley Law, Sheffield Telegram on the	13	1034

	VOL.	PAGE
Madagascar, French tariff in........	14	1732
Protective tariff in............	14	1733
Madison, James, at the Congress of 1789....................	14	1339
Biography of................	14	1404
Framer of the embargo........	11	263
On removal of civil servants....	12	788
On suppression of local insurrections...................	13	1059
On the British Treaty.........		1404
Madman, Macedonian, Alexander, as the......................	12	621
Magna Charta, alluded to by Thaddeus Stevens...............	15	1949
The Bible is the, of the poor....	15	1773
The principles of, retained in the Confederate Constitution....	15	1936
Magnanimity, room for, in South Africa....................	14	1476
Mahdi, the, his agreement with Farag Bey......................	15	1816
His army's condition before Khartum..................	15	1816
His attitude towards England..	15	1818
In arms before the Liberal ministry was prepared...........	15	1810
Lieutenants of the, attack garrisons in the Sudan...........	15	1811
Maid of Athens, Byron's, quoted by William M. Springer.........	15	1930
"Maine" Disaster, Robert G. Cousins on the...................	12	738
Majority, paramount authority of the, an essential principle of the United States Government	13	1258
Malays of Sumatra suffered from Commodore Downes, under Andrew Jackson............	11	214
Malietoa of Samoa deported by Germans.....................	13	1031
Malmesbury, Lord, his reply to M. de la Croix...................	13	996
Malignant malady of anarchy.......	13	1151
Maniacs from the Philippines, a carload of....................	13	1202
"Manifest Destiny," the plea of great conquerors...........	12	629
Man, rights of, expounded by Thomas Paine...................	14	1535
The idle, and the barren woman, no place for, in healthy community...................	15	1761
Mandan Indians, trading-houses to be established among the, by Jefferson...................	13	1261
Manila, Aguinaldo coöperates at capture of...................	15	1838
Manila, allusion to, by Senator Beveridge.....................	11	228
Capture of, imposed duties incompatible with evacuation..	15	1919
McKinley's view of, as an American Hong Kong............	13	1923
Manitoba, its grain production......	13	1071
Mannerisms, accidental character of.	13	viii
Destroy eloquence............	12	xiii
Not to be imitated............	13	viii
Mansfield, Lord, biography of......	14	1422
His high opinion of Americans..	14	1430
On the Right of England to Tax America...................	14	1422
Mantica, history of................	11	176
Mantua, Napoleon's address to soldiers during the siege of.....	11	293
Manufactories, John Randolph's ideas on........................	14	1704
Prejudicial to health...........	14	1703
Manufactures, England dependent on her.....................	14	1732
Marat, Jean Paul, biography of.....	14	1433
Defamed....................	14	1433
His Defense.................	14	1433
Marathon, Demosthenes swears by the heroes of..............	12	868
Marcy, the spoils system advocated by......................	12	786
Marianna, his view of assassination..	11	167
"Maria Stuart," Schiller's, quoted by Kossuth...................	13	1275
Market, the, of the British farmer, for buying in, should be the cheapest....................	13	1072
Reserved to Great Britain in Rhodesia...................	14	1735
Seldom monopolized by a trust.	15	1779
Marlowe, Julia, qualities of her voice.	12	vii
Marshall, John, biography of.......	14	1440
On the meaning of the term, "United States"..........	11	87
On the Federal Constitution...	14	1440
The great American jurist......	13	1217
Mars' Hill, eloquence of St. Paul on.	12	v
Martial legion condemns Antonius..	12	600
Marx, Engels, and Lassalle, intellectual fathers of socialists...	11	163
Maryland colonized by Roman Catholics.....................	13	981
General Butler's operations in..	12	446
Mary, Queen, her grief for Calais....	12	621
Masaniello, a madman.............	14	1429
Mason and Dixon's line............	14	1700
Massachusetts, House of Deputies in.	13	984
Motto of...................	13	1273
Settled by Governor Winthrop.	13	992

	VOL.	PAGE
Massachusetts and Sumner, Anson Burlingame on.	11	429
Bay, with the South against the tariff.	14	1700
Massacre, proclamation of a, by Aguinaldo's secretary of the interior.	15	1920
Boston, John Hancock on the.	13	1125
Mastership of Malta, Grand, claimed by Paul of Russia.	13	1013
Matabeleland, mines and males in.	14	1741
Sentiment of, on the African confederation question.	14	1741
Materialism, widespread, distressed George Washington.	13	1278
Mathew, Father.	13	1277
Matthew vi. 2, cited by Leo XIII.	14	1331
xi. 5, cited by Leo XIII.	14	1330
Maurice, Prince of Orange, on the Hollanders.	14	1432
Maverick, victim of British cruelty.	13	1130
Mavrocordato, a household word in America.	15	1929
Maxim, John Randolph's.	14	1717
Maximilian, his end in Mexico.	13	1031
Mayflower, the sailing of the.	13	901
Mazzini, Joseph, biography of.	14	1467
Harbored by Mr. Stansfeld, M.P.	14	1368
To the Young Men of Italy.	14	1467
Measure of value, the world's, in currency maintained by Republicans.	13	1034
Mediæval kings, more tyrannous than the Cæsars.	13	977
Meeting, public, right to a, non-existent in Ireland.	14	1376
Megara.	12	836
Melvill on the universality of oratory.	15	vi
Men, live, wanted by civilized countries	14	1589
The very greatest, studied the Bible.	15	1770
Messenians, abettors of Philip.	12	835
Memnon.	13	1164
Merchant of Venice, Shakespeare's, quoted by John Randolph.	14	1707
Mercy, corporal works of.	14	1330
Merritt, General, refused to receive Aguinaldo.	15	1840
Method, proper and improper, of preparing a speech.	12	xiii
Methodist Episcopal Church divided on the slavery question.	12	471
Mexico, Against War with, speech of Thomas Corwin.	12	724
Mexico, a monarchy in.	13	1031
And Louis Napoleon's Policy, Louis Adolphe Thiers on.	15	1974
Mexico, City of, its universities.	12	684
Democratic party desired slavery in the territory acquired from, in 1846.	15	1859
Gulf of.	14	1701
Mexican law in Nebraska.	12	553
Mezentius, the marriages of.	14	1712
Micawber policy of the Cleveland administration.	15	1908
Michigan irregularly admitted to the Union.	12	480
Midas of the century, Jay Gould the.	13	1232
Middleton, acts of, the acts of Warren Hastings.	15	1897
His cruel order to Lieutenant Rutledge regarding Begums.	15	1898
The tool of Warren Hastings.	15	1900
Migration from east to west in the United States, its toils and difficulties.	13	1249
Of England to America in seventeenth century the most numerous in history.	13	1229
The most formidable, in history.	13	1229
Mikado, the, how he maintains his position.	14	1744
Milan, Napoleon's Address to Troops on entering.	11	291
Miles, General, in Porto Rico.	14	1399
Military government extended over the Philippines in 1898.	15	1842
Military importance of the Bosphorus.	13	1093
Militia, American, regulated by the Amendment of 1789.	11	138
And standing armies.	14	1430
A well-disciplined, the best security against foreign foe.	13	1132
A well-disciplined, essential to a republic.	13	1258
Miller, General, at Iloilo.	13	1197
Mill-fires lighted at the funeral pile of slavery.	13	1140
Millionaires "the froth on the beer".	13	1231
Not producers or laborers.	13	1231
Millions, twenty-five, spent in railroad improvements in Georgia	15	1937
Milner, Lord, biography of.	14	1474
Speech of, "Never Again".	14	1474
Milton, John, his "Paradise Lost," quoted by Henry Clay.	12	645
His "Paradise Lost," quoted by Senator Hoar.	13	1200
His testimony to the truth of Christianity.	13	959
On the incarnation.	13	958

	VOL.	PAGE
Milton, John, on war, quoted by Thomas Francis Bayard....	11	137
Quoted by Daniel Webster.....	15	2076
Quoted by John Randolph.....	14	1709
Milwaukee, her wasteful gift of public service franchises...........	13	1285
Mincovich, slain in the Venetian arsenal......................	14	1368
Mine-owners, oppression of, by railroad companies...............	13	1283
Mines in Matabeleland............	14	1741
Ministers, foreign, out of 140, up to 1861, the South had 86......	15	1935
Of the Begums, cruel treatment of, by Middleton............	15	1898
Minnesota, half a century ago......	15	1769
How built up.................	15	1760
State Fair of, Address at the, by Theodore Roosevelt.........	15	1759
Mirabeau, H. G. Riquetti, biography of........................	14	1477
Speech of, Against the Charge of Treason...................	14	1477
An oratorical roarer..........	12	viii
Charged with rioting..........	14	1480
The constructive statesman of the early French Revolution..	11	ix
Ugliness of..................	14	1477
Miracle required to feed hungry office-seekers...............	12	786
Miracles, no government can perform them......................	14	1384
Misfortunes of Greece attributed to Demosthenes..............	11	39
Mission, the Turkish, its large expenses...................	15	1925
Missionary government, the government of the United States not a.....................	15	1914
Missionary Ridge, battle of........	11	228
Mississippi, governor of, B. G. Humphreys as..................	13	1057
Honor paid by, to the memory of Sumner.................	13	1289
River, opened to England by treaty.....................	14	1411
Slavery in, restricted by Congress......................	14	1340
Territory of, organized in 1798..	14	1339
Missouri, operations of the Union armies in..................	12	447
Missouri Compromise, the, abrogated by the Democratic party....	15	1861
And the Ordinance of 1787, disastrous to the South........	12	464
Missouri question, the, in 1819–'20..	14	1341
William Pinkney on the.......	14	1603
Mistresses of George II in London ..	14	1723
Mobs, signs of new national life in 1835...................	14	1593
Mock great man, statue of a........	14	1589
Model, Holland furnishes America with a.....................	14	1443
Modjeska, Madame, qualities of her voice......................	12	vii
Moltke on the German army grant..	11	136
Monarchical principle, its advantage in the Canadian government..	14	1393
Monarchies and republics, alike transitory.....................	14	1585
Monarchy, aristocracy and, not the end of government.........	14	1380
Arguments for reëstablishment of, in France................	12	512
In France, the scourge of the people.....................	12	512
Stable government not guaranteed by.....................	12	512
The President of the French republic does not aspire to..	13	1049
Money, an aristocracy of, most intolerable...................	14	1752
Change in the standard of, favors cheating...............	12	716
Enormous sums of, taken home by Chinese.................	14	1580
Its activity more important than its volume.................	12	715
Not identical with property....	12	715
Paper, monopoly of, petitioned against by Chartists........	14	1382
The creation of law...........	13	1236
Monk, victim of British cruelty, John Hancock's apostrophe to....	13	1130
Monmouth, Washington on the plains of...................	13	1306
Monongahela, Washington supports Braddock beside the.......	13	1305
Monopolies, complained of, by Chartists......................	14	1382
Monroe, James, Florida under the administration of.............	11	233
His acts in civil service appointments.....................	12	789
Monroe doctrine, the, not international law...................	15	1765
No cause for bluster.........	15	1765
President Roosevelt on the....	15	1766
Vindication of the............	13	1161
Montaigne on the end of oratory....	15	v
Montcalm, General, his death at Quebec....................	13	1306
Montefiore, Sir Moses, distinguished philanthropist.............	14	1559

VOL. PAGE

Montesquieu, Baron, on education in
republics.................... 11   203
On standing armies........11   135–136
On "tiresome annals "........ 12   729
Montezuma, Spanish despotism fol-
lowed the empire of........ 12   680
Montgomery, General, death of..... 13   1306
Morgan, John Tyler, biography of... 14   1490
On the Nicaragua Canal....... 14   1490
Morley, John, biography of........ 14   1497
On Irish Home Rule........... 14   1497
Morrill tariff, enactment of, its effects 11   270
Morris, Gouverneur, as an anti-slav-
ery man.................... 14   1343
At the Congress of 1789....... 14   1343
Morristown, Washington at........ 13   1306
Moscow, every man has his........ 14   1592
Moses and Amalek, Emperor William
II of Germany, on.......... 15   2129
Motherhood, Theodore Roosevelt on. 15   1761
Mothers, bereaved, their consolation. 14   1570
Mounier, M., Mirabeau's remarks to. 14   1481
Mountain, the, members of, defend
Marat...................... 14   1434
Mount, Sermon on the, its eloquence. 12   v
Movement, Popular Christian, the,
in Italy.................... 14   1325
Popular Christian, the, its influ-
ence on the masses........ 14   1332
Mnesiphilus, the archon........... 12   829
Murders, judicial................. 14   1732

N

Nabob of Oude, his character de-
stroyed, his country depopu-
lated by Hastings........... 15   1891
Napier, Sir Charles............... 11   325
Naples, atrocities at the British de-
liverance of................ 13   1026
Overturn of its government.... 14   1429
Napoleon, a pitiful, despicable object 14   1720
At St. Helena................ 14   1720
Cruelty of, compared with that
of Suwaroff................ 13   1008
Empire of, in 1812, likely to
stand but for England...... 12   505
Fall of, a matter of unbounded
joy to the world............ 12   496
Fall of, originated in Russian
campaign.................. 12   501
Fall of, placed England at the
head of the world.......... 13   497
His Egyptian expedition in-
spired by Louis XIV........ 13   991
His prediction of Europe's future 15   1852
Insulated policy against, power-
less....................... 12   503

VOL. PAGE

Napoleon, product of American ex-
periment................... 13   904
Universal dominion the aim of.. 13   1098
Napoleon's Overtures, Rejection of,
Charles James Fox on the... 13   994
Narrative, Hastings's, a mass of false-
hood...................... 15   1901
Nassau, a pirates' naval station dur-
ing the Civil War........... 12   449
Natal, the Progressives in......... 14   1741
National banks, free, in every city,
advocated by John Sherman. 15   1911
National life, Italian, viewed since
the American revolution..... 13   904
Nations, the great, America's obliga-
tions to.................... 13   968
Free, cannot hold dependencies. 11   87
Free Trade With All, Richard
Cobden on................. 12   698
Linked together by steam and
telegraph................. 14   1400
The Six..................... 14   1726
The Six, and the United States.. 14   1728
Natural Bridge, the, John Brown's
inscription on.............. 14   1590
Natural religion, a great common-
wealth, never established by. 13   961
Naturalization laws should discrim-
inate...................... 13   1143
Naturalized, foreigners who become. 12   652
Nature, the laws of, superior to
human contingencies........ 14   1326
Naval preëminence, England's, at the
beginning of the Napoleonic
wars...................... 12   506
Naval stations, guardians of Ameri-
can commerce.............. 11   239
England's.................. 11   239
Navigation, places convenient for,
benefited by tariff.......... 14   1704
Naylor, Colonel, witness against War-
ren Hastings............... 15   1873
Nazareth, the Holy Family of, a
splendid example........... 14   1335
Nebraska bill, the................ 13   935
Chase's amendment to the.... 13   936
Its provisions................ 13   936
Of Judge Douglas, the........ 14   1360
Needle, the, "the asp for the breast
of the poor "............... 13   1241
Negro, a, cannot sue at law, accord-
ing to the Dred Scott deci-
sion...................... 14   1356
Emancipation of the, more diffi-
cult in 1860 than during the
Revolution................ 14   1359
Equality of the, with white man. 13   940

	VOL.	PAGE
Negro, estimate of the, not higher in 1860 than during the Revolution.	14	1359
Hard condition of the, in 1860.	14	1360
Personal freedom and political rights of the.	13	1293
Political position of the, worse in 1860 than before.	14	1359
Negro race, inferiority of the, corner-stone of the Confederate Constitution.	15	1939
Negroes, according to Douglas, not included in the Declaration of Independence.	14	1361
British, Emancipation of Earl of Derby on the.	13	908
Not literally equal with whites.	13	1361
Voted in five states in 1860.	14	1358
Nelson, Justice, on the term "enemies of the government".	13	1062
Neptune, the patron of British prowess.	12	506
Nethersole, Olga, vocal qualities of.	12	vii
Neutrality, not preserved by England during the American Civil War	12	449
"Never Again," speech of Lord Milner.	14	1474
Newfoundland, the French in.	14	1737
New Mexico, acquisition of, by the United States.	13	939
Democratic party in 1850 wished slavery in.	15	1859
New Orleans, battle of.	11	119
Ladies of, protected by General Butler.	12	447
News, rapid distribution of.	14	1399
Newton, Sir Isaac, a Christian.	13	956
New World, its lesson in government to the Old.	12	514
Its partition among Europeans.	13	900
New York, civil service reform in custom-house of.	12	791
Nicaragua Canal, John Tyler Morgan on the.	14	1490
Question of the.	14	1492
Nile, the river.	13	1164
Nobiling, not a Social Democrat.	11	163
North Africa, Cecil Rhodes's plan for annexing.	14	1733
North, ascendency of the, in the government, in 1850.	12	466
And Northwest, Democratic party not a party of the free states in.	15	1857
And South, population of, in 1790, compared with that of 1840.	12	459
North, the, poor before the Revolution, rich afterwards.	14	1699
Twenty-four years of presidents from the, up to 1861.	15	1934
North Carolina, operations of the Union armies in.	12	447
Northcote, Sir Stafford, predicted Gordon's fate at Khartum.	15	1812
Norway and Sweden, how affected by American independence.	13	904
Notes, difficulty of maintaining, at par.	15	1905
Total of, issued by the United States Treasury under the Act of 1890.	15	1909
United States and Treasury, their superiority to national bank.	15	1910
November ninth, Lord Mayor's day, compared with April first.	13	1096
Nullification, birth of.	13	1176
And the Force Bill, John Caldwell Calhoun on.	12	485
Doctrine of.	12	488
Nullum Tempus bill, the.	13	1111
Numa, the law-giver of Rome.	13	1217

O

Oath, the, required from members of Parliament.	14	1550
Obedience, the spirit of, not impaired by Christian Democracy.	14	1328
Object of the Athenian funeral oration.	14	1563
Occupation of Egypt, British, its object.	12	596
Of the Philippine Islands, results of.	13	1201
Oceans, Atlantic and Pacific, to be united.		
O'Connell, Daniel, biography of.	14	1510
On Catholic Rights.	14	1510
On Justice for Ireland.	14	1522
Octavius, confirmation of the death penalty by.	14	1747
Accomplices in his crimes.	14	1747
Offenses committed by the Chinese in California.	14	1574
Offices, minor political, not public trusts, but prizes.	12	793
The Jews eligible to.	14	1553
Old Guard, Napoleon's Farewell to the.	11	295
Old Hickory, name given to Andrew Jackson by his soldiers.	11	118
Oligarchial feeling among the Dutch, fatal to progress.	14	1744

	VOL.	PAGE
Oligarchy, the slave	15	1963
Olive, cultivation of the, forbidden in Spanish America	12	681
"Olive Jane," piracy of the	12	448
Olynthus betrayed by Lasthenes	12	832
Omnibus bill, the	12	558
Onondaga (Canandaigua) Indians	14	1728
Opinion, public, and civil service reform	12	783
Public, restrict the action of Presidents	12	791
South African, change of, in the matter of expansion	14	1731
Oppression, British, in American colonies	13	1126
Italians made bloodthirsty by	11	177
Opprobrium, worse than death	14	1748
Oration, Columbian, by Chauncey Mitchell Depew	13	893
Funeral, established by law at Athens	14	1563
Orations, historic evolution of nations discerned in	11	vii
Illuminative power of, in historic works	11	vii
Orator, dominant desire of the	13	xi
How far authoritative	13	xii
Occasions for the	12	vi
Physical limitations in the	13	x
Practical object of the	11	xvi
Prerequisites of the	11	xiv
Self-consciousness in the	13	x
Training makes the	11	xiv
Oratorical illustration of history in our own country, completeness of	11	viii
Oratorical power, vanity the death warrant of	13	xi
Orators, as molders of nations	13	vi
Earliest, of Greece, poets	11	v
Great penetrative power of the voices of	12	vii
Natural	11	xv
Oratory, a continuous stream from antiquity to the present	11	vi
American, battlefield of, between 1761 and 1863	11	ix
And the press, compared	12	xii
Aristotle includes, in art of statesmanship	11	v
Cicero's definition of	11	xvi
Effort and ease in	13	x
Highest, impersonal	13	xi
Music more formal than	13	ix
Plasticity of, art of	13	ix
Political, a work dealing with actualities	11	vii
Oratory, political, the heart of great events revealed by	11	vii
Political, history of liberty contained in	11	viii
Power of	13	v
Reveals the orator	13	viii
Ordinance of 1787, the	14	1338
Condemned slavery	15	1854
Oregon, acquisition of, by the United States	13	939
Organization, character of, in the American government, as important as escape from despotism	13	1118
Of the United States Supreme Court, centennial of the	13	1138
Territorial, given to Louisiana, 1804	14	1340
Orleanists, French republican party charged with being	13	1044
Orleans, Duke of, banished by Lafayette	14	1484
Orsini and John Brown, parallel examples	14	1351
Osage Indians accused of aggression on the Delawares	13	1263
Ostracism in the Southern states	13	1060
Otis, James, biography of	14	1526
His book on taxation, full of madness	14	1429
His importance	14	1429
His speech on Writs of Assistance	11	viii
On the Writs of Assistance	14	1526
The "child independence" born in speeches of	11	viii
Oude, Chief-Justice Impey at	15	1889
Disturbances the effect, not cause, of Warren Hastings's oppression	15	1875
Province of, its condition under Warren Hastings	15	1872
Outrage, Justin McCarthy accused of conniving at	14	1366
Overtures, Napoleon's, Charles James Fox on the Rejection of	13	994
Ovid, quoted by the Earl of Derby	13	908

P

	VOL.	PAGE
Pacific Coast, the, labor among the people of	14	1576
Pacific ports, steam communication needed by	14	1402
Pacta conventa	14	1432
Paine, Thomas, biography of	14	1532
Erskine's main argument against	13	955

	VOL.	PAGE
Paine, Thomas, his "Age of Reason," blasphemous	13	958
His "Age of Reason," not addressed to good and intelligent men	13	960
Lord Erskine against	13	949
To the French National Convention	14	1532
Palace of Rest, the windowless	13	1240
Palafox, the knife of	14	1368
Palatine counties of England, and the American colonies, analogy between	11	405
Palmerston, his name, why to be honored	13	1088
Palmyra, a vanished city	14	1585
Pandours, fierce	14	1512
Paper currency, national, advantages of, at par with coin	15	1905
Paper money, issue of, profitable	13	1223
Parchment no defense against the sword	14	1702
Parents of the dead in battle, comforted	14	1569
Paris, treaty of	14	1491
Treaty of, how it bound the United States	13	1197
Treaty of, permanent occupation of Philippines not imposed upon the United States by	15	1918
Parity of silver and gold	13	1185
Parliament, British, the, sixty Irish members in	15	1866
Filipino, superior to that of Japan	15	1841
Irish, Farewell to the, speech of John Philpot Curran	12	769
Oliver Cromwell on the Dissolution of the	12	741
Seats in, bought by the wealthy	14	1706
Parliaments, annual	14	1380
Parties, political, joint-stock associations	15	1857
Sectional, Washington's warning concerning	14	1347
Two great, of the country, represented by Hayne and Webster	13	1172
Partisanship, to be eliminated in tariff reform	12	695
Party, a, defined by G. W. Curtis	12	786
Cavalier, in the Commonwealth	12	747
Democratic, betrayers of the Constitution and of freedom	15	1864
Democratic, bound to the slaveholders	15	1857
Democratic, its want of beneficent policy	15	1860
Party, Democratic, violated express provisions of the Constitution	15	1861
Republican, a party of one idea	15	1864
Spoils system a misconception of the function of	12	786
The Republican, William Pierce Frye on	13	1030
Passion, impetuosity of, urged Nero and Caligula	15	1901
Patapsco, the river	14	1701
Patriotism, Dr. Johnson's definition of	12	782
Enlightened, of Lee and Grant	13	1155
Instinctive, comes before desire of political amelioration	12	501
Patriots, true, in the United States, who they are	15	1846
Patronage, existence of, ruined Roman republic	13	970
Presidential, development of	12	784
Patterson, William, at Congress of 1789	14	1339
Paul of Russia, his indignity to Knights of Malta	13	1013
Paul, St., eloquence of	12	v
Quoted by Leo XIII	14	1327
Pax Britannica, benefits of	12	538
Peace, abroad, maintenance of, the second principle of Gladstone's foreign policy	13	1086
And industry, Jefferson counsels Mandan Indians to pursue	13	1261
Of Ryswick, tardy and futile	13	1022
With all nations, marked the administration of Andrew Jackson	11	213
Peach Tree Creek	11	228
Peel, Sir Robert, biography of	14	1539
Defends his course	14	1543
On the Disabilities of the Jews	14	1544
On the Repeal of the Corn Laws	14	1539
Opposer of Catholic Emancipation	14	1523
Peers, judgment of one's, necessary in the Confederate constitution for trial of a citizen	15	1936
Pekin, cut off from communication	14	1400
Pemberton, General John Clifford, at Vicksburg	13	1057
Pendleton, Senator, on the spoils system	12	783
Penetrative power of great speakers' voices	12	vii
Pennsylvania, colonized by Quakers	13	981
Property of, to be secured by a declaration of war	14	1715

	VOL.	PAGE
Pension laws must be discriminating.	13	1146
Pensions, economy in	14	1660
Pericles, biography of	14	1563
On the Causes of Athenian Greatness.	14	1563
Peril to foreigners, in case of withdrawal from Philippines by the United States	15	1920
Perjury, not invited by an income tax	11	361
Cromwellians not chargeable with	13	1021
Perkins, George Clement, biography of	14	1572
On the Exclusion of the Chinese.	14	1572
Persepolis, a ruined capital	14	1585
Persecutions of the Jews	14	1556
Persian invasion of Greece	14	1604
Persian war, victory in the, at Marathon, accounted for	14	1604
Personality, power of, in oratory	13	vii
Petroleurs, the French republican party accused of being	13	1044
Pew, Mr., and his writ of assistance..	14	1528
Pharaoh and abolition	15	1945
Philadelphia, gift of franchises in, wasteful	13	1285
Failure of, as a trade center, predicted by John Randolph....	14	1715
Philammon crowned at Olympia....	12	891
Philip of Macedon, Athenians deceived by	12	831
Demosthenes, anxious to ratify oath of, for peace	12	827
Greece, how conquered by	13	vii
Greek orators corrupted by	13	vi
Letter of, to Athens	12	838
Profuse bribery practiced by ..	12	825
Successful guilt of, cited by Sheridan	15	1877
Philippic, the Fourth, of Marcus Tullius Cicero	12	598
Philippine question, its several alternatives	15	1915
Philippines, American civil institutions in the	13	923
American invasion of the, slandered	13	919
Americans in the, did their duty.	15	1767
American treatment of the	15	1767
American treatment of, compared with the treatment of Cuba	13	1201
Democratic policy regarding the	15	1844
Effect of Spanish evacuation, without American occupation of the	15	1918
First problem in dealing with the	13	925
Philippines, future of the, left to decision of the President	13	923
Horrors of war in the	13	1203
How far pacificated	13	929
Independence of the, promised by United States	15	1837
Military despotism in the	13	1198
Not Spain's to sell	15	1840
Only republic in Asia	13	1209
On the Government of the, speech of John Coit Spooner.	15	1913
Popular ignorance of the geography of the	13	927
Popular mind disturbed by war in the	15	1834
Purchase of the	13	1197
Races and population of the...	11	79
Sold to the United States without consulting Filipinos	15	1840
Tubjugation of the, Iniquitous, speech of George Frisbie Hoar	13	1194
The American Occupation of the, Jonathan Prentiss Dolliver on	13	919
Their cession to the United States by treaty of Paris	15	1914
Their deliverance from Spain demanded by the country...	15	1916
Their mineral wealth should not affect the Senate	15	1914
Phillips, Charles, biography of	14	1583
Dinas Island speech of	14	1583
His eulogy of Washington	14	1586
Phillips, Wendell, biography of....	14	1588
On John Brown and the Spirit of Fifty-nine	14	1588
Spoke in conversational tone...	12	vi
Philocrates, acts of, mentioned by Demosthenes	12	825
The Agnusian	12	826
Philosophy, cultivation of, at Athens	14	1566
Of Style, Herbert Spencer's....	12	xiii
Phocians, destruction of the	12	829
Phrenology, Henry Clay on	12	633
Pickering, Colonel, agreement of, with the Six Nations	14	1728
The Six Nations and	14	1728
Pierce, General, supplants the Websters and Clays	14	1591
Piety, filial, Richard Brinsley Sheridan on	15	1894
Pilgrim Fathers, first cleared the forest	13	1217
Pilnitz, conference at, on the Napoleonic war of 1791	13	997
Pinckney, Charles, stood for slavery on the Missouri question....	14	1341

	VOL.	PAGE
Pinckney, Charles, voted against slavery prohibition in 1819–'20	14	1341
Pine Creek, an Indian murdered at	14	1727
Pinkney, William, biography of	14	1603
On the Missouri Question	14	1603
Pioneers, Americans a nation of	15	1759
Pirate orgy, John Brown's trial so styled	14	1599
Pitt, William, and war with America, Lord Brougham against	11	333
Biography of	14	1613
Character of the immortality of	11	337
On the Abolition of the Slave-trade	14	1613
Plan of the slaveholding class to keep majority in Senate	15	1855
Planters fear ruin if slavery is abolished	14	1622
Platform, free, lacking in Ireland	14	1376
Playfair, Lyon, his testimony as to American agriculture	13	1069
Pliny on perfection in oratory	15	v
Plot, gunpowder, in England	14	1350
Nefarious, against Indian princes, carried on by Hastings	15	1886
Plymouth, civilization planted at	14	1597
Poe, Edgar Allan, on oratory and poetry	14	xi
Point in a speech, demanded by the American audience	12	xi
Police, the, and anarchist conspiracies	11	172
Chief of, at San Francisco, on the Chinese	14	1574
Policy, an English, would entail English institutions	14	1706
American, towards European affairs	13	1143
A sordid, disastrous to business	14	1401
Enlightened, need in trade of	14	1401
Foreign, Gladstone's professed principles of	13	1086
Foreign, proposed by the Democratic party	15	1844
Narrow, not profitable	14	1401
Noblest, chosen by Athens in opposing Philip	12	878
Philippine, of President McKinley, exemplary	15	1923
Selfish, of Europeans towards the United States	13	1140
Tariff, of every power on acquiring a new dependency	14	1732
The Democratic, "a nefarious schedule of slaveholding designs"	15	1860
Political interest, and skill in government, active at Athens	14	1566
Political results of free-labor	15	1851
Political Situation, John James Ingalls on the	13	1229
Political support, necessity of, spoils system founded on the	12	787
Politicians, English, and South African expansion	14	1731
Politics does not concern Christian Democracy	14	1326
Polk, James K., and free trade	12	704
Polyglot Congress, as a result of foreign annexation	12	621
Pomp and precedent, inferior to popular judgment as basis of government	11	4
Pontiffs, Roman, dealings of, with different governments	14	1327
Pope, Alexander, quoted by Edward Everett	13	972
Popes, why they do not reform church abuses	12	789
Population, laboring, census of	12	690
Populists threaten the authority of the Supreme Court	12	712
Porto Rico, commissioners of	14	1389
Ports, American, closed by the British	14	1315
Of the United States, open to England by treaty	14	1410
Position of Great Britain dependent on her trade	14	1731
Post nati of Scotland, Bacon on the	14	1547
Post-office, New York, civil service reform in the	12	791
United States, the, statistics of	13	1246
Posts of the United States, their value	14	1409
Potomac, banks of the, ennobled by John Brown	14	1594
Poverty, idleness and	15	1760
Insults to, unwise	12	878
No bar to political preferment at Athens	14	1565
No disgrace at Athens	14	1566
Wide-spread, remedy for, to be found in free silver	13	1234
Power, a speaker's, depends on his hearers	12	882
Federal, limitation of, in individual states	12	488
Orator's, summary of what constitutes the	13	xiii
President's, in removing civil servants	12	789
Reforming, of the novel	13	v
Spanish, crushed by Filipino rebels	15	1840

	VOL.	PAGE
Power, unlawful, of trade combinations, to be checked by the Federal government..	13	1284
War, the, resides in the executive	11	17
Power, Mr., telegram of, from Khartum.	15	1814
Powers, great, the, America's friendly relations toward	13	1143
Praga, massacre of, under Suwaroff .	13	1008
Praise of the Athenian dead in battle	14	1564
Pratt, Mr., consul at Singapore	15	1839
Prayer, the peroration of "On the Crown" a	12	892
Precision in expression, to be gained by translating classic authors.	11	xx
Preliminaries proper to a declaration of war.	13	999
Prentiss, Sargent Smith, biography of.	14	1646
Dangers of patronage stated by.	12	785
On the Defalcations of the Government	14	1646
Preponderance of Northern representatives in Congress in 1850	12	461
Presence, personal, cannot be assumed.	13	viii
Personal, what it is	13	viii
Presents made by the Turkish minister, list of	15	1925
Preservation of the Union, Rufus Choate on.	12	575
President, the, of the Confederate States, six years' term of	15	1938
The, of the French republic, powers of.	13	1049
The, of the United States, a despot.	14	1393
The, of the United States, as a party leader.	14	1393
The, of the United States, his power of removing civil servants.	12	789
The, of the United States, in civil service appointments	12	788
The, of the United States, not responsible to his cabinet	14	1393
The, of the United States, originally visited and conferred with the Senate	11	297
The, of the United States, usually chosen from the South up to 1861.	15	1934
The, of the United States, why he does not reform civil service	12	789
Press, freedom of the, error driven away by.	13	952
Press, free, none in Irleand	14	1376
Liberty of the, enfeebled under Napoleon	12	515
New York, cited by Wendell Phillips.	14	1599
Religious, the, on slavery	12	581
Russian, hostility of the, to Germany in Bismarck's day	11	257
Prestige, English, imperiled by abandonment of Gordon.	15	1821
Preston's hand in the Boston massacre of 1770	13	1128
Preternatural being, Warren Hastings believed by Asiatics to be a	15	1875
Price, law of, discussed.	12	655
Pride, the most imperious of passions	14	1748
Princeton, Washington at	13	1306
Principles, party, in America, England, France and Spain, identical.	13	1173
Prior, quoted by Lord Chatham	12	573
Priority, unique, of Washington among his contemporaries . . .	13	1311
Privateering, among the interests of Baltimore.	14	1715
Privileges, dock and harbor, required abroad.	13	1144
Mail and post-office, enjoyed by the South	15	1935
Problem, the negro	15	2016
Problems, home, the first duty of the United States to solve	15	1914
Proclamation, the Filipino Junta's, favored Americans.	15	1837
Napoleon's, to his army	11	290
Production, how to be stimulated . . .	12	656
Products, Cape, and the Rhodesia tariff.	14	1739
The, and exports, of United States in 1860 and in 1893. .	13	1243
Progress, material, in America	13	1230
Material, of the United States from 1860 to 1880.	13	1242
The wand of	13	1240
Progressives of the Transvaal.	14	1741
Prohibition, a vote for the, of slavery, by Rufus King	14	1341
Of the slave-trade in the West Indies, considered an invasion of legal inheritance	14	1626
Prometheus, Napoleon the modern. .	12	621
Property, British, sequestration of .	14	1414
Not identical with money	12	715
Proprietary, peasant, its advantages.	13	1075
Prosperity, based on virtue.	14	1329
Of Rhodesia.	14	1737

	VOL.	PAGE
Prosperity of the United States, indicated by trade statistics....	14	1400
Of the United States, unexampled....................	14	1400
Prostitution or suicide, alternatives to dependent women........	13	1234
Protection, a Century of, James G. Blaine on..................	11	259
Advocated by James G. Blaine.	11	xi
Advocated by Jefferson and Hamilton..................	12	647
All-embracing beneficence of...	12	645
And encouragement of home industries the end of McKinley law.......................	15	1907
An exploded doctrine.........	13	1079
Benefits all classes............	12	662
Benefits of, summarized.......	12	660
Built up from July 4, 1789, to 1833......................	12	650
Established by George Washington.....................	12	646
Has no place in tariff discussion	12	695
In England did not increase exports......................	13	1084
Its duration coeval with the Constitution...................	12	646
Lord Beaconsfield on..........	13	1081
Made by slavery a sectional question....................	13	1140
One-sided, to be deprecated....	13	1081
Two-sided, an examination of the effects of................	13	1082
Protective tariff, prosperous results of the, from 1824...........	12	643
Protectorate, Madagascar as a......	14	1732
Protest, a final, against secession....	15	1936
Against Sentence as a Traitor, speech of Robert Emmet.....	13	941
Protocol, a, between Costa Rica and the United States...........	14	1493
Signed by Spain and United States......................	14	1400
Proudhon, Max Stirner, and Bakunin, intellectual fathers of anarchists......................	11	163
Provinces, subject, cannot pertain to free nations.................	11	87
Provisions, clause of treaty relating to.........................	14	1413
Of the Rhodesia tariff law......	14	1734
Proviso, Wilmot, the..............	12	664
Prudence, great crimes incompatible with......................	15	1878
Prussia, the income tax in..........	11	354
The wives of, in war-time.......	15	1961
Psalm lxxviii, quoted by Cromwell..	12	742

	VOL.	PAGE
Public abuses, remedy for..........	14	1659
Public debt, the, paid off during the Jackson administration......	11	214
Public finance, false economy in....	14	1661
Public moneys, appropriated to private use....................	14	1648
Custody of....................	14	1647
Public officers, arraignment of......	14	1652
Public opinion, omnipotent, could not save France..............	14	1589
Sensitiveness of...............	12	581
Public recreations at Athens, their object......................	14	1565
Public speaking, Albert J. Beveridge on.........................	12	v
Punishment, capital, a crime.......	14	1747
Punishments, objects of............	14	1748
Purchase of the right of subjugating a people, iniquitous..........	13	1216
Puritans, the, brought the torch of liberty to America..........	13	1217
Punic War, a Napoleonic war more than a.....................	12	507
Purse-string of the world, held by Great Britain..............	15	1911

Q

	VOL.	PAGE
Quack remedies for agricultural distress in England............	13	1073
Qualification, a property, for members of Parliament...........	14	1379
Qualifications of a voter in the French Revolution..................	14	1756
Quebec, conference at, between Americans and Canadians...	13	1300
Queen of Greece, a contra-dance with the, led by the American minister......................	15	1927
Question, slavery, the, as understood by the fathers..............	14	1338
Social, the, not merely an economic one..................	14	1329
Questions, economic, their popular discussion disturbing........	14	1323
Quincy, Josiah, biography of.......	14	1663
On the Admission of Louisiana.	14	1663
Quintilian says that oratory must suit the occasion............	14	vi
Quixotic plan of sending Gordon to Khartum...................	15	1811
"Quod Apostolici Muneris," encyclical letter..................	14	1324
"Quod facit per alium, facit per se," applied by Sheridan to Warren Hastings................	15	1900

R

	VOL.	PAGE
Rabida, Columbus, Christopher, at convent of	13	897
Races, populations and, of the Philippines	11	79
Equality of, Jefferson's views on the	15	1939
Raid, Jameson, inquiry into	12	541
Railroad extension under the Confederate constitution	15	1937
Railroads in combination, the power of, indicated by the coal trust	13	1284
Railway, the African transcontinental	14	1736
A Cape Town, to Cairo	14	1736
The Sudan, how to be built	15	1820
The Sudan, projected	15	1818
Railways, prospects for, in Africa	14	1739
Raleigh, Sir Walter, as a colonist	13	980
His colony	14	1597
His story of an internecine battle	13	1007
Randall, Samuel Jackson, biography of	14	1671
On Tariff Legislation	14	1671
Randolph, Edmund, biography of	14	1678
Edmund, speech of, In Defense of the Union	14	1678
Randolph, John, biography of	14	1697
John, moves the postponement of the tariff bill of 1824	14	1725
John, speech of, On the Tariff	14	1697
Randolph, P. B., on reasoning and rhetoric	15	viii
Ratio of gold and silver, American	13	1221
Ravaille, Father, devotion of	15	2018
Read, George, at the Congress of 1789	14	1339
Read, John Meredith, minister resident in Turkey	15	1926
Reading, wide, Charles Sumner's	13	1290
Reason, belief an act of	13	956
Rebellion, failure of the, a benefit to mankind	13	1302
State questions growing out of the	13	1056
Receipts of government under Cleveland more than expenditures	15	1905
Receivers, Austrian, no better than French thieves	13	1011
Reciprocity, a natural outgrowth of prosperity	14	1401
A quack remedy for agricultural depression	13	1078
Trade, a necessity	14	1401
Reconcentrado period in Cuba	15	1916
Reconstruction, different theories of	13	1293
Recreations, public, at Athens	14	1565

	VOL.	PAGE
Recrimination, mutual, of Whigs and Tories	12	786
Red Book, the	14	1706
Red Jacket, biography of	14	1726
His reply to Samuel Dexter	14	1726
Red Sea, crossing of the, cited by Garfield	13	1062
Redistribution, Cornwall and	15	1825
Gladstone's bill for	15	1823
John Bright on	15	1822
John Bright's plans of, illustrated by Aston	15	1824
Lord Hartington on	15	1823
Of Parliamentary seats, Scotland's share in	15	1826
Reform, civil service	12	782
Civil service, executive	12	790
Civil service, why presidents fail to achieve	12	789
Refuge for the oppressed to be found in America	14	1584
Regalia	14	1432
Registration of Chinese immigrants, required by law	14	1575
Reid, Whitelaw, one of the makers of the American treaty with Spain	13	923
Reissue of notes by the treasury imprudent	15	1909
Relations, good and brotherly, with Canada	13	1299
The, between Congress and the States compared with those of Great Britain and her colonies	14	1444
Religious freedom secured by the English Constitution	13	953
Remedies proposed for the evils of trusts	15	1778
Removal, Sir Robert Walpole, on a motion for his	15	2025
Of Senate, speech preceding the, by John Cabell Breckinridge	11	296
Rents in Scotland, speculation in	13	1072
Repeal of the Corn Laws, Sir Robert Peel on	14	1539
Repetitions, examples of, in the Sermon on the Mount	12	xiv
The power of, in eloquence	12	xiii
Reply to Lincoln, by Stephen Arnold Douglas	13	933
Representation in Congress, a three-fifths, for slaves, granted to the South	15	1933
Representative system in American colonies	13	983
Republic, a, incapable of maintaining permanent dependencies	11	85

	VOL.	PAGE
Republic, American, the, compared with Rome in its decadence..	14	1724
American, the, not to be limited in extent..	13	939
And empire, in Rome, contrasted	12	512
A, organized in the Philippines..	15	1837
French, the, due to American example..	13	969
Mexican, the, commissioners of.	14	1398
Philippine, the only one in Asia.	11	79
Representative, Chateaubriand on a..	13	984
Roman, the, destroyed by vast patronage..	12	970
Republican government, advantages of..	13	1043
The strongest of all..	13	1257
Republican Institutions, a Plea for, by Emilio Castelar..	12	517
"Republican or Cossack," whether the country will be..	12	719
Republican party, its motto, "Equal and exact justice to all men"..	15	1864
Its work in American politics..	13	1030
Republicanism and absolutism cannot subsist together..	13	1275
Republicans, Black, a term of reproach..	14	1346
Black, and Lincoln..	13	940
National, their origin, rise and progress..	13	1172
Not sectional..	14	1346
Republics, Greek and American, difference between..	13	974
Greek, short-lived..	13	973
Mediæval, of Italy, their character..	13	976
Varied classes of..	12	522
Requisites of speaking, two indispensable..	12	v
Resources, the, of the continent, the first duty of the government to develop..	15	1914
Reserve, gold, in the treasury, its object..	15	1905
"Resistance to tyrants is obedience to God."..	14	1590
Resolution, Foote's, Robert Young Hayne on..	13	1170
Restoration, of legitimate monarchy in France, abhorrent to public opinion..	13	1045
Of the South, James Abram Garfield on..	13	1054
Restraint, legislative, British farmer must be freed from all unnecessary..	13	1072
Restrictions on slavery in territory of Louisiana..	14	1340
Result of the peace of 1815..	12	508
Results, political, of slavery..	15	1851
Retrenchment, the programme of the Congress of 1876..	15	1931
Economy, and Reform, William McKendree Springer on..	15	1924
Reunion Address, by Robert G. Ingersoll..	13	1241
"Revanche," the French talk of the.	11	247
Revenue, excess of, how to utilize..	14	1402
Government, more than three-fourths of, raised in the North	15	1935
McKinley Act failed to add to, in 1893–'94..	15	1906
Requires no excessive surplus..	13	1146
Revere, Paul, the ride of..	13	985
Revision of the Constitution, in America..	15	1828
In France..	15	1828
Revolt, principle of American, asserted by John Hampden..	11	10
Revolution, American, war of the..	13	1303
Cuban, the, and the Filipino..	15	1837
French, excesses of the, made the word liberty odious..	13	989
French, influence of oratory in the..	13	vii
Greek, greatest triumph of public opinion was the..	13	990
Italian, martyrs of the..	14	1470
Right of, Vattel on the..	12	682
Spanish-American, intellectual results of the..	12	685
Or Secession, Robert Toombs on..	15	2003
Revolutionaries of Spanish America imitated United States..	12	684
Revolutionary movement, the Italian, that of Europe..	14	1469
"Rerum Novarum," encyclical letter	14	1324
Reynolds, Sir Joshua, on the fuel of oratory..	14	x
Rhodes, Cecil, biography of..	14	1730
Gladstone to..	14	1732
His efforts to secure South African union..	14	1745
In a Boer Commando..	14	1738
On the Crisis in South Africa..	14	1730
Rhodesia, by her tariff law, pays back the debt due to England..	14	1735
Prosperity of..	14	1737
The constitution of..	14	1734
Ricardo, David, political economist.	14	1717
His preëminence..	14	1718
Rich, to tax the, is to serve..	12	803

VOL. PAGE

Richardson, ruin of, politically, by
the Nebraska bill............ 14 1360
Right in logic, wrong in practice,
Gladstone so styled by Cecil
Rhodes..................... 14 1732
Rights, Declaration, of the, a provi-
sional code.................. 13 916
Equal, of all nations acknowl-
edged by sound foreign policy. 13 1087
French declaration of......... 14 1534
Of man, the, proclaimed in the
French Revolution.......... 14 1751
Of others to be inviolate...... 14 1335
Property, not impugned by
Christian Democracy....... 14 1326
Bill of, merely recommendatory. 14 1465
Riley, General, in early California
affairs..................... 12 478
Riley, James Whitcomb, his touching
and tender voice............ 12 vii
Riot, General Butler's definition of a. 12 446
Riots, reform in Hyde Park........ 14 1372
Rivalry the spur to improvement.... 14 1398
Rivardi, Major, and the Indians.... 14 1729
Robertson, F. W., on clear thinking. 15 vii
Robespierre, biography of......... 14 1746
Robespierre, Maximilian, Against
Capital Punishment, speech of 14 1746
Decree proposed by, in the Na-
tional Assembly............ 14 1756
Defamed.................... 14 1433
On the Festival of the Supreme
Being..................... 14 1756
On Universal Suffrage........ 14 1750
Prayer of................... 14 1758
Robinson, John, his church at Leyden 13 980
Rob Roy, an eminent annexationist. 12 629
Roland, patron of the Girondists.... 14 1433
Roman Catholic party, attitude of
the, toward German socialism 11 160
Roman Catholic rights, Daniel O'Con-
nell on..................... 14 1510
Roman Catholics, British persecution
of......................... 15 1867
Irish, their former hard lot..... 12 769
Irish, their sincerity and zeal... 12 771
Maryland colonized by........ 13 981
Their political position in 1807.. 15 1867
Roman race, the, still a living force.. 15 1764
Romance, Columbus uneclipsed by
figures of.................. 13 896
Romans, St. Paul's epistle to the,
quoted by Leo XIII......... 14 1336
Their hatred for the title king.. 13 975
"Roman States," Farini's.......... 14 1368
Rome, ancient Britons sold in slave
markets of................. 14 1641

VOL. PAGE

Rome and Carthage, could not live
simultaneously.............. 13 1275
And Italy, Count Camillo Benso
di Cavour on................ 12 530
Barbarian invaders of, govern-
mental changes wrought by.. 13 976
Both pagan and papal......... 14 1472
Liberty in, not firm and pro-
gressive.................... 13 975
Moral decadence of........... 14 1724
Should be capital of Italy...... 12 530
The matrons of............... 15 1961
Work done by, not suited to
modern times............... 13 1098
Roosevelt, Theodore, address of, on
Reading the Bible.......... 15 1770
Biography of................. 15 1759
Endorsed by the people of Wis-
consin..................... 13 1283
His Address at the State Fair of
Minnesota................. 15 1759
His approval of large families.. 15 1761
On equal freight rates......... 13 1285
On the Philippine question..... 15 1768
On Trusts and the Tariff....... 15 1776
Rosebery, the Earl of, biography of. 15 1785
On Questions of Empire....... 15 1785
Rossi, Minister, assassinated at Rome 14 1368
Rowan, Archibald Hamilton, Cur-
ran's speech, In Behalf of.... 12 764
Rubicon, the, passed by Cæsar...... 12 673
Rudicus, betrayer of Thessaly...... 12 832
Ruin, bound to follow on Secession.. 15 1933
National, as inevitable as na-
tional rise................. 14 1585
Of the country, threatened by
slaveholding schemes........ 15 1851
Runaway slaves, often punished with
death...................... 14 1638
Runnymede, the barons of......... 15 1949
Russell, Lord John, name of, why to
be honored................. 13 1088
Earl, Lord Lyons's letter to, on
the American Civil War..... 12 454
Russia, abstention of, from Afghanis-
tan to the credit of Lord Clar-
endon..................... 13 1091
Emperor of, the, and Batoum.. 13 1090
Friendly relations of Germany
with, since 1866............ 11 250
Geographical resemblance of, to
the United States........... 14 1714
Gladstone's opinion of........ 13 1088
Has no aggressive designs on the
east of Europe.............. 13 1092
Her position in Central Asia,
forced upon her............. 13 1090

	VOL.	PAGE
Russia, hostility of, to Prussia, at the convention of Olmutz.	11	250
How aggrandized by Tory government.	13	1089
Shuts out English manufactures.	14	1733
Suppression of capital punishment in.	14	1749
Ryan, Chief-Justice, on the pending issue.	13	1287
Rynders, Captain, checks freedom of speech.	14	1600
Ryswick, the peace of, no security against the machinations of France.	13	1022

S

Salamanca, Irish soldiers at.	15	1871
Salamis, Demosthenes swears by the heroes of.	12	868
Salaries, inadequate, of cabinet members.	15	1925
Salem, settled by Pilgrim Fathers in 1628.	13	992
Salic law, republican.	14	1608
Salisbury, Lord, biography of.	15	1808
On the Abandonment of General Gordon.	15	1808
On Tampering with the Constitution.	15	1821
Salisbury, Schouvaloff and, overrode the authority of Europe.	13	1096
Sallust, on the decay of the Roman republic, quoted.	14	1724
Samoa, Malietoa of, restored by the United States.	13	1031
Seized by Germany.	13	1031
The native chief in.	14	1737
Sancho Panza, Don Quixote and, Senators Butler and Douglas compared to, by Charles Sumner.	15	1957
Sanction, the Pragmatic.	15	2027
Sandico, Teodoro, his bloody order of extermination.	15	1920
San Domingo, insurrection in.	14	1624
Negroes of, freed themselves.	14	1596
San Francisco, bones of Chinamen sent back from.	14	1580
San Stefano, treaty of, of no value.	13	1094
Santiago, first shots fired at.	14	1400
Heroes of.	11	228
Santoro, Who was he?	11	175
Saratoga, the hero of.	13	1307
Savings-banks, large deposits in, prove prosperity.	14	1401
Rural, in Italy.	14	1325
Say, Léon.	14	1717

	VOL.	PAGE
Say, Lord, his aristocratic colonial plan.	13	984
Schurz, Carl, biography of.	15	1834
On the Policy of Imperialism.	15	1834
Pleads not only for Filipinos, but also for American honor.	15	1847
Schiller on Dionysius and Damon, quoted by Bebel.	11	168
Schools, Indian, speech of George Graham Vest on.	15	2013
School system of India and China, character and antiquity of the.	14	1589
Schopenhauer, declaration of, that style is not imitation.	14	v
On expression as more than words.	15	ix
Schouvaloff, Count, Lord Salisbury's agreement with.	13	1089
Science, success in, an international asset.	14	1399
Scipio, continence of, equaled by that of Washington.	14	1587
Scotland, the Gladstone redistribution scheme in.	15	1826
The law of, how altered.	14	1388
Scott, General, on the "Trent" affair	11	326
Sir Walter, quoted by W. J. Bryan.	11	367
Scythian, Demosthenes accused of being a.	11	40
Search warrants, the proper character of.	14	1527
Sea, the Caribbean.	14	1491
Secession, Alexander Hamilton Stephens on.	15	1932
An unwise and ill-timed measure.	15	1933
Right of, never existed.	13	1061
Seven States in.	15	1936
Secessionists, enemies in a technical sense.	13	1062
Sectional enforcement of law, unconstitutional.	13	1142
Sectionalism, tyrannical.	15	1958
Washington's warnings against.	14	1347
Seditious acts and men, to be shunned.	14	1335
See, the Holy, its authority in social discussions.	14	1334
Self-consciousness, in an orator, how to be overcome.	13	xii
Destructive to the speaker.	13	x
Self-government, the natural government of man.	12	685
To be learned by exercising.	15	1845
Self-sacrifice, claimed by Cromwell.	12	757
Selour, Mr., a philanthropic dreamer.	12	539
Semi-barbarous country, Greece a.	15	1926

	VOL.	PAGE
Semiramis.	14	1607
Senate, Alexander Hamilton advocates the creation of a	13	1119
Arguments in favor of the creation of a	13	1118
Chamber, old, of the, its associations.	11	301
Its history, as marking three epochs in that of the United States.	11	298
Of the United States, at first a mere executive council.	11	297
Place of the, in the Roman Empire.	13	975
The, condemnation of Jackson by, shameless.	11	212
The, debates of, the public not originally admitted to.	11	298
The, out of thirty-five Presidents of, twenty-four, up to 1861, were Southerners.	15	1934
Senates of Rome and Venice, the, excellence of.	13	1050
Senators for life.	14	1453
Sensibility, moral, in Charles Sumner.	13	1291
Septennat, the, in France, a dream of traditional royalty.	13	1046
Service, the end of art.	13	xi
Services, diplomatic, expenses of.	15	1925
Settlers, early American, champions of English liberty.	13	982
Early American, character of.	15	1759
Seward, William Henry, biography of	15	1849
His prophetic glimpse of American expansion.	13	932
On the Irrepressible Conflict.	15	1849
Shakespeare, mastery of, by Lincoln	15	1771
Othello of, the, quoted by William M. Springer.	15	1930
Quoted by Edward Everett.	13	975
Sharks, a nation of, Americans so styled by John Randolph.	14	1722
Sharpe's rifles.	14	1588
Shawnees, Andrew Jackson commander in the war with.	11	117
Sheehy, M. P., Mr., his speech reported.	14	1501
Sheil, Richard Lalor, biography of.	15	1865
On Ireland's Part in English Achievement.	15	1865
Sheridan, Richard Brinsley, biography of.	15	1872
Speech of, Against Warren Hastings.	15	1872
Taken ill during his speech against Hastings.	15	1886
Sherman law, repeal of the, urged by D. B. Hill.	13	1186
Sherman, John, biography of.	15	1904
On the financial situation.	15	1904
Reluctantly controverts views of President Cleveland and Secretary Carlisle.	15	1905
Sherman, Roger, at the Congress of 1789.	14	1339
Ship-money.	14	1423
Ships, free, make free goods.	14	1411
Sidney, Algernon, his immortal book.	14	1598
Silver, demonetization of, in 1873, calamitous.	13	1234
Free, favored by the South and West.	13	1235
Free, Richard P. Bland champion of.	11	x
Silver certificates, when justly redeemable by silver.	15	1910
Simplicity of great oratory.	12	v
Sincerity, absolute, necessary in the great orator.	11	xviii
Single standard of currency, established by England.	13	1222
Sinkat, a garrison in the Sudan.	15	1811
Fall of, caused by Gladstonian blunders.	15	1812
Signers of the Declaration of Independence, their fame.	13	963
Situation, financial, John Sherman on the.	15	1904
Six Companies, Chinese, the.	14	1580
Sixth seal, opening of the.	14	1599
Sixty years, presidents of, claimed by the South up to 1861.	15	1934
Slanders, American, of Aguinaldo.	15	1836
Slave, the, makes the tyrant.	13	1108
Slave code, a, forced on Kansas by the Democratic party.	15	1859
Slave power, the.	15	2000
Slaveholders, designs of, Democratic party committed to.	15	1856
The strength of the Democratic party.	15	1857
Vote of, Democratic party's reliance on the.	15	1857
Slaveholding class, struggles of the, to sway the whole Union.	15	1855
Slaveholding system, tenacity of the.	15	1855
Slave insurrection at Southampton.	14	1350
Slave law, Mexican, abrogated by the Democrats.	15	1861
Slave race, the, at Santo Domingo the only one that ever freed itself	14	1596
Slavery, a burning question.	11	x

	VOL.	PAGE
Slavery, Abolition of, Emilio Castelar on the	12	523
Abolition of, in Spanish America	12	525
African, fruits of	15	1851
African, origin of	15	1850
African, the question of, settled forever by the new Confederate constitution	15	1939
And Christianity	12	527
And free labor compared	15	1851
Aristotle on	12	526
At Rome, ameliorations of	12	526
A weight in the race of progress up to 1860	13	1241
Chinese, in Hawaii, worse than African	12	624
Condemned by the Ordinance of 1787	15	1854
Condemned by the principles of the Constitution	15	1854
Constitutional war-power over, John Quincy Adams on the	11	17
Coolie, existence of, in the Sandwich Islands	12	624
Exclusion of, and the Supreme Court	13	937
Federal control of	14	1338
Founders of the Constitution ashamed of	15	1853
Greatest evil in the world	14	1631
Inconsistent with republican form of government	14	1603
In Mississippi, prohibited by Congress, 1798	14	1339
In Russia, the cause of despotism	15	1852
In the days of Tacitus	12	526
In the Northwestern territory, forbidden	14	1347
Once universal in Europe	15	1852
Party of, political successes of the	15	1852
Plato on	12	526
Political results of	15	1851
Prohibition of, in the Northwest, approved by Washington	14	1347
Prohibition of, opposed by C. Pinckney in 1819–'20	14	1341
Question of, likely to lead to discussion	12	458
Reasons for abolishing	14	1630
Sectionalized the question of protection	13	1140
State rights and	13	937
Subserviency to, a law written on the Democratic forehead	15	1862
The curse of mankind	14	1614
The natural and normal condition of the negro	15	1939
Slavery, theory of labor in	15	1850
The propagandists of	15	1955
Throned, like the idol of Serapis	13	1055
Slaves, affection of, for their owners	14	1350
Allowance of time to	14	1620
Are property	15	2008
British, misery of	15	2122
Disproportion of sexes among	14	1617
Importation of, forbidden by Congress	14	1339
Property in, not sanctioned by the Constitution	14	1352
Right to take, into Federal territories	14	1352
Roman, of eminence	12	526
Smuggling of	14	1616
Status of	15	2008
Vote of the Democrats increased by representation of	15	1857
Slave state, each new, strengthens the Democratic party	15	1857
Slave-trade, abolition of the, in English colonies	14	1614
Abolition of the, William Pitt on	14	1613
An outrage upon justice	14	1628
British, Horrors of the, William Wilberforce on	15	2120
Foreign, forbidden by Act of 1808	15	1855
In Africa, British aim to destroy	15	1820
Parliamentary sanction given to the	14	1627
The South's demand for, granted	15	1933
Threatened repeal of the, by the Act of 1808	15	1855
Slavonic Population of Turkey-in-Europe, England's policy towards	13	1091
Slidell and Mason	12	451
Smiles, Samuel, on great oratory as of slow attainment	15	vi
Smith, Adam	14	1718
Never read by Fox	14	1719
Smucker on Clay's first speech	14	xii
Snug the joiner	12	786
Social intercourse, freedom of, at Athens	14	1565
Social war, in Rome, originated in question of suffrage	13	1061
Socialism, its dangers	14	1324
Adherents of, unchristian	14	1326
And Assassination, August Bebel on	11	159
Societies, secret, levy blackmail among the Chinese	14	1575
Workingmen's, in Italy	14	1325

	VOL.	PAGE
Society, American, becoming hopelessly stratified	13	1233
True, requires one belief and aim	14	1469
Upper classes of, must be looked after by Christian Democracy.	14	1327
Socrates	14	1441
Soil of Eastern states exhausted by careless agriculture	13	1069
Sojourn of Chinese in the United States only transient	14	1580
Soldiers and sailors of the United States, a majority of, from the North	15	1935
Soldiery, British, a scourge to the American colonies	14	1315
Solomon, quoted by Cromwell	12	749
Solon harangued people in hexameters	11	v
Sorrow, its sources	14	1570
Soul, greatness of, never grows old	14	1570
Soundness of body and mind without character, useless	15	1771
South Africa, British difficulties in	14	1730
Mr. Bryce's book on, cited	14	1740
Object of the tariff law in	14	1734
The Crisis in, Cecil Rhodes on	14	1730
South African difficulty, the	11	99
South America, Emancipation of, The, Henry Clay on	12	676
South Carolina, operations of the, Union armies in	12	447
South, the, compared to the tormented in the Hall of Eblis	14	1595
The, determined against the tariff bill	14	1710
The, how deprived of share in the territories	12	462
The, most presidents chosen from the North controlled by.	15	1934
The, political condition of, at the close of the war	13	1058
The, rich before the Revolution, poor afterward	14	1699
The, united against tax on importations	14	1701
The, wealth of, after the Revolution	14	1699
Sovereign, a, above party	14	1393
Sovereignty, each state a	12	489
Over territories vested in Congress	12	477
Popular, a fantastic term	14	1348
State, defined	12	491
The people's, and freedom of the press	13	970
The United States fighting for, in the Philippines	13	1196
Sovereigns, feudal, and the grace of God	13	977
Spain, American triumph over, and its responsibilities	13	921
American war with, sprang from devotion to liberty	15	1914
America's war with, British sympathy during, sprang from the tie of blood	13	1301
Conflict with, regarded by McKinley with fear and anxiety.	13	920
Could not be expected to relinquish the Philippines freely	15	1918
Despotism of	14	1512
Free municipalities and town governments did not save	14	1589
The United States and, relations of, in 1818	12	678
Treaty with, opposed in the Senate	15	1841
Spaniards, the, walking corpses	14	1513
Spanish America, moral causes of its emancipation	13	990
Spanish colonial despotism described	12	680
Spanish monarchy, the, absolute in the eighteenth century	12	522
Spanish territory in America, extent of, in 1818	12	679
Spartacus, his struggle for freedom	12	526
Speaker of the House of Commons, Mr. Gully, grandson of a pugilist	12	625
Speakers, great, touching and tender quality of the voices of	12	vii
Of the House, out of thirty-five, up to 1861, twenty-three were Southerners	15	1934
Speculative society, theater of debate for University of Edinburgh	11	xix
Speech, last, of John C. Calhoun	12	457
To the Chiefs of Various Indian Tribes, by Thomas Jefferson	13	1265
Speeches, great, read well	11	xxii
Political, important in the study of history	11	viii
Recent and earlier, compared in literary value	11	xi
Spirit, not form, of government essential	15	1769
Spirits, ardent, intemperate use of, by the Indians, rebuked by President Jefferson	13	1266
Spoils system, the, a misconception of the function of party	12	786
As expounded by a government officer	12	786
Calhoun on the	12	797

	VOL.	PAGE
Spoils system, defalcations result from the	14	1648
G. W. Curtis on the	12	782
History of the	12	784
Its first triumph	12	784
Its ludicrous side	12	788
Makes politics mere place-hunting	12	787
Personal favoritism its root	12	793
Second great triumph of the	12	784
Source of the	12	792
Stupendous and grotesque folly of the	12	788
The, to be remedied by competitive examination of candidates	12	796
Sponge, Squeezing the, speech of Georges Jacques Danton on	12	802
Spooner, John Coit, biography of	15	1913
On the Government of the Philippines	15	1913
Spoons, gold, purchase of, for the White House, popular indignation caused by	15	1925
Sprague, Judge, his decision in the Amy Warwick case	13	1062
Springer, William McKendree, biography of	15	1924
On Retrenchment, Economy, and Reform	15	1924
Staël, Madame de	12	673
Standard of morals based on the Bible	15	1770
Standing armies, how hurtful to a state	13	1132
Stanley, Lord	14	1523
Star Chamber, a slavery tribunal more odious than the	15	1949
Star, Morning, newspaper, cited	14	1373
Starvation the lot of one million American citizens	13	1234
Starving in a land of plenty, the Irish	13	1100
State and Federal union described	12	578
State, a free, requires a well-regulated militia for its security	11	138
State Fair of Minnesota, Address of Theodore Roosevelt at the	15	1759
State governments, relation of, to the Union	13	1120
Support of the rights of, an essential principle of the United States government	13	1258
State rights, described	12	487
Discussion of	12	482
State sovereignty	11	x
A grossly immoral and dishonest doctrine	11	16
State sovereignty, contrary to the Declaration and the Constitution	11	17
States, combination of, necessary to meet the problem of trusts	15	1782
Rebellious, dwellers in, not, therefore, enemies of the government	13	1062
Rebellious, how far to be considered enemies of the government	13	1062
Statesman, what kind of, required in the Philippines	15	1844
Statesmanship diffused generally at Athens	14	1566
State rights, difficulty of, Civil War largely brought on by the	14	1394
Statistics, trade, indicate prosperity of the United States	14	1400
Steam communication with South America, inadequate	14	1402
Steamers, new lines of, required	14	1402
Stephens, Alexander Hamilton, biography of	15	1932
On Secession	15	1932
"Corner-Stone" Address of	15	1936
Sterne, on wisdom learned through emotion	15	viii
Stevens, Thaddeus, biography of	15	1943
Speech of, against Webster and Northern Compromisers	15	1943
St. Helena, Napoleon's literary work at	14	1720
Stirner, work of, "The Individual and His Property"	11	165
St. Louis, "boodled" by criminal compact of its aldermen	13	1285
Story, an amusing, about Sir William Harcourt	14	1736
Strafford, a deserter of the people's cause	15	1870
Strawberries, cultivation of, in Scotland	13	1077
Strelitzes, the, of Moscow or St. Petersburg	14	1721
Strife and distrust between North and South, no longer room for	13	1294
Struggle of slavery with free labor, in the United States in the eighteenth century	15	1852
Stuart, Charles, his machinations in the Commonwealth	12	748
Student, the oratorical, what books he should study	11	xxiii
Success in great guilt, examples of, cited by Sheridan	15	1877

	VOL.	PAGE
Success of the world, this country the one	13	1241
Sudan, abandonment of the, by the Egyptians, demanded by Gladstone	15	1811
A good government in the, essential to British interest	15	1819
Objects of British domination in the	15	1820
The question of the, and the Gladstone ministry	15	1810
Suffrage, enlargement of, in England, due to American example	13	969
Limited by a money qualification	14	1752
Monopoly of, alleged by the Chartists to exist	14	1382
Negro, Samuel Jones Tilden on	15	1992
Question of, caused great civil war in Rome	13	1061
Universal, an agent of the people's sovereignty	13	970
Universal, and sovereignty of the people	13	969
Universal, opposed by Macaulay	14	1378
Universal, Robespierre on	14	1750
Universal, subversive of civilization	14	1380
Universal, threatens the security of property	14	1381
Sumner Assault, The, Preston Brooks on	11	328
Sumner, Charles, attitude of, towards his opponents	13	1292
Biography of	15	1952
Eulogy of, by L. Q. C. Lamar	13	1289
His high moral qualities	13	1291
Ideals of	13	1199
On the Crime against Kansas	15	1952
"Sumter," the, fitted out at Birkenhead	12	450
Superiors, respect due to	14	1335
Supervision and control the right remedy for trusts	15	1781
Supremacy, British, necessary in Egypt	15	1819
Of the laws of the states	13	1123
Of the laws of the Union	13	1123
Supreme Being, Festival of the, Robespierre on the	14	1756
Supreme Court, authority of the	15	2011
Populists threaten to overthrow the	12	712
Proportion of judges of the, from the North and South	15	1934
Surplus, a, from 1866 to 1893, existed in the treasury	15	1905
Surplus, Jefferson did not abandon protection on account of	11	262
Yielded by a protective tariff should be used for national improvements	11	262
Survivors of Athenian heroes	14	1568
Suspension of American commerce by French and British restrictions	12	647
Suwaroff, cruelties of	13	1008
Swift, Dean, on curates	14	1520
On style	14	v
Switzerland, government corruption in cantons of	14	1453
Sword, the British Empire does not live by the	15	1806
Sylla, conquered enemies condemned to death by	14	1747
Cruelty of	14	1749
Sympathy, American, promised Aguinaldo by General Anderson	15	1838
System, American, produces cheapness	12	653
Feudal, condition of people under the	13	894
Spoils, absurdities of the	12	788
The American, Henry Clay on	12	642

T

	VOL.	PAGE
Tacitus, no turpitude described by, like that of Warren Hastings	15	1891
Taft, William H., his wise administration in the Philippines	15	1768
Work of, in the Philippines	13	930
Tagalos, hostility of the, an obstacle to military occupation of the Philippines	15	1919
Improved condition of the, under American rule	15	1769
Present freedom of the	15	1769
"Tail to a London Kite," R. P. Bland's description of American finance until free silver is established	11	288
Tampering with the Constitution, Lord Salisbury on	15	1821
Taney, Chief-Justice, denies that the Federal government can hold colonies	11	93
On the political position of negroes	14	1358
On the scope of the Declaration of Independence	14	1359
Tanganyika to be reached by the African railway	14	1736
Tariff, cost of living increased by a high	12	691

	VOL.	PAGE
Tariff, lowering of the, in 1857, followed by a money panic	11	269
On importations, first instituted in 1789, with Washington's approval	11	260
On importations, would hinder exportations of tobacco or cotton	14	1711
On manufactures, abolished by the Confederate constitution	15	1937
On the, speech of John Randolph	14	1697
Protective, efficacy of a	13	1034
Revenue from, Congress felicitated upon, by Jefferson	11	261
Supposed settlement of the, in 1816	14	1700
The Porto Rico, Joseph Walden Bailey on	11	84
To be altered only if fostering monopoly	15	1779
Tariff Act of 1893, amended by the Senate, vetoed by the President	15	1906
Tariff bill, advocates of the, likened by John Randolph to a Jewish usurer	14	1712
Comparison of the, to the Stamp Act	14	1701
Of 1816, disasters following the, described by Clay and Benton	11	263
Of 1824, John Randolph moves its indefinite postponement	14	1725
Prosperity of New York threatened by the	14	1715
The, favored by the hunters of the interior	14	1714
Unconstitutionality of the	14	1702
Tariff law, the, of Rhodesia, best reply to Little Englanders	14	1734
Tariff laws, vicious and inequitable	12	688
Tariff Legislation, Samuel Jackson Randall on	14	1671
Tariff question, early history of the	14	1688
Tariff revision, Grover Cleveland advocates	11	xi
Grover Cleveland on	12	687
Would not affect oil and anthracite	15	1779
Tariffs may be applied to extend commerce	14	1402
Tariff views of Clay, holders of the, and the colored population	13	1141
Taste, oratorical, Shakespeare's description of	12	ix
Tax, ruinous, the proposed tariff styled a	14	1710
Taxation, direct, necessity of	14	1447
Taxation, English, its history obscure	14	1423
For paying interest of the national debt	14	1381
No part of the legislative power	12	566
Of America, by the British, a subversion of the Constitution	13	965
Of the rich, how it benefits them	12	803
Principle of, Adam Smith, on the	11	356
Subjects of, in Greece	15	1926
Taxes, direct	14	1535
Direct, objects of	14	1448
Reduced one-half during the Jackson administration	11	214
Tax, income, advocates of an, not hostile to corporations	11	353
Income, an, not inquisitorial	11	360
Income, an, objections to	11	355
Income, perjury said to be invited by an	11	361
Income, poor not oppressed by an	11	357
Income, the, in England	11	354
Income, the, in the Netherlands	11	354
Income, the, W. J. Bryan on	11	352
The malt, a grievance to the British farmer	13	1080
The post	14	1428
The territorial	14	1535
Taxes in 1890	13	1220
Taxing America, the Right of, the Earl of Chatham on	12	563
Taylor, Zachary, supplants the Websters and Clays	14	1591
Tecumseh, biography of	15	1970
Speech at Vincennes by	15	1970
Speech to General Proctor by	15	1971
"Telegram," Sheffield, the, on the McKinley tariff	13	1034
Telegraph, advantages of the	14	1399
Tel-el-Kebir, battle of	15	1810
Tell and Gessler	11	168
Teller resolution, the, affirmed	13	1196
Tempe, the vale of	15	1949
Tennessee, operations of the Union armies in	12	447
Popularity of Andrew Jackson in East, a rock in the sea of treason	11	116
during the Civil War	13	1062
Territorial governments, in distant possessions, Daniel Webster on the establishment of	11	85
Territorialism, foreign, attitude of the United States towards	11	xi
Territory, acquired by the United States, between the Declaration of Independence and 1850	12	463
Acquisition of, by the United States, when desirable	13	939

VOL. PAGE

Territory, Confederate, gradual reduction of, 1863–1865 .... 12 448

Terror, Reign of, in France, cause of excesses of the............. 13 904

Terry, Major-General, of Virginia, as a nullifier.................. 13 1058

Texas, admitted by the Democrats, in spite of slaveholding...... 15 1858

And the slavery question, from 1840 to 1843................ 15 1858

Thebans induced by Demosthenes to oppose Philip............... 12 873

Thebes, Demosthenes and the ambassadors of Philip at....... 12 869

Themistocles, patriotic example of.. 12 867

Theophilus, Bishop of Alexandria, and the Serapeum.......... 13 1054

Theophrastus on the injudicious orator...................... 15 v

"The rock upon which the old Union would split," said by Jefferson, of slavery............ 15 1939

Thessalians and Dolopians, abettors of Philip.................... 12 835

Thiers, Louis Adolphe, biography of. 15 1974

On Mexico and Louis Napoleon's Policy...................... 15 1974

Thieves, French, no worse than Austrian receivers............... 13 1011

Thorn of the tariff, removed from the new Confederate constitution. 15 1937

Thrift and foresight, mechanics and laborers to be taught........ 14 1331

Throne, insecurity of the Spanish, due to American influence ... 13 969

Thucydides, policy of Athens revealed in speeches reported by 11 vii

Thurman, Allen Granbery, biography of......................... 15 1986

On the Tilden-Hayes Election.. 15 1986

Tiberius, cruelty of................ 14 1747

Ticonderoga..................... 14 1318

Tilden, Samuel Jones, biography of.. 15 1992

On Negro Suffrage............. 15 1992

Timekeepers of progress, expositions are the.................... 14 1398

Timolaus, friend of Philip.......... 12 832

Destroyer of Thebes........... 12 832

Tin trade, English monopoly of..... 14 1705

Tioga Point, an Indian murdered at. 14 1727

Treaty of..................... 14 1727

Toilers, condition of, to be made more tolerable through Christian influences................... 14 1328

Tokar, a garrison imperiled in the Sudan, neglected by Gladstone 15 1811

Surrendered to the Mahdi...... 15 1812

VOL. PAGE

Tomahawk, an eternal burial of the, desired by Red Jacket....... 14 1727

Tone, conversational, adopted by Wendell Phillips............ 12 vi

Tooke, John Horne, repartee of..... 14 1711

Toombs, Robert, biography of..... 15 2003

On Revolution or Secession.... 15 2003

Tories and Whigs, their mutual recrimination................ 12 786

Toulouse, Irish soldiers at the battle of...................... 15 1871

Townshend, Charles, his reckless budget.................... 15 1787

Trade, British, excluded from the Drifts in South Africa....... 14 1738

British, fostered by Rhodesia tariff law.................. 14 1734

British, supported by British dependencies.............. 14 1732

Free, Gladstone professes a belief in........................ 14 1732

Free, has never existed........ 12 651

Indian, United States posts and the....................... 14 1409

Traitors to Greece, the fate of...... 12 834

Transatlantic English nation, America the..................... 11 304

Translation of the Bible, King James' 12 xi

Translation, value of practise in.... 11 xxi

Translating from Latin or Greek, best training for the orator ...... 11 xviii

Translation from Demosthenes, recommended by Brougham.... 11 viii

Transvaal, accumulation of armaments in the.............. 11 101

Affairs, Cecil Rhodes on 14 1739

Corruption and misgovernment of the..................... 11 100

Government of the............ 14 1737

The, cannot be a danger to the British empire.............. 14 1737

The franchise in the........... 14 1741

The President of the.......... 14 1737

"Traveller," Goldsmith's, quoted by J. J. Ingalls................ 13 1237

Treachery, British, at Castel de Novo, Naples.................... 13 1026

Treason, Against the Charge of, speech of Mirabeau........ 14 1477

Treasury, deficiencies in the, increased from 1893.......... 15 1906

The, United States, as a borrower of gold.............. 15 1908

Treaties, reciprocity, their advantages...................... 14 1402

Treaty, American, with Spain, no peace treaty................ 15 1841

	VOL.	PAGE
Treaty, British, fifteenth article of the	14	1418
British, positive evils of the....	14	1415
British, the, Fisher Ames on...	11	43
British, the, James Madison on.	14	1404
British, the, to be ratified......	14	1405
Clayton-Bulwer, the...........	14	1494
Of arbitration with the United States, advocated in the British Parliament..............	13	1032
Of Paris, its scope.............	13	1094
Of Paris, with Spain, makers of the......................	13	923
Of 1783.....................	14	1408
Of 1783, arguments for carrying into effect..................	14	1405
Of 1783, its deficiencies........	14	1406
Of 1783, its merits discussed....	14	1405
Of 1783, its objects...........	14	1406
Of Tioga Point, made in 1791...	14	1727
Of Utrecht, the, tardy and ineffectual.....................	13	1022
The Hay-Pauncefote..........	14	1495
With Spain, a declaration of war against Filipino allies........	15	1841
With Spain, opposed in the Senate.......................	15	1841
With Turkey, concluded by George H. Boker...........	15	1925
"Trent" Affair, the, John Bright on.	11	303
Trenton, Washington at...........	13	1306
Tribunal, the revolutionary.......	14	1433
Troops, African and Egyptian, not to be relied on by Gordon......	15	1816
Trophies in war, won by Andrew Jackson....................	11	118
Troubles, labor, to be met by gospel precepts...................	14	1324
Troy, living only in song...........	14	1585
Trust problem, States must combine to meet the................	15	1782
Trusts, according to Grover Cleveland, selfish schemes........	12	693
And the Tariff, Theodore Roosevelt on.....................	15	1776
Evils of, to be eliminated by supervision and control.......	15	1781
Existence of, the foremost of national problems.............	13	1284
Gigantic power of, unassailable by tariff revision.............	13	1283
Harrison on the dangers of, to the commonwealth..........	13	1142
Theodore Roosevelt on........	15	1776
Vital importance of the subject of........................	15	1776
Truth, Guesses at, passages from...	15	ix
Guesses at, passages from......	15	x

	VOL.	PAGE
Truth, tradition and conscience, guides to.................	14	1470
Turkey, England under Beaconsfield, the advocate of......	13	1091
Treaty with, of 1875...........	15	1925
Turkish mission, large expenses of the	15	1925
Turks, diplomatic presents to, not reciprocated..................	15	1925
Turner, Nat, insurrections of.......	14	1596
Turner, Sharon, on the persecutions of the Jews.................	14	1558
Tuscany, the Grand Duke of, treated with indignity by Lord Harvey.......................	13	1010
Tuscarora Nation................	14	1729
Tyrant, history of the word........	13	975
The Egyptian, and the abolitionists Moses and Aaron........	15	1944
Tyrian colonies in Africa...........	14	1424
Tyrtæus, translations from, recited to British soldiers...........	11	v

U

	VOL.	PAGE
Uitlanders, ill-treatment of, in South Africa.....................	11	100
Their grievances..............	14	1737
Their grievances to be redressed.	14	1738
Ultima ratio regum, motto on crown of Louis XIV...............	11	135
Union, a South African...........	14	1740
Colonial, with England, Washington's view of.............	12	474
Germanic, suggested by American independence...........	13	904
Implied in the Declaration of Independence.............	13	967
In Defense of the, speech of Edmund Randolph.............	14	1678
National, proposed by American colonies....................	13	1172
No magic in the word.........	14	1712
Of American colonies with England, advantages of.........	12	474
Of the United States, political, in 1850, how best effected......	12	472
On the Withdrawal from the, speech of Jefferson Davis....	12	815
Right of territories to enter the.	13	934
The, as conceived of by the people of Carolina..............	12	486
The, endangered by Southern discontent in 1850..........	12	458
The Oxford....................	14	1497
The, paramount among the several states..................	13	1119
The, threatened by slavery party	14	1351

VOL. PAGE

Union, the whole, Democratic party not a party of.............. **15** 1857
"United Ireland," published in Dublin........................ **14** 1370
United States, establishment of the, and that of Botany Bay, compared..................... **13** 980
   Migration or importation of people, as treated in the Constitution of the............... **14** 1608
   The, and Canada, good will between..................... **13** 1297
   The, in the Pan-American Exposition...................... **14** 1398
Unity, German, would have come without Bismarck.......... **11** 164
   In Italy, restoration of, due to American example.......... **13** 969
   Of England and America....... **13** 1301
Universal dominion, men in Christian times have aimed at........ **13** 1098
Universal suffrage.................. **14** 1750
   Free labor and, inseparable..... **15** 1851
Unpaid indemnity, demand for, in Jackson's annual message.... **11** 129
Unpremeditated speeches, few famous...................... **11** xv
Upper chambers, of lords and peers, in disfavor.................. **13** 1050
Utrecht, treaty of................ **13** 1022

V

Vagrant negro law of Virginia...... **13** 1058
Valfond mistaken for Mirabeau..... **14** 1480
Valley of Decision, the, entered by the nation in 1860.......... **13** 1153
Valor, not weapons, relied upon by Athenians in war........... **14** 1566
Value, agricultural, of land in France and England............... **13** 1075
Values of land in New York State and Great Britain, compared..... **13** 1070
Van Buren, Martin, abolition in the District of Columbia opposed by........................ **15** 1858
   Assailed by Prentiss.......... **14** 1646
   Corruption of his administration **14** 1652
   His election witnessed the disastrous results of the compromise tariff bill.............. **11** 266
Various Indian Tribes, Speech to the Chiefs of, by Thomas Jefferson **13** 1265
Vattel, authority of, not followed strictly in drafting Anglo-American treaty............ **14** 1412
   On the right of revolution..... **12** 682

VOL. PAGE

Vehement, when orator and statesman should be.............. **12** 883
Velasquez, of Spanish America...... **12** 684
Vendée, La, the French Convention's measures against............ **12** 803
Vengeance the spur of Athenian valor **14** 1568
Venice, begirt by foreign foes....... **14** 1467
   Unjust seizure of, by the French. **13** 1011
Vermont favored by the tariff bill... **14** 1705
Versailles besieged by Amazons..... **14** 1481
Vest, George Graham, biography of.. **15** 2013
   On Indian Schools............ **15** 2013
Veto, presidential, meaning of the, taught by Andrew Jackson.. **11** 217
Viceroys in Spanish America, their nationality................. **12** 681
Vicksburg, heroes of................ **11** 228
   Pemberton at, accepted the results of the war............. **13** 1057
Victoria, port of.................. **14** 1580
Victories in war, permanent, must be based on justice and reason.. **11** 137
Vienna, treaty of................. **15** 2027
Vimiera, Irish soldiers at........... **15** 1871
Vincennes, speech at, by Tecumseh.. **15** 1970
Vincent of Paul, the father of the afflicted.................... **14** 1335
Vine, cultivation of the, forbidden in Spanish America............ **12** 681
Virgil, quoted by Daniel Webster.... **15** 2095
   Quoted by John Randolph..... **14** 1704
   Quoted by William M. Evarts.. **13** 971
Virginia, another Algiers........... **14** 1590
   Commonwealth of, as an inverted pyramid.............. **14** 1589
   General Butler's operations in.. **12** 446
   Government of, a pirate ship... **14** 1590
   Hospitality of................ **14** 1714
   House of Burgesses, a, opened in, in 1620.................. **13** 984
   Its vagrant negro law......... **13** 1058
   Law of the General Assembly of, 1808..................... **15** 1944
   No cowards in................ **14** 1594
   Operations of the Union armies in........................ **12** 447
Virtues, public and private......... **14** 1568
Visitors and immigrants welcomed at Athens.................... **14** 1565
Voice, beauty of, described........ **13** xi
   Rules for employment of the, in oratory.................... **11** xvii
Volume of money, less important than its activity........... **12** 715
Voorhees, Daniel Wolsey, biography of........................ **15** 2021
   On the Tilden controversy..... **15** 2021

VOL. PAGE

Vote against Chinese immigration, in
California, in 1879.......... 14 1572
Voters, qualifications for, in South
Africa..................... 14 1742
White and black, proportion be-
tween, in the South........ 13 1060

W

Wages, gradual increase of, to the
workingman of the United
States..................... 13 1247
Rate of, the infallible test of
prosperity................. 12 714
Wales, the Marches of, and taxation. 14 1424
Walford, the Massachusetts pioneer. 13 992
Walpole, greatness of the name of.. 14 1548
Walpole, Sir Robert, biography of.. 15 2025
On a Motion for his Removal.. 15 2025
Wampum, amicable significance of.. 14 1727
Belt of, a token of peace....... 14 1728
Wapanakies, parties to the treaty of
Greenville................. 13 1263
War, American, with Spain, avowed
purpose of the............. 15 1835
And Armaments, in Europe,
Otto von Bismarck on...... 11 244
Arbitrament of, accepted by the
South..................... 13 1295
Balkan, only prevented by Ber-
lin Congress 11 247
British-American, of 1812..... 15 1993
Chinese, question of, under Lord
Palmerston................ 15 1830
Civil, of 1861-1865, a crime... 13 1302
Civil, of 1861-1865, a Red Sea of
slaughter.................. 13 1063
Civil, of 1861-1865, Great Britain
nearly involved in........... 12 451
Civil, of 1861-1865, liberalizing
effect of................... 13 1241
Civil, of 1861-1865, meaning of.. 15 1853
Civil, of 1861-1865, prospects of,
discussed by General B. F.
Butler..................... 12 447
Court of last resort........... 13 1061
Crimean, John Bright on the... 11 325
Crimean, American neutrality in 12 451
Danish, question of, under Lord
Palmerston................ 15 1830
Excellence in, of the Athenians. 14 1565
Honors of the Civil, common to
both sides.................. 13 1294
Mexican, and the great men in
Washington................ 14 1591
Mexican, in 1846, and the Dem-
ocratic Party.............. 15 1858

VOL. PAGE

War, offensive, Bismarck's aversion
for........................ 11 255
Philippine, a dangerous prece-
dent...................... 15 1843
Philippine, iniquitous......... 13 1194
Phocian, referred to by Demos-
thenes.................... 12 825
Seminole, Henry Clay on the... 12 672
Shawnee, Andrew Jackson com-
mander in................. 11 117
Social, at Rome, originated in
the question of suffrage...... 13 1061
Spanish-American, United North
and South................. 13 1302
Vision of, The, by Robert G.
Ingersoll.................. 13 1238
War power, the, resides in the execu-
tive....................... 11 17
Warrants, general, illegality of..... 14 1528
Search, character of.......... 14 1527
Warren Hastings, Against, speech of
Richard Brinsley Sheridan... 15 1872
Crimes of.................. 13 1215
Warriors, seven Indian, murdered... 14 1727
Warships to be built............... 13 1146
Warwick, Amy, and enemies of the
government................ 13 1062
Washington, D. C., Alaskan commis-
sion at.................... 13 1300
Washington, Booker T., eminence of. 15 2016
Washington, George, and civil service
reform.................... 12 789
George, as military leader...... 13 1306
George as President of the
United States.............. 13 1308
George, being dead, still speak-
eth....................... 13 1312
George, biography of......... 15 2032
George, complained of the pre-
dominating materialism..... 13 1278
George, controller of a great his-
toric crisis................. 13 896
George, crushes the Indians, with
Wayne as his lieutenant..... 13 1310
George, death of............. 13 1304
George, Eulogy on, by Henry
Lee....................... 13 1304
George, fame of.............. 13 1305
George, Farewell Address of... 15 2036
George, First Inaugural Address
of......................... 15 2032
George, first in war and peace.. 13 1311
George, founder of the federate
republic................... 13 1305
George, Fox's eulogy of....... 13 1025
George, glory of.............. 14 1585
George, inauguration of....... 13 1138

	VOL.	PAGE
Washington, George, in retirement	13	1309
George, in time of peace	13	1307
George, Lincoln as great as	13	1298
George, on revolutions among other nations	12	682
George, settled the difficulties with France	13	1311
George, signed the anti-slavery act of 1789	14	1339
George, slaveholder and planter	12	474
George, supporter of Braddock	13	1305
George, warning of, against sectionalism	14	1347
George, wisdom and faithfulness of in peace	13	1308
Waterloo, every man has his	14	1592
Irish soldiers at	15	1871
Wealth, calculation of its distribution in the United States	13	1232
Distribution of, in the United States uneven	13	1230
Growth of, in the United States, from 1860 to 1880	13	1231
Half of the, held by a minority in the United States	13	1232
Or manhood, which to rule	13	1287
Webster, Daniel, and the spoils system	12	784
And Northern Compromisers, Thaddeus Stevens on	15	1943
As Secretary of State, and office-seekers	12	786
Biography of	15	2053
Bought by the South	14	1595
Constitutional expositions of	13	1141
His Bunker Hill Monument Oration	15	2090
His Reply to Hayne	15	2053
On Adams and Jefferson	15	2082
On dangers of patronage	12	785
Style of, now out of date	12	xi
Wellesley, Mass., value of lands near	13	1070
Wellington, Arthur Wellesley, Duke of, biography of	15	2107
Hindered by Peel	12	791
On Catholic Emancipation	15	2107
Sheil's appeal to	15	1870
Wentworth, a tyrant in Ireland	15	1870
West Indies, American trade with the	14	1417
Condition of slaves in the, how to be ameliorated	14	1622
Dangers of importing Coromantine negroes into the	14	1623
Duty paid on imported slaves in the	14	1623
English possessions in the, security of	14	1625
West Indies, laborers in the	14	1618
Laws respecting slave-trade in the	14	1627
Mortality among newly imported slaves in the	14	1622
West, the, to be injured by tax on foreign goods	14	1704
Weylerism not adopted by Americans in the Philippines	13	927
Whately, Richard, on oratory	15	v
Wheat, per acre, less produced in France than in Great Britain	13	1074
Wheat belt, Teutonic civilization coextensive with the	12	622
Which Shall Rule, Manhood or Money? speech of Robert Marion La Follette	13	1281
Whigs and Tories, their mutual recrimination	12	786
White and negro, inequality of	15	1940
White, Luke, the leader of Irish seceders	14	1515
White man, the, why not enslaved	15	1850
White Plains, battle of	12	785
White, Richard Grant, on acquirement of style	14	v
Whittier, John G., his poetic address to Englishmen	13	1299
Widows of Athenians admonished	14	1570
Wilberforce, William, biography of	15	2120
On Horrors of the British Slave-trade	15	2120
Wilkins, J., on logic and eloquence	15	v
William II, of Germany, biography of	15	2129
On Moses and Amalek	15	2129
William the Conqueror, controller of a great historic crisis	13	896
Willmott, R. A., on simplicity in style	14	v
Wilmot Proviso, object of the	12	475
Wilson bill, the, deficiencies in the treasury caused by	15	1907
Wilson, Epiphanius, General Introduction by	11	v
On prayer and eloquence	15	x
On the preëminence of the orator	15	x
On the telling phrase	15	xi
Winslow, a religious refugee in New England	13	981
Winthrop, Governor, settled Massachusetts	13	992
Wirt, William, biography of	15	2135
Speech of, Against Aaron Burr	15	2135
Wise, Henry Alexander, addressed in a letter by Lydia Maria Child	14	1601

	VOL.	PAGE
Wise, Henry Alexander, and John Brown	14	1591
Biography of	15	2141
On Know-nothingism	15	2141
Tribute of, to John Brown	14	1598
Wolf, the, and People of the Mandan Nation, Thomas Jefferson to	13	1260
Wolfe, General, death of, referred to by Henry Lee	13	1306
Wollstonecraft, Mary	14	1608
Women, acknowledged civil rights possessed by	14	1607
Milton's praise of	14	1607
Pericles on	13	1085
Wool, tariff on, how inequitable	12	692
Woolen industry, the, in Ireland	13	1100
Work, the fundamental law of success	15	1760
Workingmen and small corporations would suffer from free trade	15	1780
Workmen, British, are imperialists, and why	14	1733
Interests of, to be considered in dealing with trusts	15	1779
World, the civilized and enlightened, must recognize slavery	15	1940

	VOL.	PAGE
World, the new, sought by lovers of liberty	13	899
World duties of the United States	15	1763
Without a slave, Ingersoll on a	13	1240
Worst men lead tumults	14	1431
Wright, Luke E., his work in the Philippines	13	932
Writs of Assistance, character of	14	1528
Wrongs, Aguinaldo's, at the hands of Americans	15	1837
Inflicted upon American colonies by England	13	1126

Y

	VOL.	PAGE
Yankee's love of the dollar	14	1597
Yorktown, battle of	14	1591
Youth, corruption of, caused by presence of Chinese	14	1574

Z

	VOL.	PAGE
Zebah and Zalmunna, cited by Cromwell	12	749
Zenobia	14	1607